Designing the Learning-Centred School

This
descr
cultu

It
centr
and
From
new

Th
exam
West
ries
differ

E
and
the
scho

Clive
Adm
the U
tancy

e
-

-
s
).
e

h
n
)-
r

n
n
y

al
it
l-

Student Outcomes and the Reform of Education
General Editor: Brian Caldwell
*Professor of Education, Head, Department of Education Policy
and Management, University of Melbourne, Australia*

Student Outcomes and the Reform of Education is concerned with the reform
of public education and its impact on outcomes for students. The reform
agenda has gripped the attention of policy-makers, practitioners, researchers
and scholars for much of the 1990s, with every indication of more to come
with the approach of the new millennium. This series reports research and
describes strategies that deal with the outcomes of reform. Without sacri-
ficing a critical perspective, the intention is to provide a guide to good
practice and strong scholarship within the new arrangements that are likely
to provide the framework for public education in the foreseeable future.

School Effectiveness and School-Based Management
A Mechanism for Development
Yin Cheong Cheng

**Transforming Schools Through Collaborative
Leadership**
Helen Telford

The Inner Principal
David Loader

The Future of Schools
Lessons from the Reform of Public Education
Brian Caldwell and Donald Hayward

Beyond the Self-Managing School
Brian Caldwell and Jim Spinks

Designing the Learning-Centred School
A Cross-Cultural Perspective
Clive Dimmock

Designing the Learning-Centred School
A Cross-Cultural Perspective

Clive Dimmock

London and New York

First published 2000
by Falmer Press
11 New Fetter Lane, London EC4P 4EE

Simultaneously published in the USA and Canada
by Falmer Press, Garland Inc.
19 Union Square West, New York, NY 10003

Falmer Press is an imprint of the Taylor & Francis Group

© 2000 Clive Dimmock

Typeset in Times by Taylor & Francis Books Ltd
Printed and bound in Great Britain by Biddles Ltd, Guildford and
King's Lynn

British Library Cataloguing in Publication Data
A catalogue record for this book is available from the British Library

Library of Congress Cataloging in Publication Data
Dimmock, Clive A. J.
    Designing the learning-centred school : a cross-cultural
    perspective / Clive Dimmock.
    p. cm. – (Student outcomes and the reform of education)
    Includes bibliographical references and index.
    1. School improvement programs Cross-cultural studies.
    2. Educational change Cross-cultural studies. 3. School
    management and organization Cross-cultural studies.
    I. Title. II. Title: Designing the learning-centered school.
    III. Series.
    LB2822.8.D56 2000
    371.2'07–dc21   99–36837
                                                CIP

ISBN 0–750–70850–6 (hbk)
ISBN 0–750–70849–2 (pbk)

Contents

List of Illustrations   vii
Series Editor's Preface   ix
Preface   xiii
The Audience for this Book   xv

1   Designing the Learning-Centred School   1

2   Designing Learning-Centred Schools: Models, Frameworks and Precepts   18

3   Recognizing Societal Culture in School Design: The Case for a Cross-Cultural Comparative Approach   39

4   Initiating the Re-Design Process: Creating the School Culture   63

5   Designing the Curriculum   78

6   Focusing on Student Learning   107

7   Targeting Informed Teaching   132

8   Integrating Computer Technology   168

9   Building Supportive Organizational Structures   184

10   Developing Personnel and Financial Resources Policies   203

11   Evaluating Teachers' Performance   233

Contents

12 Learning-Centred Leadership   250

13 Community, Connectivity and Consistency in the
    Learning-Centred School   275

    Index   291

Illustrations

Figures

1.1	The School Design Elements	4
2.1	The Relationship between Schools, Restructuring Policies and Improved Student Outcomes	24
2.2	Restructuring and the Relationship between Authority, Resources and Accountability	26
2.3	Restructuring and School Penetration: Linkage with Teaching and Learning	27
2.4	A Model of School Re-Design through Review and Improvement	30
2.5	Restructuring and Linkage with Student Outcomes	32
2.6	The School and its System Environment	34
5.1	A Model of School Implementation of a Student Outcomes' Approach to the Curriculum	92
6.1	Relation of the Phases of Learning to Instructional Events	114
6.2	Learning Styles	120
7.1	The Mastery Learning Sequence	143

Tables

3.1	Dimensions of National/Societal and Organizational Culture	57
7.1	Effects of Instructional Quality and Time on Learning	152

Series Editor's Preface

School design and learning-centred education are at the forefront of research, policy and practice at the start of the twenty-first century. They integrate much of what has occurred in the last decade of the twentieth century and place the focus for the years ahead on the central issue of how the rhetoric of creating world-class schools is to be brought to realization.

For many nations, the 1990s was the decade of restructuring in education. For the most part this occurred at levels beyond the classroom and the day-to-day experience of learners. It was concerned with relationships between different levels of government, between the centre of a school system and schools which made up the system, and among all stakeholders in respect to realignments of authority, responsibility and accountability. It occurred at the same time that education, and indeed society at large, was being transformed by the information revolution, and as realization dawned that a knowledge society was being created.

Work intensified in the education industry and a sense of urgency was apparent as governments recognized that the transformation of schooling and a capacity for lifelong learning were essential for economic success and a civilized society. This urgency was heightened in countries where most of the restructuring had occurred, for many had made little or no progress, and some had even gone backwards, in the ranks of nations on indicators of educational achievement. Nations at the top of the table continued to make progress.

Design has replaced structure as the focus shifts to schools. The term has had long currency in the workplace but has only recently been adopted to describe what is needed in schools. Its use in the United States became widespread under the aegis of New American Schools, as nine school designs were selected for particular attention in efforts to lift performance in public schools. Each design reflected a particular constellation of values, philosophy, curriculum, organizational arrangement and approach to learning. Each had proved successful on a small to moderate scale in meeting the educational needs of students in particular situations. The issue then became one of how to increase the scale on which these designs were implemented in schools across the nation.

The intention was flawed, however, as each design was initially devised in particular circumstances, and success in large scale implementation was no more likely than it was for open plan classrooms and programmed learning. Attention is turning to how each school ought to design itself to best serve its students, for it is now recognized that each school has a unique mix of students and circumstance.

Enter Clive Dimmock. A better match of scholarly enterprise and policy priority is hard to imagine. He has been a highly successful academic on three continents in the years of the great reform movements. In each instance, his work spanned the domains of research, policy and practice, with books, papers, presentations, consultancy and, where appropriate, advocacy bringing the fruits of his endeavour to a wider audience. He was in Britain before and shortly after the key marker in contemporary reform, the 1988 Education Reform Act. He moved to Australia and was similarly engaged as major change swept that nation. Finally, in Hong Kong, he engaged deeply with a new cultural perspective as a succession of initiatives was implemented in schools, with thoughtful analyses of events before and after the key marker in that setting, the return to China on 1 June 1997.

This is a remarkable book because it covers, in depth and with great authority, virtually every dimension of schooling. His exhaustive account of school design and student learning is certain to be a major source for policy makers and practitioners over the next decade.

From a Western perspective, readers will recognize the extent of Clive Dimmock's journey. His first book on restructuring and school effectiveness was one of the first to critically examine the impact of the school reform movement. The limitations of that movement were readily apparent. His co-authored book that followed on the life histories of school leaders was also ground breaking, and it brought another dimension into focus for those who sought to make the connection. In *Designing the Learning-Centred School*, he completes the journey by shifting the focus to how a school can build its own capacity or create its own design. He also adds a deep understanding of and respect for a perspective from the East, where several nations are at the top of the table on international measures of student achievement, and they have remained there throughout the years of major reform in the West.

Soundly framed by the most authoritative cultural theories and infused with an extensive repertoire of research findings, Clive Dimmock leads readers to a new level of understanding of why schools in his new setting have been so successful. Stereotypes are shattered for those who thought that learning-centredness, either for teaching or for the school as a whole, was a Western construct. His accounts of practice in the East, better described as Confucian-heritage cultures, reveal that schools as learning organizations may be more effectively modelled in this setting.

Clive Dimmock has made a fine contribution to the series on Student Outcomes and the Reform of Education. I am confident that its impact will still be felt at the end of a new decade in the further transformation of schools.

Brian J. Caldwell
University of Melbourne

Preface

Ideas presented in this book have evolved from an amalgam of personal and professional beliefs moulded by years of experience working with teachers and school leaders in England and Wales, the United States, most Australian states, especially Western Australia and Victoria, and more recently Hong Kong. They are also the product of personal research and the research findings of many others from whose scholarship I have benefited.

I consider myself extremely fortunate to have had the opportunity to work in three continents. For each of the three, I can identify a new phase in my career. The first stage took place in the UK, where I began teaching at University College of Wales, Cardiff. This exposed me to a wealth of literature, most of which was UK in origin. The second phase took place when I moved to the University of Western Australia, a move which opened up new vistas. Australian academia tends to embrace North American as well as British literature, and of course produces some world class research of its own. More recently, a move to Hong Kong has provided me with an Asian perspective – the third phase – an experience which has prompted me to question the assumed universality of many of the Western theories and prescriptions which tend to dominate much of the literature. Living and working at the Chinese University of Hong Kong has made me aware of the importance of culture in understanding people's thoughts and actions.

The impetus to write the book came from two sources. The first concerned the relative absence of books covering comprehensively and in depth the kind of knowledge which would enable schools to undertake whole-school re-design. Many books focus on school management and leadership; some focus on curriculum, teaching and learning; still others cover school improvement and change. Very few, however, connect all of these in a systematic way. Yet the reality of school life is that curriculum, teaching, learning, organization, management and leadership are all interwoven. The second prompt to write the book came from a growing awareness of the internationalization and globalization of educational policy and restructuring, while concomitantly little cognisance is given to cultural difference and diversity. Everyday living and working in different cultural environments provides convincing personal experience of the importance of culture in determining the acceptability and adaptability of ideas and practices imported from elsewhere. If this book is considered a contribution to both of these issues, it will have been worth the effort.

Many people have influenced my thinking, but three in particular stand out in terms of their collegiality and friendship. I admire the tenacity and vision of Alan Bain, who has striven to put into practice in an American school, the theories and ideals in which he believes. I have learned a great deal from Alan and find him inspiring. Likewise, I owe debts to Tom O'Donoghue and Allan Walker, both of whom I have had the good fortune to work with as research partners and joint authors. They have been excellent friends and productive colleagues, always positive and encouraging. I am also extremely grateful to Brian Caldwell, the series editor, and to Falmer Press for the opportunity to publish this book.

The author and the publisher wish to thank the copyright holders for their kind permission to reproduce illustrations and text. Extracts reprinted from Dimmock, C. (1995) 'Reconceptualizing restructuring for school effectiveness and school improvement', *International Journal of Educational Reform* 4 (3): 285–300. Reproduced with permission from Technomic Publishing Co., Inc., © 1995; Figure 6.1 'Relation of the Phases of Learning to Instructional Events' adapted from Gagnè, R.M., *Essentials of Learning for Instruction*. Copyright © 1988 by Allyn & Bacon. Figure 6.2 'Learning Styles' adapted from McCarthy, B. (1990) 'Using the 4MAT System to Bring Learning Styles to Schools', *Educational Leadership* 48 (2): 32, figure 3. Used by permission of the Association for Supervision and Curriculum Development © 1985 by ASCD. All rights reserved; Figure 7.1 'The Mastery Learning Sequence' from W. M. Bechtol and J. S. Sorenson, *Restructuring Schooling for Individual Students*. Copyright © 1993 by Allyn & Bacon. Adapted by permission; Table 7.1 'Effects of Instructional Quality and Time on Learning' reprinted from Fraser et al. (1987) 'Syntheses of educational productivity research', *International Journal of Educational Research* 11 (2): 147–247 © 1987, with permission from Elsevier Science. Every effort has been made to obtain permission to reproduce copyright material. If any proper acknowledgement has not been made, we would invite copyright holders to inform us of the oversight.

The Audience for this Book

With a book focusing on school re-design, it is important to clarify two issues, one relating to the macro-micro or multi-level nature of schooling, and the other concerning the theory–practice relationship. No school is an island. For public or government schools, even those which have experienced considerable devolution and decentralization, there is usually a keen awareness of systemic relationships involving resourcing, goal setting, monitoring, evaluating, accountability and equity. In some systems, this influence extends to staffing. Even in the independent sector, many schools are part of a system and are thus subject to influence from broader systemic policies. While much of the discussion in the book focuses specifically on the internal aspects of schools, it is important to acknowledge the complex environment within which schools function.

Equally, it is important to comment on the theory–practice relationship. There is no dichotomy between good theory and practice: good theory is grounded in, or tested by, practice; that is, theory informs and enlightens practice, and practice sharpens and reinforces theory. This is an iterative relationship. Accordingly, theory should not be the sole preserve of the scholar, nor practice the monopoly of the practitioner. A successful practitioner requires a knowledge of relevant and robust theory and research, while the academic needs a sound grasp and understanding of practice.

This book is written for a broad range of people who are likely to be engaged in, or concerned with, the task of school re-design. These include the following groups of professionals:

- change agents and those responsible for leading and managing school design or re-design, notably school principals and other senior school staff with formal leadership responsibilities;
- teachers who may be involved in the design process and who are instrumental in its implementation;
- consultants and professional developers, from both inside and outside the school, who are involved in the re-design process;

- policy makers and bureaucrats at system level concerned with re-configuring schools.

In addition, it is hoped that students and scholars interested in school restructuring, improvement and design and who are undertaking formal programmes of study at university or college for bachelors', masters' or doctoral degrees will also find the material of interest.

Most importantly, it is intended that the scope of the book embrace an international readership. By giving formal recognition to differences between, as well as similarities of, societal cultures and to the implications that these have for school design, it is hoped that the book will appeal to scholars and practitioners in many different cultural environments.

Although not specifically targeted at them, the book may also be of interest to non-professionals, such as parents, with an involvement or vested interest in the performance and operation of their local school. As parents and other community representatives are invited to play more active roles in school affairs many of the issues and ideas discussed in this book may be of relevance to them.

1 Designing the Learning-Centred School

This book focuses on the challenge of designing learning-centred schools. This apparently simple statement contains many complex assumptions and implications. The first assumption is that schools are not presently 'learning-centred', a claim which requires a clarification of what is meant by the term. A second assumption is that such complex organizations as schools can only become learning-centred if they are intentionally created or designed.

With regard to the first assumption, the 'learning-centred' school is one whose mission, organization, leadership and curriculum delivery are all singularly focused on providing successful learning experiences and outcomes for all of its students. 'Learning experiences and outcomes' include the knowledge, values, attitudes and skills considered worthwhile and desirable across the spectrum of academic, social, spiritual, moral, aesthetic and physical domains. In reality, it is extremely challenging and rare for schools to engage all of their elements in a singularly focused way; just as it is uncommon for them to provide successful learning experiences for all of their students irrespective of ability, ethnicity, age and gender. Achieving a balance of learning outcomes also presents major challenges.

The response to the second assumption largely follows from that to the first. The sheer magnitude of the challenge – involving many elements, most of which are interdependent – means that incremental or piecemeal change is unlikely to succeed; equally holistic but haphazard change is likely to be unsuccessful. Schools are complex systems of interrelated parts; to change the parts is to change the system, and vice versa. The process must be holistic and designed with intent.

Reasons for Focusing on the Learning-Centred School

A central argument of this book is that school design and re-design should be based on the concept of the learning-centred school. Attention is thus placed on the quality of teaching, learning and curriculum experienced by all students. Seven reasons are advanced below in justification for this focus.

First, previous waves of reform have generally failed to penetrate beyond school administration into the classroom. Changing classroom practice is consistent with the notion that the main enterprise and concern of schools is learning. Schools are essentially places for all students to learn. A focus on learning also signifies that many schools currently fail to give it the attention it deserves. Second, and perhaps most significant, is the recognition that successful reform of teaching and learning is predicated on a holistic view of the school, incorporating its organizational structures, leadership and management (Holly, 1990). A design focus on learning is useful, since most of the other activities that schools conduct are linked to it and can therefore be embraced in the design. This book presents such a view by mapping the connections between learning, teaching and organizational structures, while emphasizing the role of management and leadership in securing quality teaching and learning. Placed in this context, the importance of school leadership, management and administration is judged by the extent to which they nurture and support quality teaching and learning for all. Securing uniformly high quality service delivery across the whole school has been relatively neglected by school leaders in the past. Third, a learning-centred design focus is consistent with the view that the quality of a school is appropriately judged by the quality of teaching and learning (the core technology) offered and experienced by its members. It is at the points of service delivery, the interface between teacher and learner, and the outcomes of learning, that the most pertinent and poignant indicators of school quality are provided.

Fourth, increasing recognition is being given to the equity argument that *all* students, irrespective of gender, ethnicity, age and ability, have the right to experience quality teaching and learning and a quality curriculum. Large numbers of students have in the past left school without realizing this entitlement. Fifth, a policy emphasis at system level on student learning outcomes is moving schools to focus on learning processes and outcomes and ways to improve their present 'low levels of learning productivity'. Government policies of accountability now place more emphasis on the effectiveness with which schools use resources, as measured or gauged by the outcomes achieved, rather than the level of resource inputs to schools. It is argued that teachers and schools in the past have been insufficiently accountable for their use of resources and their performance in relation to promoting and achieving student learning. A consequence of this policy shift is the newly created significance of the concept 'value-added', being the difference in students' learning achievement between entry to and exit from, the school. There is growing dissatisfaction with the relatively low levels of value-added in many schools and the existing core technology which accounts for it. Research findings now provide reasonably clear insights into the characteristics of schools providing quality learning and teaching for all students (Murphy, 1991). Finally, governments, other agencies and parents are increasingly realizing the importance of successful learning – in both process and outcome terms – to the lives of students and to their social economies in the emerging global and competitive marketplace of the world economy.

Elements and Strategy in Designing the Learning-Centred School

In a book devoted to comprehensive whole-school design, it is important to distinguish the various elements. These are:

- learning outcomes and the curriculum;
- learning processes and experiences;
- teaching approaches and strategies;
- technology, especially computers;
- organizational structures;
- human (including professional development) and financial resources;
- leadership and organizational culture;
- performance evaluation/appraisal.

While the elements are listed separately, in reality they are functionally interrelated. For purposes of analysis, however, the organization of material and the content of chapters in the book is based on these elements. Figure 1.1 depicts the elements of school design listed above. It also includes an additional element for consideration, namely, societal culture.

In the centre of Figure 1.1 are the elements forming the core technology. These elements are a curriculum based on student learning outcomes, informed teaching practices and informed learning, and computer technology. All are interconnected. The school is designed around these core elements in order to maximize learning-centredness. Other elements of school design are crucial in supporting and furthering the quality of the core technology. These elements include organizational structures, organizational culture, personnel and financial resources, performance evaluation/appraisal, and leadership and management. Each of these exerts mutual or reciprocal influence, but more importantly, each influences the core technology elements. The interrupted boundary line between the core technology and other elements signifies the mutuality and reciprocity of influence between all of the elements. Figure 1.1 also includes societal culture as an additional element, on the grounds that the form, shape and practices of re-designed schools need to be sensitive to the particularities of a given societal cultural context. This aspect is elaborated later in this and subsequent chapters.

On what basis can schools be designed? The argument presented is that conventional planning is inadequate for an organization – the school –

Figure 1.1 *The School Design Elements*

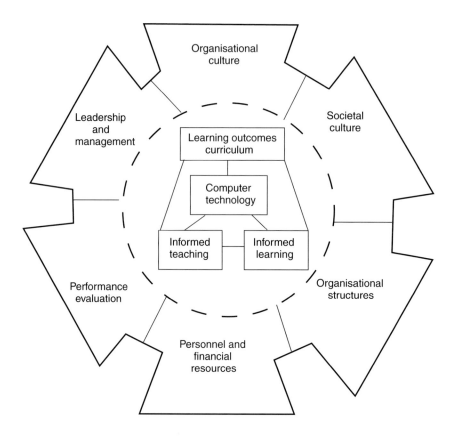

which is complex and which needs the capacity to evolve and change with time, and when environments are subject to so much change. In other words, the design needs built-in flexibility for continuous evolution and adaptability in fast changing environments. Consequently, the approach adopted throughout this book approximates to what Boisot (1995) calls 'strategic intent', as distinct from strategic planning. This approach assumes, firstly, highly turbulent environments, and secondly, high understanding on the part of the organization. There can be little dispute about the turbulence of the education environment; and it is a central theme of this book that considerable knowledge, information and understanding about effective schools exists, even though it is not always known by, or brought to the attention of, schools themselves. This knowledge – in the form of research evidence, theory, values-based prescriptions and experience – and drawn from many different sources (for example, curriculum, learning, teaching, organizational behaviour, and leadership) allows the formation of 'intuitively formed patterns or gestalt' (Boisot, 1995: 36), which give unity and coherence and which are an amalgam of the rational and the intuitive.

The design strategy advocated in this book conforms to Boisot's (1995) 'strategic intent': that is, it purports to being a coherent mix of vision, intuition and research-driven knowledge, which enables schools to make institution-wide responses rather than to rely either on the inflexibilities of strategic planning or on the opportunistic behaviour of individuals. In many chapters in this book, I refer to 'informed practice' as the manifestation of this mix. An approach based on informed practice lifts the whole enterprise of schooling from a low plane of individualism, where individuals act opportunistically and often in isolation, what Boisot (1995) terms 'intrapreneurship', to a higher level where individuals work collaboratively and, at the same time, experience greater personal satisfaction and success, while the school as an organization achieves synergy.

The School Effectiveness and School Improvement Context

A copious literature has been accumulated on what is wrong with contemporary schools, why they are failing and what is needed by way of rectification. Many pundits have offered prescriptions for reform and improvement. A careful scrutiny of this literature, however, reveals that much of it is over-reliant on opinion or personal values, some is piecemeal in its coverage of what needs to be changed, and practically all of it assumes a 'Western' perspective. There is certainly need for vigilance before particular policies, strategies or practices become endorsed.

At least two approaches to major school reform can be discerned from among advocates: one which argues that schools have failed in terms of their main mission to educate students, and another which celebrates the past achievements of schools in general but which recognizes that they are increasingly failing to meet the new challenges and agendas of future societies and economies. Both points of view arrive at the same conclusion, namely, that schools need to change if they are to meet the needs and aspirations of their clientele and remain relevant and valued institutions. They differ, however, in their assessments of school achievements in the past and present. The view adopted in this book is that past and present schools owe their design to a bygone age – the early twentieth century – when for the first time the main challenge was to educate the mass of children for the industrial society. This argument holds that schools were designed to meet the needs of the time, namely, to educate students in large numbers, and only to a limited degree, since the majority were considered to need only a basic grasp of numeracy and literacy to fulfil the economic and social requirements of the period. In this vein, and in retrospect, it could be argued that the design served society reasonably well.

Debate has also taken place over the ability and willingness of schools to change. It is often argued that a design which has served well for most of the twentieth century is inadequate for the twenty-first century as schools have generally failed to keep abreast of new developments, challenges and expectations associated with broader socioeconomic change. This has led some to claim that schools are 'fossilized' institutions; that even prisons and psychiatric hospitals have changed more than schools over the past fifty years. A counter-view, however, is the argument that schools have indeed undergone appreciable change, including reforms to the curriculum, organization and managerial decision making, and that it is all too easy to be dismissive of their flexibility and achievements.

In trying to resolve such debates, one is inevitably forced into making generalizations, and this is a dangerous practice when considering an organization (the school) which exists in hundreds of thousands across the world. By their very nature, most schools and teachers tend to be conservative and to exhibit varying degrees of resistance to change. Part of their mission is to socialize the young into adult society by introducing them to the traditions and mores which have become ingrained. On the other hand, the nature of adult society is itself changing, and another part of the mission is to prepare students for a society which is continuously evolving.

Over the past twenty years, a stream of school effectiveness studies, mostly employing quantitative techniques and large-scale samples, have provided some guidance as to the characteristics of so-called 'effective schools'. These have generated checklists which, as even the researchers themselves readily accept, represent an oversimplification of a complex process. As indicated in one commonly quoted aphorism, 'we know what makes an effective school, but we do not know how to make schools effective'. The process of making schools effective, or managing change, is the core of the so-called school improvement movement, to which increasing attention has swung over the past decade. While it is readily accepted that simple adoption of checklist characteristics will not do because each school is a unique organism with its own combination of cultural and resource characteristics, we still seem to be falling short of building robust theories of school improvement and change management which are sufficiently fine-tuned to accommodate diversity and difference found in schools and their contexts.

Growing criticism of the school effectiveness movement has been mounted in recent times. Such criticism, centred on the following, has led some to feel disenchantment with the whole movement:

- 'effectiveness' is a contested concept, and no single definition has found support;
- the research methods and procedures employed are mainly large-scale statistical studies which fail to unravel the full complexity of interrelationships;

- the same preponderance of quantitative studies fail to take account of the individuality and uniqueness of factors underlying the effectiveness of each school;
- the focus on the school as the unit of operation has failed to recognize the variability of performance *within* the school, such as exists at department and teacher levels, although recent multi-level techniques may address this problem in part.

While it is not the intention of this book to launch a full-scale assault on the body of school effectiveness research, it is worth mentioning some of the issues which continue to raise debate. There is the question of time: for how long should a school demonstrate a level of performance in order to be classified as 'effective'? There are the fundamental questions of effective at what, and for whom? Slee et al. (1998), for example, challenge the school effectiveness movement by raising these two questions. They maintain that while purporting to be inclusive and comprehensive, the school effectiveness research is flawed along with some of its assumptions. They argue that it is excluding, normative and regulatory, and that it can be bureaucratic and disempowering. School effectiveness researchers have too easily jumped to the assertion that an effective school is effective for *all* of its students, irrespective of ability, gender or age. The assertion has powerful appeal, especially in times of growing consciousness with respect to equity and equal opportunity. Many schools seem to be 'effective' in catering for some of their students, whether they be the gifted, those with special needs, or the broad group in the middle, but given finite resources and human energy, schools struggle to provide an equally high standard for all. They are indisputably effective for *some*. The question is, do such schools qualify for the title 'effective'?

Likewise, some commentators recognize problems with the school improvement research. These focus on the self-evident truth that the process of change lies at the heart of improvement, and that change ultimately reduces to the human capacity and willingness to do things differently. This means that change *inter alia* is political and cultural, realities which the school improvement research has generally failed to take sufficiently into account. Nonetheless, as with the school effectiveness research, these are not grounds for total dismissal of the findings. There are valuable insights to be gained, especially when the improvement research takes cognisance of political and cultural factors.

Some are tempted to dismiss the school effectiveness and school improvement movements outright. This is as much of a mistake on their part as are the shortcomings they allege the school effectiveness and school improvement researchers have made. For all its faults and weaknesses, the fact is that scores of effectiveness and improvement studies conducted chiefly in the US, UK and the Netherlands are broadly confirmatory. They present some useful guidelines which, when interpreted critically and cautiously, are too useful to be dismissed. Many of the findings appeal to common sense, even if they need filtering and modification in practice to accord with competing sets of values and aims.

There are other bodies of related literature besides the school effectiveness and school improvement movements, which deserve consideration. One such body focuses on restructuring, a generic and comprehensive term which embraces policy and practice aimed at transforming education across all levels from system through regional and district to school. Scholars may pay particular attention to one of these levels, while acknowledging the contextual importance of the other levels. In the case of this book, the focus is placed on the school for a number of reasons. It is the unit of operation closest to the client groups, namely students and parents; it is charged with responsibility for delivering the most important educational services, teaching and learning; and recent restructuring movements have witnessed a redistribution of powers and responsibilities from other levels to the school.

An important issue concerning the burgeoning literature on restructuring is the extent to which it embraces the school effectiveness and school improvement bodies of knowledge, and as a consequence, the extent to which it constitutes a derived or dependent, as opposed to a discrete, body of literature. Consistent with the view espoused in this book, the school effectiveness and school improvement movements can and should inform restructuring. Consequently, in this eclectic view, few clear divides exist between these bodies of literature.

Designing or re-designing a school in its entirety necessarily incorporates many ideas, theories and findings from a diverse range of literatures, including teaching and teacher effectiveness, learning theory, learning styles and learning processes, organizational theory, leadership and management of resources, and culture building. Such eclecticism is part of a whole-school approach which advocates the connectivity of the parts of a school and the imprudence of 'tinkering' with piecemeal or incremental change when the situation calls for something more. Schools, as dynamic organizations, are multi-functional; at one and the same time, they engage in learning, teaching, managing, organizing, leading, decision making and so on. In designing future learning-centred schools, it is necessary to take all of these into account. Failure to so do has been a major reason for unsuccessful reform in the past.

Terminology: 'Design', 'Restructuring', 'Reform'

It is important to distinguish between the terms 'reform', 'restructuring' and 'design.' For the purposes of the present discussion, the three terms can be seen as a continuum based on intentionality with respect to change. Thus educational 'reform' is a general term applied to any change, large or small.

Conceptually, it fails to convey definition and specificity to the change. 'Restructuring', on the other hand, as applied to the school, has become a term associated with major transformation of one or more of the following: school governance, leadership, management and school organization, and curriculum, teaching and learning. In other words, 'restructuring' brings a sense of more specificity to the change than does 'reform', but only marginally so. The concept of 'design', as used in this book, brings significantly more specificity to the process than either reform or restructuring. It has three key implications: first, intentionality to the structures, processes and practices proposed or implemented; second, connectivity or linkage between the various elements; and third, following from the second attribute, reinforcement, synergy and consistency of the different elements and parts.

Thus the concept of 'school design' not only has connotations of comprehensiveness, but also planned intentionality, which reform and restructuring do not necessarily possess. 'School design' implies forethought, planned, intended, deliberate and comprehensive change creating desired organizational patterns. The term 're-design' is used periodically throughout the book to signify that the present form and shape of most schools has been determined by the requirements of an earlier period and that a new and different configuration is now needed to meet the changed expectations and requirements of schools in future societies.

The distinction made between 'reform' and 'design' may go some way to explain the two seemingly contradictory views elucidated earlier, namely, that schools have not changed much over the last fifty years, or that on the contrary they have changed a great deal. Many school change programmes are more reforms than designs; that is, they are inadequately and only partially conceived, and are *ad hoc* and incremental rather than systematic, integral and holistic. Thus curriculum reforms may have been implemented without concomitant supportive changes to school management and organization. This again explains how some can claim that schools have been receptive to many piecemeal changes, while others maintain that schools have changed relatively little.

Why the Need for School Design?

It has already been noted that school design owes its origins to a configuration which served the industrial society and its needs for an industrial workforce. Conversely, in the post-industrial, technology-driven age of the twenty-first century, a different set of skills is necessary in order for students to become valued citizens and successful members of the workforce. The question is, what are the forces and trends propelling the move for schools to re-design?

First, schools are functioning in turbulent educational policy environments.

Policy statements underpinning school restructuring allude to the basic aim of improving student learning outcomes. Many governments have established structures and procedures to render schools accountable for their students' academic performance. Schools are expected to define their purpose in school development plans and to render accountability in terms of student outcomes. System-wide monitoring of standards and student attainments in basic subject and skill areas, such as literacy and numeracy, allow ministries, schools and parents to measure and compare the performances of individual schools against system-wide norms. These demands on schools shift the focus away from a traditional concern for resource inputs to an orientation towards student outcomes.

Second, attacks on schooling come from critics who focus on the relationship between schooling and the broad long-term changes taking place in society and the economy. These analysts place students and their learning at the heart of their arguments to reconstruct schools. The type of workforce needed for the future, for example, will require school and college programs to reflect knowledge-based, high technology competencies and skills required in a competitive global economy.

Elsewhere, Schlechty (1990) refers to the shift of American society from an industrial base to an information base in the late twentieth century and describes his vision of schools for the twenty-first century to meet this change. In an information-based society, knowledge work, work that entails expending mental effort, is the primary mode of work since information constitutes the main means for its accomplishment. Calls for major reform of the American school system are abundant. Elmore et al. (1990: 1–2), for example, argues that:

> In order to sustain our present standard of living and regain our competitive position in the world economy … we will need a better educated work force, which will in turn, mean that schools will have to dramatically improve the way they educate all children.

In a particularly succinct account of the educational implications of moving from an industrial to a post-industrial information society, Murphy (1992: 114) recognizes:

> A vision of education quite unlike the 'centre of production' (Barth, 1986: 295) image that has shaped schooling throughout the industrial age. In its stead stand metaphors of 'education as human development' (Clark, 1990: 27), school as a 'community of learners' (Barth, 1986: 295), and administrators as 'transformative intellectuals' (Foster, 1989: 1). Embedded in this emerging post-industrial conception of education and schooling are changes in 3 areas: the relationship between the

school and its larger environment, the management and organization of schooling, and the nature of teaching and learning.

A new wave of educational thinking in the 1990s reinforces this reconceptualization of teaching and learning. American scholars recognize a shift from behavioural psychology, which has been the source of thinking underpinning the traditional industrial model of schooling, to social cognitive or constructivist psychology as the inspiration for a new model of learning and teaching in the post-industrial information society (Cohen, 1988; Murphy, 1992). Murphy (1992: 117) states, 'This shift away from a "science of teaching" and toward "research on cognition as a basis for understanding how people learn casts an entirely different perspective on how the schooling process should be re-designed" (Hutchins, 1988: 47).'

Third, most social scientists predict a continuing rise in the social problems of alcoholism, drugs, crime, vandalism and family breakup in the foreseeable future. An increasing number and proportion of students will be directly or indirectly affected by these trends. If schools are simply to keep pace, let alone seriously cope with these growing problems, they will have to shift from their established customary practices.

Fourth, there is growing concern that too many students leave school with little or no success in learning (Goodlad, 1984; Sizer, 1984). Murphy (1991: 52), referring to the United States, claims that 'twenty-five percent of all students physically remove themselves from engagement in learning by dropping out of school'. Of those who stay, many fail to achieve the school graduation certificate, let alone succeed in passing a public exam, assuming it exists, for college entrance. While it has become customary to blame students for their failure to learn, more recently the spotlight has tended to shift to the school and to teachers to assume more responsibility for ensuring that all students learn (Chubb, 1988). Many disaffected students report negative attitudes toward school, finding them unfriendly and uncaring places, unreflective of their values, interests and subcultures (Cuban, 1989). Pressures for mainstream schools and classes to adopt policies of inclusion serve only to exacerbate the problem, placing ever increasing and unrealistic expectations on teachers in mainstream classes. Policies espousing equity and protection of rights for minority and underprivileged groups also serve to highlight the problem.

A fifth reason arises out of the rigidity of schools with respect to changing their core technology, that is, teaching and learning. Arguing that present school design owes much to the industrial model, critics claim that schools look much the same as they did fifty or more years ago. Elmore (1990: 8), for example, describes classroom activity for the average student as 'dull, perfunctory and disconnected from what goes on in other classrooms or in the larger community'. Faced with unachievable challenges of educating thirty, forty or more students, often of mixed ability, in the same classroom, teachers either lower their expectations of student learning or focus on smaller groups of more able students who provide them with job satisfaction. With few exceptions, the curriculum is delivered in regimented ways, for fixed periods of time unrelated to individual student needs, and at the end of each year students move in lock-step to the next grade level irrespective of their performance in mastering the material to be learned.

Finally, a growing awareness of social justice issues, particularly pertinent to minority groups and to the educationally deprived and disadvantaged, adds further momentum to the case for school re-design. In times of greater competition and marketization in education, it becomes even more important to protect the rights of those whose interests are least likely to be served. Many scholars see the goal to be the improvement of learning opportunities for all students, recognizing the entitlement of all students to a quality learning experience commensurate with ability, need and interest (Levin, 1987; Slavin, 1988). Schools are increasingly expected to cater to the needs of all students through policies of inclusion at a time when the student body is growing more multicultural and diverse.

According to the foregoing argument, a case for re-designing schools appears robust. The problematic issue, however, is how best to re-design. Are there models, precepts and frameworks which can help address this issue? Most would agree that the main goal should be to gear design to improved teaching and learning for all students. Accordingly, the following chapter presents a conceptualization of school design along these lines.

Globalization, Internationalization and Ethnocentrism

A final point in this discussion centres on two parallel and contemporary trends. The first concerns the increasing globalization and internationalization of educational policy, particularly with respect to restructuring. Dimmock (1998), for example, has noted in regard to Hong Kong that the basis of school restructuring policy owes its origins to similar initiatives in Australia, the UK and US. The globalization phenomenon generates a new conceptual language. Only relatively few countries generate new policy ideas – often the US and UK – and become policy exporters. Other countries and states which adopt the policies become policy importers. If the latter simply adopt policies with little adaptation, they resort to what I term 'policy cloning' (Dimmock, 1998).

The second relates to the ethnocentric, and largely Western (Anglo-American) bias to the ideas, policies, practices and research which have come to dominate the globalization process. Books and journal articles are written, and professional development and training provided, assuming a Western perspective. The assumption, made explicitly or implicitly, is that what applies in countries such as the US, UK and Australia is equally relevant to other countries and states with very different cultures. The problem lies not only with the 'exporting' countries, but also with the 'importers', who may be only too willing to accept the ideas and practices from the West. Herein lies a paradox: the more that education policy becomes globalized, the more important it becomes to take cognisance of each society's culture. Paraphrasing, the greater the take-up of a policy by different countries and states, the more important it is for each to juxtapose its own culture to increase the likelihood of policy acceptance and implementation (Dimmock, 1998).

Global searches for effective schools are of limited utility unless we take account of the cultural contexts within which those schools have evolved. What is an 'effective' school in one culture may not be thought of in the same way in another. What works in one culture may not work in another. 'Effective' schools need, therefore, to be seen in cultural context, a perspective requiring the development of cross-cultural frameworks. One of the purposes of this book is to explore the implications of a cross-cultural perspective.

Aims and Argument of the Book

Readers should by now have some idea from the foregoing discussion of the flavour of this book. Essentially, it provides an approach to whole-school design or re-design which aims at creating the learning-centred school, and which takes the significance of culture into account in determining that learning-centred schools may assume different characteristics in different societies. In achieving this aim, a number of sources are drawn upon. These include:

- relevant research findings from the school effectiveness and school improvement movements, the teaching and learning effectiveness literature, credible ideas on learning theory and learning processes, technology, leadership, management and organization theory;
- information gained from leading schools in different parts of the world;
- experience gained through professionally developing principals and other professionals in a wide range of contexts;
- knowledge and personal experience gained from living and working in a European, Australian and Asian culture.

The book has five main purposes, as set out below:

- to present models and precepts of school design which match the goal of improving student learning;
- to develop a framework for the cross-cultural comparison of schools in different societies;

- to provide a systematic approach to whole-school design by articulating informed practice for each of the elements in the espoused models and frameworks;
- to contextualize the elements of school design by highlighting the influence of societal culture in determining what is appropriate;
- to emphasize the connectivity between the various elements which comprise a school.

Underpinning the book is a central argument, with five premises, as follows:

- the onus to re-design is on each school;
- re-design should focus on teaching, learning and the curriculum;
- school design needs to be holistic, emphasizing the interconnections between all parts of a school;
- no single blueprint of school design is appropriate for all schools; however, there are generic precepts and approaches which provide sensible guidelines and directions;
- it is important to contextualize models and blueprints of school design within the societal culture in which they have developed; what is appropriate for one culture will probably require adaptation when implemented in another.

These premises deserve amplification. The first premise rests on the fact that, irrespective of whether a school is in the government system, is part of a religious system or is independent, the main responsibility for its re-design rests within. Support from outside the school or elsewhere in the system may be offered, but it is essentially the school community which must undertake the necessary moves. The second premise recognizes that teaching, learning and the curriculum are the most important functions of a school since they reflect the main reasons for its existence. The third takes cognisance of the fact that schools are dynamic, organic systems and that the parts are interrelated such that change in one part is likely to have effects on other related parts. The fourth premise also follows from the organic nature of schools as organizations; each school is a unique amalgam of its human, physical and material resources, and these produce a unique culture. Each school is a reflection of the individuals and groups which form its community. Consequently, no single blueprint will suit all schools. Nonetheless, it is argued that there are sound precepts and approaches on which all schools can formulate their own responses to the challenge of school design. The fifth premise parallels the fourth in extending the point of uniqueness of schools to societal level cultures. That is, no single blueprint will necessarily suit schools in different countries and states, since schools exist within cultural environments which reflect different values, customs and expectations. Again, it is argued that generic precepts and models are useful in guiding the design of schools and that these apply across different cultures.

The Structure and Content of the Book

This introductory chapter has two main purposes: to explain the aims of the book and the central argument threading through the chapters, and to establish the need for, and nature of, school restructuring and why schools are facing the challenges of re-designing themselves. In Chapter 2, a number of models are presented which are deemed helpful in understanding school restructuring and design. These provide a framework for conceptualizing the complex interrelationships which underpin the process of school design. They are thus useful in providing frameworks for, and insights to, subsequent chapters of the book. Chapter 3 raises the significance of culture at societal and organizational levels. A cross-cultural framework comprising dimensions at societal and organizational levels is introduced which, it is suggested, is useful in gauging and comparing cultural differences and similarities with repercussions for school design. The purpose of Chapters 2 and 3 is thus to frame analysis and discussion in subsequent chapters as well as to provide a structure for the rest of the book.

Initiating school reform and design is the theme of Chapter 4. Where does a school begin and how does it go about the process? An important part of this early experience is establishing an organizational culture for re-design. Chapters 5, 6 and 7 comprise the heart of the design process. Chapter 5 selectively considers some fundamental considerations of curriculum in the re-designed school. Chapter 6 shifts the focus to learning processes and outcomes and focuses on the main aim of schools, namely, the pursuit of learning for all students. Chapter 7 highlights informed teaching practices; the term 'informed teaching practices' is preferred to the commonly used 'best practices' for reasons explained in the chapter. In both Chapters 6 and 7, some important cultural differences are noted as to how students learn and teachers teach in Chinese as compared with Anglo-American societies.

Chapters 8 through 12 explore the contributions to enhancing teaching and learning made by a number of key elements. Chapter 8 introduces the role and contribution of computer technology to the enhancement of teaching and learning in the re-designed school. Chapter 9 moves to organizational structures and their significance in supporting informed teaching and learning. In Chapter 10, attention switches to the importance of appropriate personnel and financial policies supporting informed teaching and learning in the re-designed school. In Chapter 11, the importance of evaluation is emphasized while focusing discussion on teacher appraisal in the re-designed school. Chapter 12 highlights the role and contribution of leadership and management in reinforcing and promoting teaching and learning, and draws some implications from leadership in culturally diverse societies.

Finally, Chapter 13 provides an overview of the holistic nature of school re-design, in particular, the interdependence and connectivity of the different elements in its creation. The benefits of internal harmony and consistency between the elements, in order to achieve organizational synergy and efficiency and effectiveness, are extolled. It is argued that achieving and maintaining high degrees of connectivity and consistency is the responsibility of school leaders.

References

Barth, R.S. (1986) 'On sheep and goats and school reform', *Phi Delta Kappan* 68 (4): 293–6.

Boisot, M. (1995) 'Preparing for turbulence: the changing relationship between strategy and management development in the learning organisation', in B. Garratt (ed.), *Developing Strategic Thought: Rediscovering the Art of Direction-Giving*, London: McGraw-Hill.

Chubb, J.E. (1988) 'Why the current wave of school reform will fail', *The Public Interest*, 90: 28–47.

Clark, D.L. (1990) *Reinventing School Leadership*, working memo prepared for the reinventing school leadership conference, Cambridge, MA: National Center for Educational Leadership, 25–9.

Cohen, D.K. (1988) *Teaching practice: Plus ca change—*,. East Lansing: Michigan State University, The National Centre for Research on Teacher Education (Issue Paper 88–3).

Cuban, L. (1989) 'The "at-risk" label and the problem of urban school reform', *Phi Delta Kappan*, 70 (10): 780–4, 799–801.

Dimmock, C. (1998) 'School restructuring and the principalship: the applicability of Western theories, policies and practices to East and South-East Asian cultures', *Educational Management and Administration* 26 (4): 363–77.

Elmore, R.F. et al. (1990) *Restructuring Schools: The Next Generation of Educational Reform*, San Francisco: Jossey Bass.

Foster, W. (1989) 'School Leaders as Transformational Intellectuals: A Theoretical Argument', paper presented at the Annual Meeting of the American Educational Association, San Francisco.

Goodlad, J.I. (1984) *A Place Called School: Prospects for the Future*, New York: McGraw-Hill.

Holly, P. (1990) 'Catching the wave of the future; moving beyond school effectiveness by re-designing schools', *School Organisation* 10 (2 & 3): 195–212.

Hutchins, C.L. (1988) 'Design as the missing piece in education', in Far West Laboratory for Educational Research and Development, *The Redesign of Education: A Collection of Papers Concerned with Comprehensive Educational Reform*, San Francisco: Far West Laboratory, 1: 47–9.

Levin, H.M. (1987) 'Accelerated schools for disadvantaged students', *Educational Leadership* 44 (6): 19–21.

Murphy, J. (1991) *Restructuring Schools: Capturing and Assessing the Phenomena*, New York: Teachers College Press.

—— (1992) *The Landscape of Leadership Preparation: Patterns and Possibilities*, Beverly Hills, CA: Corwin/Sage.

Schlechty, P.C. (1990) *Schools for the 21st Century: Leadership Imperatives for Educational Reform*, San Francisco: Jossey Bass.

Sizer, T.R. (1984) *Horace's Compromise: The Dilemma of the American High School*, Boston: Houghton Mifflin.

Slavin, R.E. (1988) 'On research and school organisation: a conversation with Bob Slavin', *Educational Leadership* 46 (2): 22–9.

Slee, R., Weiner, G. and Tomlinson, S. (eds) (1998) *School Effectiveness for Whom? Challenges to the School Effectiveness and School Improvement Movements*, London: Falmer Press.

2 Designing Learning-Centred Schools

Models, Frameworks and Precepts

The purpose of this chapter is to present models, frameworks and precepts which help clarify the concept of a re-designed school as it is advocated in this book. Models and frameworks are abstractions and simplifications of reality. They enable analysis to focus on particular variables or parts of a system and the relationships between them, and at the same time to see the parts in relation to the whole. Furthermore, modelling can serve a useful purpose in enabling the formation of shared visions and goals among personnel working at different levels within a school and a school system.

Precepts are principles which underlie models; they are based on beliefs and values. When framing precepts for school design, it is important to explicate the beliefs and values underlying the argument. The school design precepts espoused in this book are unequivocally founded on the promotion of quality teaching, learning and curricula for all students, irrespective of age, gender or ability. In the present context, the term 'quality school' is taken to mean a school which delivers and promotes teaching, learning and curricula to all of its students to a standard that extends the achievements of both teachers and students up to or beyond what might reasonably be expected. Leadership and management should be added to this definition since, in the present context, they are considered important in facilitating the delivery and promotion of high achievement in teaching, learning and curricula. Too often, the term 'quality school' is used in contemporary parlance without adequate definition, a situation which leaves the values of those involved unarticulated and tacit.

Many school system administrators and politicians have introduced restructuring policies over the past decade which are not only intended to change the administrative and organizational arrangements of schools, but also to improve the quality of classroom teaching and learning. There is abundant evidence to date showing that relatively few of these schemes have penetrated the classroom to affect teaching and learning (Murphy, 1991; Murphy and Beck, 1995). Consequently, many now question the assumed relationship between restructuring and improved teaching and learning (Dimmock, 1995a).

A central purpose of this chapter is to advocate how the mapping and conceptualizing of such a relationship may be forged. It suggests that empirical research on the effects of restructuring should be encouraged. However, since restructuring has influenced mainly policy, administrative and organizational arrangements, then predictably, empirical research will currently yield relatively little in terms of how it affects the quality of teaching and learning and classroom variables. Instead, a more promising approach is to investigate how restructuring could be engineered to influence classroom variables. A promising way to achieve such a goal is through a systematic approach to school re-design.

The present argument is that restructuring policy is likely to fail if it does not recognize and embrace the idea of school design. That is, restructuring may reconfigure the power and influence relationships among participants, but of itself it is unlikely to improve the quality of teaching and learning. Chapter 1 referred to a number of bodies of literature ranging from those at the macro level, such as school effectiveness, school improvement and restructuring, to those at the micro level, such as effective teaching and learning research. Acknowledging these bodies of literature is helpful in reminding us that restructuring is likely to have little influence on enhancing teaching and learning if policies fail to reflect and support the conditions, cultures, structures and practices which appear to characterize effective classrooms and schools. Thus at the micro level of restructuring, re-designing teachers' work, student work and classroom conditions should take cognisance of research findings on effective teaching and learning. In regard to macro-restructuring at system and whole-school levels, the school effectiveness and school improvement research findings become more pertinent to policy design.

It is difficult to avoid the conclusion that restructuring policy initiated from system centres is, at best, likely to do little more than create the context and environment conducive for schools themselves to assume responsibility for internal re-design, especially as it relates to the micro-level of the classroom. This still leaves a number of problematic issues: which systemic policies are more conducive to school re-design? What are the linkages between the two? Why and how do schools in the same system embark on re-design while others do not? The models and frameworks discussed in this chapter will address these questions.

It follows from the above discussion that the current need is not so much to research the extent to which restructuring has influenced teaching and learning, but how such influence can be engineered. The key question is: how can schools be re-designed or reconfigured to improve the quality of teaching and learning? It will be argued here that restructuring policy and school-level practice need to be re-examined if they are to have intentional and beneficial outcomes on classroom variables. Consequently, there is need for better understanding of the linkages between system, school and class-room variables (Banathy, 1988; Scheerens, 1992).

This chapter will first establish a number of precepts for school design. Second, it will conceptualize and model the linkages between the system and school levels. Third, it will conceptualize and model the linkages within the school in order to identify the chains of variables which need to be forged for policy to thread through the school to the class teacher and student. In other words, it will explore the organizational territory of the school. According to this perspective, management is concerned with proactively forging links between the means and goals. Leadership and management are viewed as mediating and forging the practices and structures which need to be in place in order for school re-design to embrace quality teaching and learning. Fourth, an overall model of the school and its environment is presented. In proffering a number of precepts, models and frameworks, it is convenient to group them into those which focus on the relationship between the school and the system, and those which concentrate on the school *per se*. Comment is offered on the relevance of each model to the theme of school design. Finally, in the summary and conclusions, the impor-tance of societal culture is introduced as a factor in questioning the cross-cultural transferability of many policies, theories and practices of rele-vance to school design.

Precepts for School Design

What would schools geared to effective teaching and learning for all students look like? This is a far more difficult question to address than it seems, because existing practice in schools departs markedly from many of the principles underlying effective teaching and learning. A degree of imagi-nation is thus called for in reconstructing quality schools for the future. A vision of these quality schools, however, can be forged from the existing knowledge base derived from research findings on learning styles, effective teaching and learning and school effectiveness and school improvement. This vision also appeals to literature in the field of policy implementation.

From reviews of this extensive research literature, it is possible to derive seven main precepts undergirding the quality school for learning (Dimmock, 1995b):

1   student outcomes provide goal direction for learning.
2   schools exist primarily for teaching and learning; learning and the indi-vidual learner are made the centrepiece of all that happens in the school.
3   teaching focuses on learning and teaching for understanding; a balance and variety of teaching strategies is achieved, a combination of methods from didactic and expository to constructivist.

4   the curriculum is tailored to suit the diverse needs of students.
5   learning and teaching shape and dictate school structures and organiza-
     tion, including technology and the use of space, which are designed to
     support and facilitate the principles and practices of learning and
     teaching.
6   learning and teaching determine professional development, leadership
     and management, resource allocation and culture/climate, all of which
     are dedicated to supporting a service delivery designed for quality
     teaching and learning.
7   at all stages and in all activities, especially teaching, learning and leader-
     ship, the school adheres to 'informed practice'.

These seven precepts provide only a partial explanation for quality
schools of the future. Of equal importance is their interrelationship, rather
than their separateness. Connectivity holds the key to unlocking excellence
in the quality of service delivery. Furthermore, the direction and nature of
this interrelationship is critical. School systems have tended to develop
policy and practice from the top down, that is, from a central bureaucracy
down to the school. This is most conspicuous in traditionally centralized
school systems, such as the Australian states, but it is also true of schools
in decentralized systems. Consequently, policies are developed at the top
and trickle down to the classroom teacher with little regard for the problems of implementation and the classroom context. It should cause no
surprise that many policies fail to be implemented, or are only partly implemented. Likewise it is little wonder that since policies are formulated by
people far removed from the classroom who are not necessarily conversant
with the core technology of schools, top-down policy has generally failed to
deliver significant improvements to teaching and learning over the past
century. It is argued here that schools excelling in learning and teaching are
likely to be driven more by bottom-up generated policies, issues and
concerns.

The Importance of 'Informed Practice' rather than 'Best Practice'

A commonly used term in effective teaching and school effectiveness literature is 'best practices'. It enjoys ready appeal among scholars and
practitioners alike. In terms of its connotations, however, the term is problematic. A few scholars have already begun to recommend alternatives;
Davis (1997), for example, prefers 'wise practices'. However, for reasons
explained below, I advocate the usage of 'informed practice'.

One reason why the term 'best practices' is problematic is its implication
that there is only one best way of teaching, learning or managing. In this
respect, 'better practices' might be more valid than 'best practices', since

research evidence tends to be more tentative and conditional than generalizable and robust. Thus the term 'best practice' is an oversimplification of what are invariably complex phenomena, a point more fully explored below. A related reason why the term 'best practices' is unhelpful is its implication that there are right and wrong ways of teaching; for example, that direct teaching is wrong and that cooperative learning is to be preferred. This leads many critics of the term to complain that a 'best practices' approach is unduly restrictive and prescriptive on teachers, that it de-professionalizes their work and turns them into simple technicians of a 'science' of teaching. Such a view, however, represents a misunderstanding and distortion of the 'best practices' literature. Far from narrowing the range of choice available, it advocates that teachers have a wider range of practices from which to select. Evidence reveals, for example, that *both* direct teaching and cooperative learning are more likely to be successful when teachers adopt certain behaviours and factor-in certain contextual features. The 'best practices' approach therefore informs teachers about how to maximize the effectiveness of whatever approach they wish to adopt. It is therefore more likely to increase professionalism rather than reduce it.

There is now substantial research evidence to indicate that some practices are more conducive to the achievement of desired outcomes than others, a theme brought out more substantially in subsequent chapters. For our current purpose, however, we know that research findings exist on effective teaching which provide helpful guidance as to which strategies and approaches are more likely to result in student learning. The same is true of the characteristics of effective schools and of school improvement. One important hallmark of a profession is that it has a well accepted body of knowledge underpinning practice on which its practitioners are expected to draw. Teachers have traditionally failed to recognize and agree upon a set of practices to underpin their profession. Instead, they have chosen to develop their own strategies, often based on response to their circumstantial experiences rather than on informed understanding of research evidence and validated theory. With few exceptions, teaching in most societies has traditionally failed to win the level of professional status from its publics that it would like or deserve, partly because of this low level of consensus and agreement among its members as to what constitutes a body of informed practice.

While many teachers fail to acknowledge the existence of research evidence which could help underpin a body of professional practice, it is not a simple matter of their adopting such practices. This is because the research evidence itself is contextual in that a particular approach or method may have been found to work in an environment with specific characteristics, such as class size, ability grouping, physical space or resource levels. Thus the teacher whose environment differs in any of these respects would need to reflect on whether the practice is feasible in their own environment and what, if any, adaptations are necessary.

Neither is it simply a question of adaptation to different settings. Teachers need to match their own views and experiences with the research evidence on successful practice. This is what the process of reflection should mean. The teacher as reflective practitioner is a meaningless concept unless teachers first have knowledge of sound practice as a basis on which to reflect. Without such knowledge, reflection is likely to take place in a context of ignorance and inevitably become over-reliant on personal experience. Doctors and lawyers combine a technical knowledge base of medicine and law, respectively, with a process of critical reflection with regard to its application to specific cases and situations. Teachers should be no different. As professionals, they should be cognisant with the professional knowledge base underpinning teaching and learning and be able to critically reflect upon it with a view to its appropriate application in particular situations. For these reasons, the term 'informed practice' is more appropriate than 'best practice'. Teachers need to be informed in order to make judgements about appropriate strategies to adopt in given situations and contexts.

Models and Frameworks of the School–System Relationship

The first framework presented (see Figure 2.1) depicts the package of restructuring measures which have been introduced by governments in many countries and states. The framework has three parts. On the left are the present characteristics of schools; on the right is the aim of achieving improved student learning. In the centre is the raft of restructuring policies and practices. The range and diversity of measures signify that there are usually many agendas behind restructuring: increasing parental and teacher involvement in school decision making, increasing the school's control over resources and delegating certain curriculum functions, promoting school planning and accountability, and sometimes student-centred learning. These agendas may be worthy in their own right: a convincing case, for example, can be made for promoting teacher involvement in decision making. However, the pursuit of quality schools and improved teaching and learning for all students must remain the prime aim, and it is this which prompts the question as to how the different measures connect with improved teaching and learning outcomes. Attention needs to focus on how each of the policies, practices, and structures independently and/or collectively, directly or indirectly, lead to improved student outcomes. In selecting one of the measures as an example – school development planning – three levels of questions need to be addressed, as follows:

- Is school development planning likely to improve, directly or indirectly, student outcomes? If so, how?

- Are there specific characteristics which school development planning requires in order to have these effects on student outcomes?
- Are there other aspects of restructuring policy and practice which are likely to reinforce the effects of school development planning?

These types of questions need to be asked of each of the restructuring policies shown in Figure 2.1. If policymakers, practitioners and researchers focus on these levels, it may be possible to improve understanding of the linkages between policies, practices and structures, between students, teachers, managers, leaders, parents and bureaucrats, and between all of these and improved student outcomes.

A second framework, shown in Figure 2.2, introduces the relationships between the system centre and the school. This highlights some of the key policy parameters involved in the transfer of functions from centre to

Figure 2.1 *The Relationship between Schools, Restructuring Policies and Improved Student Outcomes*

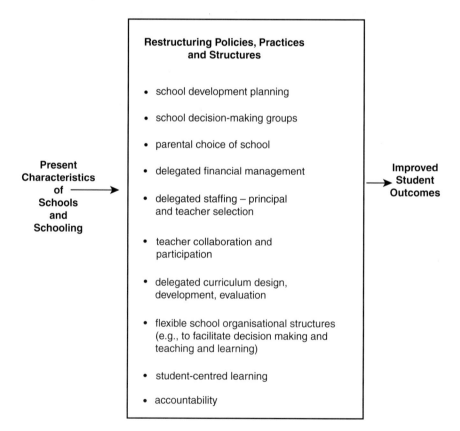

school. Depicted on a number of separate but connected continua are responsibilities, authority and power, resource levels and controls, and accountability. Synchrony between these, it is argued, is crucial. If one or more of these is shifted from the system centre to the school without a commensurate movement of others in the same direction, then the process of restructuring is likely to be asynchronous and problematic. Thus, if the centre shifts additional responsibilities to schools without furnishing the necessary powers, authority and resources, the school is unlikely to fulfil its obligations. It then becomes iniquitous for the centre to hold the school to account. Accountability should be conceived as a two-dimensional rather than uni-directional process between centre and school. Figure 2.2 also provides a list of the functions for which responsibilities, powers, resources and accountability are operationalized.

A further issue is the extent to which the four variables – responsibility, authority, resources and accountability – are shifted toward either the school or the system centre and the implications for the respective sizes of, and resources consumed by, each. In a restructured decentralized system, the school's resources may grow and the centre's diminish, while in a centralized system, the centre grows in relation to the school (as indicated by thick and thin lines in Figure 2.2). A compensatory adjustment exists between the two, assuming fixed levels of resourcing. In a restructured (decentralizing) school system, it is reasonable to assume that a larger share of the education dollar will be spent at school level rather than at the centre, despite the centre often assuming new roles such as monitoring and evaluating. In a school system bent on maximizing student outcomes, the aim would be to maximize the proportion of the education dollar dedicated to the school, and in particular to classroom teaching and learning.

Models and Frameworks to Guide School Re-Design

Since the prime aim is to ensure that restructuring policies and practices penetrate to influence classroom activities of teaching and learning, it is crucial to consider the variables internal to the school which connect system policy-making and student learning outcomes (Scheerens, 1992). These are presented in Figure 2.3, which identifies five key sets of variables within the school. These are leadership, management, resources, culture and professional development; school organization and structure, including curriculum, technology and physical space; teaching methods and strategies; learning processes and content; and student outcomes. Outside the school is another level of policy making and administration at the system level.

Figure 2.2 *Restructuring and the Relationship between Authority, Resources and Accountability*

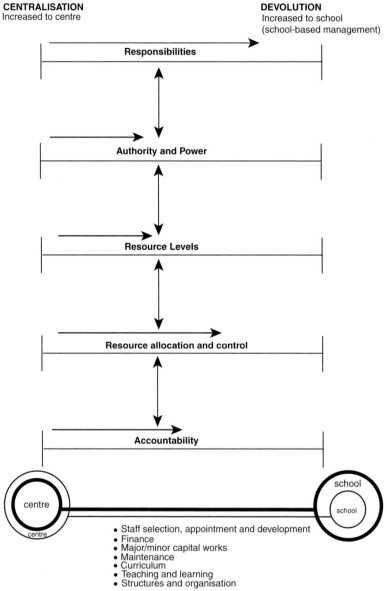

In many systems, devolution has to date increased reponsibility and resource allocation and control to school level, along with some increase in accountability. Commensurate increases in authority and resource levels appear not to have occurred. Challenge: to restructure schools in such a way that increased responsibility and control and allocation of resources are matched by commensurate increases in authority, resource levels and further increases in school accountability.

Figure 2.3 *Restructuring and School Penetration: Linkage with Teaching and Learning*

System Environment: Policy Making, Administration

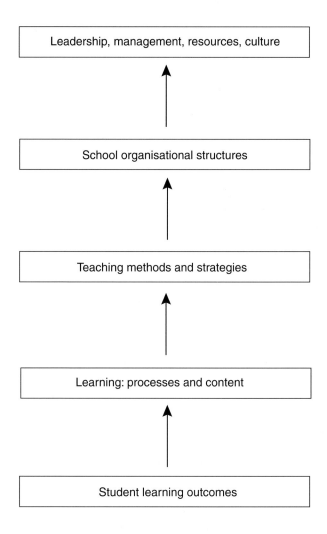

In the conventional paradigm, policy is implemented top-down, from system level into school. Even before a policy initiative has begun to permeate a school it has normally passed through many tiers of the organization, each of which may add its own interpretation. That policy will penetrate to the classroom and have the intended outcomes is therefore less likely the more tiers it permeates. Accordingly, Elmore (1979–80) has suggested a process of backward mapping to reverse the stages of policy making. In other words, begin with the end in mind and work backwards; clarify the end goals and achievements and work back from those, drawing out the implications at each stage. Dimmock (1995b) has identified the key variables at each stage in advocating the application of backward mapping to his five clusters of school-level variables, starting with student learning outcomes as shown in Figure 2.3. Since the most important stage of the policy process is the delivery of quality teaching and learning to achieve the intended outcomes, it makes sense to start rather than finish at that point, by first identifying outcomes.

Backward mapping seeks alignment and consistency at each phase and across all stages. It spotlights the most important part of the policy process, namely, implementation at the point of service delivery. System policy makers begin the policy process at the end point and work back up through the school to the system level in order to derive their own roles in supporting and facilitating the intended outcomes. This model places due importance on the implementation phase of change and on teachers' and students' contributions to the change process.

Through backward mapping, the design process starts with the expression of intended outcomes; in this case, student learning outcomes. The beginning goal and the final outcome are then one and the same. Learning is most effective when it is goal-directed. The interface between student learning outcomes (goals, skills or competencies, which may be expressed in cognitive, affective and behavioural terms) and learning *per se*, is critical in raising to pre-eminence the strategies by which learning is promoted. Key focus questions are: how do students best learn? What are the individual differences between students in how they best learn? Responses to these questions about learning and individual learning styles are necessary prerequisites for the school's next sequential stage of decisions focusing on teaching and teaching strategies. Key issues here are: how do teachers best teach in order for students to achieve the learning outcomes? What are the individual differences between teachers in how they best teach? Most importantly, at the interface between learning and teaching, how does the school's perspective on student learning shape its teaching? Teaching is therefore driven by learning and responds and reacts to the demands, needs and interests of learners.

The foregoing questions and concerns centring on student outcomes, learning and teaching constitute the core technology of the school. Further sequential stages are important in enabling and supporting the core technology. First, how do school organization and structure (including the curriculum, use of technology and physical space, timetable and so on) need re-design in order to provide the framework for delivery of this core technology? These structures should be designed for the purpose of enabling the school to operationalize its planned core technology. Pertinent questions here include: what structures are most enabling for the successful implementation of planned teaching-learning activities? Are there structures in existence which are inhibitive or obstructive of the delivery of effective teaching and learning? In this approach, core technology drives the design of organization and structure rather than the structure dictate core technology.

Second, the core technology of effective learning and teaching, with the addition of organizational structures, provides insights into appropriate leadership, management, resourcing, professional development and culture building. The nature of the school's core technology provides a framework and touchstone for school leadership and management. This provokes the following key questions: how do leadership and management best support effective teaching and learning in the school? Do effective teaching and learning provide the generic purpose of, and priority for, leaders and managers? Closely allied with leadership and management are professional development, resource allocation and culture/climate. Placing the core technology at the forefront of schools raises considerations as to whether patterns of resource allocation and utilization enable and support effective teaching and learning. Similarly, is professional development aligned towards the delivery of informed teaching and learning practices? Do school culture and climate reflect an emphasis on securing effective teaching and learning for all students?

A backward mapping process, as presented in Figure 2.3, can be appropriately applied as a school improvement model, as shown in Figure 2.4. Assume that the school in question wishes to improve the quality of teaching and learning. It currently has a set of goals and it decides to undertake a school review and evaluation. The backward mapping strategy suggests that it start the review process by attending to student learning outcomes and to student learning experiences and processes. Such a review should include cross-representation of all students by age, ethnicity, gender and ability. The issues emanating from a focus on learning might suggest that some improvement is necessary to the teaching strategies and approaches adopted in the school. At the same time, teaching and learning are closely integrated with the curriculum, and there may be some need for a change in curriculum structure and content. The changes to teaching, learning and curriculum, or core technology, may generate a need to change school organization and structure so that they fully align with, and support, the core technology. Finally, all of these changes would expectedly have implications for professional development, leadership, management, resourcing and school culture (Dimmock, 1995c).

The connectedness of the whole process, as described, has a 'ripple' effect. All of the changes cannot be made at the same time and so priorities need to be decided. These priorities become the basis of the school improvement

Figure 2.4 *A Model of School Re-Design through Review and Improvement*

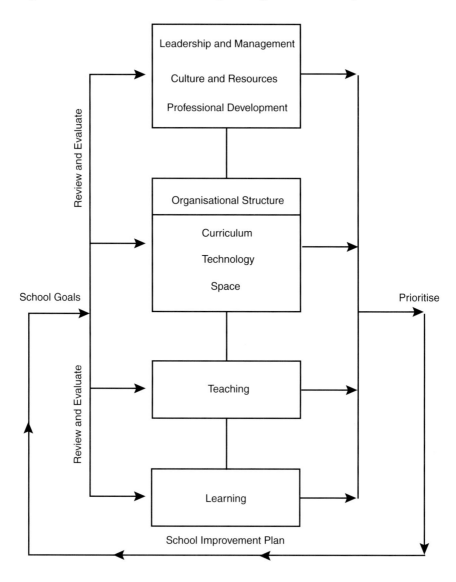

plan at any particular time. They feed back to the school goals for a check on consistency, and may even instigate a modification of the goals.

Connectedness is the key theme of the framework presented in Figure 2.5, which attempts to model the flows and linkages in a school and system environment of restructuring and improved student outcomes. Four levels are recognized: system, whole school, classroom and an intermediate level linking school and classroom. Part of the framework focuses on functions at system level, such as system goal setting, monitoring and reviewing, and regulating and legislating for social justice. Specific responsibilities and structures are dedicated to school level, such as generating a school development plan, establishing a school decision-making group, and delegating financial management, staffing and curriculum functions. These structures, processes and tasks do not appear to have a direct influence on the quality of curriculum, teaching and learning provided at classroom level. Instead, they are filtered, mediated and influenced by a number of intermediate, intervening or indirect variables which assume crucial importance in deciding how effective the school-level functions are in delivering improvements in classroom variables. It is unlikely, for example, that a school development plan and the process of planning *per se* will lead directly to improved classroom performance of teachers and students because it is essentially a whole-school activity. However, when the school development plan is subjected to the influence of the intermediate variables of participative, flexible organizational structures, planning and reviewing processes, patterns of resource allocation, school culture and climate, and professional development, all of which are assumed to be aligned to effective teaching and learning practices at classroom level, it is more likely to have the desired effect. The same analysis can be repeated for school decision-making groups, delegated financial management, staff selection, and curriculum planning. Each is more likely to influence teaching and learning if key intermediate variables are present, supportive and operational in school.

The inclusion of the key intermediate variables identified in Figure 2.5 is justified on the basis of research findings from the school effectiveness and restructuring literature. These constitute enabling variables in the securement of enhanced student learning outcomes. The importance of the first variable – participative, flexible, organizational structures – in enhancing the quality of teaching and learning for all students is emphasized by Brown (1990), Murphy (1991) and the Schools Council (1992) in Australia. This body of research emphasizes the need for school structures (student and teacher grouping, timetable, curriculum organization and delivery) to be more flexible and responsive to the needs and abilities of different students. The participative nature of these structures is also stressed, encouraging parents, teachers, students, and others to gain commitment. The second variable – planning and reviewing – is well documented in the effectiveness literature as an important means of achieving improvement in school effectiveness and student learning (Caldwell and Spinks, 1988; Fullan, 1991; Locke and Latham, 1990). These researchers endorse the value of visioning, goal setting, monitoring, evaluating and feedback as institutionalized practices, not only at classroom level but throughout the school.

The third variable – resource allocation – is considered instrumental to the achievement of improvement in teaching, learning and student outcomes

Figure 2.5 *Restructuring and Linkage with Student Outcomes*

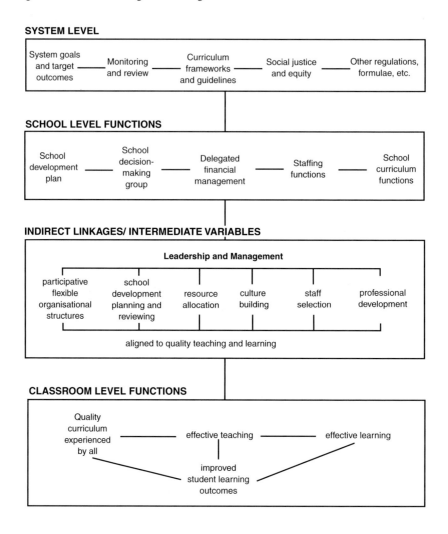

(Caldwell and Spinks, 1988). Appropriate distribution of physical and financial resources is a necessary condition enabling teaching and learning goals and outcomes to be secured. It is assumed that responsibility for resource allocation is best performed nearest to the point of service delivery (that is, the classroom teacher) where the needs of the clientele are best known. The fourth enabling variable – school culture – underlines the importance of a set of values and expectations which need to pervade the school community in its orientation toward the promotion of learning (Rosenholtz, 1989). In particular, many researchers emphasize the importance of collaborative cultures for teachers and students (Fullan, 1991; Fullan and Hargreaves, 1991; Little, 1990). These values provide the foundation for designing school structures, processes and practices, and resource allocation.

The fifth and sixth variables – staff selection and professional development – focus on the importance of the human resource, especially the quality of teachers and teaching, to the achievement of improved student outcomes (Fullan, 1991). The human resource function centres on hiring, retaining, developing and motivating the best quality teachers (Rebore, 1991). It is argued that school-site selection of staff, as opposed to centralized placement, is more likely to secure a match between teachers' attributes and the particular school ethos. Likewise, school-site responsibility for professional development enables the school to focus resources on developing teaching and learning priorities in accordance with its needs (Joyce and Showers, 1988; Louis and Miles, 1990).

Assuming the above reasoning is sound, it is pointless to look for direct links between restructuring and improved student outcomes since few, if any, exist. It is more likely that restructuring, having spawned new structures, processes and functions at school level, will exert meaningful influence on teaching and learning through indirect and mediating variables, such as those identified. Whether these indirect influences materialize is highly dependent on the quality of school leadership and management. The argument presented suggests that direct connections between restructuring and student outcomes are unlikely to exist. Researchers, as well as policy makers and school leaders, should consider the complexity of mediating variables when undertaking multi-level modelling and when searching for improvements to the quality of teaching, learning and student outcomes.

A Gestalt Model

In turning the spotlight back to the school in its restructuring environment, and summarizing many of the aforementioned issues and precepts, reference is made to Figure 2.6. Models and frameworks outlined previously in this chapter have identified key variables without and within the school, and have highlighted the importance of linkage or connectivity between them. While schools are indisputably dynamic organizations, the linkages and connections between the key variables may not exist naturally. In his seminal work, Weick (1976) recognized this phenomenon as 'loose coupling'. Consequently, the linkages and connections will need to be forged, a task which falls to school management.

While backward mapping is a sound strategy to promote the fidelity of school design to student learning outcomes, the reality of school life is rarely smooth or logical. There may, for example, be disagreement at the outset as to what are desirable or appropriate outcomes. Teachers may lack the knowledge and skills to accommodate the different learning styles of students. Formidable physical, financial and time constraints may constitute organizational and structural impediments. As Purkey and Smith (1983: 446) assert, 'most successful school change efforts will be messier and more idiosyncratic than systematic'. Moreover, schools do not exist in an insulated environment. Cultural, political and social forces constantly act upon them. Interference from outside is always possible and principals need to be vigilant and prepared for such eventualities.

Figure 2.6 *The School and its System Environment*

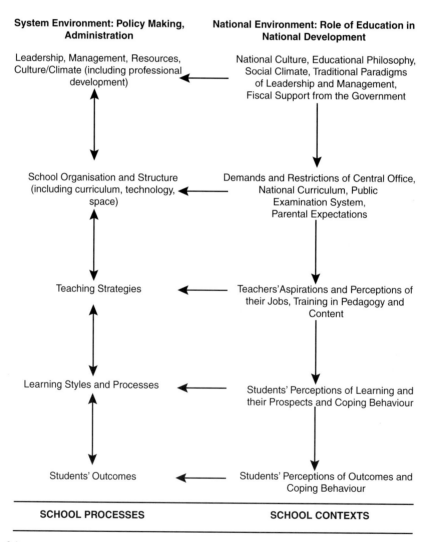

System Environment: Policy Making, Administration	**National Environment: Role of Education in National Development**
Leadership, Management, Resources, Culture/Climate (including professional development)	National Culture, Educational Philosophy, Social Climate, Traditional Paradigms of Leadership and Management, Fiscal Support from the Government
School Organisation and Structure (including curriculum, technology, space)	Demands and Restrictions of Central Office, National Curriculum, Public Examination System, Parental Expectations
Teaching Strategies	Teachers' Aspirations and Perceptions of their Jobs, Training in Pedagogy and Content
Learning Styles and Processes	Students' Perceptions of Learning and their Prospects and Coping Behaviour
Students' Outcomes	Students' Perceptions of Outcomes and Coping Behaviour
SCHOOL PROCESSES	**SCHOOL CONTEXTS**

The tiers in the left hand column of Figure 2.6 constitute the within-school variables which provide the model for the backward mapping school design strategy outlined earlier. The process begins with the desired student outcomes, and works back up through each level of the organization to leadership and management. Many practitioners might prefer an adaptation of this simple backward mapping process by advocating an iterative rather than uni-directional process. This entails starting with student outcomes and backward mapping, but recognizing a need to reverse the algorithm by referring to previous tiers. The backward mapping process then reverses and becomes an iterative, interactive mapping process. Thus learning styles and processes may guide teaching strategies, but the backward mapping process becomes iterative when teaching strategies also influence aspects of learning.

Contrary to the variables in the left-hand column, those in the right-hand column tend to work downwards or forwards, with those at or near the top setting the context for the next level below in a kind of 'nested layer' fashion. What is valued in the societal or national culture, for example, can impact the educational philosophy, leadership, curriculum, exam system, teachers' pedagogy and ultimately students' perceptions of the value of their learning outcomes. This is well illustrated in Chinese societies, such as Singapore, Hong Kong and Taiwan, where scholastic achievement, prized since Confucius's time and reinforced by the mandarin system, has become the obsession of most students and their parents. Students blame themselves more than the system for failure. Not only do the forces in the right-hand column act downwards, they also exert lateral effects on the school in the left column. Teachers' perceptions of their work, for instance, are shaped by societal culture and are reinforced by the educational and examination systems, factors which might detrimentally affect the adoption of new constructivist teaching and learning strategies. Teachers in Asia generally, and in Chinese societies particularly, see themselves as transmitters of knowledge and truth, a role which makes it almost impossible for them to treat students as equals in the pursuit of knowledge.

The point to make is that those exercising leadership in re-designing schools must constantly attend to the wider environment and respond as proactively as they can, while at the same time engineering the within-school variables in the left-hand column of Figure 2.5. They may be able to contain and mitigate some of the more negative environmental forces, while promoting the more positive. There are still other environmental forces which may be beyond their control, such as the materialism and hedonism which characterize many developed and developing societies.

Summary and Conclusion

The models presented in this chapter provide an overarching framework and a suggested strategy by which schools and their communities can address the challenge of designing schools providing high-quality teaching and learning in the twenty-first century. They address the need to understand the connections and linkages between schools and their system environments and within schools themselves. The backward mapping strategy is advocated as a means of elevating the all-important stage of delivery and implementation of classroom teaching and learning to the forefront of the policy process. Policy formulation and strategy would be improved if it first took cognisance of the end results desired. Realities of organizational life might dictate that backward mapping be compromised to become an iterative process, whereby reference is constantly made backwards and then forwards to each of the key components, in order to ensure consistency and coherence.

Individual schools can make their own responses to the frameworks presented in this chapter, depending on school context, school goals and the school's perceived strengths and weaknesses. Importantly, responses will be shaped by appeal to what works. The case has been argued for teachers to be familiar with relevant research evidence in order for them to be able to make more informed choices as to what works in given situations. A growing body of research literature on effective teaching and learning provides schools with a rich variety of informed practices to adopt. The diversity of responses made by individual schools should be celebrated, for there is great value in each school devising and owning its own path for providing a quality service delivery for all students.

It is a further theme of this book that schools in different societies are best advised to adopt policies, practices and structures which harmonize with key features of their cultural contexts. Schools are undeniably products of their own cultures and histories. Most of the research on effective teaching and learning, school effectiveness and school improvement has been conducted in Western settings, while relatively little has been undertaken, for example, in Asia. The extent to which the research findings are generalizable across different Western countries, such as the UK and US, let alone non-Western settings, remains a moot point. There is much that is generic and thus transportable across different cultures. The models, frameworks and precepts outlined in this chapter, for example, are not culture-specific; rather, they establish broad parameters and directions within which schools in different cultural settings can adapt. An emphasis on quality teaching and learning is just as acceptable in China as it is in the US or UK. However, the backward mapping strategy might well need adaptation in China, given the historical-cultural tradition of strong autocratic leadership. School leaders might, for example, use the approach simply as a planning-design strategy as a means of clarifying and determining what changes they will introduce into their schools, rather than as an attempt to democratize decision making.

It is an aim of this book to raise awareness of the significance of cultural similarities and differences in the area of restructuring, school effectiveness and school improvement and school design. The book addresses questions, such as: to what extent is it valid to draw conclusions about effectiveness with respect to schools, teaching and learning in the US and UK, and then apply them to Asian societies, such as Hong Kong, Taiwan or Singapore? And the same question is equally valid in reverse – that is, how legitimate is it for the US and UK, for example, to apply effective practices taken from Asia? To what extent does cultural diversity inhibit transferability of research findings, policies and practices to different societies? Relatively little is known about cross-cultural differences and their implications for school design, despite a strong trend towards the internationalization and globalization of educational policy. It is hoped that discussion of these issues in subsequent chapters will provide a useful contribution to this growing debate.

References

Banathy, B. (1988) *Improvement or Transformation?*, Denver, CO: McRel.

Brown, D.J. (1990) *Decentralization and School-Based Management*, Basingstoke: Falmer Press.

Caldwell, B. and Spinks, J. (1988) *The Self-Managing School*, Basingstoke: Falmer Press.

Davis, O.L. (1997) 'Beyond "best practices" toward wise practices', *Journal of Curriculum and Supervision* 13 (19): 1–5.

Dimmock, C. (1995a) 'Reconceptualizing restructuring for school effectiveness and school improvement', *International Journal of Educational Reform* 4 (3): 285–300.

—— (1995b) 'Restructuring for school effectiveness: leading, organising and teaching for effective learning', *Educational Management and Administration* 23 (1): 5–18.

—— (1995c) 'School leadership: securing quality teaching and learning', in C. Evers and J. Chapman (eds), *Educational Administration: An Australian Perspective*, Sydney: Allen & Unwin.

Elmore, R.F. (1979–80) 'Backward mapping: implementation research and policy decisions', *Political Science Quarterly* 94 (4): 601–16.

Fullan, M.G. (1991) *The New Meaning of Educational Change*. London: Cassell.

Fullan, M.G. and Hargreaves, A. (1991) *What's Worth Fighting For? Working Together for Your School: Strategies for Developing Interactive Professionalism in Your School*, Hawthorn: Australian Council for Educational Administration.

Joyce, B. and Showers, B. (1988) *Student Achievement through Staff Development*, New York: Longman.

Little, J.W. (1990) 'The persistence of privacy: autonomy and initiative in teachers' professional relations', *Teachers' College Record* 91 (4): 509–36.

Locke, E.A. and Latham, G.P. (1990) *A Theory of Goal Setting and Task Performance*, Englewood Cliffs, NJ: Prentice Hall.

Louis, K.S. and Miles, M.B. (1990) *Improving the Urban High School: What Works and Why*, New York: Teachers' College Press.

Murphy, J. (1991) *Restructuring Schools: Capturing and Assessing the Phenomena*, New York: Teachers College Press.

Murphy, J. and Beck, L. (1995) *School-Based Management as School Reform: Taking Stock*, Thousand Oaks, CA: Corwin Press.

Purkey, S.C. and Smith, M.S. (1983) 'Effective schools: a review', *The Elementary School Journal* 83 (4): 427–52.

Rebore, R.W. (1991) *Personnel Administration in Education: A Management Approach*, 3rd edn, Englewood Cliffs, NJ: Prentice Hall.

Rosenholtz, S. (1989) *Teachers' Workplace: The Social Organisation of Schools*, New York: Longman.

Scheerens, J. (1992) *Effective Schooling: Research, Theory and Practice*, London: Cassell.

Schools Council (1992) 'The compulsory years: developing flexible strategies in the early years of schooling – purposes and possibilities', Project Paper No. 5, Canberra: National Board of Employment, Education and Training.

Weick, K.E. (1976) 'Educational organizations as loosely-coupled systems', *Administrative Science Quarterly*, 21: 1–19.

3 Recognizing Societal Culture in School Design
The Case for a Cross-Cultural Comparative Approach

This chapter addresses the importance of culture in school design. It particularly focuses on culture at societal level and its effects in shaping the extent to which ideas, research findings, policies and practices can travel and be successfully adopted and implemented outside the society in which they originate. Organizational culture is also considered. At the end of Chapter 2, it was recognized that most of the research literature pertinent to school design emanates from English-speaking Western countries, especially the UK and US. Other societies, some with very different cultures, are inclined to adopt these ideas and research findings in an uncritical way. This chapter argues that insufficient attention has hitherto been paid to culture and to cross-cultural comparison in Educational Administration and Policy and related fields, such as school effectiveness and improvement, effective teaching and learning and restructuring. Accordingly, what is needed are robust frameworks for examining the similarities and differences between cultures so that more informed analysis and judgements can be made as to which ideas, research findings, policies and practices may be successfully transported, whether by adoption or adaptation, between societies.

The chapter is structured in five parts. The first part recognizes three contemporary issues and debates which illustrate the need to take greater cognisance of the similarities and differences between societal cultures. The second part suggests a way forward by arguing the case for the development of cross-cultural comparative frameworks at societal level. It acknowledges, however, that there is an absence of such frameworks in education generally and in education administration and policy in particular. A third part then outlines two well recognized cross-cultural frameworks in the field of international business management which appear helpful in generating a suitable framework for education. Accordingly, a cross-cultural comparative framework for education is proposed in the fourth part of the chapter. Finally, the fifth part outlines a framework for enabling comparison at the level of organizational culture.

Contemporary Trends and Debates: The Need to Consider Culture

In this part, focus is placed on three currently debated issues: first, the globalization and internationalization of educational policy, including restructuring; second, the tendency for Western paradigms, theories and ideas to be adopted uncritically in non-Western settings; and third, the inferences drawn from international achievement tests in mathematics and science, namely, that countries with inferior student results should selectively imitate those with superior results. These debates are generally conducted without reference to cultural and cross-cultural similarities and differences. Such debates, it is argued, would be elevated to a more informed plane if they embraced a cross-cultural perspective.

A trend towards the internationalization and globalization of educational policy, especially with respect to restructuring, has been noteworthy over the past decade (Beare and Boyd, 1993; O'Donoghue and Dimmock, 1998). Improved communications bring researchers, practitioners and policy makers around the world ever closer, exposing them to the same knowledge and ideas. In addition, international organizations such as the OECD report and disseminate country studies. As a consequence, the same policies, or variations thereof, tend to be adopted by a host of countries and states of widely varying cultures, giving rise to the phenomenon of 'policy cloning' (Dimmock, 1998). Some countries and states tend to lead, such as the US and UK, while others follow and 'clone'. In economic language, English-speaking Western countries tend to be policy exporters, while non-Western countries tend to be policy importers. In short, Western ideas and practices tend to prevail even in non-Western settings, a situation reinforced by the unquestioning assumptions made and the ready willingness on both the exporting and importing sides to regard theories, policies and practices as culturally neutral.

A marked trend over the past decade towards devolution and decentralization is discernible in English-speaking Western countries, such as the USA, Canada, the UK and Australasia. The same trend, however, is also apparent in Eastern European countries, which are democratizing after the break-up of the Soviet Bloc (Weiler et al., 1996), and in many African and Asian countries, including India and China (Cheng, 1994; OECD, 1989; Sapra, 1991). Even in highly centralized France, an OECD (1996: 36) study reports that 'decentralization, deconcentration and the growing autonomy of schools have favoured the emergence of new types of relationship between the different partners in the educational community'. Policy makers in countries with contrasting cultures have tended to follow similar policy blueprints.

Questions arise about the relevance, applicability, validity and appropriateness of theories, perspectives and policies which are adopted and 'cloned' by education systems whose cultures and socio-political-economic contexts are quite dissimilar from those in which they were conceived. Fok et al. (1996: 1), for example, found 'support for the proposition that individuals from different cultures have different equity-sensitivity orientations and different approaches to organizational citizenship'. Moreover, the impetus and intended outcomes behind such efforts to restructure vary between countries. In the USA, school restructuring has been largely motivated by the drive for school improvement, whereas in the UK and Australia, restructuring initiatives are strongly associated with economic stringency, reform of the public service and political ideology aimed at rolling back the contribution of the state. In mainland China, a similar trend towards decentralization is taking place, driven by the incapacity of the centre to adequately finance the whole system (Cheng, 1994). In other Asian states and territories, such as Singapore and Hong Kong, similar restructuring policies to those in the USA, Australia and UK have been adopted, yet economic conditions and political imperatives are quite different (Y. C. Cheng, 1995; Dimmock, 1998; Wong, 1995).

A second issue centres on the ethnocentric and Western-dominated nature of theory, research and practice in fields such as educational administration and policy, school effectiveness and improvement, restructuring, and teaching and learning effectiveness. Textbooks are written and research is conducted with an ethnocentric bias towards Western traditions and Judaeo-Christian thinking and logic (Begley and Johansson, 1997). Yet a tacit assumption is made that the results are universally applicable. For their part, academics, policy makers and practitioners in non-Western settings have too hastily adopted Western paradigms, having neglected to develop their own culture-specific approaches. Put simply, such ethnocentric research conducted purely in Western contexts disenfranchises large groups elsewhere, denies the identities of important racial, ethnic and national groups and risks restricting understanding to narrowly, even arrogantly, defined parameters (Walker and Dimmock, 1999a).

A third and further twist to the debate arises from the recent inclination of some educators, especially in Anglo-American countries, to draw inferences from international comparisons of student test scores revealing the superior performance of East Asian students in International Achievement Tests in mathematics and science (Reynolds and Farrell, 1996). Students from Japan, Korea, Taiwan and other Chinese communities, such as Singapore and Hong Kong – what Biggs (1994), citing Ho (1991), calls 'Confucian-heritage cultures' – consistently occupy the top places and outperform their Western counterparts on these tests. This has led some Western educators to advocate, somewhat crudely and simplistically, the adoption of East Asian approaches in Western schools.

In reviewing some of this work, Morris (1997) rightly raises a number of objections and concerns. First, he points out that it is a mistake to generalise across East and South-East Asian societies because there are significant cultural differences between, for example, Taiwan, Hong Kong and Singapore. In other words, important cultural differences apply among Chinese societies, let alone between them and Japan. He gives as examples, firstly, the status of teachers, which in some Asian countries is high while in others, such as Hong Kong, it is low; secondly, the amount of time teachers spend out of the class-room: in some countries, such as mainland China, it is very high – about one-third – while in others, such as Hong Kong, it is much less.

More fundamentally, cross-country studies, such as those relating to the International Achievement Tests in Mathematics and Science conducted by the International Association for the Evaluation of Educational Achievement (IEA), invariably fail to consider all of the important variables. In relation to a study by Reynolds and Farrell (1996), Morris comments:

> Further, the list of explanatory factors ignores a number of important variables. They include the length of schooling: in many East Asian societies most children attend kindergarten from the age of three, and even in kindergarten spend a significant proportion of time studying mathematics. Also, the educational enterprise is closely linked in Korea and Taiwan to the quest for national identity and survival within the context of an unfinished civil war; and in several East Asian societies the curriculum is strongly oriented to the study of a few academic subjects, with the result that other areas, such as aesthetics, creativity and physical education, are neglected. Mathematics and science are accorded a high status in schools, and are generally seen by East Asian pupils to be the most interesting and enjoyable subjects.

Morris goes on to highlight the high level of within-country variance revealed in the IEA achievement tests and evidenced in all countries, Asian and Western, before making the following telling observation with respect to the Reynolds and Farrell (1996) study:

> The authors bemoan the inability of the discipline of comparative educa-tion to explain the differences in pupil achievement across countries or to identify solutions which travel. Ironically in their own efforts to provide explanations, the analysis demonstrates the pitfalls of such an enterprise and the reasons why comparativists have been wary of providing such grand narratives. Examining other nations' educational achievements and systems is certainly a valuable exercise. However, the value may lie in the questions that it generates rather than in the ready-made answers it provides for politicians.
>
> (Morris 1997)

In summary, it is extremely difficult to make valid comparisons without a sound understanding of the multifarious culturally-related factors which account for how particular school systems function. What is being argued is that schools are products of their unique histories and distinctive societal cultures. A strong case can therefore be made for an approach which takes cognisance of cultural similarity and difference. What is required is a cross-cultural comparative framework for seeking to understand the degree to which theories, research findings, policies and practices can be successfully adopted in culturally diverse settings. Researchers, practitioners and policy makers have a responsibility to reassess the emphasis, origins and applicability of what is produced and disseminated by accounting for cultural and cross-cultural contextualization. For this to happen, research should stretch beyond its current near-exclusive grounding in Western theory and move towards more diverse perspectives incorporating the multiple cultural contexts within which educational administration and policy takes place. In this respect, reconceptualizing and strengthening the neglected field of comparative educational administration which, to date, has failed to emerge in a robust and coherent form (Dimmock and Walker, 1998a, 1998b; Hughes, 1988), offers a promising way forward.

The Case for Culture and for a Cross-Cultural Comparative Framework: The Way Forward

Much of the foregoing discussion has indicated the need for the development of a comparative approach grounded in the concept of culture. Before developing such an approach, however, it is important to clarify the meaning of culture and the benefits a cross-cultural comparative framework holds over existing alternatives.

While culture is a contested concept (for a full discussion of this, see Dimmock and Walker, 1998a, 1998b), it is here defined as the enduring sets of beliefs, values and ideologies underpinning structures, processes and practices. As culture constitutes the context in which school design and restructuring is exercised, it exerts a substantial influence over, and provides a fuller understanding of, the whole process. It helps to explain how school design and restructuring is played out in different settings. Moreover, it can be conceptualized at a number of interrelated and nested levels, from the micro (school) level to the macro (national) level.

At least three arguments support the development of a cultural or cross-cultural comparative approach to school design and restructuring (Dimmock and Walker, 1998a, 1998b). These centre on first, the suitability of the concept of culture for underpinning a cross-cultural comparative approach; second, the limitations of existing frameworks typically used in comparative educational studies, such as structural-functionalist models; and third, the pitfalls of ignoring the significance of culture in the adoption of educational practices. Each of these is now briefly elaborated.

The Suitability of Culture

The first argument is that the concept of culture appears both timely and appropriate for underpinning a comparative approach to educational administration and policy. Relationships between an organization's culture and context on the one hand, and educational management and leadership on the other, are now widely acknowledged in the relevant literature (Bolman and Deal, 1992). A move towards considering societal cultures rather than organizational cultures appears a natural extension of this line of inquiry (Hallinger and Leithwood, 1996). Since culture is reflected in all aspects of school life, and people, organizations and societies share differences and similarities in terms of their cultures, it appears a particularly useful concept with universal application, one appropriate for comparing school design and restructuring practices. The subtleties and sophistication of the concept of culture also provide researchers with rich opportunities for exploring organizational phenomena which are often blanketed by surface similarities. For example, schools in most societies look to have similar, formal leadership hierarchies and organizational structures. Such similarities, however, often mask the subtle differences in values, relationships and processes below the surface. The concept of culture is also useful for studying the relationships between schools and their micro- and macroenvironments.

Most cross-national studies of educational administration and policy ignore the analytical properties of culture. This neglect has been challenged recently by researchers such as K.M. Cheng (1995: 99), who assert that, 'the cultural element is not only necessary, but essential in the study of educational administration'. Specifically, Cheng bemoans the fact that much research in educational administration ignores culture and makes no reference to larger macro-societal, or national cultural configurations. The concept of societal culture has not been rigorously applied as a basis for comparison in educational administration, nor as a means for comparing the organization of individual schools. Neither has school-level culture been developed as a foundation for comparative analysis, its application being largely confined to school effectiveness and organizational analysis.

Limitations of Existing Comparative Approaches

A second argument justifying a cross-cultural approach to comparative educational leadership is that existing comparative education frameworks are too often concentrated at a single level only and tend to be grounded in structural-functionalist traditions. Frameworks and studies which focus on a single level risk ignoring the cultural relationships and interplay between different levels of culture, from school to national, thereby failing to account sufficiently for context. For example, Bray and Thomas (1995) claim that national or macro-comparative studies tend to suffer from overgeneralization, and therefore to neglect local differences and disparities. In short, single-level studies neglect the influence of culture on schools and on school leadership in particular.

If researchers were to study the dynamic, informal processes of schools and the leadership practices embedded within them, theoretical tools which stretch beyond structural-functionalist perspectives should be considered. Although structural-functionalist models are useful for fracturing education systems into their constituent elements (structures), they do little to explain how processes, or why various elements, interact. As a result, their analytic power is diminished through their adoption of a static rather than a dynamic view of schools. Consequently, explanation remains at a surface level only and rigorous comparison is difficult. A multi-level cultural perspective, however, holds promise for meeting these expectations.

Adoption of Educational Policies and Practices

The third justification for adopting a cross-cultural approach to comparative educational administration and policy relates to a growing tendency for policy developed and implemented in one cultural context to be adopted in a totally different cultural context (Dimmock, 1998; Hallinger and Leithwood, 1996). This phenomenon, discussed earlier in this book and appropriately labelled 'cultural borrowing' or 'policy cloning' (Dimmock, 1998), reflects a growing trend by policy makers and practitioners in countries with contrasting cultures to adopt policy blueprints, management structures and leadership practices developed elsewhere. In seeking to understand why some policies and practices appear to be workable in some contexts but not others, there is a clear need to take the cultural and cross-cultural contexts into account.

This third argument appears particularly important given the increasing trend towards globalization of educational policy, structures and practices. For example, the knowledge base utilized for training school principals is homogeneous, grounded predominantly in Western (Anglo-American) leadership thought. We appear to be heading towards a situation where, at least on the surface, policy, systems, structures and leadership practices appear to be uniform. Unless and until educators attempt to understand processes, such as leadership, as at least partially derived from and influenced by societal culture, there is serious risk that our understandings will remain too narrowly conceived. A comparative approach to educational administration and policy can expose the value of theory and practice from different cultural perspectives which may then, in turn, inform and influence existing dominant Western paradigms.

In summary, there is now wide acceptance of the importance of 'culture' and its role in understanding life in schools. Whereas considerable research into various aspects of school culture has already been undertaken, little is known about the influence of societal culture in explaining school design, restructuring, and leadership practices.

Cross-Cultural Comparative Frameworks in International Business Management

The paucity of cross-cultural frameworks in education is not replicated in the fields of international and comparative business management or in comparative psychology where, in both fields, extensive research has been undertaken for some two decades (Dimmock and Walker, 1998a). In developing a cross-cultural framework for education, it is thus instructive to take account of the work already completed in these other fields.

Hofstede's Cultural Dimensions

The most widely cited framework for exploring the influence of culture on business management is that developed by Geert Hofstede (1980, 1991, 1994). As a leading advocate of cultural comparative research in international business management, Hofstede (1991: 4–5) defines culture as, 'patterns of thinking, feeling and acting' underpinning 'the collective programming of the mind which distinguishes the members of one group or category of people from another'. His work is generally acknowledged as the most influential in the field of international and comparative business management over the last two decades. Although Hofstede's framework has been criticized on a number of grounds (Trice and Beyer, 1993), his ideas have been applied and tested repeatedly over the last fifteen years and stand, according to Redding (1994: 324), as 'a unifying and dominant' influence in the field.

In his original work, based on a large-scale survey of IBM employees in more than fifty countries, Hofstede (1980) identified four cultural dimensions which he suggests are universally applicable across all societies or nations. The four are power distance, uncertainty avoidance, masculinity/femininity and individualism/collectivism. A fifth dimension, Confucian dynamism, later termed short term/long term orientation, was added to his work by a group of Chinese scholars (The Chinese Culture Connection, 1987). Hofstede's dimensions are suggested as choices between pairs of empirically verifiable alternatives that allow the identification of patterns within and between cultures to emerge, and facilitate their meaningful ordering (Hofstede, 1980, 1995; Hofstede and Bond, 1984). The five dimensions are outlined below. Asian and Western examples of rankings, according to each dimension, are also included.

Power distance (PD). This refers to the distribution of power within society and its organizations. It is defined as the extent to which the less powerful members of institutions and organizations within a country expect and accept that power is distributed unequally. In societies with large PD values, greater inequalities of power distribution are expected and accepted in the family, in school and in the workplace. Many Asian societies are high PD cultures, while many Western societies have low PD values. The more Westernized is the Asian society, the more likely it is to experience a reduced PD. Hong Kong displays a high power distance index (PDI), being ranked 15th out of 50 countries; Singapore is even higher at 13th, South Korea is 27th and Japan 33rd. By contrast, the USA is ranked 38th, Australia 41st and Britain 44th.

According to Hofstede (1991), in societies with large PD values, greater inequalities of power distribution are expected and accepted in the family, in school and in the workplace. Thus, in the home, children are educated towards obedience to parents, whose authority is rarely questioned. In school, teachers are respected, learning is conceived as passed on by the wisdom of the teacher, and teacher-centred methods tend to be employed. In the workplace, hierarchy means existential inequality, subordinates expect to be told what to do and the ideal boss is a benevolent autocrat, a kind 'father' figure. By contrast, families in small PD societies encourage children to have a will of their own and to treat parents as equals. In school, more student-centred methods are used, teachers enjoy less respect and learning is viewed as impersonalized truth. In the workplace, hierarchy means an inequality of roles established for convenience, subordinates expect to be consulted and the ideal boss is a resourceful democrat.

Individualism versus collectivism. This dimension is the degree to which individuals are integrated into groups and to which there is closeness between persons in a relationship. Vecchio (1995) describes it as the extent to which a person is 'inner-directed' or 'other-directed'. In individualist societies, individuals place their personal goals above those of their in-group, the ties between individuals are loose, people are expected to look after themselves and their immediate families. In collectivist societies, people place group goals above their personal goals; they are brought up to be loyal to, and integrate into, strong cohesive groups, which often include extended families.

On this dimension, Hong Kong, Singapore, Malaysia and Thailand are ranked towards the collectivist end, Hong Kong being placed 37th out of 53 countries. At the individualist end of the spectrum, the USA, Australia and Britain occupy the first three places. Large power distance societies, like Hong Kong, tend to be more collectivist, while small power distance societies tend to be more individualist.

In individualist societies, people are driven by an 'I' consciousness and obligations to the self, including self-interest, self-actualization and guilt. In the school, emphasis is placed on permanent education and learning how to learn. In the workplace, values tend to be applied universally to all, other people are seen as potential resources, tasks prevail over relationships and the employer–employee relationship is described as 'calculative'. In collectivist societies, by contrast, family members are brought up with a 'we' consciousness, opinions are predetermined by the group, and strong obligations to the family emphasize harmony, respect and shame. At school, learning is viewed as an activity primarily for the young, and focuses on how to do things and on factual knowledge; and at the work place, value standards differ for in-group and out-groups, relationship prevails over task, and employer–employee relationships have a moral basis.

Masculinity versus femininity (MF). This dimension is concerned with the ways in which 'biological differences between sexes become perpetuated in differences in social and organizational roles played by men and women' (Harrison et al., 1994: 246). The assertive pole is termed masculine and the modest, caring pole, feminine. Hong Kong ranks 18th out of 53 countries and regions, compared with Britain, USA and Australia, which are 9th, 15th and 16th, respectively. All of these societies tend towards the more masculine end, indicating much less of a Western/Asian divide on this dimension.

In more masculine societies, family values stress achievement, competition and resolution of conflict by power and assertiveness. At school, norms are set by the best students, the system rewards academic achievement and failure at school is seen as serious. In the workplace, assertiveness is taken as a virtue; selling oneself, decisiveness and emphasis on career are all valued. By contrast, in feminine societies, the family places emphasis on relationship, solidarity and resolution of conflicts by compromise and negotiation. At school, norms tend to be set by the average students, system rewards reflect students' social adaptation and failure at school is taken as unfortunate; in the workplace, assertiveness is not appreciated, people are expected to undersell themselves, and emphasis is placed on quality of life and intuition.

Uncertainty avoidance (UA). This dimension relates to how people react to, manage, cope with and tolerate uncertainty and ambiguity in their lives. Uncertainty-avoiding cultures tend to proliferate laws, rules, safety and security measures and on a philosophical and religious level, tend to believe in absolute truth. Conversely, people in uncertainty accepting cultures are more tolerant of a range of different opinions, they prefer fewer rather than more rules, and on the philosophical and religious level they are more relativist and tolerant of different faiths and creeds.

Most Asian societies rank low on uncertainty avoidance. Hong Kong, for example, is ranked 50th out of 53 countries and regions. Singapore is 53rd, Britain is 48th, the USA is 43rd and Australia 37th. People in these societies do not feel sufficiently insecure and threatened by the unknown, unfamiliar or uncertain that they take measures to regulate their lives as a consequence.

In the school context, this dimension of societal culture may be overshadowed by organizational culture. By the nature of their task, schools are organizations where abundant rules and regulations are necessary, a generic characteristic which seems to cut across even the sharpest of differences in societal culture. This presents a contradiction: schools displaying characteristics of high uncertainty in societies which may be classified as low uncertainty. Such is the case, for example, with Hong Kong.

Long-term versus short-term orientation (LS). This fifth dimension was added to Hofstede's original schema after research by Chinese scholars (The Chinese Culture Connection, 1987) and is less validated than the other dimensions. Values associated with long-term orientation, such as thrift, perseverance and willingness to make short-term sacrifices for long-term gains, are counterbalanced by values associated with short-term orientation, such as respect for tradition, fulfilment of social obligations and protection of one's face. Although many of these values are associated with Chinese (Confucian) values, they also seem to apply to other societies without a Confucian heritage.

China, Hong Kong and Taiwan rank 1st, 2nd and 3rd out of 23 countries and regions on this dimension; that is, they have a long-term orientation. Australia, the USA and Britain rank 15th, 17th and 18th, respectively. Because Hong Kong and its East Asian neighbours rank very high on long-term orientation does not mean that they possess no characteristics of short-term orientation. For example, 'loss of face' is a prevalent trait among Chinese. It can be posited that cultures with a long-term orientation are more conducive to academic achievement, since students are more likely to forego short term pleasures and gains for the benefits that eventually follow from study.

Hofstede's research fulfils at least two important functions. First, it provides a much-needed empirical base for evaluating the conclusions and implications which many scholars are quick to make in regard to cross-cultural comparison. Second, it signals what is really needed in cross-cultural research; that is, a valid and reliable set of generically applicable cross-cultural dimensions. Against this, the limitations of Hofstede's work should be acknowledged. Completed in the early 1980s, the data are becoming rapidly dated as societal cultures change, albeit at different rates. Furthermore, although Hofstede's aim was to develop measures of societal culture in general, the data were based on the views, values and behaviours of business employees. To what extent, therefore, do Hofstede's findings reflect the cultural identities of educators? At this stage, it is difficult to ascertain the extent to which societal cultures contain internal variance as between major sectors of the labour force and socioeconomic groups, let alone different ethnic and racial groups. As societies become more multicultural, the difficulties increase.

Building on the work of Hofstede, Trompenaars and Hampden-Turner (1997: 6) suggest that 'culture is the way in which a group of people solves problems and reconciles dilemmas'. These authors suggest that cultures distinguish themselves from others in how people approach and solve problems.

They suggest seven fundamental categories which can be used for identifying cultural influences and for making comparisons across cultures. Five of the categories are based on how people relate to others; they are universalism versus particularism, individualism versus communitarianism, neutral versus emotional, specific versus diffuse and achievement versus ascription. The remaining two categories relate to different cultural attitudes towards time and the environment.

Although both of the foregoing taxonomies have proven utility for conceptualizing cross-cultural research, for a number of reasons they are not ideally suited for education. The first reason is that both frameworks were developed specifically from studies in comparative and international business management. In Hofstede's work, for instance, the sample consisted of IBM employees and may thus be of limited validity for those working in education. The second is that some of the dimensions or categories which comprise the frameworks have been criticized as being overly restrictive (Trice and Beyer, 1993), again limiting their applicability to education. The third reason is that some of the terms or labels used are confusing and in some cases, politically incorrect. For example, Hofstede's masculinity/femininity dimension has been plagued by misinterpretation and criticized for its discriminatory labeling (Westwood, 1992). In the framework enunciated in this book, the power distance concept is more appropriately labeled power distributed/power concentrated, thus indicating more clearly whether power is distributed across a large number of people or concentrated in the hands of a few.

A Cross-Cultural Comparative Framework for Educational Administration and Policy

Culture is a difficult phenomenon to measure, gauge or even describe. However, as the core concept for a comparative framework, it needs to be transposed into a form which will facilitate description, measurement and comparison. This can be achieved by identifying generic dimensions, as illustrated in the work of Hofstede (1980, 1991) and reported in the previous section.

Dimensions may be defined as core axes around which significant sets of values, beliefs and practices cluster (Dimmock and Walker, 1998a). They provide common benchmarks against which cultural characteristics at the societal level can be described, gauged and compared. Despite their usefulness, however, one must agree with Hofstede's (1994: 40) cautionary remarks about dimensions, when he claims that the same limitations apply to them as to culture itself: 'They are also constructs that should not be reified. They do not "exist"; they are tools for analysis which may or may not clarify a situation'. The dimensions described, therefore, should not be regarded as uni-dimensional. They do not aim to polarize cultural influence on school design, restructuring, leadership or teaching and learning, but rather to provide a basis for comparison. For example, it is argued that it is possible for school leaders within a given culture to be both aggressive and considerate at different times and in different situations. Therefore, although the dimensions are presented as pairs of alternatives, to view them as polarities along a uni-dimensional scale is too simplistic and could lead to serious misconceptions.

A decision not to adopt an existing framework for comparative study of educational administration and policy led to the fashioning of a six-dimensional model. As a first stage, existing frameworks were reviewed, labelled and their core constructs recorded. Differences and similarities between and within the dimensions and categories used in the various frameworks were identified, regrouped and relabelled in relation to their relevance to education. At the completion of this process, six dimensions were identified as the foundation of a cross-cultural comparative framework. The six dimensions are now described (Walker and Dimmock, 1999b).

Power-distributed/power-concentrated. The first dimension is modeled on Hofstede's (1991) power distance construct. This dimension is re-labeled as power-distributed or power-concentrated, since this more accurately captures the essence of power relationships in various cultures. Power tends either to be distributed more evenly among the various hierarchical levels of a society, or it is concentrated in the hands of a few. More specifically, the dimension refers to the distribution of power in a society and how the inherent inequities involved in this distribution are perceived and coped with; that is, how societies institutionalize inequity. In societies where power is widely distributed, for example, through decentralization and institutionalized democracy, inequity tends to be treated as undesirable and effort is made to reduce it where possible. In societies where power is commonly concentrated in the hands of the few, inequities are more acceptable and legitimized: people tend to accept unequal distributions of power. For example, Blunt and Jones (1997) suggest that in many African societies power structures are highly centralized with authoritarian and paternalistic leadership patterns widely accepted.

Group-oriented/self-oriented. The second dimension embraces Trompenaars and Hampden-Turner's (1997) individualism/communitarianism category and Hofstede's (1991) individualism/collectivism dimension. Both of these schemata describe whether people within a given culture tend to focus on *self* or on their place within a *group*, hence the preference for the label 'group-oriented or self-oriented'. The dimension can be taken to describe the degree to which individuals are integrated into groups and the closeness of relationships between persons. In *self-oriented* cultures, relations are fairly loose and relational ties tend to be based on self-interest. People in such societies primarily regard themselves as individuals first, and members of a group second. This does not indicate that people in *self-oriented* cultures are selfish; rather, they perceive themselves as more independent and self-reliant. In *group-oriented* cultures, ties between people are tight, relationships are firmly structured and individual needs are subservient to the collective needs. Important collectivist values include harmony, face-saving, filial piety and equality of reward distribution among peers. In *group-oriented* cultures, status is traditionally defined by factors such as age, sex, kinship, educational standing, or formal organizational position. In *self-oriented* cultures, people are judged and status ascribed more in line with individual performance or what has been accomplished individually.

Consideration/aggression. This derives from Hofstede's masculinity/femininity dimension, but is reconceptualized and re-labelled because of the confusion surrounding Hofstede's category and the possible discriminatory nature of the original labeling. In what are called *aggression* cultures, achievement is stressed, competition dominates and conflicts are resolved through the exercise of power and assertiveness. In aggression cultures, school norms are set by the best students, the system rewards academic achievement and failure at school is seen as serious; in an organizational context, assertiveness is taken as a virtue, and selling oneself, decisiveness and emphasis on career are all valued. By contrast, in *consideration* societies, emphasis is on relationship, solidarity and resolution of conflicts by compromise and negotiation. At school, norms tend to be set by the average students, system rewards reflect students' social adaptation and failure at school is taken as unfortunate. In the workplace, assertiveness is not appreciated, people are expected to undersell themselves and emphasis is placed on quality of life and intuition.

Proactive/fatalistic. The fourth dimension draws on Trompenaars and Hampden-Turner's 'attitudes to the environment' category, Hofstede's uncertainty avoidance dimension and personal thinking in respect of the concepts of 'opportunism/fatalism' and pragmatism/idealism. The labelling of the dimension reflects the proactive or 'we can change things around here' attitude found in some cultures, and the willingness to accept things as they are in others, a more fatalistic perspective. Relabelling was required to reflect more accurately the content of the dimension which drew on a complex blend of previous categories and constructs. The dimension addresses how different societies and cultures react to and manage uncertainty and change in social situations. In proactive societies, people tend to believe that they have at least some control over situations and over change. In other words, they believe that people 'make their own luck', and therefore tend to accept uncertainty without undue stress, seeking to take advantage of any opportunities associated with change. People in proactive cultures are tolerant of different opinions and are not excessively threatened by unpredictability. In fatalistic cultures, on the other hand, people believe 'what is meant to be, will be'. Uncertainty is often viewed as psychologically uncomfortable and disruptive, and people seek to reduce it and to limit risk by hanging on to the way things have always been done. This often involves the inflexible retention of rules and dogmas that breed orthodoxy. People hold that these principles are fixed and that they have little or no control over them.

Generative/replicative. This dimension, original to the schema, was so labeled to reflect the assumption that some cultures appear more predis-posed toward innovation, or the generation of new ideas and methods, while other cultures appear more inclined to replicate or to adopt ideas and approaches from elsewhere. In *generative* cultures, people tend to value the generation of knowledge, new ideas and ways of working. They are more likely to seek creative solutions to problems, to develop policies and ways of operating which are original and unique, and which stretch and challenge knowledge in various directions. In such cultures, new inventions and approaches often appear. In *replicative* cultures, people are more likely to adopt innovations, ideas and inventions developed elsewhere. Whereas these sometimes undergo partial adaptation, more often they are basically replicated *in toto* with little consideration of alignment to the indigenous cultural context.

Limited relationship/holistic relationship. This dimension builds on Trompenaars and Hampden-Turner's 'specific/diffuse' and 'performance/connection' categories and on work by Walker and Dimmock (1999b) on the importance of connections and relationships in cultures. The label reflects an assumption that in some cultures, interpersonal relationships are limited by the fixed rules applied to given situations, whereas in other cultures relationships are more holistic or underpinned by association and personal considerations. In limited relationships cultures, interactions and relationships across situations tend to be determined by firm rules which are applied equally to everyone. For example, when a leader needs to make a decision on a promotion, objective criteria are applied regardless of who are the possible candidates. Relationships are prescribed by the specific situation (business or contractual) rather than by the people involved. In holistic cultures, on the other hand, greater attention is given to relationship obligations (for example, kinship, patronage and friend-ship) than to impartially applied rules (see Walker and Dimmock, in press). Dealings in formal and structured situations in holistic cultures are driven more by complex, personal considerations than by the specific situation or by formal rules and regulations.

These six dimensions, it is claimed, enable the societal cultures of different countries and states to be compared in terms of their influence on their respective education systems. They provide conceptual tools for making culturally based comparisons. As concepts, the dimensions need operationalizing through the development of instruments which facilitate the collection of empirical data.

A Comparative Framework for Organizational Culture

A comparative framework based on dimensions of societal-level culture needs to be complemented by an equivalent set of cultural dimensions at organizational level. Qualitative differences between organizational and societal cultures stem from the fact that membership of an organization is usually subject to some degree of choice, whereas the country and culture into which people are born and bred is decided for them. In addition, national cultures differ mostly at the level of basic values, while organizational cultures differ mostly at the level of more superficial practices, as reflected in the recognition of particular symbols, heroes, and rituals (Hofstede, 1991). This allows organizational cultures to be managed and changed, whereas national cultures are more enduring and change only gradually over long time periods, if at all.

Research studies on the organizational cultures of companies found large differences in their practices (symbols, heroes, rituals), but only minor differences in their values (Hofstede, 1995). Most of the variation in practices could be accounted for by six dimensions which, Hofstede admits, need further validation. These six, while not exhaustive, provide a useful baseline on which to build an organizational culture framework. Minor adaptations to the six have been made, as indicated below. In addition, while Hofstede presents the dimensions as either/or choices along six axes, it seems more accurate to think of them as multi-dimensional rather than uni-dimensional. The six dimensions of organizational culture are outlined below.

Process and/or outcomes-oriented. Some cultures are predisposed towards technical and bureaucratic routines, while others emphasize outcomes. Evidence suggests that in outcomes-oriented cultures, people perceive greater homogeneity in practices, whereas people in process-oriented cultures perceive greater differences in their practices. In education, some schools are process-oriented, emphasizing the processes and the skills of teaching and learning, while others are results-oriented, stressing learning achievements such as exam results. Many schools and school systems are currently reforming their curricula to reflect specific student learning targets or outcomes expressed in terms of knowledge, skills and attitudes, indicating a trend towards designing curricula on the basis of, and measuring student and school performance by, a learning outcomes approach. It appears that the more homogeneous the culture, the greater its strength. Strong cultures, therefore, tend to be results-oriented or outcomes-oriented.

Task and/or person oriented. In task-oriented organizational cultures, emphasis is placed on job performance and maximizing productivity, while human considerations such as the welfare of the staff take second place and may even be neglected. Conversely, person-oriented cultures accentuate the care, consideration and welfare of the employees. Both dimensions were recognized in the 1960s literature on leadership style through Blake and Mouton's managerial grid (1964). Blake and Mouton posit that an organization or its leader may score high or low on both task and person orientation, seeing them as two dimensions rather than one. Applied to schools, a task-oriented culture exacts maximum work effort and performance out of its teachers in an aloof, uncaring work environment. A person-oriented culture on the other hand, values, promotes and shows consideration for the welfare of its teachers above all else. It is conceivable that some schools might score highly (or lowly) on both task and person orientations.

Professional and/or parochial. In professional cultures, qualified personnel identify primarily with their profession, the standards of which are usually defined at national or international level. In parochial cultures, members identify most readily with the organization for which they work. Sociologists such as Gouldner (1957) have long recognized this phenomenon in their distinction between 'locals' and 'cosmopolitans'. In the school context, some teachers, especially those with an external frame of reference, are primarily committed to the teaching profession as a whole, while others with a strong internal frame of reference are more committed to the particular school in which they work.

Open and/or closed. This dimension refers to the ease with which resources such as people, money, and ideas are exchanged between the organization and its environment. The greater the transfer and exchange of resources between the environment and the organization, the more open the culture. Schools vary between those which champion outside involvement in their affairs and maximum interchange with their environment, and those which eschew such interaction and communication, preferring a more closed, exclusive approach. Trends in education over the last decade have favoured the opening of school cultures, particularly to parental influence and involvement.

Control and linkage. An important part of organizational culture concerns the way in which authority and control are exerted and communicated between members. In this respect, Hofstede's dimension identifies only one aspect, namely, tightly–loosely controlled cultures. Two more aspects can be added, namely, formal–informal and direct–indirect, which taken together enable more sensitive and detailed accounts of control and linkage in schools.

1   *formal – informal*: organizations vary in the extent to which their practices are guided by rules, regulations and 'correct procedures' on the one hand, and the extent to which they reflect a more relaxed, spontaneous and intuitive approach on the other. Highly formalized organizations conform to the classic bureaucracies; they emphasize definition of rules and roles, tend towards inflexibility and are often characterized by austere interpersonal relationships. Staff–student relationships stress politeness and respect and reflect a certain distance. By contrast, informal organizations have fewer rules dictating procedures, roles are

often ill-defined, they display flexibility in their modes of work and interpersonal relationships tend to be more relaxed. Schools characterized by informality rely more on spontaneous decision making, rules are minimized and applied only when needed, staff roles may not be clearly defined so that teachers are expected to undertake a range of diverse tasks which may frequently change, and relationships between staff and students are casual.

2   *tight – loose*: this aspect gauges the degree to which members feel there is strong commitment to the shared beliefs, values and practices of an organization. Such strong commitment might come through supervision and control by superordinates or through members' own self-motivation. An organization which has strong homogeneity and commitment in respect of its members' values and practices is tightly controlled (whether control is externally imposed by superordinates or self-imposed by employees). Conversely, a loosely controlled culture is one with only weak commitment to, or acceptance of, shared beliefs, values and practices, and little or no control is exerted to achieve homogeneity either by superordinates or by members themselves. Schools with tightly controlled cultures have principals, teachers, students and parents believing in and working towards the same goals and sharing many of the same teaching and learning practices. In the opposite case, teachers in schools with loosely controlled cultures are inclined to 'do their own thing', resulting in a wide range of heterogeneous practices.

3   *direct – indirect*: this aspect captures the linkages and patterns of communication through which power, authority and decisions are communicated. In some organizations, managers assume direct personal responsibility to perform certain tasks and to communicate directly with their staff, often circumventing intermediate levels in the vertical hierarchy or chain of command. In other organizations, managers exert control indirectly by, for example, delegating to staff the tasks they would otherwise do themselves, or by changing the culture. Exerting control indirectly often entails working through other people and employing more subtle tactics and strategies to secure the objective. In the school context, principals may exercise instructional leadership in direct ways, by close personal involvement in teaching, learning and supervision. Other principals, however, may prefer to adopt indirect methods, by managing the quality of teaching, learning and curriculum through their staff and by employing more subtle strategies, such as involving parents in classroom activity.

Pragmatic and/or normative. This dimension defines the prevailing way an organization services its clients, customers or patrons. Some display a flexible, pragmatic policy aimed at meeting the diversity of customer/client needs. Others exhibit more rigid or normative approaches in responding bureaucratically and treating all in the same way, irrespective of their particular needs. This dimension measures the degree of customer orientation. In the educational context, some schools consciously try to meet individual student needs by offering a more diversified curriculum with flexible timetables and alternative teaching strategies. They mould their educational services to meet different student needs. Others, particularly the more traditional schools, offer more standardized, normative programs, may be less student focused and may expect students to fit into the agenda determined for them by the school. A summary of both sets of dimensions – societal and organizational – is presented in Table 3.1.

Conclusions: Culture and its Conceptual Complexities

While this chapter has presented the case for a cross-cultural foundation to underpin a comparative framework, the concept of culture is not without its ambiguities. These ambiguities, however, also offer possibilities for future research by promoting different interpretations. This is well illustrated by the disagreement among scholars as to whether patterns of organizational characteristics tend towards convergence (similarity), or divergence (difference). Put another way, are organizations culture-bound or culture-free? (Trice and Beyer, 1993; Richards, 1993).

Proponents of convergence believe that organizations are culture-free and are therefore similar across national cultures because the processes of organizing and using technologies place certain universal requirements on organizations, thereby inducing the cultures themselves to become more similar over time. By this argument, all schools are much the same, wherever they are located. Conversely, the reasons why organizations may be thought

Table 3.1 *Dimensions of National/Societal and Organizational Culture*

National/Societal Culture	*Organizational Culture*
Power distributed – Power concentrated	Process – Outcome oriented
Group oriented – Self oriented	Person – Task oriented
Consideration – Aggression	Professional – Parochial
Proactive – Fatalistic	Open – Closed
Generative – Replicative	Control and Linkage
	• formal–informal
	• tight–loose
	• direct–indirect
Limited relationship – Holistic relationship	Pragmatic/flexible/individualistic – Normative/rigid/standardized

to be culture-bound, and therefore divergent, are that their internal cultures and formal structures reflect their external environmental or societal cultures. In this event, differences persist because of unique histories, traditions, expectations, resources, demography, stage of development and cultural inertia (Trice and Beyer, 1993).

Three further propositions about culture are worth mentioning. First, cultures are not necessarily bounded by national boundaries. A common mistake is to think that cultural boundaries are synonymous with national boundaries. As Child (1981) found in an extensive review of comparative management literature, 'cultural boundaries do not necessarily overlap with national boundaries, but are usually taken to do so' (in Redding, 1994: 326). Perhaps the most common occurrence of this is the grouping of Asian countries as identical Confucian societies. As Wilkinson (1996: 427) writes: 'there is a tendency to gloss over or ignore differences between the different "Confucian" societies of East Asia. Japanese, Korean and overseas Chinese capitalism (in Singapore, Hong Kong and Taiwan) have emerged from different political contexts, and occupy different positions in the world economy ... '. Cultural differences are just as commonly found within and across national boundaries as they are bound by them. There is a danger that researchers may assume that because a school is located in, for example, a Chinese society, it will reflect a culture similar or identical to other schools in the same country, or to other schools in a Chinese society in a different country.

A second issue is that when considering the influence of culture on schools and schooling in different societies, attention is not exclusively focused on difference and divergence at the expense of important and interesting similarities. A true cross-cultural comparative approach must be balanced, taking into consideration both similarity and difference, convergence and divergence.

A third issue is that the explanatory power of culture may not be sufficient to fully explain differences and similarities, a point relating to the convergence versus divergence argument touched upon earlier (Westwood, 1992). 'Culturalists', Wilkinson (1996) claims, have a tendency to attribute rather simplistically any residual unexplained phenomena to culture and to ignore 'institutionalist' arguments to the effect that it is primarily historical, economic and political conditions that shape organizations. Examples of powerful economic, political and social forces shaping education are seen in the USA and UK, where economic growth over a much longer time period than in Asia has produced systems of mass higher education, high levels of education across populations, a large group of professional and middle-class citizens and a consequent change in societal values.

The earlier expansion of higher education in the West, where demand for and supply of places is much less pressurized than in Asia, has done much to shape the values and cultures of those countries. It is important that researchers respect both perspectives and view culture as interacting with economic, political and sociological factors to shape organizations, such as schools. An exclusive concentration on either perspective may risk the construction of an incomplete picture. *The Economist* (1996: 30) provides cautionary advice on this issue:

> The conclusion must be that while culture will continue to exercise an important influence on both countries and individuals, it has not suddenly become more important than, say, governments or impersonal economic forces. Much of its (culture) influence is secondary, that is, it comes about partly as a reaction to the 'knowledge era'. And within the overall mix of what influences people's behaviour, culture's role may well be declining, rather than rising, squeezed between the greedy expansion of the government on one side, and globalization on the other.

While the present argument does not fully endorse this view – it believes that comparative study in educational administration, for reasons provided earlier, should intimately address and be grounded in culture – it acknowledges that studies should take careful cognisance of other social, political and economic environmental factors which influence education.

The Structure of Subsequent Chapters

This chapter has focused on developing a cross-cultural conceptual framework for use in comparative studies of schools and school systems. Recognition of cross-cultural issues and of the need to contextualize school restructuring and design are regarded as key aims of this book. While many draw attention to the globalization and internationalization of educational policy and practice, there is an equal need to recognize important local forces, including culture, which may or may not harmonize with the international trends.

Accordingly, each subsequent chapter is structured around a key element of school design. As argued in Chapter 1, the precepts and principles of school design are regarded as generic. How each of them is applied and implemented in practice, however, may need to take into account the influence of societal culture. Towards the end of each chapter, therefore, attention is given to relevant cross-cultural issues and perspectives which help qualify the generic principles regarding that particular design element.

References

Beare, H. and Boyd, W.L. (eds) (1993) *Restructuring Schools: An International Perspective on the Movement to Transform the Control and Performance of Schools*, London: Falmer Press.

Begley, P. and Johansson, O. (1997) 'Values and school administration: preferences, ethics and conflicts', paper presented at the annual meeting of the American Educational Research Association, Chicago, March.

Biggs, J. (1994) 'What are effective schools? Lessons from East and West', *Australian Educational Researcher* 21 (1): 19–39.

Blake, R.R. and Mouton, J.S. (1964) *The Managerial Grid*, Houston, TX: Gulf Publishing.

Blunt, P. and Jones, M. (1997) 'Exploring the limits of Western leadership theory in East Asia and Africa', *Personnel Review* 26 (1/2): 6–23.

Bolman, L. and Deal, T. (1992) 'Leading and managing: effects of context, culture, and gender', *Educational Administration Quarterly* 28 (3): 314–29.

Bray, M. and Thomas, R.M. (1995) 'Levels of comparison in educational studies: different insights from different literatures and the value of multilevel analysis', *Harvard Educational Review* 65 (3): 472–89.

Cheng, K.M. (1994) 'Issues in decentralizing education: what the reform in China tells', *International Journal od Educational Research* 21 (8): 799–808.

—— (1995) 'The neglected dimension: cultural comparison in educational administration', in K.C. Wong and K.M. Cheng (eds), *Educational Leadership and Change: An International Perspective*, Hong Kong: Hong Kong University Press, 87–102.

Cheng, Y.C. (1995) 'School effectiveness and improvement in Hong Kong, Taiwan and mainland China', in B. Creemers and N. Osinga (eds), *International Congress of School Effectiveness and School Improvement Country Reports*, Friesland, Netherlands: GCO, 11–30.

Child, J., (1981) 'Culture, contingency and capitalism in the cross-national study of organizations', in L. Cummings and B. Shaw (eds), *Research in Organizational Behaviour*, vol. 3., Greenwich, CT: JAI Press.

Dimmock, C. (1998) 'Restructuring Hong Kong's schools: the applicability of Western theories, policies and practices to an Asian culture', *Educational Management and Administration* 26 (4): 363–77.

Dimmock, C. and Walker, A. (1998a) 'A cross-cultural comparative approach to educational administration: development of a conceptual framework', *Educational Administration Quarterly* 34 (4): 558–95.

—— (1998b) 'Towards comparative educational administration: building the case for a cross-cultural, school-based approach', *Journal of Educational Administration* 36 (4): 379–401.

Fok, L., Hartman, S., Villere, M. and Freibert, R. (1996) 'A study of the impact of cross-cultural differences on perceptions of equity and organizational citizenship behavior', *International Journal of Management* 13 (1): 3–14.

Gouldner, A. (1957) 'Cosmopolitans and locals: toward an analysis of latent social roles', *Administrative Science Quarterly* 2: 291–306.

Hallinger, P. and Leithwood, K. (1996) 'Culture and educational administration: a case of finding out what you don't know you don't know', *Journal of Educational Administration* 34 (5): 98–116.

Harrison, G., McKinnon, J., Panchapakesan, S. and Leung, M. (1994) 'The influence of culture on organizational design and planning and control in Australia and the United States compared with Singapore and Hong Kong', *Journal of International Financial Management and Accounting* 5 (3): 242–61.

Ho, D.Y.F. (1991) 'Cognitive socialization in Confucian heritage cultures', paper presented to Workshop on Continuities and Discontinuities in the Cognitive Socialization of Minority Children, Washington, DC: US Department of Health and Human Services.

Hofstede, G.H. (1980) *Cultures Consequences: International Differences in Work-Related Values*, Beverly Hills, CA: Sage.

—— (1991) *Cultures and Organisations: Software of the Mind*, London: McGraw-Hill.

—— (1994) 'Cultural constraints in management theories', *International Review of Strategic Management* 5: 27–48.

—— (1995) 'Managerial values: the business of international business is culture', in T. Jackson (ed.), *Cross-cultural Management*, Oxford: Butterworth-Heinemann, 150–65.

Hofstede, G. and Bond, M. (1984) 'Hofstede's cultural dimensions: an independent validation using Rokeach's value survey', *Journal Of Cross-Cultural Psychology* 15 (4): 417–33.

Hughes, M.G. (1988) 'Comparative educational administration', in N.J. Boyan (ed.),*Handbook of Research on Educational Administration*, White Plains, NY: Longman, 655–76.

Morris, P. (1997) Review of the book *World's Apart: A Review of International Surveys of Educational Achievement Involving England*, in *International Journal of Educational Development* 17 (4): 475–6.

O'Donoghue, T., and Dimmock, C. (1998). *School Restructuring: International Perspectives*, London: Kogan Page.

Organisation for Economic Cooperation and Development (OECD) (1989) *Schools and Quality: An International Report*, Paris: OECD.

—— (1996) *Reviews of National Policies for Education: France*, OECD: Paris.

Redding, S.G. (1994) 'Comparative management theory: jungle, zoo or fossil bed?', *Organization Studies* 15 (3): 323–59.

Reynolds, D., and Farrell, S. (1996) 'World's apart? A review of international surveys of educational achievement involving England', London: Her Majesty's Stationery Office.

Richards, D. (1993) 'Flying against the wind? Culture and management development in south east Asia', in P. Blunt. and D. Richards (eds), *Readings in Management, Organisation and Culture in East and Southeast Asia*, Darwin, Australia: Northern University Press, 256–371.

Sapra, C.L. (1991) 'The school principal in India', in W. Walker, R. Farquhar and M.G. Hughes (eds), *Advancing Education: School Leadership in Action*, London: Falmer Press, 119–30.

The Economist (1996) 'Cultural explanations: the man in the Baghdad cafe', 9 November, 23–30.

The Chinese Culture Connection (1987) 'Chinese values and the search for culture-free dimensions of culture', *Journal of Cross-Cultural Psychology* 18: 143–64.

Trice, H. and Beyer, J.M. (1993) *The Cultures of Work Organizations*, Englewood Cliffs, NJ: Prentice Hall.

Trompenaars, F. and Hampden-Turner, C. (1997) *Riding the Waves of Culture: Understanding Cultural Diversity in Business*, 2nd edn, London: Nicholas Brealey.

Vecchio, R. (1995) 'A cross-national comparison of the influence of span of control', *International Journal of Management* 12 (3): 261–70.

Walker, A. and Dimmock, C. (1999a) 'Exploring principals' dilemmas in Hong Kong: increasing cross-cultural understanding of school leadership', *International Journal of Educational Reform* 8 (1): 15–24.

—— (1999b) 'A cross-cultural approach to the study of educational leadership', *Journal of School Leadership* 9 (4): 321–48.

—— (in press) 'Leadership dilemmas of Hong Kong principals: sources, perceptions and outcomes', *Australian Journal of Education*.

Weiler, H.N., Mintrop, H. and Fuhrmann, E. (1996) *Educational Change and Social Transformation: Teachers, Schools and Universities in Eastern Germany*, London: Falmer Press.

Westwood, R. (ed.) (1992) *Organisational Behaviour: Southeast Asian Perspectives*, Hong Kong: Longman.

Wilkinson, B. (1996) 'Culture, institutions and business in East Asia', *Organization Studies* 17 (3): 421–47.

Wong, K.C. (1995) 'School management initiative in Hong Kong – the devolution of power to schools, real or rhetoric?', in K.C. Wong and K.M. Cheng (eds), *Educational Leadership and Change: An International Perspective*, Hong Kong: Hong Kong University Press, 141–53.

4 Initiating the Re-Design Process
Creating the School Culture

The first three chapters of this book have attempted to lay a framework for school design based on key precepts, principles and elements. In addition, they have introduced societal culture as a further element warranting consideration as school design initiatives spread globally. This chapter bridges between the first three, largely conceptual, chapters and subsequent chapters each of which focuses on a particular school design element. In this chapter, attention is given to how schools can begin the re-design process.

One of the most difficult stages in the school re-design process is how and where to start. Moving a school from where it currently is towards a desired future state involves first, undertaking changes in policies, practices and techniques; second, embracing the human side of the enterprise and the school community at large; and third, a time-consuming and lengthy process which is ongoing and evolving, but which will almost certainly take a minimum of five years before any significant results are achieved. As challenging as school design is, it cannot be undertaken superficially and without careful preparation and planning. Laying the groundwork for change through culture building is imperative, the aim being to gain the active support of as many of the school community and key participants as possible.

This chapter establishes guidelines as to how the re-design process can be initiated, the stages which need to be completed and the management issues that need to be faced. It focuses on the needs assessment process as the basis for recognition of the current strengths and weaknesses of the school. In particular, it highlights the need to identify the forces pushing for change inside and outside of the school. It recommends that the process be informed by research evidence as to what works at the school and classroom levels. It details some key stages involved in conducting the needs assessment. It relates the foregoing stages to school vision and mission. It connects the whole needs assessment exercise with the school vision and with the formation of school policies, which help direct the energy of the organization and its members. Finally, the chapter concludes with some cross-cultural implications for initiating the review process.

A school which works its way through this set of authentic experiences will, at the same time, be developing its culture to align with that required for the future school design. By the same token, the school will be reassessing its mission and realigning it to be consistent with new functions and different ways of working. By way of exemplifying of the above stages, reference is made to the process engaged in by Brewster Academy in New Hampshire, USA, and in particular the views espoused by Bain (1996, in press), the architect of that school's re-design.

Identifying Forces for Change: 'Drivers'

A logical starting point for a school embarking on a needs assessment exercise is to take account of the forces exerting a 'push' for change. Bain (in press) uses the term 'drivers' to refer to forces or events which cause the members of an organization to do things differently. The distinguishing characteristic of drivers is that they are forces which exert an impetus for change. It is important for a school to identify the drivers in its environment early in the process, for a number of reasons. First, it is wise to identify the forces pushing for change to counteract the possibility that the forces of resistance, which are usually well to the fore, may otherwise become predominant. Second, awareness of the nature and the form of the drivers will almost certainly shape the direction of the whole needs assessment exercise.

Forces shaping the evolution of change in schools exist both inside and outside; hence, a school conducting an analysis of its drivers would find it convenient to classify them as external and internal. Among the external drivers, one might expect to find the following:

- education policies emanating from governments and education departments, such as curriculum reforms, decentralization, devolution and school-based management;
- economic policies pursued by governments;
- changes in the economic structure of a society;
- changes in technology as used in business and industry;
- demographic and socioeconomic changes taking place in the school's target population or catchment intake;
- parental expectations;
- competition with other schools.

From the outset, a school intent on re-designing itself would need to embrace in its deliberations the key changes and trends taking place in its environment. For example, if it is a government school, what are the systemic policies with regard to devolution, decentralization and school-based management? Is the policy context tending towards more curriculum centralization, or more school-based curriculum design? In the light of recent and likely future economic policy, is expenditure on schools increasing or decreasing in real terms? How is the budgetary allocation changing? Is the occupational and economic structure of society undergoing fundamental change? For example, is the economy shifting from a manufacturing to a service base, or from a traditional service economy to a high-value added service economy? How are global forces affecting the economy? To what extent is technological change placing pressure on demands for employees with information technology skills? All of these may drive the school to reassess the knowledge and skills required of its students.

Moreover, demographic changes currently taking place, or likely in the future, may be significant in shaping school design. Is the catchment area population increasing or decreasing? Will the school be expanding or contracting? Alongside these considerations are possible changes in the socioeconomic mix of the catchment area. Is the population shifting in complexion to become more middle class? Are parental expectations providing an impetus for change? What changes are taking place among competing schools such as to warrant a response? In a similar vein, the internal school drivers might include:

- student academic performance;
- student disciplinary record;
- teacher initiatives;
- school-based curriculum initiatives;
- teacher professionalism;
- administrator initiatives;
- a new appointment.

An internal school incentive and impetus for change may come from student academic results, whether they be improving, deteriorating or stable. The key point is whether parents, teachers and students are motivated to act and react in positive and proactive ways to the status quo. The same is true with respect to student disciplinary behaviour. Another internal driver may come from an individual teacher or group of teachers keen to introduce, for example, a new teaching approach, assessment strategy or school-based curriculum project, such as individualized learning or integrated studies. If there is a school climate and culture predicated on teacher professionalism, then that might be a driver for change. A respected leader or leadership team might equally constitute a force for driving change. Similarly, the new appointment of a senior member of staff, especially a person appointed to a position with a clear and specific agenda in mind, might be a catalyst for and give an impetus to change.

In summary, 'drivers' are forces external and internal to the school which provide impetus for change. They may comprise a wide range of forces, including policy trends and mandates, pressure for the school to keep abreast of technological and employment trends in society, demand for and supply of places at the school, and leadership and personnel initiatives. A school needs to capitalize on and harness its drivers in shaping and supporting the design process. In turn, the drivers should force the school to re-examine its mission.

Schools should consider their drivers en masse. This 'big picture' or gestalt view can then form the basis of a tentative overall image, vision or goal for the future school, a vision which will gradually be refined and sharpened as the school proceeds through the following stages of the needs assessment.

Identifying What Works: School Effectiveness and 'Informed' Teaching and Learning Practices

Having identified the drivers, the school needs to begin its strategy to address them. It is commonplace for schools to look inwards and to focus on their strengths and needs. In such cases, the whole process becomes narrowly introspective early on and tends to stay that way. Rather, schools should look outwards at this stage and particularly to the research literature for what works. In keeping with one of the main themes of this book, it is desirable for teachers and administrators to become 'informed'. In this regard, engaging a whole-school design process entails familiarity with a number of bodies of research literature. These include school effectiveness, school improvement, restructuring, effective teaching, effective learning, learning theory and learning processes, organizational design and human resource management. In addition, and of particular relevance to the theme of this book, is the need for schools to consider culture at organizational, and especially societal, level, in transferring and adapting research findings to specific environments.

The aim of engaging these literatures is to broaden the school's perspective, to take account of knowledge that might be relevant and useful in shaping the school's design, and to provide some reference points, yardsticks or benchmarks for the school community to use in its deliberations. At the same time as extolling the virtues of consulting the research evidence, it is necessary to advise a cautious and questioning approach in respect of the literature. School staff might, for example, ask about the validity and reliability of the findings. Are claims being made purely on the grounds of personal opinion and prescription? Are generalizations being claimed without adequate sampling techniques? Are conclusions being drawn which do not fit the data? If case studies are used, to what extent do the contexts of the cases match that of the school?

As discussed in Chapter 1, the state of the art in some of these fields is tentative and approximate rather than exact. That does not mean, however, that useful knowledge cannot be gained. One would advocate, for example, a cross-checking of the findings and recommendations from a number of studies by different researchers. It would be wise to consult both quantitative and qualitative studies. It is now commonly realized that using checklists of school and classroom effectiveness characteristics, in ways which de-contextualize them, is fraught with the probability of failure.

Where are the likely sources of such knowledge? University education libraries are an obvious place to start. Academics might be consulted in guiding the school towards relevant and robust research in books and journals. Schools might wish to build their own libraries by purchasing books and subscribing to journals, and then making them available to the wider school community. Useful software is now available which provides a synthesis of research findings from many of the better quality journals concerned with the relevant bodies of literature. An example is the Research Assistant (Effective Schools Productivity Systems, 1994), an interactive database of Effective Schools Research Abstracts, which is updated each year. It provides an entry point for those looking to make sense of voluminous bodies of literature.

The aim of this process is for the school to develop clarity about informed practice in teaching and learning, curriculum, technology, organization and leadership, management and administration of the design process. This knowledge will serve as a reference base for identifying needs, building school policy and fashioning the model of school design to be adopted.

Examples of Informed Practice

At this juncture, it is helpful to be reminded of the seven precepts for designing quality schools geared to learning (Dimmock, 1995a, 1995b, 1995c), as set out in Chapter 2. They are as follows:

1 Student outcomes provide goal direction for learning.
2 Schools exist primarily for teaching and learning; learning and the individual learner are the centrepiece of all that happens in the school.
3 Teaching focuses on learning and teaching for understanding; a balance and variety of teaching strategies is achieved, a combination of methods from didactic and expository to constructivist.
4 The curriculum is tailored to suit the diverse needs of students.
5 Learning and teaching shape and dictate school structures and organization, including technology and the use of space, which are designed to support and facilitate the principles and practices of learning and teaching.
6 Learning and teaching determine professional development, leadership and management, resource allocation and culture/climate, all of which

are dedicated to supporting a service delivery designed for quality teaching and learning.

7   At all stages and in all activities, especially teaching, learning and leadership, the school adheres to 'informed practice'.

These precepts are themselves founded on research evidence of informed practice. The essence of, and rationale behind, referencing research evidence and eliciting precepts in this way is to adopt a model of school design which makes informed practice intentional as opposed to accidental or fortuitous.

Subsequent chapters elaborate on different bodies of this research literature. For example, Chapter 7 elucidates informed practice concerning teaching and learning approaches, methods, skills and behaviours. It is suggested that confirmatory evidence exists on how best to practice cooperative learning, mastery learning, direct teaching and problem-based learning. Evidence suggests that there are 'informed' and 'less informed' ways to practice these methods. It is known that a number of specific teaching behaviours – such as positive reinforcement, and cues and feedback – are associated with promoting student learning. Likewise, in regard to school effectiveness, almost all studies reveal the importance of the following: visibility of the principal's leadership, consistency between school mission, clear goals and curriculum and assessment, a supportive culture and climate for learning, an emphasis on feedback and evaluation, and parental support. In terms of school improvement, change efforts are more likely to succeed if there is agreement and consistency between principal and all staff, a clear plan and strategy to guide action and outside support for internal initiatives.

Reviewing relevant literature in this way provides the major participants in the school design process with a perspective on the scope of knowledge, skill and activity required. It also helps them to reconsider their mission and to establish an appropriate culture, one which is geared to school-wide adoption of informed practice in an intentional way.

Leading and Managing the Needs Analysis Process

Underlying the notion of school design being advocated is the principle of intentionality, the idea that informed practices are deliberate and consciously planned. As a consequence, importance is placed on management and leadership of the change process. In regard to management of the needs assessment, there are at least four aspects to consider: the selection and role of a change agent, the establishment of a task group, the involvement of the community and the conduct of the assessment exercise, involving evaluation of the school's strengths and needs. Each of these is now briefly discussed.

The Change Agent

The appointment of a change agent, a person who can guide and steer the needs assessment exercise as part of the change process, is crucial. Two inter-related matters concern the role expected of the change agent, and the selection of a suitable person.

The change agent plays an especially key role early in the change process by making the 'cognitive leaps' to get the process moving, establishing structures and procedures, and gaining the involvement of key personnel. The change agent should possess the knowledge and expertise which will gradually be transferred to the school community if the change process is to be sustainable in the long run.

What expertise should a change agent possess? The following are indicative of the breadth of knowledge and ability sought in a change agent, based on the key areas involved in school design: teaching, learning and curriculum; technology; organizational structures; professional development; the management and evaluation of professional staff; the use of resources; and a gestalt view of the whole change and design process and an understanding of how the parts interrelate to form the whole. For example, change agents should possess a sound knowledge of informed teaching and learning practices, such that they can recognize when a teacher is misapplying the principles of cooperative learning, peer tutoring or direct teaching, and then proceed to offer sound technical advice. In the area of human relations, they need to know how best to handle difficult interpersonal conflicts, breakdowns in communication, or resistance to and fear of change.

The aim is not to create a change agent who is seen as 'the expert on everything'. Rather, it is to provide leadership to the change process, particularly in the early stages, and for the change agent to gradually transfer that leadership to others across the school community as the process unfolds and expertise becomes diffused. Clarification of the role and skills expected of the change agent will influence the selection of an appropriate person. Two options are possible:

1   to appoint a person already on staff;
2   to make a new appointment from outside the school.

The position of change agent is likely to require at least one-half of a full-time load, and may even justify a full-time load, especially at certain stages. A change agent needs to be a senior member of staff, a person with credibility and respect and with the technical expertise and interpersonal skills to fulfil the role elaborated above. If there is not a suitable candidate who already possesses these characteristics, then it may be possible to identify someone who is capable of acquiring them, providing the time required matches the schedule for school design.

A change agent would normally have the status of a principal, a deputy principal or dean. In this regard, the particular circumstance of each school will come into play. A prime consideration is that the school needs to be routinely managed at the same time as the change process is taking place. However, whole-school change is likely to be all-consuming. Consequently, it is reasonable to expect a division of roles between the change agent with overall responsibility for managing the design process and another senior staff member who will handle the routine management of the school. Clearly, both need to share the same visions and values and to work closely. The case for division of roles in this way is stronger the larger is the school. Whether it is the principal who assumes the change agent role and a deputy who assumes the manager role, or vice versa, will depend on their relative abilities, interests and other school circumstances. It is commonplace for the principal to continue to manage the school while a deputy assumes the change agent role.

A further issue arises in the event of a suitable change agent not being available from within the school, while at the same time there is little possibility of hiring one. In this situation, a possible solution is for the change agent's role to be shared between two people or among a small group. Pragmatism may have to rule in such cases. The skills and expertise demanded of a change agent in whole-school design are formidable. There may not be one person who is capable of fulfilling the role. The more the role is shared, however, the greater the danger of inconsistencies between the various elements of the design, as differences of view may need to be reconciled.

Bringing Faculty Together

One of the biggest challenges in managing the change process, and particularly the needs assessment part, is to balance the effort expended in determining the tasks and their sequence with concern for the human management side of the enterprise. Investing in the individuals who will run with the change means that ideas and processes need to be shared and owned. That group of people should not be too narrow. It is tempting to focus only on those who show eagerness and support. Getting the job done, itself a major challenge, can easily mean that the more time-consuming task of winning broad support is neglected. Sharing information and building support is necessary to minimise the appearance of deep divisions in the staff. Securing agreement for the core values of the school is paramount. This is best achieved by appeal to the drivers, the research literature on informed practice and the precepts that emanate, and identification of the school's needs. It also means critically reviewing the school mission. Faculty, therefore, need to be brought together in one or more workshops.

Resort to the drivers and to the research literature, that is, to more objective sources, helps to defuse any tendency for the process to become overly subjective and personal. The roles of key players need to be agreed in arranging the workshop. For example:

- the change agent might plan the whole workshop;
- the principal should introduce and frame the exercise;
- a dean might act as the main facilitator for the day;
- a credible and respected teacher might present the informed practices research;
- another respected staff member might present the 'drivers';
- the dean-facilitator might conduct a review of the school's strengths and weaknesses;
- the facilitator might then categorize and prioritize the emergent themes from the strengths and weaknesses activity under the elements of school design.

The culmination of the workshop is a comprehensive record of high priority needs referenced to each of the elements of school design (curriculum, teaching, learning, technology and so on), having taken into account the drivers and research literature on informed practice.

As a large forum, the workshop is a means of sharing information across faculty, and involving all members. For the ongoing and more detailed management of the needs assessment process, a small task group is appropriate.

Appointing a Task Group

Under the leadership of the change agent, this task group has the job of completing the needs assessment which began at the faculty meeting. Its membership should reflect all levels of the school: departments, faculty members, senior and class teachers, and technology staff. It conducts the methodology of the needs assessment, devising the means of data collection and analysis, interpreting the findings and writing a report.

There are two reasons for forming a task group. First, it is a useful way of collecting more rigorous data on which to build the school design. Second, the needs assessment task if exercised properly, requires the close involvement of a number of people. Thus it serves the purpose of broadening involvement. The group should be large enough to commit two or three people to each of the school design elements: curriculum, teaching and learning; technology; professional development; organizational structures; personnel; and evaluation. The change agent coordinates the various teams.

Implementing the Needs Assessment

With the appointment of a change agent and a task group, and having brought the community together to identify strengths and needs, the next stage is to move the needs assessment exercise to data collection and analysis. This set of procedures involves six steps, each of which is now briefly described.

Develop questions for each of the strengths and needs identified at the faculty meeting

The needs assessment data collection and analysis phase is essentially a research project. As with any research project, it is helpful to begin with a list of questions. These should be based on the strengths and needs identified at the faculty meeting. Questions provide a focus for deciding relevant data and suggest ways of collecting it. For example, a question on the curriculum might be: 'What is the current level of vertical and horizontal integration of the subjects forming the curriculum?' Another question, on behaviour, might be: 'What is the current level of problem behaviour in the school?'

Establish criteria as standards–performance indicators

Early in the procedure it is important to establish standards or criteria which will serve as benchmarks of performance against which the data to be collected can be compared and evaluated. In current parlance, these standards are often called performance indicators. They may be generated from within, as expressions of the school's own expectations, or they may be taken from outside the school, such as standards laid down by professional bodies or government departments. Thus a government or professional body may have systemic figures for attrition rates, examination successes, misconduct, and so on.

Seek sources of data collection

In seeking relevant data, two sources can be distinguished: first, data that already exists in the school, and second, primary data that will need to be generated. The former includes documentary sources such as school records, minutes of meetings, school mission, curricula and syllabi. Other sources might include test scores, records of disciplinary behaviour and absenteeism, service records of teachers and parent participation rates.

Some information will need to be generated, however, and for such data the use of the questionnaire survey is often appropriate. There is the issue of deciding who will take responsibility for drafting a suitable instrument. Taking the curriculum as an example, data could be collected on:

- its breadth, depth, balance, integration, individualization and relevance to the school mission and to the adult world;
- the degree of collaboration within and between the staff and student bodies;
- the levels of technology resources in the school and their integration across the curriculum.

Decisions need to be taken as to who will collect data and by when. For this and all of the steps outlined in the procedure, appropriate pro formas are needed to register clarity of agreement and commitment as to who is shouldering responsibility and by when these responsibilities will be discharged.

Analyse the data

Decisions regarding data analysis relate to who will undertake the task and the methods they will use. With quantitative methods, all that may be needed is simple frequency counts and descriptive statistics. If interviews have been conducted, then transcripts will need to be coded and emergent themes identified. Data should be analysed in the context of the questions posed and the criteria and standards imposed at the beginning.

Aggregate and interpret the findings and make recommendations

All the findings need to be brought together and the results compared with the benchmarks and criteria established earlier on in the process. Evaluative judgements can then be made about the performance of the school in relation to those standards, and the criteria can continue to serve as the source of future progress. Comparison of the results with the standards and criteria set enables recommendations to be made and highlights those areas where current school performance falls well short of expectation.

Produce the evaluation report

A typical structure of a report would include contents, executive summary, aims, evaluation questions, implementation plan, findings, conclusions and recommendations. It is wise to tailor the language of the report to suit the particular audience. Thus, different versions of the report may need to be made. A report to parents requires brevity and plain English, while a report to a professional audience, such as the Education Department or a funding agency, would be more technical.

Formulating Policy

The series of processes and their sequence described in this chapter reveal a complex set of procedures, all of which need to be completed before a school is ready for policy development. This will surprise those who might have been inclined to believe that schools could move swiftly and easily into the policy stage. In fact, good preparation beforehand improves the quality of an emergent policy. By this stage the school will have examined its drivers, become familiar with research literature on informed practices at school and classroom levels, and identified its strengths and needs. It is now ready to move into developing policy statements, which will serve to channel the combined effort and energy of the community into achieving all aspects of the design programme. Policy statements will need to be generated for curriculum, teaching and learning, for technology, professional development, structures, leadership, management, personnel and evaluation.

At various times throughout the foregoing procedures, the school will have needed to reference its mission statement. Indeed, it will almost certainly have felt the need to modify its mission as a consequence of identifying its drivers, reading the research literature on informed practice and conducting the needs analysis. Mission statements, however, are very general and need to be fractured into a series of consistent operational policy statements on which resources and energy can be focused in the daily routine life of the school. Bain (1996) articulates this well when he argues that schools should be intentional rather than accidental or coincidental organizations. That means that if they truly believe in individual differences in student learning, then curricula should incorporate flexible grouping, multiple levels of expectation and student-oriented teaching. Policies, says Bain, are opportunities to build consensus around and bring definition to the school's intentions.

Policies need to be directional, and to reflect and be consistent with the mission statement, school outcomes, drivers and research on informed practices. The needs assessment task group is appropriate to draft the policies since it represents a cross-section of staff. Drafts will need to be presented to, and legitimized by, the whole staff. An example of a policy statement is:

> In order to respond effectively to the school-wide student outcomes, the curriculum should be outcomes-based and contain the following:

- clearly defined learner outcomes;
- knowledge, skills, attitudes and values embedded in the outcomes;
- learning activities needed to achieve the outcomes;
- suggested instructional methods and materials;
- evaluation criteria, standards and methods to check degree of achievement.

Cross-Cultural Issues and Conclusions

This chapter has focused on the conduct of a needs assessment and has adopted a somewhat technical approach. It has attempted to bring structure to a process which can easily lose its way. It is apparent nonetheless that projects such as needs assessment exercises, which are built on a sequence of procedures and tasks are in fact reliant on intensely human and interpersonal processes for their success. At the same time as the procedures and stages of the needs assessment are being implemented, the staff involved in implementation are experiencing changes in interpersonal relations and in the values underlying the change, all of which push towards the establishment of a different organizational culture. Establishing new tasks and procedures and setting up new decisional structures is an expedient way to build culture.

With regard to initiating the design process and the needs analysis, issues of societal culture merit attention. From one viewpoint, the needs assessment exercise is a technical activity requiring a number of steps. These steps in themselves do not appear to be culture-sensitive. The interpersonal and human operations underpinning the procedures, however, are likely to be subject to cross-cultural differences. How meetings are conducted and whose views prevail are more culture-sensitive than the technical or task stages of the exercise. This is particularly true for teachers and parents, as indicated below.

Teacher participation in initiating the school review process in some Asian systems is by no means easy. Dimmock and Lim (1999), for example, found in Hong Kong that opposition to higher levels of teacher participation even came from middle managers, who foresaw their roles being eroded as a result. In hierarchical power-concentrated societies (see Chapter 3) such as Hong Kong and many other Asian systems, teacher participation might be more illusory than real, lapsing into an 'administrative control mode' rather than a 'professional control mode' (Murphy and Beck, 1995).

There may of course be cultural similarities as well as differences. For example, parents appear to be reluctant players in school decision making in both the East and the West. Any differences between societies in terms of parental reluctance to participate may thus be ones of degree rather than kind. The same end result – parent reluctance – may, however, mask different motivations. In the USA and UK, arguments championing parent participation are closely aligned to their democratic rights. That is, by participating in school councils, parents are advancing their democratic rights to influence their children's education. Appeal to the same democratic rights argument is nowhere near as strong in East Asian societies. Much of the momentum for parent participation in East Asian schools comes from restructuring policies adopted from the West. The likelihood of their succeeding, therefore, is even less than in the West. A number of factors justify this conclusion. First, the push to exercise democratic rights is less.

Second, in societies such as Hong Kong, parents generally accord more respect to teachers than do their counterparts in the West. Parents tend to believe that what takes place in the school is the teachers' preserve, and that by participating they are infringing on the teachers' territory. Third, because societies such as the UK and USA developed systems of mass higher education long before East Asian societies, they have a large, educated middle class, many of whom are less inhibited about communicating with teachers and principals. Hong Kong's expansion of its university system in the 1990s means that the present generation of students is the first to go to university. Nonetheless, involving parents in initiating the school design process is generally a challenge in both Eastern and Western societies. School restructuring policies have generally escalated the push for parental participation in school decision making beyond the readiness and acceptance of parents themselves. Moreover, resistance to parent involvement comes from many teachers, who fear the erosion of their authority.

The above conclusions apply only to parental participation in school decision making and not to other forms of parental involvement in their children's education, such as support for homework and the alignment of home values with school values. As a matter of interest, on both of these latter issues, Stevenson and Stigler's (1992) research comparing Chinese, Japanese and American families and schools found higher levels of parental support and involvement in the two East Asian societies.

Finally, by acknowledging cultural differences as well as similarities, schools in different societies will generate their own lists of external and internal drivers reflecting their local policy and cultural contexts. There may be some commonality between school 'drivers' in Beijing, Tokyo, Hong Kong, London, Melbourne and New York, but there will certainly be some important differences. Subsequent chapters aim to throw light on both.

References

Bain, A. (1996) 'The Future School Institute Handbook', unpublished manuscript, Brewster Academy, New Hampshire, USA.

—— (in press) 'The school design model: strategy for the design of 21st century schools', in C. Dimmock and A. Walker (eds), *Future School Administration: Western and Asian Perspectives*, Hong Kong: Hong Kong Institute of Educational Research/The Chinese University Press.

Dimmock, C. (1995a) 'Reconceptualizing restructuring for school effectiveness and school improvement', *International Journal of Educational Reform* 4 (3): 285–300.

—— (1995b) 'Restructuring for school effectiveness: leading, organising and teaching for effective learning', *Educational Management and Administration* 23 (1): 5–18.

—— (1995c) 'School leadership: securing quality teaching and learning', in C. Evers and J. Chapman (eds), *Educational Administration: An Australian Perspective*, Sydney: Allen & Unwin.

Dimmock, C. and Lim, P. H-W. (1999) 'School restructuring in Hong Kong: a case study of the effects on middle managers', *Asia Pacific Journal of Education* 19 (1): 59–77.

Effective Schools Productivity Systems (1994) *The Effective Schools Research Assistant*, PO Box 1164, Okemos, MI, USA, 48805–1164.

Murphy, J. and Beck, L.G. (1995) *School-Based Management as School Reform: Taking Stock*, Thousand Oaks, CA: Corwin Press.

Stevenson, H.W. and Stigler, J.W. (1992) *The Learning Gap: Why Our Schools are Failing and What We Can Learn from Japanese and Chinese Education*, New York: Touchstone.

5   Designing the Curriculum

The curriculum plays a centrally important role in designing the learning-centred school, since it is the essence of what is to be learned and the substance on which teaching, learning and assessment is based. This chapter first elaborates on the place of the curriculum within the school and the key connections therein. It also affirms the general precepts undergirding curriculum design. Second, it goes on to detail how an outcomes-framed curriculum can best be operationalized in and by re-designed schools. Third, it points out the difficulties of the new approach and the criticisms it has attracted. Fourth, it argues that the adoption of a curriculum outcomes' framework by school systems is in itself insufficient, and that further input by teachers and schools is necessary to enable the approach to deliver the intended benefits of enhancing student learning. Finally, some cross-cultural implications pertinent to the curriculum are drawn.

Many school systems have recognized the need to restructure the curriculum. In England and Wales, for example, a new National Curriculum was introduced in the late 1980s. Hong Kong embarked on the introduction of what it calls a Target-Oriented Curriculum (TOC) into primary schools from the mid-1990s, a scheme which will eventually be phased into secondary schools. Australian states, such as Western Australia, have also introduced a new curriculum framework, as have many states in the USA during the 1990s.

Most of these curriculum changes reflect a prevailing move to outcomes-based curriculum frameworks. To appreciate the significance of this shift, it is necessary to understand the attributes of the traditional curriculum. Historically, the curriculum has been viewed as lists of topics under subject headings for teachers to cover (Barnett and Whitaker, 1996; Sizer, 1992). Typically, syllabus documents have laid out the curriculum in this way as material for teachers to teach. Emphasis has been placed on expressions of the curriculum in terms of what is relevant for teaching and teachers. Differences between the curriculum and the syllabus have thus been minimized.

In the new approach to curriculum design, a fundamentally different orientation has superseded the former one. Curricula are now being framed in terms of learning outcomes, that is, what students are expected to learn and achieve. There are thus two very different emphases: one relates to the switch from a preoccupation with what teachers should teach to what students should learn; the other is a more explicit concern for outcomes achieved rather than material covered.

Government schools functioning in systems where central bureaucracies have reconfigured the curriculum according to an outcomes framework will have already had their curriculum contexts shaped for them. A large residual responsibility still exists within the school, however, to translate and implement the new curriculum, since in most cases it is a framework rather than a detailed prescription which is provided by the system centre. Indeed, in some systems the central bureaucracy asserts that it is only interested in the learning outcomes being achieved, and that it is up to each school to take control of the processes or strategies by which these outcomes will be accomplished. There may thus be a larger element of school-based curriculum decision making than before, particularly with regard to methods, processes and strategies.

For independent and private schools, and for schools not directly required to follow a particular curriculum, many of the principles to be discussed in this chapter are equally applicable. Some may decide to follow the same curriculum as is prescribed for government schools, since they may be preparing students for the same public examinations and entrance to the same universities and colleges. Others may not be working within the confines of a particular curriculum, but will still regard the outcomes curriculum as a design imperative. For these schools, there may be no system-level outcomes framework: instead, their own school-wide outcomes become the main framework.

The Curriculum and its Connections within the Re-Designed School

Of the elements which constitute the school, those most closely linked to the curriculum are teaching and learning. Figure 5 in Chapter 2 shows the interplay between the curriculum, teaching and learning as the crucial triumvirate of elements which operate at classroom level and which thereby determine the quality of service delivery to students. While the crucial relationship between curriculum, teaching and learning may appear rather obvious, its implications for school design are significant. It is somewhat futile to introduce informed teaching practices, or to create new learning experiences for students if the curriculum with which teachers and students are working is itself outdated. The same argument applies in reverse to the other elements; changing the curriculum is somewhat pointless and its potential benefits will be unrealized if curriculum change is not accompanied by concomitant innovations to teaching practices and learning processes.

The key point to make is the integration and connectivity of these elements. There needs to be alignment, for example, between the curriculum, teaching and assessment (Barnett and Whitaker, 1996). Critics complain that students are currently collecting graduation certificates based on accumulated seat time. Wiggins (1989: 43), cited by Barnett and Whitaker (1996), makes the point thus: 'The high school diploma, by remaining tied to no standard other than credit accrual and seat time, provides no useful information about what students have studied or what they can actually do with what was studied.' As Barnett and Whitaker argue, in the typical curriculum, teachers cover the list of topics with the additional aid of textbooks or notes; students rote learn or memorize and regurgitate in some form of normative test. They go on to note:

> This model has created a misalignment and lack of integration among curriculum, instruction and assessment. In fact, assessment has become separate from curriculum and instruction. Educators are continually in-serviced on new models of instruction, such as cooperative learning and problem-based learning ... without a firm grasp of how these instructional approaches align with curriculum and assessment.
>
> (Barnett and Whitaker, 1996: 92)

The curriculum, however, has many other important linkages besides teaching and learning. These three – curriculum, teaching and learning – taken together form what is known as the core technology of the school, which in turn requires appropriate organizational structures for its support. Curriculum change may well pre-empt major modifications to the timetable, to groupings of students and teachers, and to the use of physical space. Likewise it may also signal the need for fundamental rethinking of resource allocation within the school, of professional development, of the prevailing school culture and, more generally, of leadership and management.

Precepts for and Dimensions of Curriculum Design

A number of important precepts are invoked in re-designing the curriculum:

1   Every child is entitled to a broad, balanced and relevant curriculum. This means that the design must allow for flexibility and adaptability in order to respect student diversity. A degree of individualization is therefore necessary. The curriculum should connect with students at wherever they presently are and take them on from there, making allowance for individual difference in terms of ability and rate of progression.

2   There needs to be clarity and intentionality in the curriculum in respect of its structures, processes, values and content, all of which need to be made explicit at various levels of planning from system to school and teacher. In this respect, the framework, emphases and values embedded in the curriculum should reflect the school mission and overall policy.

3   Intentionality and clarity imply purposeful direction and goal orientation on the part of designers and planners and active involvement rather than passive consumption on the part of students. The curriculum therefore needs to be goal-oriented and outcomes-oriented.

4   There needs to be alignment between the curriculum on the one hand and teaching, learning and assessment, and computer technology on the other.

A set of curriculum dimensions by which to compare different curricula has been developed by the present writer (Dimmock, 1998). These same dimensions serve as a useful set of curriculum design principles for curriculum developers at system and school levels. The six design principles are goals and purposes, breadth, depth, integration, differentiation and relevance. Each is briefly summarized below.

Goals and purposes of the school curriculum. Curriculum goals may vary in line with differences in how curriculum developers conceive the nature of knowledge and with how the purpose of the curriculum is defined. The curriculum may be seen, for example, as having primarily instrumental functions related to future employment, or it may be seen as having more intrinsic cognitive priorities. The relative emphasis placed on knowledge, skill and attitude goals and on cognitive, affective–expressive–aesthetic and psychomotor goals may differ, as might the balance between academic and pastoral development.

Curriculum breadth. This refers to the range or spread of subjects and disciplines offered to students. Decisions need to be taken as to how broad an education is desirable.

Curriculum depth. This dimension concerns the levels, standards or grades at which the curriculum is offered. Curriculum developers invariably encounter trade-offs between breadth and depth. They must decide whether it is better to cover more subjects and topics at a superficial level, or fewer subjects and topics at a deeper level.

Curriculum integration. Levels of curriculum integration vary *vertically*, that is, the extent to which the content and teaching methods for individual subjects are coordinated and coherent from one grade level to another, and *horizontally*, that is, the extent to which coordination and coherence is achieved between different subject areas at the same grade level. A well-designed curriculum will achieve as much vertical and horizontal integration as possible.

Curriculum differentiation. This refers to the degree to which the curriculum caters for students of different abilities and needs. A well-designed curriculum should ensure all students experience core or essential knowledge while allowing for individual differences in aptitude.

Relevance. This is an elusive concept which applies both to individuals and to the wider society in respect of present and future education, employment, adult citizenship, social stability and social change. A well-designed curriculum meets the needs of individuals with respect to their present and future expectations of education, employment, social, ethical, spiritual and aesthetic development, and meets societal expectations regarding the preparation of future citizens to play full and responsible adult roles.

Discussion of Key Design Issues

While the current trend towards re-designing curricula in terms of student outcomes is strong and widespread across different cultures and societies, there are many who caution against its worst excesses. O'Donoghue (in press), for example, makes a plea for all curriculum development to take place within the context of the broader aims of education. It is essential that each society at periodic intervals re-examines its view of what are these aims. In this context, it is spurious to argue, as some governments currently espousing a students outcomes' approach do, that they are only interested in the outcomes achieved and are indifferent to the means and processes employed. O'Donoghue makes the point in relation to the context of the aims of education, that the means and processes are as crucial in education as the content. Thus, to the extent that outcomes do not embrace both means and content, they offer an impoverished framework and perspective of the curriculum.

Indeed, reiterating a previous point, it is necessary for each society – Western or Asian – to rediscover for itself the meaning of education. Such a process will yield multiple purposes flowing from the fundamental aims of education, purposes which create tensions in terms of inclusion in the limited confines of the curriculum. The key concept at this point is *balance*, a concept already implied in the previous section of this chapter when the tension between breadth and depth of the curriculum was introduced. Consequently, there can be no shortcuts to successful curriculum design. It requires a complex, comprehensive and coherent approach.

Confusion over the means–ends distinction is commonplace. Technology, for example, is probably more appropriately thought of as a means rather than an end, although it too can be an end in terms of content to be learned. The same phenomenon can be both the means and the end. More often, however, education is beset with opposing dualisms: academic versus vocational, humanities versus sciences, leisure versus work. According to O'Donoghue (in press), the curriculum should embrace all of these. An adequate reform strategy must be based on an understanding of the fundamental interrelationships between many of the alleged opposites. He cites Hughes's (1992) generalization that the short history of universal education is one of a broadening of focus, of an extension of purposes, which illustrate well the competing sets of demands which need balancing. Hughes asserts:

> In the broad sense, those purposes have always been threefold: for vocational preparation, for social participation and for personal development. However, all of these requirements have themselves become more complex and the shifting balance between them more difficult to define and maintain.
>
> (Hughes 1992: 4)

O'Donoghue goes on to recognize that the complexity will be compounded for future generations, who will change occupations and hence their competencies many times during their careers. Equally, however, as Hughes recognizes, there is a need for a closer focus not only on issues for society but on issues for the individual:

> Increasingly, education is the means by which individuals can shape and direct their future .... Can we meet the dual requirements for education: to provide the requirements, vocationally and politically, for an industrial democracy; to meet the personal needs of individuals for growth and development?
>
> (Hughes 1992: 4)

He adds:

> Not only have geographical horizons opened up – we are equally conscious of economic horizons, of the extensions and conflicts of cultural roots, of the broadening of political alliances and associations, of the ultimate sharing of a common and fragile planet. We are all part of a common society, obsessed not only with the need to make wider and stronger associations with groups and nations, but also, and in apparent contradiction, with establishing closer, more manageable, more caring communities .... Can we prepare students for these broadening demands, even though we cannot predict how they might change, only that they will? ... The implication of these wider horizons is that education is a concern for the whole society. No single group in society, not even teachers or students, can claim the right to shape it exclusively .... All will want and deserve a voice.
>
> (Hughes, 1992: 3)

Hughes's observations are instructive in explaining and justifying current moves towards national curricula throughout much of the world. O'Donoghue (in press) continues:

> In many countries where the curriculum has always been a matter of explicit national policy, its position in this regard has been solidified. Such countries include France, Italy, the Netherlands, Spain and the Scandinavian countries, along with Japan, Thailand, Malaysia, and Papua New Guinea. Many of these countries define the curriculum in national legislation. In other countries where the tradition has been very different, the trend has become very much one towards defining a national curriculum. Indeed, in England and Wales, the 1988 Education Reform Act defined both a national curriculum and national assessment while there have been very definite moves in this direction, too, in both the USA and Australia.

The whole picture is made more complex by the growing multiculturalism within nations and states. As societies become more multicultural, they must value the various elements of the different cultures within, while balancing these with the need to establish a clear national identity for all.

In achieving these delicate balances, O'Donoghue appeals to the work of Eisner and Vallance (1974), whose curriculum orientations, he argues, provide criteria for deciding balance. He reduces their five orientations to four, as follows: academic rationalism, the development of cognitive processes, self-actualization and social reconstruction. Each is briefly considered below, together with their interrelationships.

Academic rationalism

This orientation is concerned with enabling the young to acquire the tools to participate in the cultural tradition through providing them with access to the great ideas and objects created by the human race. The argument is that the major function of the school curriculum is to enhance the individual's intellectual abilities in those subject areas most worthy of study. The academic disciplines, such as English, history, mathematics and so on, are considered to be the depositories of our accumulated wisdom which we have systematically organized into bodies of knowledge over the years. What should be emphasized in schools is the knowledge, skills and values to be found in these disciplines, with knowledge being viewed as consisting of the central concepts of the discipline rather than just information.

Cognitive processes

Those who argue that the curriculum should be concerned with the development of cognitive processes contend that the mind consists of many cognitive faculties, such as the ability to synthesize, to evaluate and to solve problems. The major emphasis is on the importance of helping pupils to learn the numerous skills that enable us to conceptually address the world. Hence, the current emphasis in many Western countries in particular, is on the learning of generic skills and the development of key competencies. Those who are admirers of the educational ideas of John Dewey would argue that all of these skills and competencies are subsumed in his notion that education is ultimately about the development of 'the problem-anticipating, problem-solving individual'.

Self-actualization

This perspective 'supports the view that the school curriculum should provide learners with intrinsically rewarding experiences to enhance personal development' (Print, 1993: 51). It is based very much on the work of the humanistic 'third force' psychologists and their view of education as being concerned with the development of 'fully functioning human beings'. The notion is that individuals need to be exposed to experiences which will enhance their personal growth, integrity and autonomy. This in turn is consistent with the ideal of developing the self-actualizing person.

Social reconstruction

Social reconstructionists argue that the school curriculum should help to promote social reform and a more just society. The aim is to make students critically aware of their environment and the social inequities which exist because of the nature of power relations. The outcome, it is hoped, will be students who, when they leave school, will be knowledgeable about societal problems and motivated to deal with them.

These orientations are not contradictory. In all cultures and societies, they need to be accommodated in a balanced curriculum. To focus on one of them would be detrimental to the proper development of students. As O'Donoghue (in press) notes, 'This has been a problem in the past, particularly in the case of those who have been proponents of Deweyian pragmatism as the only orientation to curriculum. In its most extreme form, this position suggests that the content of learning is less important than its various processes; that what matters is that certain skills and abilities are nurtured.' The danger is that the processes of learning as espoused by the 'progressivists' are seen as disproportionately important in relation to the content. Murphy (1990) argues that this has a long ancestry in education and is associated particularly with 'progressivist' theory in its most extreme forms. He goes on:

> That there is a tension between factors relating to individual interests and needs and those dictated by the nature of knowledge itself – between the subjective processes of learning and the objectivity of its content – is of course a central principle of curriculum theory and design, and is generally expressed as a fruitful tension in learning, the conflicting elements of which must be maintained in a balanced synthesis. Its distortions are of two main forms: first, the 'banking' model of education which conceives of teaching as a crude transmission of knowledge from a dominant and virtually omniscient teacher to a passively recipient learner; and, secondly, the progressive model which sees the child's spontaneous interests as determining the whole process of learning.
>
> (Murphy 1990: 24)

Curriculum theorists argue for a balancing of the individual needs of the learner and the general principles of learning emanating from the nature of knowledge itself. O'Donoghue argues convincingly that individual needs and interests are a powerful dynamic in all learning, and that these must be fully accommodated in the kind of teaching that occurs in the classroom and in the kind of curriculum which is taught. But equally, there are different kinds of content, some of which are imaginatively and intellectually enriching, some of which are trivial, shallow and ephemeral and lacking the capacity to stimulate, enrich or deepen individual potentiality. Decisions on the kind of content selected are just as crucial as identifying the various learning abilities one wishes to foster.

Equally, the self-actualization and social reconstruction orientations cannot be neglected. What they both share is a recognition of the interpersonal and moral dimension in education (Buber, 1965). Teachers are moral agents who initiate students into the human conversation, into a way of life and a culture (Kerr, 1987; Burke, 1992: 212). Similarly, Goodlad (1988: 108) believes that 'the craft of teaching must be honed within the context of moral intention. Otherwise, it is little more than mechanics and might be performed better by a machine.' This leads O'Donoghue to the realization that a high burden is placed on teachers, yet schools and teachers have to take 'stands' on major cultural, moral and political issues.

To return to the original question: how does all of this relate to student outcome statements? The four curriculum orientations outlined above provide some useful guidelines. Many of the aims of education contained within these orientations can and should be represented as outcome statements. This approach is consistent with outcome-based education (OBE), which Raburn (1993) defines as follows:

> OBE is an education philosophy organized around several basic beliefs and principles. It starts with the belief that all students can learn and

succeed. Schools control the conditions of success, and the student's success is the responsibility of the teacher. Organized from a focus on student exit outcomes and designed downward to the subject and unit levels, it focuses instructional strategies on clearly defined learner outcomes, getting high standards with high expectations for all students and includes expanded opportunities for enrichment and remediation.

However, the gist of O'Donoghue's argument here is that while many of the aims can be represented by an outcome statements' approach to curriculum design, there are some provisos – four in particular – which need to be taken into account. The first is to guard against the tendency in outcomes approaches to organize segments of learning hierarchically, which emanates from the view that the student must learn the simple basics first before progressing to the higher order skills and knowledge. This sequential view of knowledge is an oversimplistic misconception of how students learn. Rather, what is needed, in keeping with recent cognitive approaches to learning, is an integrated code which fosters deep structures and under-standing of knowledge. Most subjects can be reduced to relatively few central concepts, which should be revisited in a spiral way at progressive levels of advancement. This gives students more scope and freedom to apply and develop higher order skills when they are ready and when the opportu-nity arises, rather than strictly following a sequence from lower order to higher order.

A second note of caution is that outcome statements may not embrace all possible educational objectives from across a wide array. It may be difficult, for example, to express in outcomes form a notion of knowledge as open-ended inquiry. It certainly is difficult, if not impossible, to predict the unpredictable and spontaneous events which happen in classrooms when students' imagination is suddenly captured by the unexpected.

A third proviso relates to the arts and humanities, where in certain situa-tions the objective may be to develop standards of judgement, criticism and taste rather than to reach an exit outcome. Advocates of the outcomes approach might claim, however, that such intentions can still be phrased in outcome terms, although of a qualitatively different kind.

The fourth concern is the truism that some objectives are not realized until well after the completion of formal schooling. While this should not stop schools pursuing them, it is as well to understand that either the outcome statements will necessarily be incomplete or their attainment will not be realized within the period of formal schooling.

These cautionary arguments do not destroy the case for a student outcomes approach. They merely serve to warn that there are rarely perfect panaceas in education and that a student outcomes approach might be improved the more it is able to take them into account. The crux of the present argument, however, is that curriculum design using an outcomes framework still wrestles with the same tensions and considerations as alternative approaches. There is still the need to achieve balance and to set the whole process within the larger context of the aims of education. Finally, an outcomes approach does not preclude unintended, experiential or even constuctivist approaches to knowledge. The main point is that both teacher and student have a sense of purpose, a set of aims and a structure within which to work.

Operationalizing an Outcomes-Oriented Curriculum

Contexts within which schools operate a student outcomes approach vary widely. In the case of some government schools, the curriculum may be tightly prescribed for subjects and teachers and consequently minimal adaptability and individualization is built in. In other cases, the government provides a framework based on student outcomes and leaves each school to design its own curriculum in detail. This situation is more akin to those independent and private schools which have a large measure of discretion in designing their own curriculum.

Generally, the introduction of outcomes-oriented curricula poses major challenges for schools and teachers. As previously noted, not only does the approach demand a fundamental reconceptualization from what the teacher must teach to what the student must learn, but in those situations where only a framework is provided by the system, a large responsibility is placed on teachers and administrators to undertake school-based curriculum development in order to operationalize the whole approach.

Some will argue that it is not the teachers' responsibility to develop curricula in this way. Many teachers will protest that they do not have the time to fulfil this role. On the positive side, however, it can be argued that it increases the capacity of schools and teachers to provide a more adaptive and individualized curriculum for their particular students, and that it increases the professionalism of teachers by giving them a greater influence and control over their professional practice.

The problem, however, is particularly acute for teachers having to transform from a traditional teaching syllabus approach to a student outcomes curriculum framework, with the expectation that they develop their own curricula within the outcome guidelines provided. In the course of time, schools may have the choice to purchase their curricula from a range of commercially developed packages produced elsewhere, even internationally. Schools will have to be satisfied that such packages will meet the outcomes specified in their own particular framework. Many such packages are already available in the United States (Wang, 1992). The purchase of curricula in this way will extend the trend, already noted in previous chapters, towards globalization and internationalization of education policy and practice. Even then, many schools and teachers may prefer to undertake their own school-based curriculum development believing that they achieve ownership over the process and the ability to tailor it to their own situation.

For those schools and teachers undertaking their own curriculum development within an outcomes framework, there may be little assistance provided as to strategy and process. There is also a dearth of published material on which teachers can rely for practical assistance. Few texts on school restructuring give any attention to this important issue. Accordingly, the remainder of this chapter is devoted to outlining a suggested approach by which schools and teachers can operationalize an outcomes curriculum. It is assumed that the curriculum is intentional, that it is adaptive and flexible, that it is dedicated to promoting the achievement of learning outcomes by all students, irrespective of ability, and that student grouping is heterogeneous.

In the first place, it is helpful to set the context. Reference to the case of Western Australia (WA) provides a pertinent example. In WA, learning outcomes, or what students are expected to learn, have been embedded in the curriculum framework which all schools, public and private, must adopt by the year 2002. The framework is neither a syllabus nor a curriculum. It identifies common learning goals for students across thirteen years of schooling and for the following eight learning areas: mathematics, English, the arts, health and physical education, languages other than English, science, society and environment, technology and enterprise. The same eight areas are accepted by all Australian states and territories. In keeping with restructured curricula elsewhere (see Bechtol and Sorenson, 1993), the new WA curriculum places an increasing emphasis through the thirteen years on problem-solving and higher order thinking skills and on learning how to learn, all of which are seen as imperatives for the twenty-first century. In the words of one WA bureaucrat, 'the framework was intended to give schools and teachers flexibility and ownership over curriculum in a dynamic and rapidly changing world environment'. Schools and teachers would be able 'to use the framework to develop their own learning and teaching programmes according to their circumstances, ethos and the needs of their students' (WA, Curriculum Council, 1998: 6).

The framework lists a set of overarching learning outcomes that children are expected to know and value as a result of programmes they undertake. The thirteen desired outcomes are as follows (WA, Curriculum Council, 1998: 18–19):

1   Use language to understand, develop and communicate ideas and information and interact with others.
2   Select, integrate and apply numerical and spatial concepts and techniques.
3   Recognize when and what information is needed, locate and obtain it from a range of sources and evaluate, use and share it with others.
4   Select, use and adapt technologies.

5 Describe and reason about patterns, structures and relationships in order to understand, interpret, justify and make predictions.

6 Visualize consequences, think laterally, recognize opportunity and potential and test options.

7 Understand and appreciate the physical, biological and technological world and have the knowledge and skills to make decisions in relation to it.

8 Understand their cultural, geographic and historic contexts and have the knowledge, skills and values necessary for active participation in life in Australia.

9 Interact with people and cultures other than their own and have the ability to contribute to the global community.

10 Participate in creative activity of their own and understand and engage with the artistic, cultural and intellectual work of others.

11 Value and implement practices that promote personal growth and well-being.

12 Self-motivated and confident in their approach to learning and have the ability to work individually and collaboratively.

13 Recognize that everyone has the right to feel valued and be safe, understand their rights and behave responsibly.

In addition, a set of five core values is included to shape the development of the person: a commitment to the pursuit of knowledge and achievement of potential; self-acceptance and self-respect; respect and concern for others and their rights; social and civic responsibility; and environmental responsibility.

A more detailed set of outcomes for each of the eight learning areas is provided. An example for English is the learning outcome aimed at encouraging students to read a wide range of texts with purpose, understanding and critical awareness. The texts selected and the way students reach this learning goal is left to the discretion of the school. A Catholic school, for example, might achieve this outcome very differently from an Islamic school, or a school in a city very differently from a remote rural school. Students in different year groups are also expected to achieve the outcome at different levels. An early childhood student might achieve it by looking at photographs or television programmes, while a final year student might be expected to critically review and analyse an adult text.

Implementing the framework means that teachers and schools design learning and teaching programmes to suit the needs of their students, but they must do so while achieving the outcomes and core values. The document setting out the framework (Western Australian Curriculum Council, 1998: 9) states: 'How a school structures learning opportunities in terms of time and the range of courses and programmes provided, remains the school's responsibility. This will depend on the school or teacher's assessment of students and their particular needs.'

It is the school's and teachers' responsibility to bring definition and intentionality to an outcomes' framed curriculum. As previously argued, this is a major challenge for a number of reasons: few teachers are experienced in this kind of work, they may have little support in the way of written materials and professional development, and they are already overloaded with work. Against this backcloth, the following suggestions offer a strategy as to how definition and intentionality can be achieved.

A vital and key part of the equation is often overlooked by most curriculum developers. Governments and curriculum councils may construct frameworks, but the quality of outcomes-oriented curricula are firmly in the hands of teachers and schools. For reasons already stated, this is likely to be challenging work. Teachers are not only charged with bringing definition to, and designing curricula within, designated learning outcomes; they are increasingly expected to enable all students (other than a few exceptional children with severe physical and intellectual disability) of varying abilities to achieve them. There are thus two new and separate responsibilities for teachers: designing curricula within an outcomes framework and ensuring that all students achieve the outcomes at a level commensurate with their ability.

A Model for Implementing a Student Outcomes' Curriculum Approach

The first task – designing curricula – is achievable by working downwards from the outcomes framework, with ever greater levels of specificity. The second task – ensuring that all students achieve the outcomes – demands that learning goals and outcomes be clarified and specified for individual students and groups of students. There are thus three separate but related processes: (1) curriculum design; (2) student learning goals and outcomes; and both of these are connected through (3) instructional strategy. The three elements are represented in Figure 5.1.

One of the most important features of the model is the iterative nature of the relationships between the elements. Any model is strengthened if there is constant backward and forward referencing and cross-checking between the connected parts. Each of the three elements in the model – curriculum, student learning goals and outcomes, and instructional strategy – is now briefly elaborated.

Curriculum Design

Many government (and private) schools function within a framework of system-level outcomes which can also be taken as school-wide outcomes. If this is not the case, the school will need to develop its own school-wide outcomes. Schools should then cross-check that these school-wide outcomes

Figure 5.1 *A Model of School Implementation of a Student Outcomes' Approach to the Curriculum*

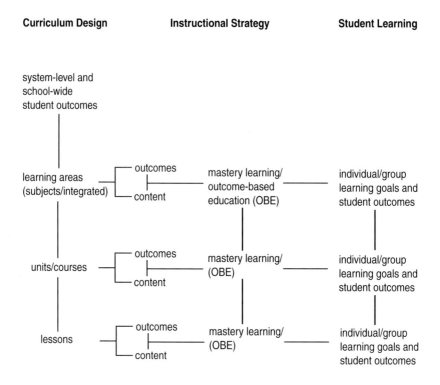

are consistent with the school mission. Below the school level are three sub-levels, each of which brings progressively more detail to the curriculum, as follows:

1   Learning areas – subjects and/or integrated subjects;
2   Units or courses;
3   Lessons.

The process of curriculum design entails at first working from the outcomes desired from each of the learning areas to identifying the broad content associated with the outcomes at that level. These outcomes and content then serve as a base for deciding on the outcomes and associated content for units or courses. In other words, the broad learning areas need to be broken into manageable units or courses for teaching and learning in a school context. Decisions about the scope and sequence of knowledge, skills and values in the units and courses will need to be made. Finally, the same process is repeated to move from the units or courses to individual lessons. The outcomes and content at unit level serve as the reference points for the development of lesson outcomes and content, and for the scope and sequence of lessons. At this juncture, the process involves fundamentally transforming the curriculum by working downwards in ever increasing degrees of specificity to bring greater definition to the curriculum.

A host of resource materials will be required along the way, including texts, audio-visual material and software and learning packages. Decisions on whether to adopt a strict subject approach or an integrated approach, or a combination of the two, will need to be taken. Teachers best work collaboratively to enrich and refine the curriculum by transforming it through a sequence of stages from general outcomes, as expressed in the framework, to detailed lesson outcomes. Close teacher collaboration is a key element, not only to ensure vertical integration within the same learning area, but also to achieve horizontal integration across learning areas.

Setting Student Learning Goals and Outcomes

The approach envisaged is not one which merely advocates translating from the curriculum framework downwards in ever increasing degrees of specificity to courses and lessons. To do this and no more would simply constitute a passive approach on the part of the teacher; students would reach whatever level of outcomes they were comfortable with, which would bring little if any improvement in learning. The only difference from the status quo would be defining the curriculum in terms of student outcomes.

Rather, if student learning is to improve, teachers need to be proactive in firstly, matching their particular students with the unit/course and lesson outcomes, and then secondly, in pushing students to as high a level of achievement within their potential, as possible. This involves a further set of processes beyond that of curriculum design and development: it requires that account be taken of the students, their abilities, needs and interests. It also involves teaching strategies, as indicated in Figure 5.1.

A key to the success of the outcomes approach is recognition of the need to develop student learning outcomes or student learning goals at the classroom level to apply to lessons, units/courses and learning areas (see Figure 5.1). Goal-oriented learning has been shown to be an effective means of learning; students learn best when they have clear, challenging but achievable learning goals to aim for. The goals can be set for individual students or groups of students; the more personal and individual they are, the better. These goals can be matched or fused with the curriculum outcomes as defined at lesson, unit and learning area levels.

The teacher will thus need to cross-reference the curriculum outcomes with the abilities of the particular students in the class so that learning goals can be set at an appropriate level for individual students or groups. The learning goals will then match with specific levels of achievement of the outcomes. The merit in setting learning goals for individual students or for groups of students, as already stated, is that it takes advantage of the known efficacy of goal-oriented learning, it personalizes and individualizes the learning process and it presents challenging but achievable goals to extend student performance. It also happens to fit well with the defined curriculum outcomes at unit and lesson levels.

Instructional Strategy

The third component of the set of procedures centres on the application of an appropriate teaching technology to link student learning with the curriculum outcomes. Since the approach being advocated recommends the setting of student learning goals and the matching of these with curriculum outcomes, it stands to reason that harmony as well as consistency demands a teaching strategy which is itself outcome-oriented and goal-oriented. Fortunately, there are strategies with proven efficacy which meet these requirements, particularly mastery learning (Block et al., 1989; Guskey, 1995) and outcome-based education (OBE) (Spady, 1995). Both operate at learning area and unit/course levels, but they are particularly relevant at lesson level, where they link student learning goals and outcomes with the outcomes framed in the curriculum. It is surprising that few have seen the potential connection between outcome-based curriculum frameworks and, at the level of teacher–student interface, mastery learning and outcome-based education. In fact, the two seem to dovetail well.

It is instructive at this juncture to give a brief account of some of the salient features of OBE and mastery learning which illustrate their harmony with the outcomes approach and the precepts of school design advocated in this book. Both strategies share much in common, but they also have some marked differences.

According to Spady (1995), OBE has the following features:

- successful learning results as the source of all planning, priorities, design, delivery and evaluation;
- schools define and communicate to students and parents the performance criteria and standards that represent the intended learning and outcomes expected;
- assessment is matched to these criteria and every student is eligible for high marks;
- programme design is carried out backwards; it begins at the culminating point of student learning and moves systematically back from there to work out appropriate teaching, resources, organizational support and so on;

- time is treated as a variable; differences in student learning rates are seen as crucial rather than inherent limitations in ability to learn;
- a broad array of teaching methods are advocated to enable all students to learn;
- acknowledging student progress and formative assessments are important in encouraging all students to attain high performance.

OBE thus has a number of premises underpinning it. First, all students can learn. However, they learn in different ways and at different rates. Second, success breeds success. If students experience success, they are more likely to be motivated to seek further success. Prerequisite learning therefore needs to be sound. Third, schools control the conditions for success. They can establish a context which is conducive for learning success or one which is inhibitive. Teachers, for example, control four crucial classroom conditions for learning (Spady, 1995: 375):

- where they place their instructional focus;
- how long, how often and when they provide students with opportunities for learning;
- what learning they expect from which students and how they reward it;
- how they design and organize curricula.

Spady (1995: 376) goes on to emphasize the importance of teachers applying the following principles 'consistently, systematically, creatively and simultaneously':

1 clarity of focus on outcomes of significance – distinguish the core outcomes from the rest;
2 expand opportunity and support for learning success, by flexibility over the time it takes to teach and to learn and over the eligibility of students to learn;
3 high expectations for all to succeed without compromising standards and within a quality curriculum;
4 design back from the culmination of student learning outcomes – these can be from a lesson, unit or course, or learning area, and the higher the level, the more teachers as a group are able to emphasize integration of higher-order and interdisciplinary outcomes.

Without labouring the point, it is clear that all of the OBE axioms and principles of practice accord with the precepts of curriculum design advocated in this chapter. The axioms leave open the question of which teaching methods to adopt; instead, they focus on principles of instruction within whatever teaching approach is adopted and on principles of curriculum design.

Mastery learning emanates from the work of Benjamin Bloom (1968), who found that under typical group learning conditions, only about 20 per cent of students learned successfully. He set out to determine what critical elements of the ideal one-to-one teaching situation of a tutor/student could be transferred to group-based instructional settings. He also looked at the learning strategies employed by academically successful students in group-based learning environments (Guskey, 1995). From these, Bloom identified the main characteristics of mastery learning as follows:

1   material to be learned is divided into small segments based on objectives of, for example, one or two weeks;
2   tests are given at the end of each segment;
3   feedback and corrective procedures apply for each test, and the test results are used to diagnose individual learning difficulties (feedback) and to prescribe specific remediation procedures (correctives);
4   the test is a formative assessment, indicating how well the student has learned the material;
5   as a result of the test, students who have demonstrated understanding receive an enrichment experience, while those who have not receive an individualized corrective programme, entailing different instructional strategies and approaches (this phase might last two extra lessons);
6   a further test is then given to ascertain mastery, defined by a percentage on the test (often 80 per cent).

Bloom (1971, 1976) believed that by providing these classroom conditions, nearly all students could achieve mastery. Grading standards are not changed, but instead of only 20 per cent of a class gaining understanding, Bloom claimed this could rise to 80 per cent.

Both OBE and mastery learning have certain common elements: they espouse the belief that all can learn to a high standard, they emphasize learning outcomes, expressed as objectives in mastery learning, both include more flexibility of time, allowing extra time to learn if it is needed, both recognize the value of formative assessment, both are essentially group-based or class-based strategies which allow for more individualization in learning achievement, and both leave open the question of teaching methods. On the other hand, there some small differences between the two. OBE has as its rationale the curriculum design principle of planning back from key outcomes desired, whereas mastery learning designs by parcelling material into small segments for instruction and testing based on curriculum objectives; hence there is no implied backward mapping process. Mastery learning places special emphasis on feedback, correctives and enrichment as its principles, whereas OBE is less specific in this respect in advocating greater flexibility of time taken to learn. This is only an outline account of OBE and mastery learning. Both are re-visited in later chapters, particularly Chapter 7 on teaching.

Cross-Cultural Implications

As discussed earlier in this chapter, all school systems make choices as to what subjects to include in the curriculum. There is always a tension between too many subjects and too little curriculum time available. Decisions as to which subjects to include and the relative time to give each tend to reflect the values and culture of a particular society. Values and culture may change over time, albeit slowly, and so therefore may the curriculum.

In some Asian school systems, including those with fast economic growth rates over the past thirty years, such as Hong Kong, a strong focus on the so-called academic subjects including mathematics and science has tended to marginalize subjects such as music, physical education and the arts. There are many contributory reasons for the academic emphasis. In societies, such as Hong Kong, the Confucian tradition places high value on academic learning and achievement. The industriousness of the Hong Kong Chinese has elevated financial prosperity and material well-being above almost everything else. Success in education, especially in the academic subjects, is viewed as a passport to material wealth.

In comparison with much of Asia, curricula in the relatively more mature Western societies, while still placing a strong emphasis on the academic subjects, gives more recognition to the promotion of health and well-being and to environmental concerns. Consequently, school curricula in Western societies tend to be more inclusive of the arts, music, physical and health education, and environmental issues. With the continued economic growth of Asia, the expansion of higher education, the emergence of a middle class and a growing awareness of pollution and health problems, pressure will mount in future to broaden and liberalize the curriculum in Asia.

Indeed, major changes in curriculum policy are already in train in some Asian societies. In Hong Kong, for example, what has been described as the most ambitious curriculum reform ever – the Target-Oriented Curriculum (TOC) – was introduced into the first group of primary schools in 1995. The substance of the reform, described below, emanates from similar reforms in the West. It is largely driven by the desire to change the economic and occupational structure of Hong Kong in order to secure continued growth. Even before the Asian economic crisis of 1997, and with the imminence of the new millennium, many of the Asian 'Tiger' economies had begun to reconsider the relationship between their education systems and their economies. Global competition and structural economic changes were dictating that their prosperity in the twenty-first century would rest more on knowledge-based work, high-technology and high valued-added industries and services. In Hong Kong and Singapore, for example, it was recognized that the knowledge and skills required to develop and sustain this new economic structure have not received sufficient emphasis in schools. Accordingly, the 1990s has seen new curricular initiatives bearing marked similarity to those introduced into Western countries. However, questions arise as to the appropriateness of these reforms for the cultures into which they are introduced (Dimmock, 1998). Hong Kong provides an excellent example; the discussion that follows is illustrative of the issues at stake.

Hong Kong's Target-Oriented Curriculum (TOC)

In line with similar curriculum developments in Britain, Australia, and North America, the TOC is an attempt to introduce a form of outcome-based education and to radically shift the way in which curricula are planned, taught and learned. However, as Morris et al. (1996) argue, the similarities with other countries mask important differences. In the UK, for example, the move was associated with an intent to decrease teacher autonomy and increase central control over the curriculum. However, in Hong Kong the curriculum is already centrally controlled and has been so since the 1940s. In contrast to the UK National Curriculum, the intent of the TOC is to increase teacher professionalism, autonomy and school-based curriculum development. While the UK reforms were introduced through legislation (the 1988 Education Reform Act), the TOC is reliant on exhortation, guidelines and administrative fiat. Finally, while each policy shares a common language of accountability and student outcomes or targets, each advocates very different pedagogies. As Morris et al. (1996) recognize, the National Curriculum advocates the reintroduction of whole class teaching and traditional subject boundaries, while TOC encourages the use of student-centred learning, including cooperative learning and the development of generic, non-subject specific skills. Ironically, the English National Curriculum and its emphasis on whole-class teaching seems more suited to the Hong Kong culture.

The TOC owes its emergence in 1993–4 to various policy initiatives starting in 1989 (see Morris et al., 1996). It is aimed at enhancing the effectiveness of teaching and learning. From 1995 onwards, a phased introduction was planned to all primary schools. In 2001, secondary schools will be included in the policy. TOC is based on the following features (Morris et al., 1996: 27):

- planned and progressive learning targets and objectives for 4 Key Stages of learning;
- development of curriculum content, teaching and learning strategies, and assessment related to the learning targets;
- balanced development of students' higher thinking abilities, skills and attitudes, in addition to a sound base of subject knowledge;
- a developmental approach to student capabilities and integrative use of knowledge;

- a learner-centred approach in all aspects of curriculum planning, teaching and assessment;
- the construction of knowledge through the *processes* of learning are as important as the product of these activities, thereby shifting the emphasis of teaching and learning;
- five interdependent ways of learning and using knowledge are emphasized: communicating, inquiring, conceptualizing, reasoning and problem solving;
- individual differences and the needs of individual students;
- criterion-referenced assessment with systematic formative and summative assessment procedures (rather than norm-referenced assessment);
- charting and reporting of students' progress through the 4 Key Stages with reference to learning targets.

The use of learning and assessment tasks with systematic reporting procedures is advocated, instead of just exercises, tests, and examinations presently adopted in Hong Kong. But perhaps the most important theme is the emphasis to be placed on student-centred learning and a more individualized curriculum. Indeed, a recent review of the Aims of Education (Education Commission, 1999: 11) reaffirmed the following directions:

- Cater for the needs of individual students so that each and every one of them can have all-round and unique developments, a balance of ethics, intellect, physique, social skills and aesthetics as well as the cultivation of independent thinking and creative abilities.
- Provide equal opportunities leading to social mobility and cohesion.
- Cultivate life-long learning interest.
- Allow diversified developments, assimilate the best of East and West, and provide students and parents with more choices.
- Be outward-looking whilst firmly rooted in Hong Kong.

These are future directions, but the gap between them and the status quo is dispiritingly large, as indicated below. Nonetheless, individualization is a worthy aim, providing it can be adapted to fit harmoniously with the Hong Kong culture.

How appropriate is an individualized curriculum for Hong Kong and other Asian school systems? For generations, Asian students have been expected to mould to a standardized curriculum. In Hong Kong, secondary students are streamed and segregated into different schools referred to by five Bands: Band One schools take the most able students, while Band Five take the least able students. The disparity in the ability range between Band One and Band Five students is enormous, yet a standardized curriculum is provided for all. Moreover, provision of a standardized curriculum appeals to many Chinese parents and teachers, whose cultural interpretation of equity and fairness is that all should receive the same.

Yet there are powerful forces pushing for change towards a more individualized curriculum. First, the future structure of the Hong Kong economy, based on information technology and high-valued added services will demand high-level cognitive skills. Second, the emergence of a wealthier, more educated citizenry and of socio-environmental problems in Hong Kong, as elsewhere in Asia, will tend to push for a broadening of the curriculum to incorporate the arts, environmental and health education.

Third, many Asian students, including those in Hong Kong, are under incredible pressure to achieve academic success. This is manifested in rising stress and suicide rates. More individual support is needed. Finally, as more Hong Kong students stay in school beyond the minimum school-leaving age, increasing numbers of lower-ability students are experiencing failure and a curriculum inappropriate to their needs. Behavioural and disciplinary problems are increasing alarmingly, especially in the lower Band schools. The curriculum, as indeed teaching and learning, must move to cater for the diversity of student abilities.

Important adjustments to teaching and learning are also foreshadowed in the TOC policy, and these are discussed below. In addition, the implications for individualization within a context of large class sizes and lack of classroom resources are also addressed. Further discussion of cultural differences as they affect learning and teaching are included in Chapters 6 and 7, respectively.

Expectations that Hong Kong teachers will cater to individual differences by – being sensitive to each student's needs, evaluating each student's development of cognitive ability, judging the materials to challenge each student, arousing each student's interest, responding to and helping students who need extra attention, and appraising each student's capacity to learn and improve – are remote from present practice (Dimmock, 1998). How well adapted are current teaching-learning methods in Hong Kong's schools to meet these expectations? And what influence might culture have?

These questions are addressed by referring to the prevailing cultural characteristics of Hong Kong's classrooms, to recent research showing significant differences between how Chinese, British and American teachers teach and students learn, and to current classroom conditions. According to Hofstede (1991), in large power-distance societies such as Hong Kong (see Chapter 3), teachers are traditionally expected to take all the initiatives in class and they tend to be seen as gurus transferring their personal wisdom. Students are not expected to speak up unless invited by the teacher, and are more comfortable speaking in small groups than large. Harmony and preservation of relationships is important at all times (Hofstede, 1986: 312). The attainment of those student-centred learning methods which are dependent on assertive expression, persuasion and argument between group members may thus be more difficult to attain. By the same token, however, the collec-tivist values of Chinese students appear to be receptive to more cooperative methods of learning. It has been noted that Chinese students work well in groups to achieve collective goals. They are particularly good at forming informal networks and support groups outside of class.

Hong Kong's students and parents place high value on examination results. Thus new teaching/learning methods which emphasize processes of learning and higher-order skills may not find ready acceptance among parents, unless they can be transparently integrated into the public exams. Although, according to Hofstede (1991), Hong Kong society in general is classed as a low uncertainty avoidance culture, the organizational culture in its schools displays many characteristics of high uncertainty avoidance. School life, including the teaching syllabus, is regulated by an abundance of prescriptive rules and regulations. This degree of prescription may be coun-terproductive in fostering more exploratory forms of teaching and learning. In addition, Hong Kong students tend to feel more comfortable in tightly structured learning situations. Finally, the long-term orientation of Hong Kong educators is characterized by an innate conservatism and by values such as perseverance and observing the ordering of relationships by status, all of which tend to militate against the easy acceptance of new more partic-ipative and democratic relationships between teachers and students.

The prevailing ethos in East Asian societies values effort rather than innate ability and competition is seen as a way of improving results and as a means of socialization in order to prepare the young for tougher competi-tion in society (Cheng and Wong, 1996). Students are ranked according to their academic scores and in Hong Kong this ranking is important in allo-cating primary students to secondary school. This leads Cheng and Wong (1996: 44–5) to conclude:

> In this context, individualized teaching, where students work towards diverse targets at different paces, is almost inconceivable in East Asian societies. Therefore, the emphasis on the administration of teaching is more on how students of different abilities could learn to adapt them-selves to the common curriculum and common examination, rather than adapting the curriculum and teaching to the diverse needs of the students.

While Cheng and Wong's argument is convincing, the forces pushing for more individualization appear equally strong. What seems at first sight to be an impasse may be resolvable, however, by adapting the concept of individu-alization to fit the Asian cultures and classroom contexts. Greater emphasis on students as groups rather than as individuals or whole classes might be one possible solution.

Recent research findings on differences between Asian and Western students in how they learn (Watkins and Biggs, 1996) are also instructive in throwing light on the question of the cultural appropriateness of recent educational policy directions in Hong Kong. As shown in Chapter 6, the emphasis in Asian classrooms on rote learning and memorization may mask an important cognitive process leading to deeper understanding. Hence, there is need for caution before rejecting some of the present practices. We know that present methods serve these students well in international tests of mathematics and science. They may be less successful, however, for languages, the arts and humanities.

How teachers motivate students may also differ between Western and Asian societies. In Chapter 6, it is noted that Watkins and Biggs (1996: 273) claim, 'Western ways of categorizing motivation do not travel well, at least not to the Orient'. Westerners tend to see motivation in extrinsic/intrinsic terms as the precursor to meaningful deep understanding. The Chinese student, however, takes a more pragmatic and holistic view, being motivated by a mixed set of forces including personal ambition, family face, peer support, material reward and interest. Teachers of Chinese students may well have to adopt a multiplicity of methods as motivators, including reminders of the students' responsibilities to their families.

It is also noted in Chapter 6 that the collectivism in Hong Kong's culture affects the teacher–student relationship which, although hierarchical, can also be warm, caring and supportive (Chan, 1993). Tang (1996) found that Chinese students collaborated much more outside the classroom in helping each other to obtain material useful for the completion of homework assignments than did their Western counterparts. In addition, although it is seldom attempted, Winter (1996) found that organized peer learning can work very well in Hong Kong schools. Watkins and Biggs (1996: 275) conclude: 'Hong Kong secondary school students would in fact prefer a more collaborative learning environment which they consider would promote the deeper, more achievement-oriented approach to learning.' In these ways, some of the new directions for teaching and learning espoused in recent policy reforms might well find support from prevailing cultural characteristics.

If there are at least some cultural characteristics which appear supportive of policy changes in core technology, current classroom conditions in Hong Kong's schools do not favour the student-centred and individualized methods. Most Hong Kong classrooms are cramped and crowded. It is commonplace to find 40 to 45 students in a class. Desks are formally arranged in rows. Classrooms are typically small, so that both students and teachers work in confined spaces. Opportunities for mobility and flexible classroom layouts are therefore severely restricted. Most classrooms are not well equipped by Western standards, having no more than the bare essentials of a blackboard, desks and chairs. Lesson periods last 35 or 40 minutes, barely enough time for teachers to introduce methods such as problem solving, group work or cooperative learning. Few alternatives exist to direct teaching methods supplemented by discussion in pairs or small groups. At present, much of the class work in pairs and groups is in fact, disguised individual work, and the challenge remains for teachers to create genuine cooperative learning. Catering to the variability of student needs and abilities as well as introducing more flexible student-centred learning approaches will remain a daunting challenge for some time, even in a system which is banded or streamed.

Given the prevailing cultural characteristics of Hong Kong, how appropriate are reforms to teaching and learning recommended in Hong Kong's restructuring policies? Evidence suggests that the collectivist dimension of the Chinese culture seems well suited to cooperative learning and peer tutoring, both of which are consistent with the reform policy. Present classroom conditions of large class sizes and confined spaces will, however, present major difficulties to teachers when implementing these methods. However, peer tutoring and cross-age tutoring are convenient and appropriate teaching methods for overcoming large student/teacher ratios and would seem to fit well with the culture. While it can be argued that the current over-reliance on didactic teaching needs to be reduced, there is a useful base from which to develop best practices of direct teaching, in itself a highly effective teaching method.

Although it is early days in what is a long-term reform strategy, it is clear that teachers are struggling to implement TOC in the classroom. At least four strategies appear to be necessary (Dimmock, 1997). First, as Morris et al. (1996) argue, more money needs to be spent on resourcing Hong Kong's schools, which are grossly under-resourced compared with their Western counterparts. Typically, Asian countries spend proportionately less of their gross national products on education – around 3 per cent compared to about 5 per cent in the West. Second, in overcoming the barriers to implementation in classrooms, teachers deserve much better professional development than they are currently provided. Third, bridging the school–classroom divide is also a matter of good quality support provided by principals and senior staff through school leadership and management. Teachers have a right to expect nothing less. Finally, it is the central point of the present discussion, that reforms need to be adapted to fit the societal culture.

Conclusions

A chapter on curriculum design is imperative in a book concerned with re-designing schools. Yet it is not commonplace to find such discussion, despite the curriculum being the keystone to other aspects of schooling. This chapter has acknowledged the shift to outcomes-designed curricula around the globe. It has pointed out the dangers and pitfalls of schools and teachers passively adopting the new frameworks and simply moulding their past and present practices to fit the new paradigm. The curriculum has high connectivity with other elements of schooling; if the curriculum is changed, then consequential changes in the connected elements are also foreshadowed.

The chapter began by outlining a number of precepts and dimensions which, taken together, provide a set of guidelines for school personnel to design and to bring definition to an outcomes curriculum. It went on to recognize a number of criticisms of an outcomes approach and the challenges placed on contemporary curriculum designers by the multiple purposes deriving from ever more complex, pluralistic and multicultural societies. The chapter presented a model outlining a proactive, collaborative role for teachers in fulfilling and fusing three tasks: designing an outcomes curriculum from school-wide learning areas down to courses/units and lessons; setting individualized learning goals to match the curriculum outcomes; and finally, adopting an instructional strategy which connected both. In the latter case, it is suggested that OBE and mastery learning constitute invaluable tools and technologies for enabling the whole process.

Finally, in capturing a cross-cultural angle to the curriculum, it was noted that curricula in some Asian societies – Hong Kong as an example – place heavy emphasis on a narrow academic curriculum at the expense of a broad, liberal approach. Thus students in these countries do well in mathematics and science, but art, music, physical and health education and environmental education tend to be neglected. In addition, recent policy reforms introduced in Hong Kong signal a shift to a more student-centred, individualized curriculum. It was noted that opposition is expected from teachers and parents whose culture seems in many ways antipathetic to such trends. Overcrowded classes and the lack of classroom resources will also present major difficulties. For both cultural and resource reasons, the introduction of a student-centred, individualized curriculum will be painful and slow. If such a curriculum is to be successfully introduced, then it would be wise for it to be adapted to harmonize with the particular cultural setting; thus individualization and student-centredness would assume a distinctive Chinese form and shape rather than clone Western models.

References

Barnett, B.G. and Whitaker, K.S. (1996) *Restructuring for Student Learning*, Lancaster, PA: Technomic.

Bechtol, W.M. and Sorenson, J.S. (1993) *Restructuring Schooling for Individual Students*, Needham Heights, MA: Allyn and Bacon.

Block, J.H., Efthim, H.E. and Burns, R.B. (1989) *Building Effective Mastery Learning Schools*, New York: Longman.

Bloom, B.S. (1968) 'Learning for mastery', *Evaluation Comment* 1 (2): 1–12.

—— (1971) 'Mastery learning', in J.H. Block (ed.), *Mastery Learning: Theory and Practice*, New York: Holt, Rinehart and Winston, 47–63.

—— (1976) *Human Characteristics and School Learning*, New York: McGraw-Hill.

Buber, M. (1965) 'Education', in M. Buber (ed.), *Between Man and Man*, New York: Macmillan.

Burke, A. (1992) *Training of Trainers*, Dublin: Department of Education.

Chan, S.L. (1993) 'Approaches to learning of medical and business students in a Guangzhou university', The University of Hong Kong, M.Ed dissertation.

Cheng, K.M. and Wong, K.C. (1996) 'School effectiveness in East Asia: concepts, origins and implications', *Journal of Educational Administration* 34 (5): 32–49.

Dimmock, C. (1997) 'Hong Kong: rigid copying not the answer', *International Directions in Education*, Melbourne: Australian Council for Educational Administration, 2–3.

Dimmock, C. (1998) 'Restructuring Hong Kong's Schools: the applicability of Western theories, policies and practices to an Asian culture', *Educational Management and Administration* 26 (4): 363–77.

Dimmock, C. and Walker, A. (1998) 'Comparative educational administration: developing a cross-cultural comparative framework', *Educational Administration Quarterly* 34 (4): 558–95.

Education Commission, Hong Kong (1999) *Education Blueprint for the 21st Century: Review of Academic System Aims of Education – Consultation Document*, Hong Kong: Government Printing Department.

Eisner, E.W. and Vallance, E. (eds) (1974) *Conflicting Conceptions of Curriculum*, Berkeley, CA: McCutchan.

Goodlad, J.I. (1988) 'Studying the education of educators: values driven enquiry', *Phi Delta Kappan* 70 (2): 105–11.

Guskey, T.R. (1995) 'Mastery learning', in J.H. Block, S.T. Everson and T.R. Guskey (eds), *School Improvement Programs: A Handbook for Educational Leaders*, New York: Scholastic, 91–108.

Hofstede, G.H. (1986) 'Cultural differences in teaching and learning', *International Journal of Intercultural Relations* 10: 301–20.

—— (1991) *Cultures and Organisations: Software of the Mind*, London: McGraw-Hill.

Hughes, P. (1992) 'Creating our future: wider horizons-closer focus', in *Creating Our Future: A Curriculum for the 21st Century*, conference sponsored by Centre for Advanced Teaching Studies, Australian College of Education, Department of Employment and Training, and the British Council at University of Tasmania, Hobart, 22 December 1992.

Kerr, D.H. (1987) 'Authority and responsibility in public schooling', in J.I. Goodlad (ed.), *The Ecology of School Renewal*, Chicago: University of Chicago Press.

Morris, P. et al. (1996) *Target Oriented Curriculum Evaluation Project: Interim Report*, In-Service Teacher Education Program, Faculty of Education, The University of Hong Kong.

Murphy, D. (1990) 'Junior certificate English', *Studies in Education* 7 (1): 23–33.

O'Donoghue, T.A. (in press) 'A gestalt view of planning curriculum and pedagogy', in C. Dimmock and A.Walker (eds), *Future School Administration: Western and Asian Perspectives*, Hong Kong: The Chinese University Press.

Print, M. (1993) *Curriculum Development and Design*, Sydney: Allen and Unwin.

Raburn, R. (1993) 'Outcomes-based education: some questions answered', *OASCD Journal*, 5: 23–30.

Sizer, T.R. (1992) 'Horace's school: redesigning the American high school', Boston, MA: Houghton-Mifflin.

Spady, W.G. (1995) 'Outcome-based education: from instructional reform to paradigm restructuring', in J.H. Block, S.T. Everson and T.R. Guskey (eds), *School Improvement Programs: A Handbook for Educational Leaders*, New York: Scholastic, 367–98.

Tang, C. (1996) 'Collaborative learning: the latent dimension in Chinese students' learning', in D.A. Watkins and J. Biggs (eds), *The Chinese Learner: Cultural, Psychological and Contextual Influences*, Hong Kong: Comparative Education Research Centre, University of Hong Kong, 183–204.

Wang, M.C. (1992) *Adaptive Education Strategies: Building on Diversity*, Baltimore, MD: Paul Brookes.

Watkins, D.A. and Biggs, J.B. (eds) (1996) *The Chinese Learner: Cultural, Psychological and Contextual Influences*, Hong Kong: Comparative Education Research Centre, University of Hong Kong.

Western Australia, Curriculum Council (1998) *Curriculum Framework for Kindergarten to Year 12 Education in Western Australia*, Perth, WA: Curriculum Council.

Wiggins, G. (1989) 'Teaching to the authentic test', *Educational Leadership* 46 (7): 41–7.

Winter, S. (1996) 'Peer tutoring and learning outcomes' in D. A. Watkins and J. Biggs (eds) *The Chinese Learner: cultural, psychological and contextual influences*, Hong Kong: Comparative Education Research Centre, University of Hong Kong, 221–42.

6   Focusing on Student Learning

A central focus of this chapter is to explore how the design of schools as specialized organizations concerned with maximizing student learning, can enable students to realize their learning potential. Accordingly, the chapter is structured as follows. First, the place of learning in school design is explicated and its connections with other school components is recognized. Second, some general conditions are identified for successful learning to take place. Third, the importance to schools of adopting a learning theory to underpin their practice is emphasized, and Gagnè's learning theory in particular, is given special attention. Fourth, focus is placed on the significance of student learning styles and their implications for understanding how individual differences may be accommodated. Finally, the chapter reports research, some of which has only recently surfaced, showing cross-cultural differences in learning, especially between Western (Anglo-American) and Chinese students. Cross-cultural differences in learning deserve increased attention, since they signal the pitfalls and dangers of narrow ethnocentric, especially Western, accounts of teaching and learning as though they have universal application. If learning processes are influenced by culture, then important ramifications follow. Western research on effective learning may not apply in entirety to some processes of learning as experienced by, for example, Chinese students. Scholars will therefore have to exercise greater caution before making generalizations, bound the limits of their theories and take more care before assuming cross-cultural transferability of results.

At the heart of re-designed schools is the intention to improve student learning. This can be gauged in quantitative terms, concerning the amount of learning, and in qualitative terms, related to the skills and processes of how learning takes place. The principles of school design advocated in this book incorporate improvement in both dimensions of learning – quantitative and qualitative – for individual students across the ability spectrum. If improvement in student learning is the main intention, then this is appropriately defined in terms of student outcomes, as explained in Chapter 5.

Other terminology which might be used is 'effective' learning. Mortimore

(1993) uses the term 'effective learning' and defines the term *effective* to apply to the acquisition of knowledge, understanding or skill with economy of time and effort, in ways that foster assimilation and accommodation with other learning, and with endurance for as long as it is found relevant by the learner. To this definition of 'effective' can be added both the quantitative and qualitative dimensions relating to 'more' and 'how'. In addition, it is worth acknowledging the difficulty of measuring learning because of its largely covert nature. What is it, for example, that has been learned? Is it specific information, deeper understanding and linkage with other knowledge, or the process of learning itself?

The view espoused in this chapter is that well-designed schools place learners at the centre of their operation. Accordingly, a number of precepts follow:

1   formal learning should be geared primarily to defined outcomes, as established in the curriculum;
2   all students in the school, irrespective of their age, ability, gender or culture have the right to equal opportunity to learn;
3   individual differences in how students learn have to be recognized and catered for;
4   teaching needs to focus on securing effective learning;
5   the school has an obligation to create conducive conditions for all students to learn successfully;
6   important cultural differences as to how students learn deserve recognition.

Many of these precepts will be reflected in subsequent discussion in this chapter. Some might argue that school quality is best judged by the learning achievements of students, measured in terms of defined outcomes. The problem with this argument is that student achievement might only tenuously be related to school factors and more dependent on individual ability, home and socio-economic background. Thus the statement might be more appropriately put as follows: the quality of a school is best judged by the value added by school-related factors to student learning between entry to and exit from the school.

If the re-designed school is to become more effective at improving and enhancing student learning, then a number of implications follow. First, the key questions for the school to address are: how do students learn? More specifically, how do students best learn in order to achieve the student outcomes? While generic conditions conducive to the learning of all students can be identified, there is robust evidence to show that students best learn in different ways. That being the case, it follows that the school needs to be informed about the learning characteristics of its students. For example, how does each of them best learn? What are their particular learning styles? Indeed, do they have a learning style? This type of information comes from multiple sources, but is most useful when available for all students as soon as possible after entry to the school and when regularly updated. Crucial in this data-gathering exercise is information about student learning styles. A number of schools already identify student learning styles and preferences by using learning style inventories.

The Place of Learning in School Design

Schools are essentially organizations concerned with promoting learning. Learning is the central purpose of schools. Increasingly, curricula are being defined in learning outcomes, and these provide the context within which schools increasingly function. At this juncture it is worth making two points: first, an outcomes emphasis should not preclude attention to processes, such as cognitive skills and higher order thinking skills (indeed, these processes may even be included as outcomes); and second, the outcomes should be as all-embracing and inclusive as possible, embracing academic, social–affective, personal values, aesthetic and physical outcomes.

The key linkages involving learning are with student outcomes and with teaching, as indicated in Figure 4. Student outcomes highlight the focus of what is to be learned, while learning processes, experiences and styles, along with teaching methods, determine how these outcomes will be attained. However, just as learning is geared to specific outcomes, so should teaching take account of learning processes and learner characteristics. If schools confront the all-important question – how do students best learn? – they may have to modify other elements as well, in order to promote learning. These include organizational structures, such as the timetable and student and teacher grouping, as well as school culture and patterns of resource allocation.

Context and Conditions for Learning

Addressing how students best learn involves creating favourable conditions for learning. These conditions include the physical and emotional state of the student, the physical classroom environment, the characteristics of the teacher and teaching and the students' own motivation. Students best learn when they are free of undue worry and stress, and when they feel safe, secure and comfortable at school. While the former may be outside the school's control, the latter is clearly within its remit. Every student should be entitled to feel safe, comfortable and free from harassment, intimidation and bullying while in school.

Equally, teachers and schools have a duty to create favourable physical environments for students to work. This involves a host of factors, such as ensuring enough fresh air in classrooms by opening windows, or presenting classrooms in bright cheerful ways and displaying students' work. In hot climates, such as those found in parts of Asia and Australia, air conditioning is an indispensable means of making the learning environment tolerable. In densely populated, heavily polluted urban areas, such as parts of Hong Kong, Tokyo, Taipei and Beijing, air conditioning fulfils an additional purpose of enabling windows to be closed, thus excluding external traffic noise and fumes.

Also pertaining to the physical environment is the use of space. By rearranging desks and classroom layout, more space can often be provided for students. Changing the classroom layout might also open up more innovative possibilities for learning, such as, peer and cooperative learning. However, lack of physical space is a feature of many Asian schools in particular. In Hong Kong, for example, schools with one thousand pupils may only have playground space the size of two basketball courts. Classrooms may accommodate forty to fifty students with barely enough space to walk between the desks. While culturally the students in these cities are used to living and working in close proximity to one another, principals and teachers complain of the restrictions imposed on their ability to provide enough classrooms let alone to create stimulating learning environments. While material resources, such as equipment, are not a sufficient condition for learning to take place, their availability is a necessary condition for creating more options for learning. A further factor in the promotion of learning is the provision of a relatively quiet classroom atmosphere, free of interruptions and disturbances, where student concentration is enhanced.

As well as the physical conditions of the students and the school classroom environment, psychological and pedagogical factors affect learning. Contemporary cognitive psychology indicates the following principles or conditions which favour learning (Ornstein, 1995):

1   a positive perception of self-concept and belief about personal abilities on the part of the student.
2   a motivation and interest to learn.
3   goal direction and focus to what is to be achieved.
4   meaningful connections between prior knowledge and new information.
5   metacognition – where students are able to organize and structure their thoughts, as well as develop successful learning strategies, as aids to gaining understanding.
6   the state of 'readiness' to learn is related to the student's stage of development and previous levels of learning; knowledge or skills to be learnt need to be within the student's capabilities.
7   opportunities for appropriate practice or rehearsal; learning is generally enhanced by the learner practising the skill or applying the knowledge.

8   opportunities for the transfer of learning to new or different situations, whether horizontally (across subject areas) or vertically (more difficult applications within the same area).

9   appropriate amounts of reinforcement are provided; students differ in the amount of instructional help and time that they need to learn.

10   appropriate amounts of positive feedback, realistic praise and encouragement are received by the student; the family, home and classroom environment may be relevant in determining how much feedback a student may need.

These factors are not exhaustive, but they do suggest that the phenomenon of learning is influenced by a complex array of physical, social and psychological forces, some of which relate to the student and others of which relate to the student indirectly through the teacher or parent. They reflect the importance of connections: for example, the link between new and existing knowledge, and between the processes, strategies and skills of learning and resultant outcomes. In designing learning-centred schools, it is helpful to assemble these principles and conditions of learning into a coherent theory. Beforehand, however, it is worth emphasizing the importance of goal-directed learning.

Goal-Directed Learning

Research findings strongly support the efficacy of setting organizational and individual goals (Locke and Latham, 1990). Performance is generally improved when goals are set and prioritized, and strategies planned and developed, for goal achievement. Research evidence suggests that setting specific, challenging (but achievable) goals is more likely to lead to improved performance than general or 'do your best' goals (Locke and Latham, 1990). Furthermore, where specific, challenging goals are accompanied by regular feedback on performance in relation to the set goals, the effects on performance and goal attainment are even greater. School development planning and the subsequent plan are more likely to improve student outcomes if specific, challenging goals aligned to teaching and student learning are set, followed by regular feedback on performance, for both teachers and students.

In order to capitalize on the benefits of goal setting, and to promote the learning of all students, goal setting needs to be incorporated at the classroom level for teachers and individual students. There is convincing research evidence (Locke and Latham, 1990) to support the efficacy of goal setting through its generally positive effects in:

•   directing attention to specified activities and behaviours;
•   arousing effort;

- increasing task persistence and commitment;
- motivating people to devise strategies and plans;
- enabling measured feedback against the goals.

Teachers and students in special education and some regular classes have experienced the efficacy of goal-directed learning, outcomes-based education, and mastery learning (Block et al., 1989; Spady, 1988). Emphasis is placed on setting clear, specific, challenging learning goals for students, at individual and group levels, and ensuring that they master and achieve the goals before proceeding further. Where appropriate goal setting takes place, it provides purpose, direction, commitment and, when feedback is given, reinforcement, encouragement and a sense of accomplishment, for students and teachers.

Goal setting and feedback usually take place in the school development planning process, which is aimed at raising student performance outcomes across the whole school. While school development planning targets the whole-school perspective to improving student outcomes, it may fail to induce change to filter down to affect classroom activity, teaching and learning. There is greater likelihood of gains to student learning when goal setting and feedback occur at classroom and individual student levels as well as in whole-school planning, and when the two levels enmesh and mutually reinforce.

Learning Theory

There is no shortage of learning theories, most of them developed by psychologists. Mortimore (1993) cites the following: Piaget (1955) and his notion of children proceeding through complex stages of learning; Vygotsky (1978), whose theory links language and thought as twin processes, and whose concept of proximal development claims to enable children to perform tasks normally beyond them with the help of adults; the behaviourists (Thorndike, 1898; Skinner, 1938) and social learning theorists (Bandura, 1974), who argue that learning occurs as a response to stimulus; and Carroll (1963), whose model links learning with teaching and in so doing, spawned further models associated with Bruner (1966), Bloom (1976) and Glaser (1976). More recent theories focus on self-efficacy (Wood and Bandura, 1989), stressing an association between learners' and teachers' belief in themselves and level of achievement; Wang et al.'s (1990) theory of adaptive instruction, on the other hand, stresses the importance of match between the individual's learning and school learning environment. Other work has examined domain-specific and general thinking skills, and the differences between learning in general and school learning, which tends to assume a more pure than applied and individual than collaborative form.

From a practitioner viewpoint and from a school design perspective, this is a somewhat bewildering collection of theories on learning. There are, however, two promising directions on learning for practitioners to follow. First, given the complexity of competing and complementary learning theories, schools may well be advised to settle on *one* learning theory, one with which staff feel comfortable, and for teachers to implement this theory across the whole school in a consistent way, than for teachers in the same school to adopt different theories. Second, teaching is more effective when it is responsive to the range of student learning styles. Both of these issues are worth elaborating.

Beneficial effects come from the synergy resulting from consistent application and reinforcement of the same principles by different teachers. A school might, for example, choose Gagnè's learning theory as a basis for common, shared practice across all teachers and curriculum learning areas. Gagnè (1974) recognizes a number of phases which are needed for successful learning to take place. Although he subsequently modified these phases (Gagnè, 1976; Gagnè and Briggs, 1979), his original version is worth attention here because it links learning with instruction.

An attraction of Gagnè's theory for the school design paradigm is the connection between eight learning phases and seven instructional events (see Figure 6.1). In effect, the learning phases shape teachers' instructional responsibilities, thus conforming to the backward mapping and iterative process described in Chapter 2. Each of the learning phases and instructional events are briefly described below.

The eight learning phases – motivation, apprehension, acquisition, retention, recall, generalization, performance and feedback – are sequential (Slavin, 1991):

1   motivation phase: the learner must be motivated to learn in the expectation that learning will be rewarding. For example, it may be useful, satisfy a curiosity, or secure a better grade.
2   apprehending phase: the learner must attend to the essential features or main points of what is to be learned. The teacher or writer can help the learner by emphasizing key ideas.
3   acquisition phase: information being learned is not stored directly in memory; it needs to be transformed into a meaningful form that relates to information already in the learner's memory. Various devices help link the new with the old, including mental imaging, advance organizers, seeing or manipulating objects, or teachers pointing out the links.
4   retention phase: the newly acquired information must be transferred from short-term to long-term memory. This can take place by means of rehearsal, practice or elaboration.
5   recall phase: once the information is stored in the long-term memory, ways of accessing it need to be developed. Subsequent access is assisted

Figure 6.1 *Relation of the Phases of Learning to Instructional Events (after Gagnè, 1976: 285). Reprinted by permission.*

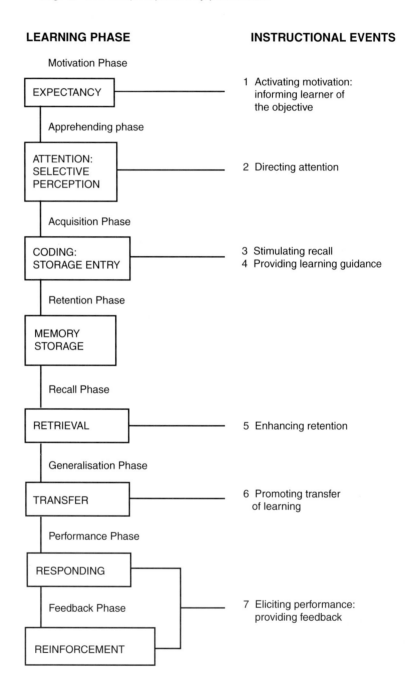

by ordering and structuring the material around concepts or categories, and noting their links.

6 generalization phase: transferring and applying the knowledge or skill gained to other situations is an integral part of learning.

7 performance phase: learners must demonstrate that they understand by performing the skill or completing a task.

8 feedback phase: learning is greatly enhanced when feedback is given on performance and understanding. This acts as a reinforcer for future successful learning.

Based on his ideas of the critical phases of learning, Gagnè proposed a sequence of crucial instructional events. In the same way that the learning phases can apply to all forms of learning, such as discovery learning, independent learning or learning from direct teaching, so instruction can apply to others besides teachers. However, the Gagnè model is best understood by assuming a teacher in control of a class or group of students. The seven instructional events, each dovetailing with specific learning phases (see Figure 6.1), are as follows:

1 activating motivation and informing the learner of the objective: students' interest needs to be aroused in order to motivate them; this can be achieved by relating the content to their own interests, citing a real life example, setting a problem, or pointing out the usefulness of the outcome. Students should also be made aware of what knowledge and skills they will possess as outcomes, and *why* they are being asked to learn something. Students thus need to realize the objectives of the learning task at the outset; knowing this will also help them focus on the salient points.

2 directing attention: the teacher must direct students' attention to relevant information and their focus on salient points.

3 stimulating recall: in order to assimilate new information, students need to recall related information already in their memories. Teachers should therefore encourage students to recall previous learning and to relate the new material to it.

4 providing learning guidance: this is the stage where new information is presented and discussed. The objectives will shape what form this takes. For example, in discovery learning or problem-based learning, the teacher might provide advice, guidance and materials, while in a direct teaching lesson based on concept learning, the teacher might provide rules or examples.

5 enhancing retention: teachers can aid retention by giving students plenty of practice, or by providing many examples, and by periodically testing retention.

6   promoting transfer of learning: once information is retained, the teacher should ensure that the student can apply it to different situations and can draw inferences about generalization. Problem solving is extremely useful in this respect.

7   eliciting performance and providing feedback: at the end of the instructional cycle, students should demonstrate their knowledge or skill so that the teacher can give feedback on how well they have achieved the outcome.

These events of instruction are designed to lead learners through the necessary cognitive steps to successful learning, namely coding, storing, retrieving and transferring information. A worthwhile objective is to develop in students a capability of leading themselves through this process – as independent learners – but this would likely only develop after teachers have reinforced the model in the students' cognition.

In summary, the Gagnè model is consistent with a backward mapping and iterative approach to school design. Sound principles of learning are dovetailed with informed teaching practices. If all teachers in a school incorporate these phases in the learning experiences of the same groups of students across the whole curriculum – in a synergistic way – then a reinforcement effect is likely to raise the quality of learning. These principles of learning underpin all teaching and can be applied irrespective of the teaching/learning strategy or style used. Learning style, however, is an important consideration for other reasons, as the following section testifies.

Learning Style

Every effort is made in the re-designed school to enhance learning across the spectrum of the student body. Towards this end, increasing attention is being paid to the importance of learning and teaching styles. Bechtol and Sorenson (1993: 204), for example, citing O'Neil (1990: 5), assert, 'As dropout and student "disengagement" rates persist at alarmingly high levels, attending to style is being viewed as one way to expand teaching methods and curriculum to reach more students.' Furthermore, in times of increasingly diverse student populations, the style movement is attractive because of its emphasis on a more personalized view of education. An additional appeal of learning styles is their concentration on students' strengths rather than weaknesses. In this regard, Dunn (in O'Neil, 1990: 6) suggests that all children have strengths, but the typical classroom design and rules that restrict student movement and learning are primary reasons why many are under-achievers and turn out to be problems. Silver (in O'Neil, 1990: 5–6) asserts that at-risk students learn best through concrete experiences, collaboration, cooperation and high levels of interaction, but that typical classrooms value competitiveness, independence and abstraction as students move through the grades. The question posed by Bechtol and Sorenson (1993) is, 'have we designed schools to militate against the success of these students?'

At-risk students often reject the typical classroom teaching–learning environment of lecturing, textbooks, classroom seating and grouping. These students may have styles that are mismatched with the prevailing conditions in schools. They are not able to work in the ways they prefer: for instance, instead of working with peers, they may have to work alone (Bechtol and Sorenson, 1993).

While most scholars acknowledge the significance of learning style, and many practitioners claim to have developed effective instructional strategies which utilize the concept, there is still a dearth of well-validated research on how best to use the learning style knowledge base in the classroom. Other difficulties relate to agreement on definition of style, on the reliability and validity of instruments used, and on relevant characteristics of learners and instructional settings. Yet, as Bechtol and Sorenson (1993: 205) claim, 'most everyone agrees, styles hold great potential for improving the education of students'.

Learning Style Differences

At the heart of the concept of learning style is the notion that children and adults have preferred ways of learning which, particularly when learning something difficult or for the first time, make it easier to learn. Thus students in the same class have a predisposition to learn the same material in different ways. Dunn and Dunn (1975: 74) define learning style as 'stimuli that affect a person's ability to absorb and retain information, values, facts, or concepts'. They identify four basic stimuli – environmental, emotional, sociological and physical – and eighteen style elements. Dunn's research suggests that between 20 and 30 per cent of students learn best from what they hear (auditory); 40 per cent learn best by visual means; and the remaining 30–40 percent rely on touching or physical contact (kinesthetic).

Undoubtedly, the most compelling conclusion of the learning styles research is that because the typical class will contain learners with a wide spread of learning style preferences, the teacher should provide learning opportunities for all by adopting a variety of methods and approaches. Loper (in Dunn, Beaudry and Klavas, 1989) suggests that teachers who teach and evaluate in only one mode serve only students who prefer to learn in that mode. If teachers are to give all students the chance to learn, they need to:

1 include a variety of learning modes in their lessons;
2 be aware of their own learning styles and how these affect their teaching styles, and;

3   help students move from one preferred mode to several modes so that they can improve their learning capacity and benefit from a variety of instructional styles.

It is not the present writer's intention to provide a full exposition of the major work on learning styles (see Bechtol and Sorenson, 1993 for a fuller exposition). Rather, the purpose here is to illustrate the potentiality of learning style for individualizing learning with the aim of improving the learning of all students. Accordingly, reference below is made to two of the more prominent research thrusts in the area of learning styles, namely, the work of Dunn and Dunn and colleagues, and McCarthy's 4MAT system.

Learning style elements: Rita Dunn and Kenneth Dunn

Dunn and Dunn (1975), using a learning style inventory, identified four stimuli and eighteen elements, as follows: the environmental stimulus, including elements of sound, temperature, light and design; the emotional stimulus, including motivation, responsibility, persistence and structure; the sociological stimulus, comprising peers, pair, adult, team and varied learning situations; and the physical stimulus, comprising perceptual, time, intake and mobility elements.

In summarizing their findings, Dunn et al. (1989) report that knowing students' learning styles helps teachers organize learning experiences in classrooms to respond to individual preferences for certain levels and types of noise, light, temperature, seating arrangements, mobility or grouping preferences. Teachers become more aware of who in their student group prefers to learn individually, in pairs or small groups, or in large groups. Some learn better in the early morning, others later in the day. Performance can be impaired if, for example, a student best learns maths in the afternoon, but is scheduled in a morning class. Some learn best by hearing, seeing, writing, experiencing, manipulating or a combination of these.

Rather than seeing learning style as locking people into a restricted mode of learning, this view assumes that it is a necessary asset. Possession of an effective learning style is an invaluable tool by which to learn. Many students with learning difficulties may never have developed an effective learning style. A re-designed school for quality learning assumes responsibility for developing an effective learning style for all students. This can best be achieved by encouraging teachers across the school to consistently adopt the same practices derived from the same learning theory or theories, so that students experience reinforcement of the same principles of learning as they move between subjects and teachers.

The 4MAT system: Bernice McCarthy

For more than twenty-five years, Bernice McCarthy and colleagues have developed and applied the 4MAT System, which offers a battery of instruments to assess learning styles and, in addition, a fully developed curriculum structured in content and method to allow for differences in student learning styles (McCarthy, 1990). 4MAT accommodates, as well as challenges, all types of learners by appealing to their accustomed or preferred learning styles while stretching them to function in less comfortable modes. It rests on two fundamental premises, namely that people have major learning styles and hemispheric (right mode/left mode) processing preferences, and that designing and using multiple teaching strategies in a systematic framework to teach to these preferences can improve teaching and learning (McCarthy, 1990).

Two major dimensions underpin the model: people perceive knowledge differently, and they process it differently. Some perceive by sensing and feeling (that is, in concrete ways), while others prefer to think things through and reflect on them (that is, in abstract ways). Similarly, people differ in how they prefer to process and internalize experiences. Some are watchers first, while others are doers. When one dimension is superimposed across the other, quadrants are formed, each with a unique combination of perception and process characteristics. Four different learning styles emerge from the quadrants: Type 1, imaginative learners; Type 2, analytic learners; Type 3, common sense learners; Type 4, dynamic learners (see Figure 6.2 on the following page).

Type 1, imaginative learners, are driven by the question, 'why' or 'why not'? They need to be convinced that learning is interesting, important and purposeful. They seek meaning, need to be involved personally and learn by listening and sharing with others. For these students, the curriculum is often divorced from their experienced lives. They want to study life as it is and reflect on it.

Type 2, analytic learners, are motivated by the question, 'what'? These people perceive information abstractly and process it reflectively. They generate ideas and theories and reflect on them. They seek facts, need to know what experts think and learn by thinking through ideas. They are usually thorough, well organized and industrious and do well in traditional classrooms.

Type 3, common sense learners, are driven by the question, 'how'? They perceive information abstractly and process it actively. They combine theory and practice by testing theories and applying common sense. They start with an idea, try it out and test to see if it works. They need to know how things work, are usually excellent problem solvers and learn by testing theories in ways that seem to make sense. They often find school frustrating because they want to know how learning is of practical use.

Type 4, dynamic learners, are motivated by the question, 'what if'? They

Figure 6.2 *Learning Styles*

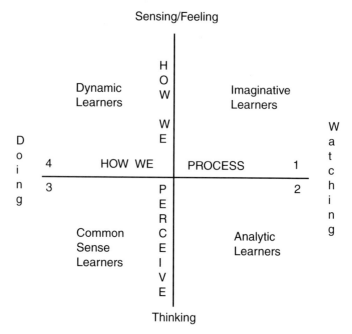

Source: adapted from McCarthy, 1990

perceive information concretely and process it by doing. They start with what they see or feel and then seek hidden possibilities; they are creative in exploiting applications and learn by trial and error and self discovery. They seek to influence others with their own ways of doing things and often find schooling frustratingly restrictive.

Based on the ideas of David Kolb (1984), 4MAT proposes firstly, that people have a dominant or preferred learning style with a supporting style, and secondly, that for complete learning to occur and to become more proficient learners, not only do students need opportunities for learning through their preferred mode, but they also need the challenge of learning in the other modes. In fact, for students to become complete or 'master' learners, they need exposure to and a degree of competence in all four learning styles.

Teachers need the ability to locate individual students in their preferred style, and to design curricular experiences which tap into that style as well as the other three styles. In fact, the 4MAT system consists of structured curricular experiences which conform to the four quadrants of the model and lays down specific approaches for principals, teachers and students to follow. For example, Quadrant 1 relates to the question, why? Students in this quadrant value connecting school work to their personal lives. Thus teachers should connect meaning to content and clarify learning objectives, while principals should replicate the same at school level, explaining the meaning, purpose and vision of the school.

Students with Quadrant 2 learning styles are motivated by the what? question; they need to understand the content. Teachers therefore should be instructional leaders or subject knowledge specialists, and principals should be instructional coordinators who align curriculum with the school and district mission statement. Meanwhile, Quadrant 3 students are users of content and skills and ask, how does this work? Teachers should be coaches and principals should facilitate resources, including multiple methods of instruction, time, money and materials. Students in Quadrant 4 are the innovators and ask, if? Teachers need to be facilitators of creative options and principals should refocus and coordinate evaluations and enlarge diffusion networks (Bechtol and Sorenson, 1993).

Many important implications for teachers follow from 4MAT. First, teachers need to identify the learning styles of their students as early in their courses as possible. Second, curricula need to be designed in ways which ensure each student is exposed to all four quadrant learning modes. It may be better to start students with experiences reflecting their preferred learning styles before extending them to styles in which they feel less confident. Third, teachers can use learning style differences to decide how to group students for cooperative learning and other team approaches. Is it better to group students with the same learning style or with different styles? In the former case, the learning process is likely to be more harmonious, but different approaches and diverse views may not be forthcoming. In the latter case, a group of four or more students who together represent the four learning styles would each contribute qualitatively different inputs to the learning task. This enriches the learning experience, providing it does not lead to breakdown and disharmony in the group. In general, there are appreciable benefits to ensuring that all four learning styles are represented in each group. At the very least, students come to realize that their peers learn in different ways and that each can make a distinctive and valuable contribution to task completion. Finally, teachers are faced with the task of adjusting their teaching styles to provide learning experiences across all four quadrants. This calls for considerable flexibility on their part. The following section pursues this issue further.

Teaching Styles and their Match with Learning Styles

A voluminous literature has grown on teaching style over the past two decades. It is not the present intention, however, to review this literature (see for example Bechtol and Sorenson, 1993). Rather, the aim is to present an example of the range of teaching styles which have been identified and to raise the importance of matching learning with teaching styles.

Most classifications of teaching styles are based on definitions of who controls the teaching–learning process: the teacher, the student, or both. The five variables in the teaching–learning process (Bechtol and Sorenson, 1993) are taken to be:

- goals and objectives;
- materials and activities;
- time and space;
- presentation method;
- how evaluation is determined.

A typical schema for teaching style is that used by Sorenson et al. (1988), who distinguish the following:

1   *Teacher-centred style*: where the teacher makes the decisions on all five variables and the student simply carries them out. This is the traditional and most common form of teaching. While it is an efficient way of conveying information to a large number of students, many fail to be motivated to learn by such an approach. Its usefulness in a technological society is also seriously questioned, as other sources of information become readily available and students need hands-on skills to exploit more opportunities.

2   *Self-instructional style*: the student works with a computer or with programmed material. Teacher and student work together to decide on the programme and the level of difficulty. Although the programme determines the objectives, the student has considerable control over options and over the other variables. Advantages of the style are that the student gets immediate feedback and that materials can be matched to the ability and age of the student. Thus remediation, enrichment and acceleration can be built in.

3   *Inquiry teaching style*: the teacher forms a partnership with the students as individuals, pairs or in small groups. The teacher presents ideas to stimulate students to think and problem solve. The lesson often starts in a large class, and eventually breaks into small groups to raise and address questions and to collect data necessary in the research process. Each student has a clearly defined role within the inquiry team, and these roles may be rotated.

4 *Co-operative learning style*: this is an extension of the inquiry style. Students work together in small groups and the development of social skills, self-esteem and independence are valued alongside cognitive achievement.

5 *Student-centred style*: this is claimed to be the ultimate goal of every teacher, the development of a lifelong learner, independent and self-motivated, where the student takes the initiative in all five decisional areas. The teacher acts as a resource and provides guidance and direction. The style incorporates elements of other styles and students may work alone, in pairs, groups or class. Not all students have the motivation or aptitude to benefit from this approach.

Bechtol and Sorenson (1993: 230–1) conclude:

> Every classroom ... has students who function well with teachers who use one, two, or all five teaching styles .... Every lesson and unit of instruction a teacher plans should provide opportunities for students to learn in more than one style – preferably, three or four different styles. When these opportunities are built into the learning plans, the idea of teaching styles has true meaning. And student learning styles can easily be matched to these five practical teaching styles.

These authors almost certainly underestimate the difficulty of matching teaching with learning styles. The teaching styles of teachers are usually dependent on their learning styles. Students with the same learning style as their teacher are likely to find learning more amenable and vice versa. Teachers can work towards achieving equity for all students by developing flexible and adaptable teaching styles. Thus teachers should provide a variety of options and choices to meet the same goals and objectives in lessons and course units so that students with different learning styles can all be engaged.

Team settings may offer the best chance of matching students' learning and teachers' teaching styles. Where teachers team teach, students can be assigned to teachers who cover the range of teaching styles. This may obviate the need for individual teachers to cover all styles.

The nature of the subject matter to be learned may also affect learning styles. Some material, such as instructions, safety procedures and rules, is best taught by direct teaching to the whole class, even though students may prefer to learn alone, in pairs or small groups. In this respect, there are compelling arguments for providing a range of learning settings from individual, paired, small group and whole class. Not only does this capture the different preferences of students, but it develops more complete learners who, in later life, might find themselves having to learn in any or all of these situations.

The quality school for learning, therefore, places the student at the centre of its operation in two ways. First, it identifies, collects and applies information about individual students' learning styles and uses this information to decide how its individual students best learn. In some cases, especially students with learning difficulties, the quality school accepts responsibility for developing an effective learning style where none already exists. Second, teachers adapt their teaching styles to accommodate student learning style differences, while mindful of the need for students to gain learning experiences in a full range of settings.

While the foregoing discussion about learning is based on Western (Anglo-American) theory, research and practice, an important question to ask is, to what extent is student learning culture sensitive? The following section addresses this question in terms of students in Confucian-heritage cultures in Asia.

A Cross-Cultural View of Learning

A considerable interest in cross-cultural comparisons of, and differences between, student achievement began to flourish in the early 1990s. Much of this focused on the apparently superior performance of students in Confucian-heritage cultures (that is, Japan, Korea, Taiwan, Singapore, Hong Kong and mainland China) compared to those in Western societies on international achievement tests in mathematics and science (reported in Reynolds and Farrell, 1996). It is interesting how, during the 1990s, a rising tide of awareness grew in the West as the Asian economic miracle continued unabated. Countries such as the UK and USA, after decades of introspection in relation to their respective education systems, suddenly became interested in the fact that the superior academic achievement of students from Confucian-heritage cultures might be associated with the economic performance and growth rates of the Asian economies. What was it, then, that the West could learn from school systems in Confucian-heritage cultures? The dangers of rash judgements being made about what could be transferred without understanding culture were readily apparent (Dimmock, 1998). Then in 1997, the Asian economic miracle unexpectedly went into reverse, a condition that is expected to last for some time. Will the same Western observers who, a few years earlier, were so covetous of educational achievements in Taiwan, Korea and Singapore now just as quickly lose interest?

Irrespective of the dramatic turn of events reported above, recent research has begun to uncover important learning differences between Western students and those in Confucian-heritage cultures. One avenue of this research is of a socio-cultural kind associated with parental and family upbringing, and recognizes major differences in study habits and attitudes to education. A second is of a cultural-cognitive kind and relates to the ways in which students process information when learning. Each of these will now be elaborated, but in so doing it is worth bearing in mind that there are always dangers associated with generalization. When claiming cultural differences, one is bound to be referring to the broad picture and to the aggregate of individuals in a defined group or population. Indeed, the nature of culture itself rests upon broad patterns of values, beliefs and practices. Much of the time, therefore, one is referring to differences of degree rather than kind. It is also the case that there are many gaps in our knowledge in this area and that much more research is needed. One such weakness is that the research evidence collected to date from the Confucian-heritage societies is exclusively urban and omits rural populations (Stevenson and Lee, 1996).

A number of socio-cultural aspects of Confucian-heritage societies help explain the generally high academic performance of students in comparison with Western students. The first is a cultural emphasis, reflecting Confucian beliefs, on the role of effort and the importance of individuals striving and working hard. Second, students are highly motivated to succeed at school. Third, parents have particularly high aspirations for their children. Fourth, a more restricted interpretation tends to operate in Confucian-heritage cultures. Emphasis is placed on academic subjects, particularly mathematics and science, with much less attention than in Anglo-American societies given to environmental issues, health, music and art, all of which are marginalized. A full discussion of many of these factors is presented by Stevenson and Lee (1996). Discounting arguments that the differences in performance are due to superior intelligence, they acknowledge that the 'everyday experiences' of Chinese differ greatly from American children and are rooted in 'contrasting cultural conceptions of child development and education' (Stevenson and Lee, 1996: 131). These authors reported major differences between students in Taipei and Minneapolis, as follows:

1   In the pre-school years, American parents take a more active interest in their children's education by reading to them and taking them on outings than do Taiwanese parents. However, after school entry the situation reverses, as reasoned below.

2   The amount of time Taiwanese students devote to study is appreciably greater than their US counterparts. For example, they spend 14 hours more at school each week than their American counterparts. Taiwanese students also spend about 10 hours more per week of after-school time in studying than do US students; in addition, 36 percent of high school students in Taiwan pursue after-school classes, compared to 3 percent in Minneapolis. In sum, Chinese students spend more time studying and less time socializing, engaging in sports and working in part-time jobs than do their US counterparts. The same results hold for Chinese students living in the USA.

3   Chinese students are highly motivated to do well at school, as this is seen to be the route to social and economic advancement as well as

improvement in the person. Aspirations are high despite the fact that many know they cannot be realized; in Taipei, 83 per cent of high school students hoped to enter university, yet only 49 percent were able to pass the college entrance exam. In Beijing, 86 per cent want to attend university, yet only 3 per cent will be able to.

4   Academic success is equated with prestige for family and society, and thus individual student success is viewed in the context of family and society. Equally, failure brings shame and 'loss of face' on the family. Parental expectations are thus a strong driving force complementing individual motivation.

5   Good role models are revered; hence parents make every effort to expose their children to good teachers, and to live in a good neighbourhood. The environment is seen as crucial in the child's success.

6   Individual differences are acknowledged, but in a different way from the West; rather than seeing them as constraints or restrictions, they are meant to signal the need for adjustments to planning the future. Thus the less able child should start to study earlier than the more able child.

7   Effort, rather than ability, is looked upon as the key factor in achievement; Chinese children are exhorted to dedicate themselves to their studies. The virtues of working hard are extolled. Research shows that the Chinese believe that working hard not only leads to success, but also increases one's ability, whereas Americans surveyed thought that working hard was an indication of lack of ability.

8   Despite the relative success of Chinese students in international comparisons, as many Chinese parents were critical of their children's performance at school as is the case with American parents. This provides insight into the high standards of expectation held by Chinese parents of their children.

9   Chinese parents tend to be more restrictive, authoritarian and disciplinarian than parents in Western cultures (Chiu, 1987; Wu, 1996). Thus children in Confucian-heritage cultures tend to be more obedient to their parents, more parent-controlled and willing to conform to their parents' wishes.

10   There is contradictory evidence about the effects on Chinese students of the strong cultural emphasis placed on education. Some argue that East Asian societies, and Taiwan in particular, have high rates of youth suicide; they also point to the fact that newspapers are full of tragic stories of young people taking their own lives and suffering stress. On the other hand, Stevenson and Lee (1996) produce evidence from a number of studies showing that while research shows that Chinese students experience higher levels of depressed mood and psychosomatic disturbance, on other measures such as calmness, tension and adjustment to school work, they are no different to students in other cultures.

A further socio-cultural characteristic of Confucian-heritage students is their apparent willingness and ability to adapt their learning priorities to suit different situations. Numerous studies of Chinese students studying overseas reveal their ability to adapt quickly to the learning goals and expectations of the different culture, while maintaining their higher work ethic and higher drive for academic achievement than Western students (Volet and Renshaw, 1996). These authors agree with Watkins and Biggs (1996) that Chinese students are able to distinguish and switch between memorization for understanding and surface learning geared to examinations. They go on to report that Asian students in a university context, compared with their Australian counterparts, had higher cognitive goals, were more able to match higher level goals with compatible learning contexts, had more extensive help-seeking strategies and support systems and contrary to stereotype, did not participate any less in tutorial discussions.

A further explanation comes from Hofstede's (1980, 1991) cross-cultural research (briefly referred to in Chapter 3), which recognizes dimensions of culture, some of which are relevant to socio-cultural factors affecting learning. On the power distance (PD) criterion, which measures the spread of power and authority in a society and its institutions, Confucian-heritage cultures tend to have high PD, that is, power and authority are distributed unequally. Children are more likely to respect their parents and students respect their teachers than is the case in the low PD Western societies. In regard to the collectivist–individualist dimension, which measures the extent to which people think of themselves primarily as group members or individuals, most Confucian cultures tend to be collectivist. This helps explain why Chinese students are more likely to help one another and to establish support mechanisms than are their more individualistic Western counterparts.

Recent research findings on cultural-cognitive differences between Asian and Western learners (Watkins and Biggs, 1996) are also instructive in throwing light on the dangers of making cross-cultural generalizations and assumptions. Watkins and Biggs (1996), basing their work on Hong Kong students, claim that many of the views typically held by Westerners in relation to Chinese (and other Asian) learners, are in fact, myths. Hong Kong students, it is argued, are representative of students in other Confucian-heritage cultures.

The first misconception centres on the contribution that repetition and rote learning make to memorization and understanding. All agree that Chinese and Asian students in general have a tendency to rote learn. Western interpretation of rote learning is derogatory, implying that little understanding, reflection or deep learning takes place. Asian students use repetition more than Westerners, but quite why is difficult to ascertain. Marton et al. (1996) claim that memorization leads to understanding, although whether it deepens understanding or is a precondition for it is not clear. There is evidence that for some Asian students, the relationship between memorization and understanding is a two-way cause–effect phenomenon. That is, while memorization is used to deepen understanding, at other times, students may already have understanding but resort to memorization for purposes of passing exams. In other words, the Asian student is sufficiently sophisticated to vary the process to suit the objective. Westerners have failed to see the advantages of rote learning in enhancing understanding. Rote learning is to be discouraged in schools, as it signifies that the student has achieved no more than surface learning. In the Western mindset, rote learning is regarded as lower order learning and is contrasted with higher order learning skills associated with deep learning and learning for understanding. In contrast, evidence from Kember and Gow (1990) and Watkins and Biggs (1996), all of whom studied Hong Kong students, shows that rote learning is a necessary part of memorization, which is in turn linked to deeper understanding. In other words, the Hong Kong student memorizes in order to understand; the two processes are functionally connected, the one is a prerequisite for the other. For Western students, it is assumed that no such link exists; rote learning and deep learning are two separate entities.

A second myth held by Westerners relates to motivation to learn. On this matter, Watkins and Biggs (1996: 273) assert, 'Western ways of categorizing motivation do not travel well, at least not to the Orient'. Westerners tend to see intrinsic motivation as the precursor to meaningful deep understanding. The Chinese student, however, taking a more pragmatic view, may be motivated by a mixed set of forces, including 'personal ambition, family face, peer support, material reward, and yes, possibly even interest' (Watkins and Biggs, 1996: 273). In addition, Confucian characteristics of diligence and receptiveness help in this process. In short, Watkins and Biggs claim, 'the familiar extrinsic/intrinsic polarity collapses'. Whereas Westerners in individualistic societies tend to be driven by achievement motivation and the ego-enhancing feeling of success in education defined in competitive terms, the Chinese have a more holistic sense of achievement, one less driven by their own ego alone but more cognisant of the way significant others, such as family members and even society as a whole, define success.

Collectivist notions also affect the teacher–student relationship, which although hierarchical can also be warm, caring and supportive (Chan, 1993). Tang (1996) also found that students collaborate spontaneously outside the classroom, helping each other to obtain material useful for the completion of, and entering discussion on, assignments. This amount of collaboration appears to be far more extensive than Western students would engage in. In addition, although it is seldom attempted, Winter (1996) found that organized peer learning can work very well in Hong Kong schools. Watkins and Biggs (1996: 275) conclude, 'Hong Kong secondary school students would in fact prefer a more collaborative learning environment which they consider would promote the deeper, more achievement-oriented approach to learning.'

Implications of Cross-Cultural Learning Differences

A major premise of this book is that schools be re-designed around student learning. If important differences in learning exist between students with different cultural backgrounds, then these need to be reflected in school design. They may not lead to dramatic differences in design, but they may well affect the fine tuning of classroom practices. Clearly, different cognitive strategies used by students in learning have implications for teachers in their choice of teaching strategies. Inescapably, the practices associated with core technology in the re-designed school are at least partially culture dependent and culture sensitive.

It follows that restructuring policies designed in the West, particularly those intended to change teaching, learning and curriculum, may need to be rethought before they are adopted wholesale and introduced to learning environments with different cultural ambience. This issue is discussed further in the following chapter on teaching.

Conclusion

It has been argued that the generic principles of school design referred to in this chapter are not culture-dependent. In designing learning-centred schools, learners and learning are placed at the heart of school activity. The key mission becomes how to facilitate and promote the learning of all students towards achievable goals. Towards this end, the school displays a number of important characteristics:

- student outcomes are converted into meaningful learning goals for individual students;
- every student is valued as a learner;
- relevant information is collected on each student's learning characteristics and achievements;
- research findings are sought on effective learning principles as guides to practice;
- wherever possible, school-wide policies and shared practices on learning are adopted for consistency and reinforcement;
- the whole school is viewed as a learning community.

Ultimately, the notion of the school as a learning community embraces all members, including the principal, senior staff and teachers as learners in the broadest sense. How they approach their professional work – as inquirers, researchers, questioners and seekers of knowledge – will have dramatic effects on those they are responsible for inducting into learning, namely, their students.

References

Bandura, A. (1974) 'Behaviour theory and the models of man', *American Psychologist* 29: 859–69.

Bechtol, W.M. and Sorenson, J.S. (1993) *Restructuring Schooling for Individual Students*, Needham Heights, MA: Allyn and Bacon.

Block, J.H., Efthim, H.E. and Burns, R.B. (1989) *Building effective mastery learning schools*, New York: Longman.

Bloom, B. (1976) *Human Characteristics and School Learning*, New York: McGraw-Hill.

Bruner, J.S. (1966) *Towards a Theory of Instruction*, New York: W.W. Norton.

Carroll, J.B. (1963) 'A model of school learning', *Teachers' College Record* 64: 723–33.

Chan, S.L. (1993) 'Approaches to learning of medical and business students in a Guangzhou university', The University of Hong Kong, M.Ed. dissertation.

Chiu, L.H. (1987) 'Child-rearing attitudes of Chinese, Chinese-American, and Anglo-American mothers', *International Journal of Psychology* 21: 167–76.

Dimmock, C. (1998) 'Restructuring Hong Kong's schools: the applicability of Western theories, policies and practices to an Asian culture', *Educational Management and Administration* 26 (4): 363–77.

Dunn, R. and Dunn, K. (1975) 'Educator's self-teaching guide to individualizing instructional programs', West Nyack, NY: Parker.

Dunn, R., Beaudry, J. and Klavas, A. (1989) 'Survey of research on learning styles', *Educational Leadership* 47 (6): 50–7.

Gagnè, R.M. (1974) *Essentials of Learning for Instruction*, New York: Holt, Rinehart & Winston.

—— (1976) *The Conditions of Learning*, 3rd edn, New York: Holt, Rinehart & Winston.

Gagnè, R.M. and Briggs, L. (1979) *Principles of Instructional Design*, 2nd edn, New York: Holt, Rinehart & Winston.

Glaser, R. (1976) 'Components of a psychological theory of instruction: towards a science of design', *Review of Educational Research*, 46–124.

Hofstede, G.H. (1980) *Cultures and consequences: International differences in work-related values*, Beverley Hills, CA: Sage.

—— (1991) *Cultures and organizations: software of the mind*, London: McGraw Hill.

Kember, D. and Gow, L. (1990) 'Cultural specificity of approaches to study', *British Journal of Educational Psychology* 60: 356–63.

Kolb, D.R. (1984) *Experiential learning experiences as the source of learning and development*, Englewood Cliffs, NJ: Prentice Hall.

Locke, E.A. and Latham, G.P. (1990) *A Theory of Goal Setting and Task Performance*, Englewood Cliffs, NJ: Prentice Hall.

Marton, F., Dall'Alba, G. and Tse, L.K. (1996) 'Memorizing and understanding: the keys to the paradox', in D.A.Watkins and J.B. Biggs (eds), *The Chinese Learner: Cultural, Psychological and Contextual Influences*, Hong Kong: Comparative Education Research Centre, University of Hong Kong, 69–84.

McCarthy, B. (1990) 'Using the 4MAT system to bring learning styles to schools', *Educational Leadership* 48 (2): 31–7.

Mortimore, P. (1993) 'School effectiveness and the management of effective learning and teaching', *School Effectiveness and School Improvement* 4 (4): 290–310.

O'Neill, J. (1990) 'Making sense of style', *Educational Leadership* 48 (2): 4–9.

Ornstein, A.C. (1995) *Strategies for Effective Teaching*, 2nd edn, Dubuque, IA: Brown & Benchmark.

Piaget, J. (1955) *The Construction of Reality and the Child*, trans. M. Cook, London: Routledge and Kegan Paul.

Reynolds, D. and Farrell, S. (1996) *World's Apart? A Review of International Surveys of Educational Achievement Involving England*, London: Office for Standards in Education (OFSTED).

Skinner, B.F. (1938) *The Behaviour of Organisms*, New York: Appleton.

Slavin, R.E. (1991) *Educational Psychology*, 3rd edn, Englewood Cliffs, NJ: Prentice Hall.

Sorenson, J., Engelsgjerd, J., Francis, M., Miller, M. and Schuster, N. (1988) *The Gifted Program Handbook*, Palo Alto, CA: Dale Seymour.

Spady, W.G. (1988) 'Organizing for results: The basis of authentic restructuring and reform', *Educational Leadership* 46 (2): 4–8.

Stevenson, H.W. and Lee, Shin-ying (1996) 'The academic achievement of Chinese students', in M.H. Bond (ed.), *The Handbook of Chinese Psychology*, New York: Oxford University Press, 124–42.

Tang, C. (1996) 'Collaborative learning: the latent dimension in Chinese students' learning', in D.A. Watkins and J. Biggs (eds), *The Chinese Learner: Cultural, Psychological and Contextual Influences*, Hong Kong: Comparative Education Research Centre, University of Hong Kong, 183–204.

Thorndike, E.L. (1898) 'Animal intelligence', *Psychological Monograph* 1 (8): 300.

Volet, S. and Renshaw, P. (1996) 'Chinese students at an Australian university: adaptability and continuity', in D.A. Watkins and J. Biggs (eds), *The Chinese Learner: Cultural, Psychological and Contextual Influences*, Hong Kong: Comparative Education Research Centre, University of Hong Kong, 205–20.

Vygotsky, L. (1978) *Mind in Society*, Cambridge, MA: Harvard University Press.

Wang, M.H.G., Haertel, G.D. and Walberg, H. (1990) 'What influences learning? A content analysis of review of literature', *Journal of Educational Research* 84 (1): 30–43.

Watkins, D.A. and Biggs, J.B. (1996) *The Chinese Learner: Cultural, Psychological and Contextual Influences*, Hong Kong: Comparative Education Research Centre, University of Hong Kong.

Winter, S. (1996) 'Peer tutoring and learning outcomes', in D.A. Watkins and J. Biggs (eds), *The Chinese Learner: Cultural, Psychological and Contextual Influences*, Hong Kong: Comparative Education Research Centre, University of Hong Kong, 221–42.

Wood, R. and Bandura, A. (1989) 'Impact of conceptions of ability on self-regulating mechanisms and complex decision-making', *Journal of Personality & Social Psychology* 56: 407–15.

Wu, D.Y.H. (1996) 'Chinese childhood socialization', in M.H. Bond (ed.), *The Handbook of Chinese Psychology*, New York: Oxford University Press, 143–54.

7 Targeting Informed Teaching

If the re-designed school is to achieve improvement and enhancement of learning for all students, then a major responsibility falls on teachers and teaching. In this regard, the key questions are:

1   If the school is clear about how its students best learn, then how do teachers best teach to secure learning?
2   How do teachers best teach in order to achieve the student learning outcomes expected?

This chapter aims to address the foregoing questions, and is structured in a sequence of steps moving from the broad to the particular. First, it discusses issues related to how teaching and 'informed teaching' in particular, can be viewed. Does teaching, for example, conform to a body of professional practice? What is the place of artistry in teaching? Second, major models of teaching approaches and learning environments are identified as useful frames for subsequent discussion. Third, a number of teaching approaches are described as an indication of what is meant by informed teaching practice. Fourth, research evidence is reported of specific teaching skills and behaviours which have demonstrated effectiveness in enhancing student learning. The importance of teachers possessing good subject content knowledge as part of informed teaching is given prominence at this point. Finally, issues relating to informed teaching are set within a cross-cultural context, enabling Confucian-heritage cultures to be compared with Western environments.

In the school design process, the reconfiguration of learning principles and practices is closely integrated with informed approaches to teaching. The principle of backward mapping (see Chapter 2) combined with an iterative process of checking backwards and forwards between student outcomes, learning and teaching will help ensure that the school possesses a sound and informed base for building its core technology.

This chapter will argue, *inter alia*, that teaching in learning-centred schools displays the following characteristics:

- teaching focuses on student learning and understanding;
- teachers share responsibility with students for their learning;
- a wide repertoire and range of teaching methods is practised;
- research findings on effective teaching principles, techniques and behaviours are sought as guides to practice;
- school-wide instructional policies and shared practices are adopted;
- teachers evaluate their own and their colleagues' teaching.

In short, this is what is meant by 'informed' teaching practices, referred to in Chapter 2.

In schools, for quality learning and teaching, the 'focus of schooling must shift from teaching to learning' (Carnegie Forum, 1986: 3). The re-designed school moves from a teacher-centred to a learner-centred pedagogy, the purpose of which is to meet the learning needs of students. Teachers become 'managers of learning experiences' (Hawley, 1989: 32) thereby sharing with students the responsibility for learning. Teachers enable students to accept more control over their learning, a condition which Elmore (1988: 11) calls 'teaching for understanding'. An emphasis on understanding requires teachers to construct learning experiences which enable students to draw connections between new and previously acquired knowledge and to encourage them to reflect on and apply that knowledge (Marton and Ramsden, 1988).

A concerned, caring approach on the part of the teacher highlights the importance of the quality of the teacher–student relationship. While emphasis is currently placed on students accepting responsibility for their own learning, it is important for teachers to assume a share in that responsibility. Students feel supported when teachers demonstrate their commitment to, and concern for, the achievement of learning goals and outcomes. Research confirms the importance of the environment created by teachers, principals and others in influencing students' perceptions of learning (Marton and Ramsden, 1988).

As this chapter will show, creating and maintaining a learning-directed rather than teaching-directed model of instruction requires a broad range of teaching strategies and a more personalized and individualized approach to learning (Brophy and Evertson, 1976; Brophy and Good, 1986; Harvey and Crandall, 1988; Murphy, 1991). A range of teaching-learning strategies is required for student engagement, taking into account individual student learning styles. The implications for teachers centre on the extent to which they possess a wide rather than narrow repertoire of teaching-learning strategies and on their ability to switch flexibly, selectively and appropriately, between them. A pertinent question for many teachers is the degree to which they are operating within a comfort zone, placing undue reliance on just one or two teaching methods. A clearer picture of the range and balance of teaching-learning strategies required in the re-designed school is provided by the array of teaching models and research findings on effective teaching presented in this chapter.

Teaching as Artistry and Professional Practice

Teachers have traditionally argued – on grounds of professionalism – that they deserve independence and autonomy in how they teach. This line of argument, however, hinges on the connotation of the term 'professionalism' for its justification. A true profession is, *inter alia*, underpinned by a set of generally accepted, agreed and proven practices which have demonstrated effectiveness and which derive from a body of theoretical and research knowledge (Hoyle, 1969). Such is the case, for example, with medicine and law. Each is underpinned not only by a body of substantive and procedural knowledge, but also by a code of ethics which guides successful practice. Teachers and teaching, however, have not reached this position. While it is argued below that a reasonably sound body of confirmatory research on successful teaching practices does exist, and could form the basis of an 'informed' approach to teaching, its existence is rarely acknowledged by practitioners. Hence, as far as teachers are concerned, there is no generally agreed and accepted set of teaching procedures and practices which they regard as equitable, ethical and effective, and which rest on a well-estab- lished body of theory and research. Teachers' lack of awareness or disregard for the effective teaching literature makes their traditional arguments for autonomy challengeable at the very least.

In presenting a counterview to the case for traditional teacher autonomy, it is worth acknowledging that in many instances, perhaps even the majority, the grounds on which teachers adopt particular teaching methods are mani- fold, but rarely do they include knowledge based on informed practice. Rather, teaching methods are based on teachers' past teaching and learning experiences as well as on personal traits and preferences. Some of these reflect the way they were taught at school and later at college. Others reflect their own learning style preferences and how they conceptualize their subject. Their peers and colleagues might also help shape their teaching repertoire. Over the passage of time, however, it appears that teachers come to rely on a narrower rather than broader range of methods, and especially on those from which they derive confidence and comfort and which offer them economy and efficiency of effort in coping with the daily pressures of lesson delivery.

As described later in this chapter, the literature on effective teaching prac- tices (that is, effective in enhancing student learning) is diverse. It embraces empirical evidence of a quantitative kind, including meta-studies of specific teaching behaviours and skills, as well as qualitative. It includes broader approaches to teaching, such as mastery learning and cooperative learning. It also contains work of a more theoretical kind, such as a number of pedagogical or instructional theories. All of these provide a basis for a more informed set of practices among teachers. They also provide an anchor point for placing the professionalism of teachers on a more secure footing. More robust practices underpinned by research and theoretical knowledge not only enhance the practice of teaching, but also create a more informed profession of teachers and reinforce the claims that there are sets of professional procedures and a body of professional knowledge about which teachers can become informed. These provide anchor points for informed practice. If acknowledged and adopted, they would lay to rest the myth that just about anyone can teach.

Some critics of the foregoing account like to claim that the recognition of what is here called 'informed practice' denies teachers autonomy by locking them into a narrower range and more rigid set of practices which, in turn, denigrates their professionalism. They go on to argue that it restricts the opportunity teachers have to impart their own personalities, individualism and personal strengths into their teaching and that these are vital in enabling teachers to cultivate their own distinctive style.

There are a number of misconceptions, however, in the position taken by these critics. First, the relevant literature tends to be inclusive rather than exclusive. Far from narrowing the range of teaching approaches advocated for use in classrooms, the literature indicates how best to implement the many different approaches for enhancing student learning. In so doing, it increases choice. For example, it does not claim that direct teaching is preferable to, for example, cooperative learning. Rather, it signals that both direct teaching and cooperative learning are desirable, providing that they are practised and implemented according to specific methods and conditions. In other words, there are more and less effective ways to practice each of the teaching methods, from direct teaching through cooperative learning to peer tutoring and discovery/experiential approaches. It informs teachers of the full range of methods available and offers advice on how to practice them for the sake of student learning. For many reasons, this adds to, not detracts from, professionalism. First, it extends teachers' repertoire and knowledge of a range of pedagogical methods and offers advice on ways to practice each of them. Second, it focuses the attention of teachers on the main purpose at stake: not the right of teachers to do whatever they want, but the responsibility to teach their 'client' group, the students, in ways which are most beneficial for learning.

Nothing which has been said so far necessarily contradicts or conflicts with the view that teaching should involve creativity and promote the exercise of personal judgement by the teacher. These attributes are also necessary for teacher professionalism. There is a compelling case for blending the notion of 'artistry' with informed teaching. Artistry has been defined as the process whereby teachers match the conditions for effective learning with those for effective teaching; students may be able to learn effectively without effective teaching, but if the two can be synchronized, the results are more likely to be guaranteed and more successful. Harris (1998) cites Rubin's (1985) definition of artistry, namely:

> There is a striking quality to fine classrooms. Pupils are caught up in learning; excitement abounds, and playfulness and seriousness blend easily because the purposes are clear, the goals sensible and an unmistakable feeling of well-being prevails. Artist teachers achieve these qualities by knowing both their subject matter and their students, and by guiding the learning with deft control. This control itself is born out of perception, intuition and creative impulse.

Artistry reminds us that teaching is a highly creative and personal activity. It speaks to the reality of teachers' lives in classrooms where spontaneity, capturing the moment and demonstrating flexibility and insight must all co-exist with sound planning and preparation. It involves the teacher in the classroom situation, bringing together multiple considerations to make intuitive, final decisions. These considerations include the particular characteristics of the students, the subject matter and informed teaching practices. Thus, informed teaching practices enhance rather than hinder artistry.

The most sophisticated level characterizing the re-designed school is reached when teachers make judicious and informed judgements about their selection of teaching methods after first taking into account the characteristics of their students as learners, the subject matter, their knowledge regarding the relative merits of different approaches to teaching, and the learning characteristics that the school is intending to develop in its students. When this situation is reached, artistry is combined with professionalism. At this point, teaching becomes a true profession.

In the following sections, attention is focused on 'informed practice' at three successive levels, working from the macro to the micro. These are models of teaching, teaching approaches and teaching skills and behaviours.

Models of Teaching

Charging the school with responsibility for developing different forms of learning characteristics in its students can form the basis of a desirable student outcome. At stake here are issues to do with the development of students as independent learners capable of learning on their own; as cooperative and collaborative learners, capable of learning as part of a team or group; and finally, as learners in a large group or class setting. A justification for this is not difficult: in adult life it is likely that students will encounter, and need to function effectively in, all three situations. Hence the school has a preparatory obligation in this respect.

Since the late 1980s, these issues have been investigated under the mantle of teaching models. Joyce and Weil (1996) describe 'models of teaching' as particular types of learning environment and approaches to teaching. Teaching models are concerned with the creation of different types of learning environment in order to extend student experiences and skills as learners. Their aim is to encourage teachers to adopt a wide repertoire of teaching approaches in order to develop in students different approaches to learning.

In a recent review (Joyce et al., 1997), four families of teaching models are recognized, together with research evidence on their effect sizes in producing learning. Each is based on the type of learning it promotes and on different orientations people may have to learning. Harris (1998: 177) summarizes the four families of teaching models as follows.

The information processing family

Information processing models develop students' capacity to organize data, to think conceptually and to generate and solve problems. Students may have to seek information themselves, or they may have to make sense of information given them. Students learn how to construct knowledge and to think creatively. Advance organizers and mnemonics belong to this family, both of which have demonstrated modest to substantial effect sizes.

The social family models of teaching

This family of models emphasizes the social context to learning. Teachers organize interactive settings for promoting learning, with the premium on working together in teams or groups. Cooperative relationships are valued and the individual is expected to learn through interaction with others as a team member. Cooperative learning approaches are examples of the social family models; their effect sizes range from modest to high. The more complex the intended outcomes, such as higher-order thinking, problem solving and social skills, the greater the effects.

Personal family models of teaching and learning

These models are predicated on individuals taking responsibility for their own learning, for discovering and developing themselves and for encouraging productive independence, leading to self-awareness and responsibility for their own destiny. Models from this family include non-directive teaching aimed at self-concept and student creativity.

Behavioural systems family of models of teaching and learning

This group of models relies on behavioural theories, where learning is considered to take place through feedback and adjustment. Models such as 'pause, prompt and praise' and 'stimulus and response' are examples. Direct instruction is a model from this family; it yields modest effect and has been shown to increase general aptitude to learn.

Evidence points to the conclusion that when the models are combined, rather than adopted individually or separately, in a practical school situation the quality of teaching improves, as does the potential for improving student learning (Joyce et al., 1997).

The Student-centred, Teacher-centred and Constructivism Debate

Recognition of the different models of teaching is of limited use unless we draw some valid conclusions from them regarding practice in the re-designed school. Building on the benefits of combining the models, as mentioned above, a further positive and fruitful outcome of the models of teaching is that debates between the relative merits of teacher-centred versus student-centred learning, and traditional teacher-mediated knowledge versus constructivism, become sterile and unhelpful. In short, students need to experience the range of these learning environments. This conclusion follows from the argument that there are at least three bases on which knowledge rests. First, students need the opportunity to develop their own thinking and to construct their own meanings; that is the essence of constructivism. Second, some knowledge is esoteric and specialized and for this, subject expert knowledge deserves recognition and respect; hence the important role for teachers with expert knowledge who can induct students into the intricacies of their subjects. Finally, knowledge is culture-bound; knowledge considered worthwhile in one society may not be so regarded in another. In this latter case, a society will filter what it considers valuable, worthwhile knowledge to distil into the curriculum.

Teaching Approaches

In this section, a number of approaches to teaching and learning are described. These are illustrative of the range of such approaches which have been shown to have demonstrated positive effects on student learning. Teaching 'approaches' are distinguishable from teaching 'behaviours' or 'skills' (discussed in the following section) in that they are sets of ideas and procedures which possess a degree of coherence and a rationale. They are broad pedagogical strategies which, in turn, embrace a number of individual teaching behaviours and skills in different combinations and with different emphases.

Four teaching approaches are singled out for focus in this section. The four are:

- mastery learning;

- direct instruction;
- cooperative learning;
- problem-based learning.

While not comprehensive, together they provide a cross-section of alternative approaches to teaching. Each has been sufficiently researched to provide reasonably good insights into what constitutes informed practice. In the confined space of this chapter, it is not the intention to provide an exhaustive account; rather, the purpose is to highlight a few of the major characteristics of each and to advocate its adoption as a basis for informed practice in the re-designed school. The key point is that for each of the approaches, specified procedures are recommended, often in a sequence. It is these procedures and sequences about which teachers need to be informed.

First, however, reference is made to the concept of adaptive education which overlays all of these approaches and provides a context for them.

Adaptive Education: The Context for a Range of Teaching Approaches

In contemporary thinking about the future direction of pedagogy and learning, there is a strong consensus of opinion on the need to cater for all students, whatever their ability, age, gender, race and ethnicity. Catering for all students entails, in effect, catering for their individual differences. Two conclusions result from this: first, schooling becomes more individualized (this does not necessarily mean that each student follows a different curriculum and relies on individual attention from the teacher); and second, that teaching and curricula are more flexible and accommodating of the different abilities and needs of students. These two phenomena are captured in the concept of adaptive education.

Wang (1992: 3–4), a leading advocate of adaptive education, defines the concept as:

> providing learning experiences that help each student achieve desired educational goals. The term 'adaptive' refers to the modification of school learning environments to respond effectively to student differences and to enhance the individual's ability to succeed in learning in such environments.

She goes on to deny the misconceptions held by some critics of the concept, that it relies solely on individualized planning and excludes group-based instruction:

> The adaptive education approaches utilize group-based instruction, as well as individual tutoring, problem solving and exploratory learning

processes .... Group lessons are included among a variety of instructional delivery and management strategies to develop academic and social skills among students who differ in multiple dimensions .... In fact, by definition, effective implementation of the adaptive education approach mandates the incorporation of a variety of instructional methods that provide learning experiences matched to individual characteristics, talents, interests, and knowledge.

(Wang, 1992: 3–40)

The variety of alternative instructional strategies and curricular options thus includes teacher-directed lessons, individualized approaches and cooperative learning. A variety of approaches is needed to meet the diversity of student needs, learning styles, abilities and interests. Underpinning the concept is the belief that pedagogy and curriculum need to be flexible to accommodate student difference, rather than students accommodating to a standardized approach to curriculum and instruction.

Mastery Learning

Mastery learning owes its origins to the work of Benjamin Bloom (1968, 1976). The approach has also been developed by Block and Anderson (1975), Block et al. (1989) and Thomas Guskey (1985, 1995). It also forms the basis of Spady's (1988) approach to outcome-based education.

Mastery learning, like other teaching approaches, is underpinned by a fundamental assumption, that all students have the ability to learn if teachers adhere to certain basic principles. Traditionally, educators believed that a spread of ability would manifest itself in learning differences. On this assumption, teachers used normative assessment and normal curves of distribution to obtain a range of student performance. Some students quickly master the material to be learned, while others are much slower and some may never achieve mastery. This practice was endorsed by the prevailing view of the function of education, namely, to select and classify students in preparation for the labour force. The idea that all are capable of learning is therefore quite radical.

It was Carroll (1963) who challenged the idea that student aptitude determined the level to which a student could learn a subject. His major contribution was that all students have the potential to learn if given enough time. Bloom combined this idea with structure, units and time variance to develop the Mastery Learning Model. More than this, however, Bloom reckoned on the cognitive and affective importance that early learning experiences had on subsequent learning. If students consistently succeeded in learning, they developed positive self-concepts as learners which stood them in good stead for subsequent learning. Equally, if they consistently failed, they developed negative self-concepts as learners, which held them back. Bloom believed that by giving students the time they needed and appropriate quality of instruction, especially in their formative period as learners, they would develop strong positive attitudes towards learning.

Mastery learning involves dividing the content of a course into units, each of which represents one or two weeks of work. The material is then taught, a stage in the process which deserves more importance than is typically recognized. In the context of more individualized, adaptive approaches, the teacher is advised to adopt a range of strategies in order to extend students' learning capacities and to appeal to students with different learning styles. Some interpretations of mastery learning, however, emphasize and advocate heavy reliance on direct teaching, but this does not necessarily have to be so.

The next stage is to administer a formative test, the purpose of which is to give immediate feedback to both students and teacher. Those students who mastered the material (often defined or measured by a minimum percentage grade, such as 80 per cent) are offered enrichment activities or are expected to serve as peer tutors. Those students who failed to achieve mastery are assigned corrective activities. When students have completed corrective and enrichment activities, they are given a summative test, which assigns them a grade or assesses their competence in a skill.

A central aspect of mastery learning is the need for considerable planning and preparation on the part of the teacher both before and during delivery and implementation of the curriculum unit. The sequence of planning and preparatory stages is set out in Figure 7.1. Each stage is described in more detail below (Bechtol and Sorenson, 1993: 118–19).

1   *Divide the curriculum into sections.* Instructional units of one or two weeks are formed, each with clear objectives or outcomes detailing the content or skill to be learned. What students must be able to do and the level of proficiency expected are clearly expressed.
2   *Construct formative tests.* Test items are constructed for each objective or outcome and then arranged in a formative test. Standards expected for mastery need to be determined. A second formative test needs to be devised for those who failed to achieve mastery in the first test.
3   *Implement instructional strategies to enable students to achieve the outcomes or objectives.* There are many interpretations as to how the instructional delivery phases of mastery learning should be conducted. Whole-class direct teaching is often emphasized, but many variations are possible. What are appropriate teaching strategies, in keeping with the concept of informed teaching and adaptive education, would depend on the teacher's consideration of the students' abilities and learning characteristics, the outcomes to be achieved and the resources available. Emphasis is placed on providing practical activities and exercises for students. These should reflect, firstly, the skills and knowledge

embedded in each outcome or objective and secondly, if appropriate, the overall set of outcomes taken together.

4   *Corrective activities.* These need to be planned and prepared for those who fail to achieve mastery on the first formative test. Essentially, they should cover the same material as before but by using different teaching approaches, since the original instructional strategies had not resulted in the desired level of achievement. It might also be the case that more time is needed to learn the material. It is particularly important to match the instructional strategy and learning mode with the students' learning styles. Hence, different techniques from the first round might include using peer or volunteer tutors, computer-assisted instruction, more individualized tutoring, or different textbooks or materials. The main aim is to boost the students' confidence and to prepare them to achieve the learning outcomes required.

5   *Enrichment activities.* These are provided to students who have already demonstrated mastery in the first round, by offering them a limited list of choices. It is essential that they be seen as a reward rather than more of the same thing. They should be interesting, exciting and challenging in raising students to higher-level cognitive skills. Appropriate activities might include peer tutoring, problem-solving, developing materials such as games and models for other students, projects and reports, and computer-assisted learning assignments.

6   *A summative test.* The purpose of this examination is to gather cumulative information on students' learning so that grades can be assigned or competence in a set of skills determined, usually for the units of curriculum covered to date.

Some critics of mastery learning focus on the incidence and frequency of the testing, arguing firstly that it consumes excessive time, and secondly that not all of the objectives and outcomes desired can be captured in the tests. In rebutting these points, it can be argued that frequent testing has been shown to be effective in producing learning, providing that teachers give ample positive feedback and reinforcement. It is the teachers' responsibility to contain the amount of time devoted to testing. In addition, the extra time – usually between one and three days – given to students to learn the material through corrective feedback, and the enrichment time given to those who learn faster, has strong appeal.

Some criticize the mastery learning sequence as too structured. The process, however, does not necessarily have to be wholly teacher-centred and behaviouristic, especially during the instructional sections – the initial phase and the subsequent corrective and enrichment phases – where there is wide scope for the full range of teaching approaches, including those which are more student-centred. Although the effectiveness of mastery learning has been disputed, in general, the results are quite positive, especially for

Figure 7.1 *The Mastery Learning Sequence*

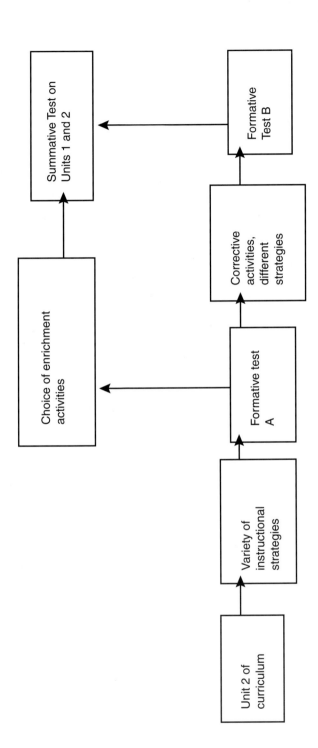

Unit 2 of curriculum

Variety of instructional strategies

Formative test A

Corrective activities, different strategies

Formative Test B

Choice of enrichment activities

Summative Test on Units 1 and 2

low achievers, who seem to benefit from more structured and guided learning strategies (see reviews by Block et al., 1989; Good and Brophy, 1991).

Direct Teaching

Direct teaching has been the most common teaching approach advocated over the past few decades. It is a structured, sequenced approach based on behaviourist learning theories. When followed and faithfully practised, it is highly effective in promoting learning. Misconceptions commonly arise, however, and many proponents claim to be practising direct teaching when they are in fact lecturing.

The direct teach model, a version of direct teaching attributed to Madeleine Hunter (1982), is well planned, systematic and intensive (Bechtol and Sorenson, 1993). It allows the teacher to receive immediate feedback during the lesson, enabling corrective changes to be made to increase student learning. Instructional and curriculum materials can be adjusted to allow for individual student differences. A key aspect of the approach is its highly efficient use of instructional time and engaged time on task.

The model requires teachers to use clear instructional objectives which centre on student outcomes. Clear instructional objectives contain three elements:

1   the behaviour the learner is to achieve is stated;
2   the conditions under which learning is to occur, are given ... for example, the materials or information the learner will be given;
3   the criterion for acceptable performance is specified (for example, 80 per cent or more correctly answered).

Bechtol and Sorenson (1993: 106) provide the following example of an objective for direct teaching:

> Given ten multiple choice questions about the Direct Teach Model, the learner will answer eight correctly.
>
> The behaviour in the objective is 'answer'. The conditions are 'given ten multiple choice questions about the Direct Teach Model'. The criterion is 80 per cent or higher.
>
> Having clear objectives enables instruction to be guided towards the desired outcome.

In explaining the Direct Teach Model further, Bechtol and Sorenson divide the process into three stages: the focus stage, the teach stage and the practice stage.

The focus stage. The main purpose of this stage is to focus the attention of the students on the learning task at hand. This is achieved by invoking three devices, in any sequence which is deemed appropriate:

- an anticipatory set;
- explaining the lesson objectives to the students;
- justifying the purpose of the learning.

Anticipatory sets gear the students into the lesson by first, getting their active participation in the lesson; second, linking with past knowledge; and third, imparting relevance by relating the content to the background of the learners.

Explanation of lesson objectives is likely to gain student commitment and effort. Without knowing what the objective is, it is unrealistic to expect students to give their commitment. Students cannot be expected to guess the objective. Likewise, wherever possible the purpose of the lesson should be justified to students, preferably by linking with relevance to their lives and how they might benefit from the knowledge. When the students are focused, the teacher can move to the teach stage.

The teach stage. Three elements constitute this basic part of direct teaching: the teacher provides:

- input of information;
- models the information or process;
- checks for student understanding.

The teacher can provide input of information by lecturing, audio-visual presentation and demonstration. Basic or essential information has to be selected and presented as simply and clearly as possible. Material should be organized in small steps, going from simple to more complex. Advance organizers, such as note-taking guides, are helpful.

Modeling is a key part of the teach stage. Models may be physical reconstructions, pictures or diagrams, or verbal or written, such as good examples of previous essays. They must highlight the critical attributes of the phenomena to be learnt: for example, the characteristics of a triangle and what distinguishes it from other shapes. Non-exemplars are introduced so that the student can contrast with the examplars. The sequence by which this is accomplished is important, however, and is set out below:

1 the model is presented and critical attributes identified;
2 more examples are given with the teacher and then students identifying the critical attributes;
3 the teacher introduces non-exemplars and has the students contrast exemplars and non-exemplars.

Imparting meaning is the essence of this part of the lesson.

The third part of the teach stage is checking understanding. This allows the teacher to adjust the lesson as it proceeds so that students understand. Student understanding can be elicited by signals (thumbs up if they understand and vice versa), by group response and by questioning the whole class and selecting individuals to respond. Good questioning technique is important. The stages of good questioning technique are as follows:

1   ask the question;
2   pause to give students time to think;
3   then name a student to answer;
4   praise the student if the correct answer is forthcoming, or stick with the student and help them if they have difficulty answering.

It is no use teachers asking the class if they understand, or using OK?, or asking, 'Does anyone have a question?' Students are unlikely to speak up.

The practice stage. Guided practice is vital to achieving expected standards of outcomes. Hunter (1982) suggests four principles of good practice:

1   short meaningful amounts of content or skill to avoid overload;
2   intensity over short time spans;
3   practice new learning regularly, older material less so;
4   teachers provide feedback initially, then students self-evaluate.

For guided practice, Hunter (1982) advises teachers to do as follows:

1   guide the group through each step;
2   monitor group responses and give feedback;
3   sample group understanding through individuals' responses;
4   monitor individuals' written responses.

Every lesson should finish with a summary, where students think about the main points of the lesson. Teachers can first model the summarizing process and then later ask students to take over the role.

Direct teaching provides a strong illustration of the main point of this chapter. Correctly applied and to gain maximum effect, direct teaching involves the practice of a number of sequenced procedures. Informed teaching is thus predicated on teachers knowing and applying these practices.

Cooperative Learning

In many schools around the world, the traditional teaching format of passive class listening to teacher and students engaged in competition with each other, has given way to more cooperative forms of learning with students working together. However, in the same way as many teachers confuse lecturing with direct teaching, so many mistakenly consider group work to be cooperative learning.

Bechtol and Sorenson (1993) give three reasons for the widespread take-up of cooperative learning. First, it is effective in promoting student learning; second, it mirrors the real world of work, where there is an increasing need for people to problem-solve together; and third, it meshes with contemporary curricular and structural changes emphasising higher-order thinking skills, learning for understanding and the push to make schools responsive to student diversity by promoting more democratic and collaborative ways of learning.

There is strong research evidence to confirm the efficacy of the approach. Slavin (1990, 1991) has shown that student academic achievement increases especially when group goals and individual accountability are incorporated in the cooperative methods. Other achievements are particularly enhanced, such as promotion of friendship choices, increased social interaction among students of different races and abilities, and greater acceptance of handicapped students by mainstream students. Affective outcomes also improve, including self-esteem, academic self-confidence and social cooperation. It also appears that these benefits apply to students across the ability range.

There is no doubting the need for people to have high capacity for cooperation in all walks of life. Successful work lives, family lives and friendships are dependent on it (Johnson and Johnson, 1985). Cooperative learning also reinforces three current curriculum themes with an emphasis on active learning, higher-order thinking skills and learning for understanding. The approach is also in line with two organizational developments: heterogeneous grouping and environmental responsiveness to student diversity. Cooperative learning provides a context for promoting democratic citizenship by enabling students to gain confidence, independence and responsibility.

A hallmark of cooperative learning that distinguishes it from group work is that all students in a team or group are involved in making a contribution. Typically, a problem with group work is that some students 'ride on the backs of others' and take equal credit. Vasquez et al. (1990) identify three structural features of cooperative learning:

1 *positive interdependence*: tasks are structured so that each student makes a contribution to the success of the group effort, and students help one another learn.
2 *individual accountability*: each student has objectives to master the material and to be held accountable for that, and thus students cannot hide.
3 *social skills*: students are taught interpersonal and group skills to foster communication, give and accept support and to solve conflicts.

Most cooperative learning procedures involve breaking the class into groups of four or five, and assigning tasks to each group member, each of whom then reports back to the group. The group collectively renders a response in the form of a public/private oral/written report for a collective grade. Peer pressure to perform should be strong. Skills involve gathering information, making sense of it, interacting with others and developing a joint product.

Three well-known versions of cooperative learning are described by Slavin (1990) and summarized by Bechtol and Sorenson (1993) as follows:

Jigsaw

Students are placed in groups, which are given a problem to solve or a question to address. Each student in a group is prescribed a specific task, for example, some reading. Then students with the same readings from different groups form new 'expert groups', where they spend time sharing and honing their knowledge with each other. Then they return to their regular groups and take turns to teach their group members. Peer teaching is the only way their fellow group members will learn the material outside their own briefs. Quizzes are sometimes given to test the knowledge of individual students.

Learning Together

Johnson and Johnson (1985) formulated a procedure whereby students in heterogeneous groups of four or five study materials on a controversial issue. Two group members take one side of the issue, and two take the other. Then they switch roles and argue the other side. Finally, the group comes to a consensus. In the process, students learn to criticize ideas, not people, and to have a group rather than individual purpose. This has been shown to result in more learning, greater retention of information and greater attitude change than typically results from debate or individual study.

Student Teams-Achievement Divisions (STAD)

STAD is built on five components: class presentations, teams, quizzes, individual improvement scores and team recognition. Class presentations are mostly undertaken by the teacher. Teams are four or five students who represent a cross-section of the class by ability, gender, race and ethnicity. The teams study notes, attend to the teacher and to other materials. Quizzes are given after one or two periods of teacher presentation and one or two periods of team practice. Students answer the quizzes individually so that every student is accountable for mastering the material. Individual improvement scores give each student a goal to achieve and to work for. The students are awarded points for their teams if they exceed their individual base scores. Team recognition is based on team members' improvement scores, and rewards are usually provided for good team performances.

Problem-Based Learning (PBL)

Recent developments in cognitive research have induced many teachers to adopt PBL as a strategy for part of a course, or even all of it. Certain features and procedures central to the approach, as outlined below, constitute a knowledge base for informed teaching. Bridges and Hallinger (1992) recognize five features of PBL: (1) a problem is the starting point for learning; (2) the best problems conform to the real world; (3) knowledge is organized around problems rather than disciplines; (4) students, individually and collectively, assume more responsibility for their own instruction and learning; and (5) learning takes place in small groups rather than through direct teaching.

First, a problem is the starting point for learning. Traditional approaches to teaching and learning begin with the transmission and acquisition of knowledge, after which the student might be expected to apply the knowledge to solve problems. PBL advocates argue that this is not what happens in the real world, where people are first confronted by problems and then search for solutions by applying knowledge which is either already possessed or which needs to be acquired. PBL is thus a better replication of the real world than the traditional paradigms of curriculum, teaching and learning.

It follows that the nature of the problems around which learning is constructed is vitally important. Teachers should formulate problems which are as realistic as possible. This often means that they are complex, involving many different aspects, a feature which lends itself to an integrated approach to the curriculum. The problem(s) should arouse the interest of students and be meaningful to them. For example, issues, dramas and disasters related to adventure, the outdoors and the environment are usually guaranteed to capture attention.

Second, knowledge is organized around the problem rather than around disciplines. Knowledge is selected for relevance according to its capacity to inform the problem. The sequence of stages involves clarifying the problem, searching for, acquiring and making sense of information which is relevant to the problem, thinking reflectively and creatively about possible solutions and choosing the best from among alternatives. Knowledge based on the disciplines might still be appropriate, especially where the problem is best tackled by a multi-disciplinary approach. The key point, however, is that the process begins with a problem and resort may be made to the disciplines as a means of informing and solving the problem. The teacher has a responsibility to structure the whole exercise into tasks, so that the students are provided with a framework.

Third, the nature of the learning objectives can be broad, encompassing both cognitive and affective domains. Problems can be couched in ways which engage ethical and moral issues while still demanding substantive subject knowledge to be learnt. Developing students' conceptual and analytical skills are central objectives, as is the ability to work both independently and collaboratively. In this respect, a premium is placed on skills related to communication and conflict resolution.

Fourth, teachers need to plan and prepare appropriate learning materials and access to appropriate information. The teacher plays a key role as facilitator, resource provider and creator of learning opportunities to assist the students to collect and analyse the appropriate material. This may entail access to library and computer materials, the provision of references and readings, the supply of video and audio materials, field work exercises and class notes.

Fifth, teaching–learning strategies may involve a range of approaches, including direct teaching, but the main vehicle is usually group work in the form of cooperative learning. The process should contain a rich blend of problem solving, self-directed and team-directed learning, cooperative learning, personal reflection and multi-media presentations. Throughout the process, the aim is to encourage students to take more responsibility for their own learning and to promote active rather than inert knowledge.

Finally, assessment outcomes and products differ from the conventional. In keeping with cooperative learning, both individual and group assessment and accountability are stressed. Thus individual students, as well as the groups to which they belong, are expected to produce assessable work. Assessment might also encompass oral presentations as well as written assignments, and might be more imaginative than the traditional essay.

As is the case for all informed teaching approaches, informed PBL teaching is predicated on teacher familiarity with the esoteric procedures and practices which underpin the approach, and the sequence in which to apply them.

Teaching Knowledge, Behaviours and Skills

Informed teaching involves more than a conceptual and practical grasp of broad strategies and approaches. Specific behaviours and skills are necessary in combination with the various approaches for teaching to be effective. These behaviours and skills have been identified by meta-analyses, incorporating the results of many individual studies (Fraser et al., 1987; Porter and Brophy, 1988). This concern for and interest in research as the guide to practice yields many benefits. It provides a more sound footing for innovation and practice than trial and error, intuition, subjective opinion or simply following practices in other schools. It is likely to reduce the risk element in any innovatory situation, since effects may have already been documented in sampled schools. Informed teaching practices need to be grounded in the research findings on effective teaching and learning.

In this section, reference is made to three studies: Shulman's emphasis on teachers' content knowledge and pedagogy, meta-analysis identifying teacher behaviours and their effect sizes on learning (Fraser et al., 1987), and the different behaviours exhibited by expert and novice teachers.

Shulman's Combination of Subject Matter and Pedagogy

Throughout the 1970s and 1980s attention focused on generic principles and methods of effective teaching, and for the most part researchers ignored the importance of content knowledge. However, in the late 1980s Lee Shulman (1986, 1987, 1991) argued the case that teachers' knowledge of subject matter was important for successful teaching. Coining the phrase 'pedagogical content knowledge', Shulman sparked a new wave of thinking. Accordingly, the 1990s has seen a shift in interest to specialized content-based methods courses, where issues of subject matter and teaching are seen as interdependent.

In Shulman's theoretical framework, teachers need to master two types of knowledge: first, content, or 'deep' knowledge of the subject itself, and second, knowledge of curricular development. Content knowledge includes what Bruner called the 'structure of knowledge', that is, the theories, principles and concepts of a particular discipline. Of particular importance is content knowledge that relates to the teaching process, especially the forms of representing and communicating content and how students best learn the specific concepts and topics of a subject. In short, as Ornstein (1995: 445) says:

> the teachers' orientation to their subject matter influences their method of planning, their choice of content, the way they use textbooks, the supplementary materials they use, their pedagogical strategies, and their perceptions of students' instructional needs. Likewise, it determines the way the teacher formulates, demonstrates, and explains the subject so that it is comprehensible to learners.

The relevance of Shulman's contribution to informed teaching is that subject-matter content cannot be divorced from pedagogy. From the school design viewpoint and in the pursuit of quality teaching, it is necessary to factor in strong subject content knowledge. Exclusive focus on pedagogical skills yields a partial and incomplete explanation of what makes for quality teaching, primarily because informed teaching practice is founded on the interdependence of content knowledge and teaching methods.

Effects of Teaching Behaviours and Skills on Learning

A meta-analysis conducted by Fraser et al. (1987) attempted to measure the effects of instructional quality and time on learning. The indicators of instructional quality mainly consisted of teaching behaviours and skills. Their findings are set out in Table 7.1.

Topping the list of effect sizes was reinforcement or reward for correct performance. Also near the top, in fourth place, was instructional cues, engagement and corrective feedback. Both of these are regarded as Skinnerian or behaviouristic in orientation, and both are essential components of mastery learning. The conclusion to be drawn is that teachers cannot give too much praise where it is due, or too much detailed feedback pointing out where and how students' work could be improved. Second on the list is acceleration programmes for academically gifted students, while third is reading training, where students are coached in the different skills of skimming, comprehension and seeking answers to questions.

Other major effects (defined as 0.3 and above) include teaching approaches such as cooperative learning (0.76), personalized (0.57) and adaptive instruction (0.45), tutoring (0. 40) and individualized instruction (0.32). Asking higher order questions (0.34) also has a significant effect.

The setting of graded homework has a very large effect size (0.79), especially when compared with assigned homework (0.28). Graded homework is closely integrated with class work and is structured; it has clear purposes and dates for handing in, and is evaluated and commented on in detail by

Table 7.1 *Effects of Instructional Quality and Time on Learning*

Method/Behaviour	*Effect Size*
Reinforcement	1.17
Acceleration	1.00
Reading training	0.97
Cues and feedback	0.97
Graded homework	0.79
Cooperative learning	0.76
Personalized instruction	0.57
Adaptive instruction	0.45
Tutoring	0.40
Higher order questions	0.34
Diagnostic prescription	0.33
Individualized prescription	0.32
Assigned homework	0.28
Advanced organizers	0.23

Source: adapted from Fraser et al. (1987).

the teacher, who returns it quickly to the students. Assigned homework, by contrast, is often set by the teacher because it is expected, and lacks most of the rigour associated with graded homework. The difference between the two in effect size is appreciable and suggests that if homework is set, it should be of the graded kind.

Instructional time has a moderate effect on learning (0.40). Time appears to be a necessary ingredient, but is not sufficient by itself to produce learning.

An important conclusion is that learning is responsive to several behaviours and factors in concert. That being so, informed teachers take careful note of research evidence and will plan to adopt and integrate as many of these techniques and behaviours as possible into their teaching practice.

Expert Versus Novice Teacher Behaviour and Skills

Although the terms 'expert' and 'novice' lack appeal, many researchers use them for want of better alternatives. This avenue of research compares experienced and successful teachers with the inexperienced and less successful. That is not to say that all experienced teachers are expert, or that all inexperienced teachers are novice. Research evidence suggests that the thinking and decision making of expert and novice teachers differ in all three stages – before, during and after teaching (Westerman, 1991). Differences are found in three areas in particular: integration of knowledge, student behaviour and interaction in the three stages of decision making.

In Westerman's (1991) study, the expert teachers thought about learning from the student's perspective and performed a cognitive analysis of each learning task during planning, which they subsequently adapted to the needs of students during teaching. In contrast, the novice teachers used specific lesson objectives to form structured lesson plans that they did not adapt to meet student needs during teaching. Effective teachers had developed expertise in both pedagogical and content knowledge and successfully blended the two. The expert teachers were more confident in reaching the goals in their own more flexible ways. The novice teachers lacked appreciation of the integration of knowledge; that is, how one part of the course related to other parts. They also experienced more difficulty handling student behaviour. Whereas the expert teachers exerted a range of strategies to minimize off-task behaviour of students, allowing maximum time on task, the novice teachers found it more difficult to manage student classroom behaviour which then took more of their time. In short, expert teachers seem to possess a wider range of abilities which they adapt and use flexibly, according to the needs of particular classroom situations. These competencies allow them to focus more time and effort on the higher order aspects of learning rather than on classroom behaviour and lower order teaching–learning behaviours.

In setting out the contrasting behaviours exhibited between the two types of teacher, Westerman's study offers specific guidance as to what teachers need to do in order to improve. Informed teachers apply the 'expert' teacher behaviours.

A Cross-Cultural Perspective on Teaching

A central theme of this book is the need to take cognisance of, and conversely, the danger of underestimating, the importance of societal culture when ideas, policies and practices are transplanted from one system to another. This issue is particularly apposite at present with the proliferation of debates about the relative merits of so-called high performing school systems in Confucian-heritage societies in comparison with their Western counterparts. Indeed, as we head into the next millennium, a new phenomenon is beginning to emerge: many Asian educators and policy makers are looking to the West for ideas on which to base their future school designs; at the same time, many of their Western counterparts are looking towards the East for similar inspiration. Each is driven by different motives.

The collapse of the Asian economic 'miracle' from 1997 onwards affected many of the countries which have topped the International Achievement Tests in mathematics and science, namely, Singapore, Japan, Taiwan, Korea and Hong Kong. This turn of events has forced a realization that their futures increasingly depend on workforces with skills based on technology, information and creativity, skills and abilities which have not been sufficiently emphasized in the past. Western countries, on the other hand, are increasingly concerned about the continued failure of their students to match the performance of their Asian counterparts on the international tests. As each looks towards the other, the likelihood that comparisons might be ill-informed and superficial, failing to appreciate deep-seated cultural differences and to contextualize each country's practices within its unique culture, is very real.

Indeed, the tendency to polarize discussion between Asian and Western is itself a gross over-generalization that tends to distort any meaningful comparison. Significant variations, for example, are found within both the Confucian-heritage cultures and Western cultures. Japan and Hong Kong have very different cultures and have education systems which reflect these differences. The same is true for the USA and UK. Such diversity has two effects. First, it obliges us to be more specific when choosing examples. Second, it suggests the need for a set of cultural dimensions to act as a universal benchmark against which all cultures can be gauged and then compared.

In fact, as presented in Chapter 3, Hofstede (1980, 1991) has generated a set of universally recognized societal cultural dimensions. Although these dimensions are today seen to have limitations (the data are increasingly dated and cultures change, albeit slowly; in addition, the data were confined to IBM employees in 53 countries), Hofstede was able to generate cultural dimensions and to suggest how these related, *inter alia*, to education and schooling. This section begins by noting some of Hofstede's conclusions in relation to teaching and learning in different cultures. It then moves on to look at other research evidence relating to cross-cultural differences as they affect teaching and learning.

Hofstede's Cultural Dimensions and their Implications for Teaching and Learning

An explanation of Hofstede's (1980, 1991) five cultural dimensions is given in Chapter 3. However, some repetition is justified at this point. According to his first dimension – power distance (PD) – most Asian societies, including Hong Kong, are high. That is, they have an unequal distribution of power, most of which is concentrated in the hands of a few. Inequalities of power distribution are expected and accepted in the family, in school and in the workplace. Thus in the home, children are educated towards obedience to parents, whose authority is rarely questioned. In school, teachers are respected, learning is conceived as passed on by the wisdom of the teacher and teacher-centred methods tend to be employed. By contrast, families in low PD societies encourage children to have a will of their own and to treat parents as equals. In school, more student-centred methods are used, teachers enjoy less respect and learning is viewed as impersonalized truth.

According to Hofstede's second dimension – individualism–collectivism – most Western societies are individualist whereas most Asian societies are collectivist. In individualist societies, people are driven by an 'I' consciousness and obligations to the self, including self-interest, self-actualization and self-guilt. In the school, emphasis is placed on permanent education and learning how to learn. Thus lifelong learning fits the individualist culture. In the workplace, values tend to be applied universally to all, other people are seen as potential resources, tasks prevail over relationships, and the employer-employee relationship is described as 'calculative'. In collectivist societies, by contrast, family members are brought up with a 'we' consciousness, opinions are predetermined by the group, and strong obligations to the family emphasize harmony, respect and shame. At school, learning is viewed as an activity primarily for the young (hence lifelong learning is not valued), and focuses on how to do things and on factual knowledge; and at the work place, value standards differ for in-group and out-groups, relationship prevails over task and employer–employee relationships have a moral basis.

On Hofstede's third dimension – masculinity–femininity – there is much less of a divide between Western and Asian societies. Most Asian and Anglo-American societies veer towards the masculine end of the spectrum. In more masculine or competitive societies, family values stress achievement, competition and resolution of conflict by power and assertiveness; at school, norms are set by the best students, the system rewards academic achievement and failure at school is seen as serious; and in the workplace, assertiveness is taken as a virtue; selling oneself, decisiveness and emphasis on career are all valued. By contrast, in feminine societies the family places emphasis on relationship, solidarity and resolution of conflicts by compromise and negotiation; at school, norms tend to be set by the average students, system rewards reflect students' social adaptation and failure at school is taken as merely unfortunate; and in the workplace, assertiveness is not appreciated, people are expected to undersell themselves, and emphasis is placed on quality of life and intuition.

In the case of Hofstede's fourth dimension – uncertainty avoidance (UA) – most Asian and Western societies rank low. The validity of this dimension for education is questionable. By the nature of their task, schools are organizations where abundant rules and regulations are necessary, a generic characteristic which seems to cut across even the sharpest of differences in societal culture. This presents a contradiction: schools displaying characteristics of high uncertainty in societies which may be classified as low uncertainty. Such is the case, for example, with Hong Kong.

Finally, in the case of the fifth dimension – long term–short term – Chinese societies rank extremely high on long-term orientation compared with Anglo-American societies. It can be posited that cultures with a long-term orientation are more conducive to academic achievement, since students are more likely to forego short term pleasures and gains for the benefits that eventually follow from study.

In spite of the acknowledged shortcomings of Hofstede's work, it has highlighted significant differences between societies in their attitudes towards education. Although some of these differences are measured by degrees, they are still noteworthy. Cultural connections between the family, home and workplace are central to Hofstede's argument, and this seems an important feature. For example, in small power distance societies, such as the USA, UK and Australia, children are brought up to have a will of their own and parents are accorded less respect; this lack of respect is repeated for teachers in schools, and as a reflection of the culture, student-centred methods are more prominent; in regard to the school as a workplace, teachers expect to be consulted in a more democratic milieu and hierarchy is seen as expedient. By contrast, in large power distance societies, such as those of East Asia, children are educated towards obedience to parents, who are treated as superiors; this spills over into school, where teachers are accorded more respect, teacher-centred methods prevail, and the teachers' role is to pass on their knowledge to the young. In the school, hierarchical relationships and autocracy are accepted as natural and teachers expect to be told what to do.

While the above analysis may still hold in general, societal cultures are dynamic, fluid and changing. For example, many of the Asian cultures are increasingly permeated by elements of Western culture, brought about by the electronic media, education and increased travel opportunities. Visitors to schools in Hong Kong, for example, might be surprised by the unruly behaviour of many children and the lack of respect for teachers, especially in those schools whose intakes are of lower ability. Moreover, generational gaps are increasingly conspicuous; the older members of Hong Kong society are staunchly Chinese in their values and customs, while the younger generations are a complex mix of traditional Chinese and more recently grafted Western culture. In the West, too, societal cultures are becoming more difficult to distinguish as the USA, UK and Australia become even more multicultural than they have been hitherto. In these latter countries, multiculturalism enters the school and classroom, presenting principals and teachers with difficult challenges.

Similar analyses apply to the other Hofstede dimensions. For example, the mainly individualist societies of the USA, UK and Australia contrast with the mainly collectivist societies of Asia and reflect differences for teachers, students and their relationships. Asian teachers and students are more inclined to reference their motives and behaviours to the family and group context. They are relationship oriented, so that harmony, respect and shame are accorded importance. An instrumentalist view of education is taken – people learn how 'to do' for a purpose – and education is seen as a service for the young. In contrast, Western cultures are inclined to be more task-oriented; relationships are treated as calculative and useful for functional and task purposes; individuals act more on the basis of self-interest, and there is a growing tendency to see the process of learning over a lifetime as important in enabling individualism.

Cross-cultural Differences and Teaching: Research Evidence

Recent research has begun to challenge the stereotypical image Westerners have of Asian teachers and students (Biggs, 1994; Stevenson and Stigler, 1992). Major differences between teachers in America and China, Taiwan and Japan have been explicated by Stevenson and Stigler (1992), who conducted research in scores of elementary classrooms in these countries from 1980 onwards. It is necessary to point out that their research applies only to primary schools, and that there are major differences within and between Asian and Western countries. Below is a summary of their conclusions:

1   Asian teachers have significantly fewer class contact hours than their Western counterparts. In Japan and Taiwan, teachers teach about 60 per cent of the lesson time. In China, a teacher might only teach three or four hours each day. This allows them to plan lessons more carefully, spend more time seeing students who need help, and to discuss teaching techniques with their colleagues. This is not the practice, however, throughout Asia; Hong Kong teachers have class contact hours similar to Western teachers, often amounting to 90 per cent of the lesson time.

2   Asian teachers spend more time working together and helping each other design lessons. This is facilitated by firstly, the existence of a national curriculum, which means that they are often teaching the same material at about the same time, and secondly, their close proximity in the same work room. American teachers, by contrast, lack the time and incentive to engage in such collaboration; they are often following different curricula, they lack the preparation time and their work rooms are often spread out across the school.

3   Primary school teachers in Asia are not expected to be expert in a number of subjects. Whereas elementary teachers in the USA are expected to teach across subjects (specialist teaching normally starts at the secondary level), this is not so in Asian primary schools. This, together with the fact that Asian teachers can prepare their lessons during their free periods rather then in the evenings when they are tired, as their Western counterparts have to do, explains why East Asian teachers tend to do their jobs remarkably well.

4   Asian teachers come closer to practising the principles of informed teaching than do their American counterparts. In general, they are well informed and well prepared, guiding their students through the material. Lessons are clearly structured: each lesson starts with a purpose and finishes with a summary. During the lesson, there is interaction and discussion and students are active participants in problem solving.

5   The technical superiority of Asian teachers is one factor in explaining why Asian students concentrate and pay attention for an average of 80 per cent of the time in class compared to American students' 60 per cent. A further reason is that the school day in Asia tends to be punctuated by shorter but more frequent rest and recreation periods; thus students do not have to study for such long continuous periods as in the West.

6   Asian children have more opportunity to interact with their teachers than do American students. US teachers structure their lessons so that they teach concepts during the first part, and then require students to undertake seatwork (that is, work at their desks) in the second part. Asian teachers, however, intersperse seatwork in brief periods throughout the lesson. Seatwork is used as a practice for the skill or

knowledge just learned, and affords diagnosis and early corrective feedback if the student demonstrates a lack of understanding.

7   Asian teachers are observed to give far more corrective feedback than their American counterparts and this serves to motivate the students. In addition, Asian teachers are more inclined to make use of concrete objects and other devices that children find enhance their learning.

8   Asian teachers are more likely to make subjects more relevant and interesting by relating material to be learned to the children's everyday lives. In mathematics, word problems often serve this function, turning the lesson into an active problem-solving exercise.

9   When Beijing teachers were asked to rank the most important attributes of good teaching, they ranked 'clarity' first, whereas Chicago teachers ranked in first place 'sensitivity to the needs of individuals'. Beijing teachers ranked 'enthusiasm' second, while Chicago teachers chose 'patience'. These results suggest that American teachers see their main role as catering to the needs of individual children at the expense of whole class teaching, while Asian teachers devote their attention to the principles and processes of whole class teaching, while still acknowledging the needs of individual children.

10 Asian teachers tend to stick to the well-known principles of teaching, and have more time and energy to apply them. They incorporate a variety of teaching techniques into a lesson, rely more frequently on discussions rather than lectures, achieve smooth transitions from one activity to another and spend more time on task.

Many of these conclusions sit uncomfortably with the cherished beliefs and stereotypes held by Western educators about Asian education. They also pose challenges for comparisons between East and West. On the surface, there seem to be many contradictions between what we see and believe, and what results and outcomes appear to be indicating. A valid explanation of reality may therefore be much more complex than we have hitherto been willing to acknowledge or accept. In mounting such a complex explanation, it is instructive to turn to the work of Biggs (1994).

The core problem is summarized by Biggs (1994) as follows: there is a high degree of consensus about what constitutes conditions for good teaching and learning (indeed, this is one of the main themes of this present book); yet, if these conditions were to apply in Asian contexts such as Hong Kong, the results would be poor. However, as we know, students from Confucian-heritage cultures (CHC) outshine other students on international tests. How, then, to explain this paradox?

Biggs (1994) begins his answer by laying out the conditions for successful learning and teaching which have emanated from Western research:

- teaching methods are varied, emphasizing student activity, self regulation, student-centredness, cooperative and group work, with minimal expository teaching;
- content is presented in a meaningful context using concepts and familiar examples;
- classes are small, a desirable but not sufficient condition for more teacher–student interaction;
- classroom climate is warm, firm and structured, but not authoritarian;
- assessment addresses high cognitive level outcomes and is non-threatening, unlike public examinations.

These conditions, it must be remembered are based on Western research findings. How well do they apply to Asian classrooms?

First, most class sizes in Asia are far larger than Western research advises or contemplates. In China, classes may rise to 60 or even 70 students. In Hong Kong and elsewhere in East Asia, classes of 40 or 45 are quite commonplace. However, it is not class size that really matters; more important is teacher–student interaction. Second, teachers appear to rely heavily on teacher-centred, expository, authoritarian methods, but again, as we shall see, and as Stevenson and Stigler's work (1992) confirms, this is a somewhat misleading picture. Third, East Asian schools, students and parents place inordinately high stress on public examinations, leading many Westerners to suppose that high-level cognitive outcomes cannot be attained. Again, this may be masking the reality.

The Western perception of the Asian student as a rote learner, passive, compliant, failing to speak up, adopting unquestioning attitudes towards their teachers, is well documented. Yet against all of this, their superior performance on international tests, plus the evidence from a number of other studies, reveals that Asian students report a stronger preference for high-level, deep learning strategies than do Western students (Watkins and Biggs, 1996). This leads Biggs (1994: 26) to assert:

> The central paradox is that highly adaptive modes of learning emerge from CHC classrooms, and this does need explaining. Large classes, exam pressure, expository teaching … do not sound like good news …. But these features … are reliably associated with high level outcomes.

How then to explain the high performance? Biggs (1994) constructs his explanation around the following themes: repetitive learning, learning environments, teaching methods and teacher–student relations, and the relationship between school and society. Elaboration on each of these is worthwhile.

Repetitive learning

Biggs argues that rote learning for students in Confucian-heritage cultures is a form of surface learning which affords economy in achieving examination success. Repetitive learning, on the other hand, is to be contrasted with rote learning, since it is a form of deep learning which enables 'deep-memorization', itself an aid to understanding and a base for higher level cognitive skills. The Chinese student is inclined towards this form of learning, given the thousands of characters in the Chinese language which have to be mastered. Biggs's point is that the Chinese student is adept at using and distinguishing between both forms of learning – rote and repetitive – as the situation demands. Rote learning is an efficient means of surface learning for examination success; repetitive learning is a necessary step towards memorization of information, leading to deeper understanding and higher-level cognitive skills. Such distinctions are not as clearly recognized in the West.

Learning environments

Major differences are noted between Chinese and Western learning environments, well illustrated by examples drawn from music and the arts. There are two principal differences. First, Chinese teachers believe that learning is an imitational skill and the task of the teacher is to guide and 'hold the student's hand' through each stage in order to render a successful performance. Western teachers are more concerned with process than product; exploring and creating are seen as more important than honing particular skills in order to render a superb performance. Second, the two cultures tend to differ in the sequence of learning. The Chinese believe in mastering the skills first, then applying them in practice; Western teachers encourage exploration first, and then subsequently the development of skills.

Teaching methods and teacher–student relations

Stigler and Stevenson (1991) highlight the Western misperception of the Asian teacher as an authoritarian transmitter of information and the students as just memorizers. Instead, they use the term 'constructivist' to describe the hundreds of teachers they observed in China, Taiwan and Japan. While the teachers were 'authoritarian' in the sense of insisting on the 'one right way' and on close supervision, theirs was a far more subtle form of authoritarianism than is normally conceived in the West.

Teachers, for example, posed provocative questions, allowing reflective 'wait time' and varied techniques to suit individual students. They were student-centred, frequently engaging all students in the class in problem solving, and pushing for high-level cognitive thought processes. In regard to teacher–student relations, the Western observer tends to focus on the hierarchical ambience, but misses the otherwise warm, caring nature of the interactions. In other words, there are two dimensions: hierarchy is evident, but this does not mean that teachers are aloof and cold towards their charges. Stevenson and Stigler (1992) found that despite class sizes of fifty or more, Chinese and Japanese teachers found more time to interact one-to-one when walking round the class than do their Western counterparts, who tend to rely on lower-order questions to the whole class. Lighter teaching loads also enable the Chinese and Japanese teachers to be better prepared and to assist students out of class time.

Hess and Azuma (1991) report a practice in Japan, called 'sticky probing', which illustrates first the curious mixture of authoritarianism and student-centredness pervading classrooms, and second the collectivist rather than individualist elements of the culture. In this practice, the work of a student who has made a mistake is focused upon by students under the adjudication of the teacher, a process which may go on for hours. Whereas students in the West might be mortified to have their work so paraded, Japanese students accept it as an opportunity for everyone to learn.

All of this leads Biggs to conclude that large classes, authoritarianism and exam pressure exist, but the teacher in Confucian-heritage societies has developed culturally adaptable ways of teaching to circumvent what is regarded in the West as unfavourable conditions. In their own way, they integrate hierarchy with warmth and care; they blend whole-class teaching with student-centredness and group work; they develop a functional mentor–mentee joint responsibility for learning; they push for high-cognitive level outcomes; and they plan and cooperate with their colleagues as part of a professional community.

The relationship between school and society

The final part of the answer to the paradox concerns the harmony between school and society. Hess and Azuma (1991) use the term 'predisposition to learn' to describe Japanese children, who are socialized to be obedient, to conform and to persist, all characteristics which schools the world over try to instil in their pupils. There is thus a reinforcing and compatibility effect between home and school. Students are predisposed to accept the conditions for learning in school before they even arrive. This is the case too with the other Confucian-heritage societies, although in Westernized Hong Kong there are semblances of change taking place. In the West, children are often brought up to be assertive, independent, curious and exploratory. They are socialized one way out of school, and another way inside school. Classroom conditions need to be constantly exciting and stimulating, and elaborate systems of positive and negative reinforcement are needed, to hold their attention.

As we have seen earlier, Chinese students are motivated in different ways from their Western counterparts. For Chinese students, success is bound up with family and social status; it is more than just individual achievement. This places even more pressure on them to succeed. A number of other learning-related factors are found in the Confucian-heritage cultures (CHC) which are transmitted through socialization. First, the belief that success is related to effort much more than ability. Hau and Salili (1991) found that Hong Kong secondary students rank ability only fifth, after effort, interest, study skill and mood, in accounting for success. This leads the CHC student to try harder when faced with failure, while the Western student is more inclined to give up, believing that lack of ability cannot be compensated for.

Two other consequences follow from the effort attribution. First, Asian teachers and students tend to be more task-oriented and to spend more time on tasks – in both classwork and homework – than their Western counterparts. Second, as part of their effort strategy, Asian students become adept at cue-seeking, especially in regard to assessment. They work out what is required in order to meet their teachers' expectations. Finally, they are predisposed to collaborate with each other in order to overcome unfamiliar situations.

Conclusions from research on culture and teaching and learning

Where Asian students are predisposed to being taught, the features of schools in the West which are associated with poor outcomes – large class sizes, low expenditure, expository teaching, emphasis on formal examinations – are of reduced importance. In other words, culturally adaptive and sensitive practices compensate for these otherwise adverse features. Equally, many of the positive features of schooling in the West, which on the surface do not appear to exist in the CHC schools, have in fact been adapted in some culturally equivalent form.

The moral, according to Biggs (1994), is that cultures are systems. This means that it is of little use looking at specific practices or features and trying to identify their presence in another culture. If certain Western features do not seem to be present in Asian settings, it might be that they exist in a disguised or different form, or that they are compensated for by another set of factors. The dynamic interplay between all of the parts, not the presence of any one part, is what makes it all work. In short, culture provides the context within which the parts interact.

There is little doubt that many Asian cultures achieve harmony between the school and home environments to a degree that the West should envy. Some of the CHCs (for example, Japan and China) have achieved other commendable features, such as decreased teaching loads allowing for better quality preparation; informed teaching practices, such as more wait time and more individual attention within whole-class teaching; more peer interaction and a belief in greater effort when faced with failure. None of these on their own makes a significant difference. Rather, it is the harmony achieved between teaching and learning in the CHC cultures and between the school and society, which matters. There is much about the methods of teaching and learning in CHC schools which would be unworkable in Western schools. In Japan, for example, the student is seen as the 'twig to be bent'. Western cultures, receptive to the notion that the school accommodate the child, continue to grapple with the problem of putting this ideal into practice. CHC schools have not had to face these problems, which threaten equilibrium in the balance and harmony between school and social life.

Conclusions: Informed Teaching and a Cross-Cultural Perspective

This chapter has had two aims. First, it has argued the case for teachers to adopt informed teaching practices; in this regard, a number of teaching approaches, skills and behaviours have illustrated the importance of successful teaching technique grounded in teachers' professional knowledge of pedagogy and learning. Second, it has ventured to set informed teaching within a cross-cultural context, and in so doing it has raised important contemporary issues in a fast globalizing world about the wisdom of trans-ferring policies and practices from one culture to another.

In regard to the first of the aims, it is argued that all teachers have a professional obligation to adopt informed teaching practices. If this is to be realized, then a number of issues need to be addressed. First, the research base on which informed practice rests has to be made available and acces-sible to teachers in a readily understandable and digestible form, but without dilution of the technicalities. Teacher training and professional development programmes are obvious places to start. Much of the research knowledge base exists in the universities, but is needed in schools. How can the gap be bridged? University–school partnerships in various guises are fruitful ways to proceed.

In relation to the second of the aims – the cross-cultural aspect – it is noteworthy that Western and Asian systems are currently displaying recip-rocal interest in each other's policies and practices. What transpires is that systems of teaching and learning evolve in ways reflective of cultural norms. If these cultural norms are not well understood, then ill-informed and misleading pronouncements can easily be made, since observers are inclined to make judgements according to their own cultural reference points.

This chapter has argued that a range of teaching and learning approaches and practices should be applied in the pursuit of successful learning. The body of knowledge on which these approaches rest tends to transcend cultures and in this respect can be considered generic. It is unlikely that any school system has yet achieved a state of the art whereby its teachers are adopting informed practices as envisaged in this chapter. In reality each society, in response to its own norms and values and to solving its particular conditions for learning, has evolved and shaped a unique combination of elements which go together to make a system of teaching and learning. Thus, many teachers and schools in Confucian-heritage cultures have responded to large classes, lack of equipment and emphasis on examinations, by adapting and adopting a particular form of whole-class direct teaching which seems to work. Students likewise have developed effective methods of learning to suit requirements. Taking a single element on its own, rather than looking at the system as a whole, tends to give a distorted picture.

Neither is the success of a school system simply dependent on achieving harmony and alignment among its various elements. Consistency between the norms and values espoused by schools and by the broader society will further enhance successful teaching and learning. Such consistency is probably higher in many of the Confucian-heritage cultures than it is in many Western societies. While acknowledging that each society has developed its own system of responses to meet its own conditions and cultural values, the fact remains that no school system has attained an ideal state, and that in any case each is continuously evolving within a turbulent global society and economy. This returns our focus to the body of knowledge upon which informed teaching rests. It is for each society and school system to strive towards adopting informed teaching and learning practices, referencing the relevant knowledge base and grounding its response in culturally appropriate ways.

References

Bechtol, W.M. and Sorenson, J.S. (1993) *Restructuring Schooling for Individual Students*, Needham Heights, MA: Allyn and Bacon.

Biggs, J. (1994) 'What are effective schools? Lessons from East and West', *Australian Education Researcher* 21 (1): 19–39.

Block, J. and Anderson, L. (1975) *Mastery Learning in Classroom Instruction*, New York: Macmillan.

Block, J., Efthim, H. and Burns, R. (1989) *Building Effective Mastery Learning Schools*, New York: Longman.

Bloom, B. (1968) 'Learning for mastery', *Evaluation Comment* 1 (2): 74–86.

—— (1976) *Human Characteristics and School Learning*, New York: McGraw-Hill.

Bridges, E.M. and Hallinger, P. (1992) *Problem-Based Learning for Administrators*, Eugene: ERIC Clearinghouse, University of Oregon.

Brophy, J. and Evertson, C. (1976) *Learning from Teaching: A Developmental Perspective*, Boston: Allyn & Bacon.

Brophy, J. and Good, T. (1986) 'Teacher behaviour and student achievement', in M.C. Wittrock (ed.), *Handbook of Research on Teaching*, 3rd edn, New York: Macmillan, 328–75.

Carnegie Forum on Education and the Economy (1986) *A Nation Prepared: Teachers for the 21st Century*, Washington, DC: Carnegie Forum.

Carroll, J.B. (1963) 'A model of school learning', *Teachers College Record* 64: 723–33.

Elmore, R.F. (1988) *Early Experiences in Restructuring Schools: Voices From the Field*, Washington, DC: National Governors' Association.

Fraser, B.J., Walberg, H.J., Welch, W.W. and Hattie, J.A. (1987) 'Syntheses of educational productivity research', *International Journal of Educational Research* 11 (2): 147–247.

Good, T. and Brophy, J. (1991) *Looking in Classrooms*, 5th edn, New York: Harper Collins.

Guskey, T.R. (1985) *Implementing Mastery Learning*, Belmont, CA: Wadsworth.

—— (1995) 'Mastery learning', in J.H. Block, S.T. Everson and T.R. Guskey (eds), *School Improvement Programs*, New York: Scholastic, 91–108.

Harris, A. (1998) 'Effective teaching: a review of the literature', *School Leadership and Management* 18 (2): 169–83.

Harvey, G. and Crandall, D.P. (1988) 'A beginning look at the what and how of restructuring', in C. Jenks (ed.), *The Re-Design of Education: A Collection of Papers Concerned with Comprehensive Educational Reform*, San Francisco: Far West Laboratory.

Hawley, W.D. (1989) 'Looking backward at educational reform', *Education Week* 9 (9): 32–5.

Hau, K.T. and Salili, F. (1991) 'Structure and semantic differential placement of specific causes: academic causal attributions by Chinese students in Hong Kong', *International Journal of Psychology* 26: 175–93.

Hess, R.D. and Azuma, M. (1991) 'Cultural support for schooling: contrasts between Japan and the United States', *Educational Researcher* 20 (9): 2–8.

Hofstede, G.H. (1980) *Culture's Consequences: International Differences in Work-Related Values*, Beverly Hills, CA: Sage.

—— (1991) *Cultures and Organisations: Software of the Mind*, London: McGraw-Hill.

Hoyle, E. (1969) *The Role of the Teacher*, London: Routledge & Kegan Paul.

Hunter, M. (1982) *Mastery Teaching*, El Segundo, CA: TIP Publications.

Johnson, D. and Johnson, R. (1985) 'Cooperative learning and adaptive education', in W. Wang and H. Walberg (eds), *Adapting Instruction to Individual Differences*, Berkeley, CA: McCutchan, 105–34.

Joyce, B. and Weil, M. (1996) *Models of Teaching*, 4th edn, Englewood Cliffs, NJ: Prentice Hall.

Joyce, B., Calhoun, E. and Hopkins, D. (1997) *Models of Teaching Tools for Learning*, London: Open University Press.

Marton, F. and Ramsden, P. (1988) 'What does it take to improve learning?' in P. Ramsden (ed.), *Improving Learning – New Perspectives*, London: Routledge & Kegan Paul.

Murphy, J. (1991) *Restructuring Schools: Capturing and Assessing the Phenomena*, New York: Teachers College Press.

Ornstein, A.C. (1995) *Strategies for Effective Teaching*, 2nd edn, Dubuque, IA: Brown & Benchmark.

Porter, A.C. and Brophy, J. (1988) 'Synthesis of research on good teaching: insights from the work of the Institute for Research on Teaching', *Educational Leadership* 45 (8): 74–85.

Rubin, I. (1985) *Artistry and Teaching*, New York: Random House.

Shulman, L.S. (1986) 'Those who understand: knowledge growth and teaching', *Educational Researcher* 15 (March–April), 4–14.

—— (1987) 'Knowledge and teaching: foundations of the new reform', *Harvard Educational Review* 57 (1): 1–22.

—— (1991) 'Ways of seeing, ways of knowing, ways of teaching, ways of learning about teaching', *Journal of Curriculum Studies* 23 (5): 393–96.

Slavin, R. (1990) *Cooperative Learning: Theory, Research and Practice*, Englewood Cliffs, NJ: Prentice Hall.

—— (1991) 'Synthesis of research on cooperative learning', *Educational Leadership* 48 (5): 71–82.

Spady, W.G. (1988) 'Organising for results: the basis of authentic restructuring and reform', *Educational Leadership* 49 (2): 67–72.

Stevenson, H.W. and Stigler, J.W. (1992) *The Learning Gap: Why Our Schools are Failing and What We Can Learn from Japanese and Chinese Education*, New York: Touchstone.

Stigler, J.W. and Stevenson, H.W. (1991) 'How Asian teachers polish each other to perfection', *American Educator* 15 (1): 12–21, 43–7.

Vasquez, B., Slavin, R. and D'Arcangelo, M. (1990) *Cooperative Learning: Facilitators' Manual*, Alexandria, VA: Association for Supervision and Curriculum Development.

Wang, M. (1992) *Adaptive Education Strategies: Building on Diversity*, Baltimore, MD: Paul Brookes.

Watkins, D.A. and Biggs, J.B. (eds) (1996) *The Chinese Learner: Cultural, Psychological and Contextual Influences*, Hong Kong: Comparative Education Research Centre, University of Hong Kong.

Westerman, D. (1991) 'Expert and novice teacher decision making', *Journal of Teacher Education* 42 (4): 292–305.

8　Integrating Computer Technology

This chapter aims to provide a coherent explanation of the potentialities of computer technology for enhancing teaching and learning, and how these potentialities may be realized, all within an holistic concept of designing the learning-centred school. First, the chapter establishes key principles for computer use in schools. Second, it discusses the creation of a school technology plan. Third, it provides examples of schools which have integrated technology into the curriculum. Fourth, the problems posed by resource constraints are acknowledged. Finally, some cross-cultural implications are drawn for the growing importance of technology in designing the learning-centred school.

Creating an improved learning environment in the learning-centred school can be approached by using powerful catalysts for change. One such catalyst is computer technology. Schools have generally been slow to adopt computer technology, especially when compared with the pace at which the business world and industry have forged ahead. This has led to the justifiable criticism that schools are not preparing their students appropriately for their adult lives and to meet the needs of businesses and employers. Indeed, it has been estimated in the United States that only 22 per cent of people currently entering the labour market possess the technology skills that will be required for 60 per cent of new jobs in the year 2000 (Zuckerman, 1994). As Hancock (1997) argues, there is a mismatch between schools and the workplace, such that we need to design new 'information age' schools.

A further problem beyond their slow introduction of computers into schools concerns the under-utilization and misappropriation of those computers which are already in schools. For many reasons, including a lack of skills training on the part of teachers, but more fundamentally a failure to plan a technology policy for the school which integrates technology across the curriculum, schools fail to make full use of what is a valuable resource. The value of this resource generally escapes the typical teacher and administrator. Its potential to improve the quantity and quality of learning in the school cannot be overstated. In one respect, it is a tool for improving student learning. In another, it is a valuable resource capable of improving the quality of teaching. And in a further respect, it is an invaluable tool for administrators in aiding their running of the school. Computer technology has capacity, therefore, to promote improved performance in learning, teaching and administering. There are few comparable innovations with the capability of realizing such multiple and profound benefits.

Although technology can act as a catalyst and a driver for school restructuring, it should not be seen as a final goal in itself. In other words, technology is important in schools as a means of enhancing teaching and learning, and consequently needs to be connected to both. There are well-meaning but misguided computer buffs in schools who advocate and champion the use of computers simply for their own sake.

Evidence to date on the effects of computer technology on learning has proven somewhat disappointing. This, however, is more a reflection of the failure to use and apply the technology productively than the value of the technology itself. It reinforces the need for schools to lay down clear and sound principles, goals and expected outcomes to guide their technology policy.

Key Principles for the Use of Computers in Schools

For the realization of the potentialities of computer technology in schools, four principles are paramount. These are: that technology serves teaching and learning; students and staff need ready access; technology must be embedded and integrated in the curriculum; and staff require training (Bain, 1996).

Technology serves teaching and learning

Technology should serve the more important goals of quality teaching and learning, rather than be an end in itself. Careful thought is therefore needed first as to how the school intends to re-design its teaching and learning approaches before it can elicit how technology can inform them.

Access

While providing access is not sufficient to ensure meaningful use by students and teachers, it is clearly a necessary prerequisite. Universal access to technology for both students and staff requires a systemic approach. Ratios of one computer per ten students or per class are clearly inadequate. Likewise, concentrating computers in just one laboratory in the school is seriously restrictive on access. Universal access therefore has two dimensions: first, all students and staff, not just a limited number, should be able to 'log on' at any time, and second, they should be able to do so in many sites around the school. In other words, design should focus on a campus-wide network which maximizes access for teachers, students and administrators.

Technology embedded and integrated in the curriculum

In schools which are maximizing the potential of technology as a tool for enhancing learning, teachers in all subjects are integrating it in a myriad of ways into their curricula. By contrast, many schools timetable technology as a separate subject, the effect of which is antithetical to integrating it across the curriculum. Bain (1996) illustrates the point well by suggesting the following questions to test the intent of schools:

- Is expertise with technology intentionally represented as a school-wide student outcome? What should students know and be able to do at graduation?
- Are these skills and competencies represented in the daily activities of students within the context of teaching and learning in all subjects? Do students learn about spreadsheets and databases through science experiments and math simulations used regularly as part of an intentional, integrated curriculum?
- Do students acquire skills in networking and information retrieval while undertaking research for authentic assessment projects that are connected to school-wide learner outcomes?
- Can teachers design a curriculum unit to incorporate a HyperStudio stack created for different levels of reading ability to be used by all students in the class, or in small groups?
- How does the HyperStudio stack fit with the school-wide and unit student outcomes?
- Is quality software combined with informed practices to create a complete teaching–learning picture?

The aim therefore is to ensure that technology becomes a routine and meaningful part of the daily life of teachers, students and administrators.

Training

There is a pressing need among many teachers and students for training to exploit the potentialities of technology. Such training does not just concern the procedures and technical operation of the equipment, but also involves making connections between the technology, curriculum, teaching methods and materials. It relates to the uses and capabilities of the hardware, and the availability and development of suitable software for use in classrooms.

Creating a School Technology Plan

If technology is to be closely integrated with and support curriculum, teaching and learning, then it is important for the school to develop a clear strategy in the form of a technology plan. A school must graduate through a number of sequential stages in formulating such a plan. The following stages of the planning process are based on the experience at Brewster Academy in New Hampshire (Bain, 1996; Bain, 1999).

The groundwork for producing such a plan should be based around a needs analysis survey or review, which includes:

- the present levels of access to, and usage of, technology in the school;
- the extent to which technology is integrated in the curriculum;
- the readiness of faculty to use technology at different levels;
- the point of evolution of the school with respect to technology.

This situational analysis is necessary to the next stage of forming a vision and a set of goals with respect to four key aspects (Bain, 1996). These are access, integration, school evolution and faculty readiness and training. Examples of Brewster's goals for each of these areas are:

- Access: to develop a fully computer literate community by providing all faculty and students with a 1:1 access to personal computers.
- Integration: to ensure that technology is meaningfully integrated into all levels of the curriculum from school-wide outcomes through units and lessons.
- Evolution: to create conditions whereby technology is used routinely by faculty, students and administrators in all aspects of school life.
- Readiness and professional development: to introduce students and faculty to information processing, database management, and spread-sheets.

Key Elements of a Technology Plan

Bain (1996) distinguishes the following components comprising a school technology plan:

- needs, curriculum and existing infrastructure analysis;
- facilities audit: review existing and new facilities;
- campus and classroom architecture and design, including remote access and connectivity, furniture, equipment, classroom layout and use of space;
- library: its place in, and contribution to, school technology and teaching and learning;

- professional development planning, including student and staff requirements;
- school technology support: position descriptions of technical support staff;
- hardware and software design;
- economic analysis, costings and budget development;
- implementation timeline.

The planning process itself demands careful and skilful management. A school technology task group might, with the help of a change agent guiding the school design process, oversee and orchestrate the strategy. While acknowledging the existing level of technological expertise currently found in schools, the expertise required to plan and build networks and to configure hardware and software is almost certainly beyond the scope of most. Outside consultants will therefore be needed, and it is important that schools make a judicious choice in this respect. Ideally, an expert should be someone with knowledge of curriculum and instructional design and teaching methodologies as well as up-to-date knowledge of hardware and software availability.

Finally, it is helpful for the school to be able to evaluate the levels of take-up of technology at various points in time. Using Hall and Loucks's (1977) model of levels of use, the following stages may be recognized, from beginning to most sophisticated:

- Orientation: the individual (or organization/unit) acquires information about the innovation and considers the demands and benefits.
- Preparation: the individual (or organization/unit) prepares to use the innovation.
- Mechanical: the user focuses most effort on the short term, day-to-day use of the innovation, with little time for reflection; the user is engaged in step-by-step implementation, which is often imperfect.
- Routine: use of the innovation is stabilized and few changes are made; little effort is made to adapt or extend the innovation.
- Refinement: the user varies or modifies the innovation in order to increase immediate and long-term benefits to students.
- Integration: the user combines the efforts with related activities and with colleagues to achieve a collective impact on students.
- Renewal: the user re-evaluates the use and impact of the innovation and seeks major modifications to produce increased benefits for students as well as the larger system.

Descriptions of Integrated Technology Schools

A number of innovative schools around the world are enacting the vision of technology integrated with curriculum and with informed teaching and learning. This section describes a few of them. For the most part they tend to be private schools with the resources to bring their visions and plans to reality. Nonetheless, such schools serve as invaluable models and pilot schemes for future school design. As noted earlier, Hancock (1997) recognizes the mismatch in terms of knowledge and skills between schools as presently designed and the workplace. She asks, 'What should Information Age schools look like?' and on the basis of six innovative schools in North America, identifies six attributes. This section describes the six attributes identified by Hancock. It then reports on two schools, one American and the other Australian, which have used technology as an integral component of school design.

Hancock synthesizes research by Breivik and Senn (1994), Glennan and Melmed (1996) and Cuban (1997) to point to six attributes of the Information Age school, as follows:

Interactivity

Students are highly interactive, communicating with other students through formal presentations, cooperative learning activities and informal dialogue. Students and teachers talk to one another about learning tasks in large groups, in small groups and one to one. Students have constant access to and know how to use print and electronic information resources to inform their learning activities. They realize the local and international communities as valuable sources of information and access all kinds of community members: business people, government officials, athletes and so on. Students at Sun Valley Elementary School in Winnipeg, Canada, for example, communicate with peers in other countries.

Self-initiated learning

Students take charge of their own learning. They, rather than the teacher, ask the initial questions. They gather their own data rather than the teacher transmit or prescribe it; they analyse, interpret and synthesize the data in the context of the problem. They experience the higher order skills involved in the process of learning. At Taylorsville Elementary School, Indiana, students work at their own pace and learning is individualized. Teachers use multi-age and multi-year groupings and team-based project work. They facilitate rather than direct. Two days a year are devoted to technology training, and the school employs a technology coordinator and three part-time aides to assist teachers.

A changing role for teachers

The teacher's role changes, as previously mentioned, from director to coach and facilitator. Information is obtained by the students from the computer, not from the teacher. Teachers stimulate and prompt the students to ask the right questions and set about solving them. This process creates excitement and gives a purpose to learning. At Adlai Stevenson High School, Illinois, a specialized laboratory for teachers is staffed by a full-time trainer and there is a commitment to raising all staff to a high level of technological competence within three years. Use of technology has permeated all aspects of school life: instruction, assessment, exploration and management.

Media and technology specialists as central participants

Media and technology specialists are critical in the Information Age school. They work with students to prompt the right questions and to guide in the availability and use of information resources. With teachers, they are instructional designers, developing curricula and helping to plan units. They can also organize in-service professional development for teachers. Computer skills are acquired and required by students for all subjects, not just for those lessons devoted to information technology. At Christopher Columbus Middle School in New Jersey, the school day has been divided into blocks of ninety minutes to two hours so that teachers can create a project-based, integrated curriculum approach. In addition to a central school computer lab, each of the twelve classrooms has five computers, a printer and a video machine. Students have access to multimedia production equipment, computer video editing capabilities, and Internet connectivity from all PCs. Teachers receive three days of paid technology training each year and the school has a technology coordinator.

Continuous evaluation

Teachers and schools engage in ongoing evaluation of the materials they use and those which are available. They collaborate in software development and exchange information about new products. The Maryland Virtual High School of Science and Mathematics is a collaboration of fifteen schools whose teachers collaborate in these ways.

A changed physical and human environment: a different classroom configuration and use of space

The classrooms in high-technology schools look and feel different from traditional classrooms. They are geared to information access and retrieval, analysis and application. Strategies such as cooperative learning, guided inquiry and thematic teaching are used. Computers are central to the ambience of the classroom, and desks and chairs are arranged around them. Brewster Academy, described in more detail below, has re-designed desks to fit round technology posts carrying cables and wiring into classrooms. The physical appearance of classroom layout, the furniture and pattern of student interaction, all change. Students and teachers focus on the learning task and problems at hand; the traditional role divisions between teaching and learning disappear.

In her conclusion, Hancock (1997) suggests a school wanting to become an Information Age school should start by improving the connections between curriculum content and school process. Among the measures suggested are: lengthen class periods, consider multi-age grouping, experiment with integrated curricular planning, develop individualized instruction plans for all students, implement continuous and authentic assessments, provide incentives to teachers and administrators to acquire the necessary skills, pay teachers to engage in relevant professional development and hire technology support staff with teaching experience. These are good illustrations of the principles set out early in this chapter. A more in-depth description of two leading technology schools follows below.

Brewster Academy, New Hampshire, USA

At Brewster Academy, a long-established independent preparatory school in New Hampshire, USA, the principles of technology serving teaching and learning, universal access and embedding technology in the curriculum have been the backbone to the technology policy adopted as part of the school's re-design. The school has engaged in holistic re-design since 1992, and technology is playing a key role in every aspect. For all of its prominence, however, technology is seen as serving the more important goals of enhancing the curriculum, teaching and learning, rather than being an end in itself. As Bain (1996), the architect behind the school design process, asserts, weaving technology into the core of school operation breaks down the barriers to curriculum integration.

Both teacher and student roles have been fundamentally changed. The school has a campus-wide network, which involves 1,766 ports covering every classroom and dormitory (Brewster Academy is a boarding school) and which gives access to both the Internet and Campus Intranet. Irrespective of whether the student is in class, in the school library or in her own dormitory, there will be a port to which she can connect. Likewise, teachers have ports in their work rooms and in their homes, many of which are located on campus. Every student and staff member has a laptop computer, affording transportability and increasing the ease and flexibility of use. Learning is no longer confined to the classroom.

Paper and pens have all but disappeared from the school. Students now carry their laptops with them as they move between classes and between their lessons and dorms. Through the Intranet, they can call up a resident tutor and request help if they encounter problems with homework. When the homework is complete, they e-mail it to their tutor, who grades, comments and returns it via e-mail.

A system which allows universal access empowers teachers to change their ways of working. For example, when teachers know that they can assign homework activity that involves spreadsheeting data from a science experiment, given that students have access to the necessary hardware and software, technology becomes a key factor in teachers' rethinking their pedagogy inside and outside of the classroom. Similarly, when teachers can develop computer-based presentations at home with the certainty that the facilities exist in the classroom for all students to gain access, there is an incentive for them to do so. Technology-prepared lessons are more likely to become part of the day-to-day teaching practice.

The use of classroom space has been radically reconfigured. The architecture and layout of desks has been re-designed in ways conducive to new teaching–learning approaches integrated with maximal use of technology. In most classrooms, cables are hidden below the floor and rise from the floor to desk height in technology posts, positioned at strategic points. Butting up to each technology post, and to each other, are four desks, one for each of four students, who are able to plug their laptops into the post. This configuration favours maximum flexibility for a variety of teaching–learning methods: students may work on their own laptop, or in pairs or groups of four; or they may attend to whole-class instruction.

Teachers are grouped in core teams of seven, with each team taking responsibility for the whole curriculum of a group of students assigned to them. All seven teachers in a team share the same staff work space, enabling collaborative and integrative curriculum planning to take place. Likewise, the team meets regularly to discuss student progress, welfare, disciplinary and counselling issues. All student assessment data for all subjects is fed onto the campus Intranet, as is information about student welfare and behaviour. Access to this information is restricted for obvious reasons. But when a team sits down to make decisions about individual students, all members have their laptops open on the desk in front of them, all have the same detailed information charting the progress of the student on their screens, and the level of informed and professional decision making consequently far surpasses that found in most conventional schools.

Methodist Ladies College (MLC), Melbourne, Australia

MLC is a large independent school of 2,000 girls from mostly middle to high socioeconomic backgrounds, ranging in age from 5–18 years. McDonald and Ingvarson (1997) describe how the school has used technology as a catalyst for whole-school change involving the introduction of constructivist principles and independent learning as the philosophical base to school re-design. Computer technology was adopted for its capacity to reinforce the philosophical principles underpinning the design model.

Like students at Brewster Academy, every MLC student has a notebook. Students use a software programme which allows them to operationalize the constructivist philosophy built on encouraging students to predict, experiment, take risks, and construct and create. In subjects as diverse as mathematics and humanities, students work at their own pace and experience more individualized programmes. Students work more independently and problem solve using cooperative and peer tutoring methods. Teachers relinquish control and monopoly over knowledge and become facilitators of learning with time to assist individual students. A teacher monitors the progress of thirty students, each pursuing an individualized programme.

In the humanities, blocks of two or three forty-five-minute periods have been formed and a more integrated studies approach combines English, history, geography and Biblical studies. Teachers pair together to teach. The result is a change from traditional classroom structures with their short time periods, lack of subject integration and teacher isolation. These structural moves in turn lend support to the principles of independent learning and constructivism.

Changes such as these fundamentally reconfigure both student and teacher roles. Technology is not the end goal, but is instead a means of achieving the more important aim of fundamental change in teaching and learning. Technology forces changes in teachers' and students' classroom behaviours in a way that few other catalysts seem able to do. Students become less reliant on the teacher to create or transmit knowledge; they are more likely to develop into active learners and problem solvers; the emphasis is switched from teaching to learning; responsibilities for teaching and learning are shared between teachers and students; students engage in more individualized learning and work at their own pace; and teachers undertake more varied roles as tutors, facilitators, advisers and monitors.

McDonald and Ingvarson (1997) conclude that strong connectivity between expanded goals, changed structures and additional resources is the key to why traditional classroom teaching and learning has been transformed. It took a few years for teachers to adjust and for many former constraints, including reluctance on the part of some teachers, to be overcome. Technology has been integrated into the curriculum, teachers have re-examined the learning process and greater attention is now given to individual needs. By these standards, technology as part of larger school re-design has been a success. It has freed teachers from the constant demands exacted by whole-class teaching, and enabled them to provide support at the individual student level.

Coping with Resource Constraints

In respect of technology, the above scenarios of leading edge schools are far removed from the reality facing many others, perhaps the majority, which are poorly endowed. Nonetheless, the examples of these schools are critical, firstly in presenting working models of how technology can be harnessed to achieve fundamental changes in curriculum, teaching and learning, and secondly in posing a challenge for other schools which can be captured in the following questions, 'how closely can our school approximate to the situation described in the leading edge schools?' and, 'given our circumstances, how can we adapt and compromise so as to achieve at least some of these beneficial effects?'

Introducing computers into schools with one thousand students or more, and class sizes of thirty and above, is a massive challenge. The inadequacy of government funding for schools is driving more to look for private sponsorship and to fall back on fundraising. Even so, they may still fall well short of the capital investment required. Re-allocating expenditures which formerly would have gone to library books may only make a small contribution, and in any case, many believe that it is not wise to use the introduction of technology as a *quid pro quo* for restricting the flow of books into the school. Although computer technology may save expenditure in some directions, it more than increases it in others. For example, technicians are needed to maintain the system and its equipment. Some effort has gone into schemes whereby schools contract with manufacturers and lease them on to students at favourable rates, thereby avoiding heavy initial outlays of capital.

For the majority of schools at present, a computer for each student is not realistic. The challenge for them is to decide what is the lowest ratio of students per computer that can be achieved and how, given that ratio, technology can best support the curriculum, teaching and learning programme.

A Cross-Cultural Perspective

The place and importance of technology in re-designing schools does not appear to generate significant cross-cultural issues. The arguments spelled out in this chapter appear to be as valid for Asian schools as for Western ones. Indeed, the leaders of Confucian-heritage economies, such as Hong Kong, Singapore and Taiwan which, prior to the 1997 Asian economic crisis, experienced some of the fastest economic growth rates, have since realized even more strongly the importance of technology to their future economies and therefore to the present and future curricula.

Many technology issues confronting schools in Asian societies are well illustrated by the case of Hong Kong. A Massachusetts Institute of Technology (MIT) study (Berger and Lester, 1997) of the economic future of Hong Kong concluded that its economic base must shift to high value-added products and services, since a number of emerging economies, some in Asia, are increasingly capable of producing, with lower labour and other costs, many of the existing goods and services produced by Hong Kong. There is a need, said the MIT report, for Hong Kong to create new products and processes, and for the capabilities of the workforce to be upgraded. The new economic structure dictates new skills among the workforce, which in turn places new expectations on the education system and the curriculum. Among the skills needed are higher-order thinking, communication, creativity and problem solving (Levin, 1997).

In one way, Hong Kong presents an even more stark example of the under-utilization of computer technology in schools than any Western country. It is a wealthy society, with an income per capita as high, or even higher, than most Western countries, but it allocates only about 3 per cent of its GDP to education compared with 5 per cent in many Western nations. Hong Kong's schools are deprived of audio-visual and technological resources. Only since 1997, when the Hong Kong Special Administrative Region Government took over from the departing British, has there been a concerted effort to install computers in every school. Even so, the ratio of students to computers is depressingly high.

One of the problems faced by many Asian schools in introducing technology, and those in Hong Kong are cases in point, is the lack of space to accommodate computers. Few schools have any spare classrooms. Indeed, many Hong Kong schools have more classes in operation at any given time than rooms to accommodate them. The excess classes spill over into halls, playgrounds and makeshift 'rooms'. In addition, classrooms are small and overcrowded, often with forty-five students packed in tight rows. These physical constrictions of space, as well as the numbers of students in classes, provide an additional hindrance to the use of computers.

Yet in another important respect, technology can be seen as instrumental in assisting Hong Kong schools to achieve new aims set out in recent curriculum policy pronouncements, notably the Target-Oriented Curriculum (TOC) (see chapter 7). TOC represents a student-centred curriculum, a more individualized approach to learning, which emphasizes the development of constructivist learning skills such as problem-solving, communicating, reasoning and inquiring (Education Department, 1994).

The policy is undergoing a phased introduction into primary schools in the late 1990s and will eventually be extended into secondary schools. Many are concerned, however, that with class sizes of forty or more and a teaching force traditionally versed in expository teaching, achieving the aims of TOC is one of the biggest challenges ever to confront the schools of Hong Kong. There is little doubt, however, that the introduction of computers into classrooms would enable students to undertake project work both individually and in groups; it would therefore encourage changes to teachers' and students' roles along the lines advocated in the TOC. In short, infusing technology into classrooms might act as a catalyst for inducing the kind of changes required in teaching and learning which might otherwise fail to materialize. Much would depend on teachers' adoption of the technology.

The example of Hong Kong is instructive in that it represents an affluent Asian society which, despite or perhaps because of its affluence, has so far failed to embrace technology in its schools to anything like the extent of schools in the UK, USA and Australia. Singapore, however, another affluent Asian society, has progressed further than Hong Kong in realizing the benefits of infusing technology into its schools. It has produced a master plan for information technology (IT) in its schools, realizing that an IT-enriched school environment for its students is vital if its economy is to meet the challenges of the twenty-first century. The master plan has four goals:

- to enhance linkages between the school and the world around it, so that teachers and students will communicate with other institutions to acquire richer perspectives;
- to encourage creative thinking, lifelong learning and social responsibility, so that IT will be used to develop pupils' ability to think flexibly and innovatively, to cooperate with one another and to make value judgements;
- to generate innovative processes such as new teaching and learning strategies in curricula and assessment; schools will be given autonomy to deploy IT flexibly;
- to promote administrative and management effectiveness.

Four key dimensions of the master plan are as follows:

- Curriculum and assessment: the aim is to shift the curriculum towards a better balance between acquisition of factual knowledge and mastery of concepts and skills, to encourage pupils to engage in more active and independent learning, and to include assessment modes that will measure abilities in applying information, thinking and communicating.
- Learning resources: the aim here is to acquire and stimulate development of a wide range of curriculum software, to facilitate use of relevant Internet resources for teaching and learning, and to help schools obtain software.
- Teacher development: the aim is to train every teacher in the purposeful use of IT, to equip trainee teachers with core IT skills, and to involve institutions of higher learning and industry partners in schools.
- Physical and technological infrastructure: the aim is to provide a pupil–computer ratio of 2:1, to provide pupils with access to IT in all learning areas in the school, to provide a teacher–computer ratio of 2:1, to provide school-wide networks and to link all schools throughout

Singapore, enabling high speed delivery of multimedia services to all schools.

The Plan to integrate IT into the curriculum began implementation in 1997 with twenty-two demonstration schools. In 1998, a further ninety schools came on stream. It is planned that 250 more schools will join in 1999. By the year 2000, core training for teachers in every school will be completed, and by 2002 it is intended to achieve the 2:1 pupil–computer ratio in schools, with 30 per cent of curriculum time being IT-based. It must be added that the small population of Singapore is advantageous for the implementation of such schemes.

Singapore's policy of introducing technology into its schools seems well established. Hong Kong, while lagging in comparison, certainly has the resources to achieve such a policy, even in times of economic downturn. Contrast both of these societies, however, with Thailand, a relatively poor and less developed economy compared to Singapore and Hong Kong. Gipson's (in press) account of an adventurous attempt to create an innovative school based on integrating technology with informed practices of teaching, learning and curriculum in Chiang Mai, Thailand, provides a stark contrast to Singapore. The project eventually failed, but why?

The template for the design of this Thai school was an American model, namely, that developed at Brewster Academy in New Hampshire and described earlier in this chapter. It is a model which fuses student-centred teaching and learning principles with a whole-school approach to technology, involving universal access, curriculum integration and a campus-wide network. The visions and plans were coherently designed.

However, the move from design to implementation provided many frustrations and costly mistakes, and the original vision quickly disappeared. Among the reasons for the failure were poor leadership and limited expertise among the staff who were hired to bring the curriculum and technology visions to reality: it proved impossible to recruit teachers and leaders with the necessary skills. Consequently, the technology was poorly utilized and the curriculum vision and constructivist teaching–learning model was never implemented. In addition, installing a campus network in a school in a remote part of northern Thailand called for the forging of reliable partnerships between the school and computer hardware and software suppliers. In the event, this proved too much to expect. As a result, inadequate infrastructure support and ongoing training compounded the problems. In addition, the project required large capital injections just at a time when the Thai economy became the first casualty of the Asian economic crisis in 1997.

Even more fundamental, according to Gipson (in press), was the failure to address issues of cultural disjuncture that arose out of conflicting understandings of the nature, function and value of constructivist, student-centred curriculum approaches and pedagogies. In many Asian cultures, the very idea that the teacher may not know all, and that knowledge may be a contested and relative concept, threatens traditional beliefs that the teacher is 'the fountain of all knowledge'. As Asian countries adopt Western ideas and education policies in an effort to re-skill their workforces, they should not underestimate the inherent difficulties that their indigenous cultures present in successfully adopting or adapting innovations designed elsewhere.

Conclusion

According to Van Horn (1991), citing Heuston (1986), there are three possible ways in which the education delivery system can be made more productive. The first is to increase the number of workers. The authors conclude that where this has been tried, it has usually failed. When parent volunteers, paraprofessionals and others are added to the workforce, the benefits are rarely reaped because the division of labour in classrooms is usually badly organized and because there are so many other inhibiting factors to improving instruction. However, where additional labour is well organized and trained, it can effectively complement the teacher. The second is to make teachers more efficient. One could also add to make them more effective. The authors argue that teacher training institutions have tried to do this for a long time without much success. Again, one could add that many teacher preparation programmes have not trained teachers in the ways of informed teaching as advocated in this book. Since he has little faith in these two ways, Heuston (1986) strongly champions the third, namely, to pursue changes in the tools of learning. If teachers are to secure significant gains in student learning they need, he says, more powerful 'teaching-learning tools'. Computer technology has the capacity to be such a 'tool'.

While one might be slower than Van Horn (1991) and Heuston (1986) to dismiss the first two strategies – there is, after all, something to be said for employing all three – one agrees with their advocacy of the third. However, as this chapter has argued, it is not just a matter of installing computers in schools. Turning them into powerful tools for teaching and learning entails a judicious and informed approach to their place within the broader philo-sophical and strategic context of the curriculum, teaching and learning in the school. It involves a process of integration into and across the curriculum, and as much as possible, universal access.

Integrating technology into school design does not appear to pose issues of a cross-cultural kind in a direct way. Rather, the cross-cultural factor may come into play in a more indirect sense, in that technology may be viewed as an integral part of a student-centred, constructivist curriculum approach to school re-design, the ideas and values of which may challenge traditional cultural notions of knowledge, teaching and learning. While poverty and remoteness in many parts of the world, including rural areas of China, are obstacles to the inclusion of technology in schools, it is precisely the drawbacks encountered in these areas which makes technology an attractive possibility in the long run. In the end, technology may prove useful in helping overcome the problems of shortage of skilled teachers, over-large classes, and communication with the outside world. As more people become connected to the Internet, especially in countries and states formerly isolated from the Western world, a clear challenge to culture is presented. It will become increasingly more difficult for governments and teachers to control the flow of knowledge and to be the arbiters of what students think and believe.

References

Bain, A. (1996) 'The school design model at Brewster Academy: technology serving teaching and learning', *Technological Horizons in Education* 23 (10): 72–9.

—— (1999) 'The Future School Institute Handbook', unpublished manuscript, Brewster Academy, New Hampshire, USA.

Berger, S. and Lester, R.K. (1997) *Made by Hong Kong*, Hong Kong: Oxford University Press.

Breivik, P. and Senn, J. (1994) *Information Literacy: Educating Children for the 21st Century*, New York: Scholastic.

Cuban, L. (1997) 'High-tec schools and low-tech teaching', Education Week on the Web (http://www.edweek.org/ew/current/34cuban.h16).

Education Department (1994) *Report of the Advisory Committee on Implementation of the Target-Oriented Curriculum*, Hong Kong: Education Department mimeograph.

Gipson, S. (in press) 'Tridhos School Village: lessons from importing a Western model of school design into Thailand', in C. Dimmock and A. Walker (eds), *Future School Administration: Western and Asian Perspectives*, Hong Kong: Hong Kong Institute of Educational Research/The Chinese University Press.

Glennan, T. and Melmed, A. (1996) 'Fostering the use of educational technology: elements of a national strategy', Santa Monica, CA: Rand.

Hall, G.E. and Loucks, S.F. (1977) 'A developmental model for determining whether the treatment is actually implemented', *American Educational Research Journal* 14 (3): 263–76.

Hancock, V. (1997) 'Creating the "information age" school', *Educational Leadership* 55 (3): 60–3.

Heuston, D.H. (1986) 'The future of education: a time of hope and new delivery systems', unpublished paper, WICAT Systems, Orem, Utah.

Levin, H.M. (1997) *Accelerated Education for an Accelerating Economy*, Education Policy Studies Series, Occasional Paper No. 9, Hong Kong: Hong Kong Institute of Educational Research.

McDonald, H. and Ingvarson, L. (1997) 'Technology: a catalyst for change', *Journal of Curriculum Studies* 29 (5): 513–27.

Van Horn, R. (1991) 'Educational power tools: new instructional delivery systems', *Phi Delta Kappan* 72 (7): 527–33.

Zuckerman, P. (1994) 'America's silent revolution', *US News and World Report* 117 (3): 90.

9 Building Supportive Organizational Structures

This chapter highlights the importance of adaptive organizational structures to support new configurations of teaching, learning and curriculum in the learning-centred school. It begins with a discussion on the bureaucratic and professional elements of schools and the tensions between them. It goes on to elicit principles for adapting structures to support core technology. Accounts are then provided of how the grouping of students and teachers can be re-designed along with the flexible use of time and curriculum structures to enhance learning-centredness. A further section considers changes in architecture, physical space and furniture. Three case studies are then presented of innovative schools whose structures have been re-designed to support teaching and learning. Finally, in the conclusion, the integrative nature of the elements of school design is emphasized, as is the need for culturally sensitive solutions to structural change.

The capacity to re-design schools depends, *inter alia*, on an understanding of the complex and dynamic relationships between curriculum, teaching and learning methodologies, technology and the organizational structures of schools. Although these are all intertwined (Cardellichio, 1995), there is surprisingly little research on how they interact. Implementation of new approaches to the curriculum, teaching and learning will be severely constrained as long as traditional school structures remain intact. The importance of structures is indicated by Carroll, who cites Deming's finding concerning systemic change, that 85 per cent of an organization's problems are usually caused by the system and only 15 per cent are related to the poor performance of staff (Carroll, 1994).

Reference was made in Chapter 1 to the rigidities of traditional school structures. Examples include inflexible standardized timetables; the regularity of thirty-five or forty-minute lessons; one teacher to each class, which in places such as Hong Kong, may have forty-five students or, in mainland China, as many as sixty; and a subject-oriented curriculum as the organizing unit around which bureaucratic departmental structures are built. A subject-oriented curriculum reinforced by departmental structures often results in a demarcated and competitive internal organizational environment.

Large schools in particular assume many of the organizational character-istics of the classic bureaucracy. Owens (1995), for example, recognizes the following trends of bureaucracy in school organization:

1   Maintenance of firm, hierarchical control of authority and close super-vision of those in the lower ranks. Administrators assume a supervisory and inspectorial role.
2   Establishment and maintenance of adequate vertical communication. Instructions to those lower in the hierarchy are important via a smooth flow of communications down through the system. In practice this may not occur, but the introduction of computers and e-mail may help in this respect.
3   Development of clear written rules and procedures to set standards and to guide actions. These are exemplified in curriculum guides, policy handbooks, and rules and regulations.
4   Promulgation of clear plans and schedules for members to follow. These include teachers' lesson plans, bell schedules, meeting schedules and the like.
5   Addition of supervisory and administrative positions to the hierarchy and extensions to the vertical structure to meet changing conditions confronting the organization. Over the last fifty years, for example, as schools have grown in size and as their functions have expanded, a number of such positions have been added, for example, deputy princi-pals with specialist functions, deans and faculty coordinators, directors of specific functions, such as special education, psychologists and school social workers. In this way, the number of vertical links in the organizational chain have grown.

If school organizational structures appear to have been shaped by bureaucratic design principles, they have also been influenced by Frederick Taylor's scientific management ideas. Referring to reform initiatives in the USA in the 1980s, Doyle and Hartle (1985: 24) argue:

> The explicit model for such reform was the factory; Frederick Taylor's scientific management revolution did for the schools the same thing it did for business and industry – created an environment whose principal characteristics were pyramidal organization ... the teacher was the worker on the assembly line of education; the student, the product; the superintendent, the chief executive officer, the school trustees, the board of directors; and the taxpayer, the shareholder.

There is little doubt that as schools grew larger and became more complex organizations in the latter half of the twentieth century, they displayed more elements of scientific management. A clearer divide opened up between those who managed and administered and those who taught and instructed.

Yet, at the same time as schools assumed the organizational characteristics of bureaucracy and scientific management, those who taught in them were beginning to struggle for an improved professional status. When teachers were not so well qualified, and while they were expected to deliver a ready-made or prescribed curriculum using methods laid down for them, it was no surprise that they were seen in terms of 'workers on the factory floor of education'. However, the conception of the informed teacher or practitioner promulgated in this book rests on the notion of teacher as true professional. School-based management, school-based curriculum development, collaborative and team-based decision making; all of these concepts and policies are threatening to change the status and role of teachers. More recent conceptions of re-designed schools, including the one espoused in this book, built on the notion of the informed teacher, envisions teachers playing expanded professional roles.

The very notion of a professional conjures connotations of a qualified person with expert knowledge, who is able to apply that knowledge in generally accepted ways which are deemed to be in the clients' interest; who keeps abreast of recent developments in their field; and who conforms to a body of professional practice as laid down by a body of theoretical knowledge and a code of ethics and practice supported by a board or council (Hoyle, 1969). Above all, trust and respect are placed in the professional to make the best judgements *in situ*, given the nature of the clients' interests. By these criteria, most teachers are pushing hard to attain professional status. The more they push, the greater the tension with the bureaucratic structures within which they are expected to work.

Teachers are often compared unfavourably to doctors and lawyers, who seem to conform more closely to the criteria of professionals. But neither medicine nor law has to cater to the hundreds of clients who are assembled in one place at the same time, as teachers must. Moreover, the hundreds of clients are young, socially immature students, who often see little reason to be in school at all. A degree of bureaucracy is therefore necessary; but it has to be combined with flexibility, so that teachers can exercise their knowledge, skills and judgements in the interests of the students in ways which meet the highest professional standards. In addition, the development of strong school cultures oriented to learning and conducive to desirable behaviour can compensate for the loosening of rigid bureaucratic rules.

There has been a growing awareness among schools undertaking reform of the need for whole-school re-design and at the same time, the need to understand the connectivity between the parts that form the whole. For example, Brickley and Westerberg (1990) report the efforts of one American high school whose plan included purposes, goals and organization with respect to the curriculum and assessment, methods of instruction, technology, organization, decision making, community involvement and accountability. Holistic change, however, is more challenging and can often fail (see Dimmock, 1997, for an account of one school's attempt which failed).

Principles for Re-Designing Structures

A school which has decided on the configuration of its core technology, based on informed practice with respect to the curriculum, teaching and learning, is then in a position through the process of backward mapping to design appropriate organizational structures conducive to its effective delivery. A key question to be posed in the context of the present chapter is, what organizational structures best facilitate informed teaching and learning?

In schools attempting to achieve informed teaching and learning, the present analysis supports Murphy (1991) in suggesting that the following conceptual and ideological principles of core technology guide the design of structural characteristics in the re-designed school:

- structures grounded in mastery (or outcome-) based learning;
- structures facilitating developmentally-paced learning;
- structures conducive to individualization and personalization of learning.

Each of these powerful concepts provides the rationale for designing more flexible structures and is discussed further below. Flexibility is the key concept in designing learning-centred schools. Murphy (1991: 63) argues that, 'for schools concerned with restructuring educational processes, learning theory and student needs take precedence over the custodial interests of parents, administrative convenience, and market forces ... in the creation and reshaping of structures to house teaching and learning'. Emphasis on learning theory and student learning outcomes is endorsed by Spady (1988), who advocates outcome-based learning and demonstrated student mastery. These concepts replace the calendar as the learning unit, so that the key issue is whether all students reach the outcomes successfully, not when or how long it takes.

According to Murphy (1991), the second principle for re-designing delivery structures is developmentally-paced learning. This allows students to progress from one skill level to the next, regardless of age or grade, but only when they have demonstrated readiness. A third principle for changing structures concerns the individualization and personalization of learning. This has two objectives: first, to humanize the organizational climate by creating a caring learning community between adults and children so that each student feels supported and valued by teachers and school leaders; and second, to differentiate delivery in such a way that students experience an appropriate curriculum.

At least twelve different but interwoven strands constitute organizational arrangements with potential for flexibility. These are:

- school clustering;
- student grouping;
- teacher grouping;
- student and teacher role changes;
- volunteers and aides;
- use of space;
- use of technology;
- calendar and time;
- timetable;
- curriculum;
- classroom and out-of-classroom learning;
- student assessment.

A school context in which flexible structures and their underlying principles find favour and expression is central to the responsibility of school leaders and managers. Hence these quality schools are characterized by leadership and management which realizes that flexible structures need to be created, accepted, workable and regularly reviewed in terms of their efficacy in regard to quality teaching and student learning.

Operationalizing these concepts requires flexible organic structures quite different from the rigid bureaucratic structures currently shaping most schools (Murphy, 1993). Each school should consider its own preferred structures in response to the learning needs of its students. Inter-school cooperation in the form of clustering may offer opportunities to share knowledge and resources. In future, clusters of schools may share students and specialist teaching staff, offering wider curriculum choices and making teacher expertise more widely available. A Schools Council report (1992) in Australia on the need for flexible strategies in the primary sector provides a useful range of options available for schools. Below, a few of these flexible structures are discussed.

Grouping of Students

Research findings suggest that students differ in their learning style preferences, some preferring to learn on their own, in pairs, in small groups, in whole classes and large groups. The dominant pattern of whole-class grouping is beginning to break up in some schools. In addition, schooling which prepares children for adult life should provide a range of experiences for students to work in groups of different size. At one end of the range, students should assume individual responsibility for their own learning and be able to work on their own; equally, at the other end, they should be able to contribute to very large teams. In between the two extremes, they should be able to work collaboratively with their peers in small teams. More opportunities need to be provided for students to study individually, especially since individualized learning figures prominently in research findings on informed teaching.

Small group work is already widespread. In Australia, a Schools Council report (1992) acknowledges that small cooperative group learning is sometimes constrained by lack of space and the physical configurations of schools and classrooms. The report also endorses the educational benefits from multi-age and non-graded grouping, which may be undertaken on the basis of family members or mixed ability.

One of the purposes of flexible student grouping is that students can be encouraged to learn from each other. These patterns of fluid grouping allow students of different grades, year levels and abilities, to interact. Two particularly effective methods in this respect are cross-age tutoring and peer tutoring, both of which have proven to have consistently positive results on learning. New conceptions of teaching and learning demand changes in traditional roles for both students and teachers. Students become workers, active learners and, occasionally, teachers. Teachers, for their part, assume a stronger learning orientation than in the past.

On a larger scale, there is interest in the extended grouping structure along with the idea of sub-schools. Students in extended groups remain with a small group of teachers for a number of years, thereby securing greater continuity and closer understanding between teachers and students. Sub-schools or mini-schools may also improve the closeness of relations between teachers and students and provide a greater sense of identity for both students and staff, particularly in large schools.

Strong advocacy for persistent, stable teacher and student groups is made by two well-known American researchers (Wynne and Walberg, 1994). These authors argue that, 'Schools should try to keep discrete groups of students and teachers together over long periods of time. The size of the groups is not as important as their continuity' (1994: 529). They continue, 'persisting groups can be formed even in large schools. A variety of organizational options – e.g. divisions, homerooms, houses, or sub-schools – may serve to foster small-group life' (1994: 530). Furthermore, effective teaching techniques geared to small group settings can be employed, such as cooperative learning.

Grouping of Teachers

Efforts to re-design schools in many different systems have placed strong emphasis on greater teacher collaboration and teamwork. This leads some to predict that teachers' work organization in the future will be more team-oriented, in contrast to the traditional privatized and individualized teacher role. Among the most canvassed ideas for regrouping teachers is the team of teachers, as distinct from team teaching. The latter has had a fairly long and chequered history in practice. Attempts in the past have tried to introduce team teaching at the classroom level by grafting new teaching methods on to existing structures and practices, which remain intact. In an environment where the principle of backward- and iterative-mapping operates between core technology and organizational structures, where change is supported at each level, both teams of teachers and team teaching hold promise for teachers to plan, deliver and evaluate educational programs collaboratively (Little, 1990; Rosenholtz, 1989).

A version of teaching teams is to combine them with extended grouping so that teams of, say, four teachers take responsibility for the delivery of the whole curriculum to between 80 and 120 students. The same team then moves through the school with their group of students. In this arrangement, teachers may teach other subjects besides their own. Consequently, they grow closer to students and become more aware of their learning difficulties and needs. Each team is usually able to 'buy in' specialist help, such as music and physical education teaching. Specialist teachers in one Canberra school in Australia have formed themselves into a team to 'service' groups of mainstream teachers. These arrangements help break the rigidity of subject departments as the predominant form for organizing curricula and for grouping staff in secondary schools.

Other developments include the creation of specialist teachers. While one version of team teaching invites teachers to become more generalist, other trends favour more specialization, especially in areas such as languages, music and physical education. There is considerable scope to involve more parents and other adults in assisting teachers and students. Adding more adults to the classroom does not reduce class size. However, more importantly for informed teaching, it reduces the student/adult ratio, which seems more critical in enhancing learning. In addition, schools providing quality teaching and learning might employ more part-time and casual teachers and teachers' aides, thereby releasing other teachers to use time more flexibly.

Flexible Time

More flexible use of time and timetabling is a *sine qua non* for improving teaching and learning. Present patterns of the school year and school day are under increasing attack for their inflexibility (Knight, 1989). Typically, schools open for only 180 days, approximately half the year. Moreover, they normally function between limited hours of 8.30 a.m. and 4 p.m. There are, however, numerous examples in many parts of the world where the rigidity of these school hours is breached. In New Zealand, for example, properly supervised homework classes are organized in the school after hours for students whose home conditions are not conducive to study. In parts of mainland China, students may not leave school until after 6 p.m., as they spend the last two hours of the day on extra-curricular activities. Interestingly, they are helped in withstanding the long day by enforced sleep for one hour at lunchtime. As many of the students are 'only children' – a manifestation of China's one child per family policy – this period at the end of the school day is probably the only chance they have to socialize with other children, since most of them do not have brothers and sisters at home.

Access to school facilities, including libraries, is normally difficult after these hours. Yet, it is after school that students are expected to complete homework and when parents are more likely to be available to provide support. Extending the school day and introducing shift patterns would enable students and teachers to make better use of facilities and to capitalize on preferred learning styles. Learning-centred schools make their facilities, including libraries and computers, as easily accessible as possible. That may entail opening longer hours, including holidays, evenings and weekends.

Introducing flexitime for teachers, restructuring the curriculum to cycles of between six and nine days, dividing the school day into two parts, so that one-teacher-per-class activities take place in one half and whole-school or sub-school activities take place in the other, offer more flexibility for group-ings of different size. The large student group taught by one or two teachers can release other staff to undertake joint lesson planning and preparation. The occasional 'special program day' abandons the normal curriculum and instead, adopts a particular theme to guide learning across the whole school. This facilitates cross-age tutoring and other more flexible forms of teaching and student grouping.

Many of these flexible structures threaten to break the pattern of the traditional one-teacher class with lessons of forty minutes. The introduction of new conceptions of learning and teaching, involving higher-order thinking skills, renders the standard lesson time obsolete and inadequate. Problem-solving activities, for example, may take considerably longer than forty minutes. Standard lesson times often appear to be more for administra-tive expedience than for enhancing the learning of all students. Flexible lesson time is necessary for self-paced learning.

In the USA, many schools have dispensed with the Carnegie structure, where teachers typically teach five classes, each approximately forty-five minutes in length, and encounter 125 or even 180 students each day. The Carnegie structure militates against the principle of greater individualization of learning. Students may be in nine different locations during a school day without ever experiencing close personal attention from a teacher. Some of these schools have adopted the Copernican Plan (Carroll, 1994), where classes are taught for much longer periods – ninety minutes, two hours or even four hours – and they meet for only part of the school year – 30, 45, 60 or 90 days. Students experience fewer classes each day, and teachers likewise encounter fewer students. Re-organizing time in this way is not an end in itself. It is designed to improve relationships between teachers and students, to give more manageable workloads and to allow for more varied instructional techniques.

Furthermore, the typical pattern of a school day promotes fragmentation and wastage of time. Effective learning time is significantly reduced by the school day being structured into as many as seven or more lesson periods. At the end of each thirty-five or forty-minute lesson, there is often a change of teacher and/or classroom, generating multiple disruptive movements about the school, and difficulty in regaining the momentum for learning at the beginning of the next lesson. When allowance is made for time lost between lessons, movements about the school, break times, class time devoted to administrative and behavioural issues, the proportion of the school day students actually spend engaged in learning or time-on-task is a surprisingly small fraction of the total.

Flexible Curriculum Structures

More flexible arrangements for student and teacher grouping and timetabling enmesh with curricular changes. Change in any one of these structures can block or facilitate change in the others. Team teaching, for example, can promote the feasibility and workability of an integrated curriculum. Conversely, the introduction of an integrated curriculum is likely to work best with team teaching. The introduction of problem solving greatly enhances the efficacy of individualized and small group collaborative learning and is favoured by an integrated curriculum approach.

A wider range of teaching–learning venues offers more flexibility. Individualized and small group learning, as well as problem solving, may require more flexible approaches to learning taking place outside classrooms in libraries, resource centres, in workplaces and in the field. Laptop computers promote learning outside of the classroom. Some schools have established student and staff research and publications centres. The more varied uses of technology, especially CD-ROM and other multimedia developments, foster changes in teaching and learning. Much of this technology facilitates individualized and small group work, self-paced learning, and problem solving. Technology affects teachers as much as students by offering more ways of transmitting lessons (one teacher in a school might teach a lesson to schools throughout an entire system), of presenting information to be learned and of recording student progress.

Flexibility extends to student assessment. In more flexible structures, instead of all students sitting examinations at the same time once a year, irrespective of their progress, they can be assessed when they are ready.

Flexibility of assessment is matched by profiling each student's achievements against agreed and negotiated learning goals.

A major managerial and leadership challenge is presented by changing organizational structures in these diverse ways and ensuring their effective operation in meeting goals of quality teaching and learning.

Architectural Design, Physical Space and Furniture

New conceptions of curriculum, teaching and learning can either be helped or hindered in implementation by the architectural design of schools. Many schools have been designed with standard size rooms, rather than a range of different sized classrooms. This makes flexible teacher and student groupings more difficult. In Hong Kong, for example, almost all schools are built to standard specifications, involving a multi-storey structure with an undercover assembly area on the ground floor. Playground space is very limited too, often extending to no more than one or two basketball courts. Likewise, classroom space is tight, and students sit in rows with little space between. Desks and chairs are designed in ways that limit their flexibility for multi-purpose learning environments.

By contrast, schools such as Brewster Academy in New Hampshire have purpose-designed buildings with classrooms of different sizes to accommodate different types and functions of instructional groups. Classrooms and dormitories reflect the school's philosophy embodied in principles of individualized and small group instruction, with high emphasis placed on computer technology as a powerful learning tool. Thus classroom furniture has been designed, as explained in Chapter 8, to promote this instructional philosophy. A classroom layout contains clusters, each of four desks, butting up against technology posts into which students plug their computers. This physical layout fosters small group work, peer tutoring, cooperative learning and individualized learning, but the desks can also be moved apart to form a more conventional configuration suitable for direct teaching.

The majority of schools do not have the resources or the capability to change their architecture, physical space or even their furniture to any significant extent. This does not necessarily mean, however, that they need be defeated in achieving some re-arrangement of classroom layout, even using their existing desks and chairs. Teachers should be encouraged to experiment to see whether they can still accommodate the same number of students in clusters or circles instead of rows. The point being made is that reconfiguring the use of physical space and the layout of classrooms can symbolically as well as structurally convey very different orientations to teaching and learning.

Three Case Studies of Innovative Schools where Structure Supports Teaching and Learning

An increasing number of schools around the world have already chosen to depart from traditional organizational patterns. These schools have succeeded in designing structures which are not just consistent with, but actively promote their conceptions of informed teaching and learning. They have intentionally designed their organizational structures to reflect and connect with their visions, values and practices concerning core technology.

These new forms of school design include different approaches to teaching and learning, groupings of students and teachers, the school day, teachers' work organization and their professional relations, curricular programmes and school management. In all cases, the prime motivation has been to improve the quality of learning experienced by all students. In line with views of informed teaching and learning espoused in earlier chapters of this book, a common design feature of these re-designed schools is the creation of smaller, more personal units for the conduct of teaching, learning and counselling. Walker et al. (1996), for example, describe the attempt by one school in Australia to reorganize around the sub-schooling principle, where groups of 130 students are cared for and taught by a team of five or six teachers who move through the school with them. The advantages of these smaller operating units is found to be particularly beneficial within large schools, whose enrolment may be between 1,000 and 3,000 students. Below is a snapshot of three such schools.

Oatlands School, Tasmania

Reform at this school provides an interesting case of school re-design linking structural with pedagogical change. The following summary is based on an account of the school by Scott et al. (1997). Oatlands is a middle school, meaning that its students straddle the primary and secondary age range. The middle school is itself a re-design concept, emanating from the view held by many that the switch from primary to secondary stages is too dramatic a leap for many students and that there is need for a more progressive and gradual change. Oatlands takes students who would otherwise be in the senior primary school years and the junior secondary school years. The structural remodelling of the school was underpinned by a clear philosophy centred on the cognitive and affective needs of adolescents (Scott, 1994).

Teacher and student grouping

Teachers work in pairs, each pair being the principal teachers of a group of 25–30 students. They teach these students for 60–75 per cent of their class time in mixed-year groups of 5/6, 6/7 and 7/8 classes. Principal teachers take their classes for English, maths, science, social studies, health education and all pastoral care roles. The use of physical space has been altered to accommodate the new philosophy. Teachers work in pairs in double classroom units which have been created by building a sliding door between two adjoining classrooms. Each team of two is chosen on the basis of a male/female combination, and one must have expertise in the sciences and maths while the other is more language and humanities oriented. Each principal teacher and their students has one side of the double classroom as their home base where the core subjects are taught.

Within the unit, teachers are free to determine student groupings and when and how they will teach particular subjects. The two classes may be taught separately, as a composite group or as multiple groups utilizing other teachers, students or parent help. In addition, one teacher can work with individuals or small groups while the other works with the rest of the class.

Use of time

Oatlands has a flexible timetable designed to accommodate small group learning. Sixty to seventy-five per cent of the time is dedicated to the core learning areas. The school day is divided into four periods. Principal teacher periods are for the core subjects, and these always occupy the first period of each day. Language and mathematics are central to the curriculum and an integrated cross-curriculum approach is encouraged. The second period (one hour) each day is given over to tutorial time. A key philosophy of the school is that there should be flexibility of time for teachers to assist students by catering to individual needs, including those who need remediation and those who need extension.

Tutorial groups run for periods of about two weeks. The principal teacher might work with a small group having difficulty with mathematics, or another group requiring extension in poetry. The remainder of the classes combine with a different group of teachers and adult tutors to study two-week courses which the parent community has deemed important. These may be content-based (for example, Japanese) or skill-based, such as keyboarding and library research.

On two days each week, two periods are assigned to arts and design. Students are scheduled out to specialist teachers in these areas at the same time. This allows the arts and design teacher team to collaborate or to work independently with the students. Equally important, it enables all of the principal teachers to be off class at the same time, thereby opening up possibilities of joint planning, preparation and professional development.

Holweide School, Cologne, Germany

Strong interest in school re-design developed in many countries during the 1990s. However, the Holweide Comprehensive school in Cologne began its life in the mid-1970s. The German school system is renowned for its divisive three-tier structure: the Gymnasium schools cater for the upper social classes and most academically able; the Realschule are for the middle classes and the Hauptschule are for the lower classes and immigrant groups. Since the 1970s, however, a number of comprehensive schools (Gesamtschulen) have been established, mainly in response to concerns that the traditional system was failing to meet the economy's needs for scientists, engineers and technologists. Consequently, about 15 per cent of secondary schools are now comprehensive.

Staff at Holweide began to re-design with the question, 'how can children from all social classes and abilities be educated in one school, in regular classrooms?' The school incorporates structural features of small unit design, facilitating greater teacher knowledge of students, a sense of community among students and higher rates of academic achievement and attendance. Structural reorganization is responsive to newly adopted instructional methods. The following account is based on descriptions of the school given by Ratzki and Fisher (1990) and Oxley (1994). Holweide is a large school with a nine-form entry, an enrolment of under 2,000 students and 200 teachers. It had formerly been a Gymnasium with a selected population of middle- and upper-class children. In deciding to go comprehensive, the staff agreed on a number of design principles (Ratzki and Fisher, 1990), as follows:

- teachers work in tightly functioning groups;
- each group or team forms a small semi-autonomous unit within the larger school;
- teachers and students stay together for the whole six years of the school programme;
- students are organized into cooperative groups for learning, socializing and counselling.

These principles are embodied in the basic organizational work unit called the 'Team-Small-Group Plan'. Each grade level comprises of approximately 200 students and 18–20 teachers. A grade leader is given six periods (one-quarter of a class load) to coordinate instruction and to sit on the school council. Within each grade unit, teachers form teams of six.

The team-small-group plan: re-grouping teachers and students

This basic organizing unit aims, firstly, to solve the anonymity of a large school, and secondly, to enable students of widely differing abilities and backgrounds to work together. Thus, the school is organized into teams or units. Teams are composed of small and stable groups of teachers, usually about six, who are responsible for about ninety students, divided into three classes of thirty. This arrangement is designed to allow teachers and students to establish close working relationships over a long period of time. They stay together for six years, from Grade 5 to Grade 10.

Students are also organized into teams or 'table groups', with five or six students per table. The table group concept is the key organizing device forming the instructional core of the school. Each table group will normally stay together for at least a year, enabling close supportive relationships to develop.

School management

School management is in the hands of the head teacher, two deputies and a governing panel of about twenty senior colleagues, some of whom are elected and others are appointed by the authorities. Their managerial roles are also different from the traditional ones of control and supervision. Rather, they coordinate and support teachers, monitor the school's progress and seek and solve problems before they become serious. The head teacher, besides having a reduced teaching load, has to justify the high level of discretion enjoyed by each team.

Teaching teams

Each team of teachers covers all the subjects and assumes responsibility for the whole curriculum of their ninety students (organized into three classes of thirty). Their level of autonomy is high. The team decides the timetable or schedules, teaching allocations and student placement in classes, how the curriculum will be organized and taught (whether in single periods or longer blocks of time), cover for absent colleagues, lunchtime activities, and parent involvement and field trips. While all six teachers cover the subject teaching of ninety students, they also pair up to work together as class tutors (home class or homeroom teachers) for a given class. A special education instructor is assigned to each team, enabling each to cope with the school policy of mainstreaming students with behavioural problems and physical and intellectual disabilities.

All teachers meet every second Tuesday afternoon for team meetings. While each team is given autonomy, consistency is gained across teams by means of separate curricular and counselling conferences, to which teams send delegates. These meetings establish school-wide standards and guidelines and attempt to solve problems of a general nature.

Student table groups

A student group of six will contain a mix of abilities, gender and ethnicities. Students tutor and help each other. Unlike cooperative learning groups, the table groups stay together for all subjects for at least a year. Group members thus get to know each other's learning differences. Both individual and group results are important, and students take responsibility for their own as well as their group's performance. If the performance or behaviour of an individual is unsatisfactory, the teacher might discuss the matter with the group as well as the individual.

Each table group meets once a week to discuss problems and to suggest improvements in their processes. During lessons, the more able are expected to help the others, allowing the teacher to work intensively with those who need attention. Such is group pride that students undertake a lot of personal and peer coaching. The belief is that the more able benefit by reinforcing their own learning, while at the same time helping the slower learners.

Attention is paid to the need to train students in effective team work. Periodically, a teacher will work with a group on undertaking learning tasks, dividing up the work and deciding on how best to work. In addition, twice a year one day is set aside for informal group consultation. Groups discuss their progress with a teacher. On other days throughout the year, the timetable is relaxed and each table group thinks of a common activity for the whole team. Certain days are set aside for project work, where students are offered a choice such as undertaking a social project or improving the local environment.

Individual plans: learning how to learn

Recognition is given to individual learning differences and time is set aside for developing individual learning strategies in addition to the table groups. Students have some choice as to whether they prefer to learn individually or in table groups, and the way they prefer to learn.

At the start of each week, the tutors present the weekly plan which structures each student's work for the next few days. They also detail the tasks for each of their subjects. Students internalize these so that they become their own plans and goals. In this way, students undertake responsibility for their own work and set personal goals. They also choose individual learning tasks for their free periods. Tutorial lessons are opportunities for students to discuss any problems with their tutors. Students decide the agendas.

Parents are involved

Parental involvement is encouraged. Parents in each class elect five representatives to sit on a council, which provides a link between team teachers and the parents. They also become involved with teachers in running an array of lunchtime activities, including music and sports.

School time

Holweide has a slightly extended school day, from 8.15 a.m. to 4.15 p.m. Students spend about the same time in class each week as do US students, the extra time being allocated to staff meetings, lengthy lunchtime activities and a mid-morning break. Over the year, however, students receive more hours of formal class instruction than US students as the school year is several weeks longer.

As previously mentioned, learning time is organized flexibly throughout the week, ranging from several double instruction periods to periods of individualized work, tutoring, community projects and student guidance. Students also have free periods when they can catch up or undertake enrichment activities. In this way, all are able to master the work. All teachers offer two periods a week of student guidance as an integral part of their schedule. Other uses of time include team meetings to discuss group process.

Professional development

Both new and beginning teachers receive no special training before assuming their duties. However, the teacher teams provide a powerful means of introducing new members to the Holweide methods. Teams are stable and cohesive and they hold regular planning meetings, all of which provides a high level of support for new teachers. Likewise, the inclusion of special education students in mainstream classes is successful partly because of team support. Special educators much prefer to be included in instructional teams rather than teach special classes in isolation.

Costs and benefits

Holweide school is well cited in the literature. It has been operating longer than most re-designed schools and represents a democratic model in a German culture noted for its hierarchical emphasis. Teachers, students and parents are all involved in decision making. This degree of democracy comes at a price: it is a time-consuming model. But on the other hand, teachers claim that their work is more satisfying, that they have more control over the rules and ideas they apply, and that they are collegial and collaborative in helping each other.

Students, likewise, speak to success. They feel more supported and self-confident, and consequently the drop-out rate has reduced to less than 1 per cent. Furthermore, 60 per cent go on to qualify for three-year college entrance (compared to 27 per cent for the country as a whole).

Brewster Academy, New Hampshire, USA

Brewster Academy has, since 1991, been undergoing whole-school re-design. The basic unit for delivery of the curriculum is the teaching team, a multi-disciplinary group of four subject teachers plus a learning specialist attached to each team whose purpose is to assist students encountering difficulty. Each team works with a group of 50–60 students and meets four times a week for an hour to jointly plan and deal with student-related issues (Bain, 1996). Every team has a team leader who is charged with the implementation of the programme and successful operation of the team process. The teams are expected to follow an institutionalized collaborative decision-making process, called the collaborative consultation model (explained in Chapter 12) and to develop action plans to deal with the needs of students and the programme. Team work is a core part of the professional life of Brewster teachers and is written into the position descriptions (see Chapter 10). Team members are given regular opportunity to evaluate the working of the collaborative consultation process. Teaching teams may create task groups for particular assignments.

Besides teaching teams, there is a raft of other teams concerned with developing policy and administering school affairs. They are headed by the school executive team, whose job is to coordinate the work of other teams and to formally adopt school-wide recommendations from these teams where appropriate. Other teams with policy and administrative responsibilities are:

- Teaching and learning (headed by the academic dean);
- Community living (headed by the dean of student affairs);
- Technology (headed by the manager of information systems);
- Management and policy (headed by the academic dean);
- Personnel (headed by the director of personnel);
- Admissions (headed by the director of admissions).

It is the prime responsibility of each team to develop Brewster policy in the area of its specialization while ensuring its fidelity to the school mission of offering every student a quality curriculum experience. The *modus operandi* of the team process is described further in Chapter 12.

Conclusions and Associated Cross-Cultural Issues

Placing the present argument in context, reconfiguring structures such as student and teacher grouping and use of space and time for alignment with new conceptions of teaching, learning and curriculum, is a necessary but not sufficient condition for successful design of the learning-centred school. Structures sympathetic to informed practices can make the difference between success and failure of reforms. Many innovations have failed to become institutionalized in the past because new practices have been grafted on to stable and unchanging structures. Importantly, it is informed practices with regard to curriculum, teaching and learning which should direct and drive the shape of organizational structures rather than the reverse. The case study of Holweide School in Cologne well illustrates how successful school re-design is dependent on a close, seamless integration of ideas, philosophies, practices and structures, all of which are mutually reinforcing.

Many observers have recognized that schools in different cultures display a remarkable similarity in their structures, the inference being that structures are not particularly culture sensitive. There may be justifiable reasons for this conclusion: culture is more likely to be present in the values, attitudes and behaviours which characterize the processes and practices of schools rather than the structures. Nonetheless, the present argument proposes that structures reflect and support core practices associated with informed teaching and learning. They also convey powerful symbolic messages to students as well as teachers about the desired orientation to teaching and learning, and their respective roles. However, the similarity of structures in schools in different cultures may be more apparent than real, especially if the similarity masks different underlying cultural preferences. A fitting example is provided by the emphasis in designing the learning-centred school given to collaborative work groups and teams for both teachers and students. In the case of schools in Anglo-American societies, cooperative student groups are usually formal, short term and change from subject to subject. However, in the case of cooperative work groups in East Asia, they are often informal but enduring, lasting from one year to the next, and founded on trusting and close supportive networks.

Many schools in Asia are undoubtedly caught in something of a conundrum as far as moving to new structures is concerned. Their over-large class sizes and lack of space, coupled with the growing expectation that they individualize their curricula, render them prime beneficiaries of restructuring. At the same time, however, these same factors serve to inhibit such change. In Hong Kong, as elsewhere in Asia, dual sessions, where two schools use the same buildings but at different times of the day, create added complications. Nonetheless, teachers and administrators need to be more alert to the possibilities that can flow from experimenting, even within current resource constraints, with the reconfiguring of space and classroom layout. Spatial rearrangements can and need to powerfully support the informed practices of core technology espoused in this book. While these informed practices are founded on principles which appear to be generic, exactly how schools in different cultures assimilate to and operationalize those principles should necessarily reflect cultural sensitivity and difference.

References

Bain, A. (1996) 'The schools design model at Brewster Academy: technology serving teaching and learning', *Technological Horizons in Education 23 (10): 72–9.*

Brickley, D. and Westerberg, T. (1990) 'Restructuring a comprehensive high school', *Educational Leadership*, 47 (7): 28–31.

Cardellichio, T.L. (1995) 'Curriculum and the structure of school', *Phi Delta Kappan*, 76 (8): 629–32.

Carroll, J.M. (1994) 'The Copernican Plan evaluated: the evolution of a revolution', *Phi Delta Kappan* 76 (2): 105–13.

Dimmock, C. (1997) 'Leading and managing restructuring at the school site: a Western Australian case study', in L. Logan and J. Sachs (eds), *Meeting the Challenges of Primary Schooling*, London: Routledge, 19–35.

Doyle, D.P. and Hartle, T.W. (1985) 'Leadership in education: governors, legislators and teachers', *Phi Delta Kappan* 67 (1): 21–7.

Hoyle, E. (1969) *The Role of the Teacher*, London: Routledge & Kegan Paul.

Knight, B. (1989) *Managing School Time*, Harlow: Longman.

Little, J.W. (1990) 'The persistence of privacy: autonomy and initiative in teachers' professional relations', *Teachers' College Record* 91 (4): 509–36.

Murphy, J. (1991) *Restructuring Schools: Capturing and Assessing the Phenomena*, New York: Teachers' College Press.

—— (1993) 'Restructuring schooling: the equity infrastructure', *School Effectiveness and School Improvement* 4 (2): 111–30.

Owens, R.G. (1995) *Organizational Behavior in Education*, 5th edn,. Needham Heights, MA: Allyn and Bacon.

Oxley, D. (1994) 'Organizing schools into small units: alternatives to homogeneous grouping', *Phi Delta Kappan* 75 (7): 521–6.

Ratzki, A. and Fisher, A. (1990) 'Life in a restructured school', *Educational Leadership* 47 (4): 46–51.

Rosenholtz, S. (1989) *Teachers' Workplace: The Social Organisation of Schools*, New York: Longman.

Schools Council (Australia) (1992) 'The compulsory years: developing flexible strategies in the early years of schooling: purposes and possibilities', *Project Paper 5*, Canberra: NBEET.

Scott, L. (1994) 'Middle schooling in Tasmania: not just a case of structural reorganisation', *Unicorn* 20 (2): 43–51.

Scott, L., Davis, K. and Andrewartha, D. (1997) 'The middle years of schooling', in L. Logan and J. Sachs (eds), *Meeting the Challenges of Primary Schooling*, London: Routledge, 79–100.

Spady, W.G. (1988) 'Organising for results: the basis of authentic restructuring and reform', *Educational Leadership* 46 (2): 4–8.

Walker, A., Templeton, B. and Stott, K. (1996) 'A move to sub-schooling: tracking the change', *Planning and Changing* 27 (1/2): 101–14.

Wynne, E.A. and Walberg, H.J. (1994) 'Persisting groups: an overlooked force for learning', *Phi Delta Kappan* 75 (7): 527–30.

10 Developing Personnel and Financial Resources Policies

While earlier chapters in this book have focused on the more technical aspects of school design involving precepts, principles, approaches, methods, practices and skills, it is a truism that all of these are fundamentally dependent on the qualities of teachers and administrators for their successful delivery. Re-designing schools is thus an integration of the two: a combination of the technical, methodological and practical with human endeavour. Both need to be integrated and mutually reinforcing. Even the most carefully conceived models of practice come to nought if personnel do not have the knowledge, skills and disposition to implement them. On the other hand, without well conceived curriculum, teaching and learning models, even the most able and energetic staff is likely to be misguided and ineffectual.

This chapter begins with an introductory discussion on the significance of a personnel policy to the re-designed school and an exposition of the key stages and functions which comprise an integrated personnel policy. It goes on, secondly, to outline three position descriptions – one for teachers, another for senior teachers, and a third for administrators. Thirdly, it argues the need for career paths in schools. Fourthly, attention is switched to the principles of selecting teachers. Fifthly, a brief discussion is presented on teacher appraisal in the learning-centred school. Sixthly, new approaches to professional development are noted and their importance as part of a personnel policy are recognized. Seventhly, cross-cultural issues connected with personnel policy are discussed. Finally, some implications of the learning-centred school for the management of financial resources are raised.

There is much wrong with current practice in regard to personnel policy in education. In reference to the USA, Darling-Hammond (1996) identifies five barriers which together account for there being no real system for recruiting, preparing and developing America's teachers. These are:

* inadequate teacher education;
* slipshod recruitment;
* haphazard hiring and induction;

- lack of professional development and rewards for knowledge and skill;
- schools structured for failure.

This is a formidable list covering the field of personnel policy.

It follows that an intentional approach to personnel is as crucial as it is to curriculum design and to informed teaching and learning practices. It is only through the appointment of appropriate teachers and administrators that the principles, methods and practices which are intended and seen as desirable are transformed from a state of theory and ideas to enactment and delivery.

In keeping with the backward mapping and iterative process promulgated in this book, a personnel policy which is consistent with the precepts and informed practices of school re-design is imperative. At stake here is an unequivocal philosophy: that only when the school has determined the form and structure of its curriculum, only when informed practices of teaching and learning have been identified, and only when the place of computer technology within the core has been decided, can it seriously begin to formulate a consistent and supportive personnel policy. It is argued that this philosophy and the following developmental stages of the model are applicable generically across all cultures.

The development of a personnel policy involves the following stages:

- clarification of position descriptions at different levels from teacher to principal;
- selection, appointment and induction of staff;
- introduction of a stepped and structured career progression;
- appraisal and evaluation of staff;
- operation of a professional development programme;
- promotion.

While it is relatively straightforward to formulate a coherent and consistent policy on paper, authenticity and legitimacy comes only when the principles and precepts embedded in each of the stages are truly put into practice. For example, position descriptions are derived from the principles of informed practice. New teachers are selected on the basis of their ability to meet the criteria in the position descriptions. Teachers are promoted, appraised and developed on the basis of performance and merit in relation to criteria underscored by informed practice. Importantly, too, recognition and reward systems should be faithful to and embedded in the principles and precepts underlying the re-designed school. Thus teachers are rewarded when they excel in terms of the practices which are valued.

Each of the stages recognized above as constituting a personnel policy is now discussed in more detail. Three sample position descriptions are provided: teacher, senior teacher, and academic leader (dean).

Position Descriptions for Teachers, Senior Teachers and Administrators

Decisions regarding position descriptions and recruitment procedures are more straightforward once the school has clarified and confirmed its approach to curriculum and to informed practices in respect of teaching and learning. With these in place, it is possible to identify the roles, functions and qualities expected of present and prospective teachers. Schooling is essentially an interactive and human enterprise: it is through human endeavour that the school's vision, mission and programme is enacted and implemented. The quality of personnel employed and their suitability for the task, given the particularities of the school's culture and context, are thus instrumental in ensuring its success.

Procedurally, the following iterative and backward-mapping process is suggested as a means of generating position descriptions for teachers (Bain, 1996):

- review the school mission and goals;
- review the intentional curriculum;
- review the list of informed practices in respect of teaching and learning;
- after considering these reviews, draw up position descriptions;
- disseminate to relevant others in the school, such as the teaching and learning team.

The format of a position description for a teacher might include the following (Bain, 1996):

---

1 Title of the position: Teacher of.....

2 Responsible to:

   Name of the person to whom the teacher will be responsible.

3 General functions and responsibilities: This should clarify that the appointee is responsible for implementing the policy of the school with respect to the curriculum, and informed teaching and learning practices; that they should strive to model excellence in so doing, and that they are expected to participate in and contribute to the school's on-going efforts to improve practice.

4 Specific responsibilities:

   i   Teaching
   •   Demonstrates variety and balance in teaching in keeping with informed practice

---

- Possesses good subject knowledge
- Presents in clear and coherent fashion
- Manages and organizes effectively and efficiently at the class-room level
- Displays and models skills valued in the school curriculum
- Provides ample and timely feedback and evaluation to students
- Skilled and comfortable using technology in the class setting
- Assumes responsibility for student performance – is outcomes oriented
- Skilled at individualizing instruction and in multi-level teaching in whole-class situations
- Instruction is based on the school curriculum

ii Programme implementation
- Demonstrates understanding and acceptance of the school handbook and precepts and principles underlying informed practice
- Acts and fulfils responsibilities to meet schedules and deadlines
- Performs all responsibilities to a uniformly high standard
- Seeks assistance from Team Leader when necessary
- Adheres to collaborative procedures when involved in team work and problem solving

iii Team work
- Works collaboratively to achieve team goals
- Assists others in the team when necessary
- Promotes and advocates collaboration and team work
- Promotes and advocates joint problem-solving
- Communicates effectively
- Is able and willing to compromise

iv Technology
- Demonstrates skills in the use of various applications e.g. Power Point
- Uses technology effectively in instruction
- Is skilled in accessing and retrieving information
- Uses and develops appropriate software

v Curriculum (academic and extra-curricular or community education)
- Actively participates in the implementation of the school's curriculum development process in the academic and community areas
- Develops units and courses in line with the school curriculum
- Demonstrates skills in the review and selection of curriculum resources
- Shows ability and willingness to problem solve and adapt the curriculum when necessary

vi Professional growth
- Seeks assistance with theory and practice
- Seeks information on informed practices and educational resources
- Translates professional development into practice
- Shares exemplary practice with colleagues

Career Progression: Senior Teacher

Irrespective of whether the re-designed school is part of a government system or is independent, it needs to think about the career progression of its staff. How will outstanding teachers be rewarded? What titles and responsibilities will they carry? Is there a clear progression of steps for excellent performance to be rewarded? Systemic schools are likely to be more constrained by external rules and guidelines governing promotion positions and criteria than are independent schools. However, in some decentralized systems, not only has the school total budgetary control but it also has the flexibility to decide its staffing structure. It may be able to decide, for example, to dispense with a senior administrator and employ two extra teachers.

Many government school systems have joined independent schools in creating master teacher or senior teacher positions. These positions provide at least two benefits: first, they enable some able people who wish to remain teachers to be promoted without leaving teaching and entering administration; second, incumbents can act as role models and mentors to teachers. Clear criteria are needed to decide who to promote to such positions. In line with the basic precepts of school re-design, all positions should be referenced to the delivery of the curriculum using informed teaching and learning practices. According to the backward-mapping process, even position descriptions of instructional leaders, including master teachers, deans, deputy principals and the principal, should be referenced to teaching and learning. It follows that schools should strongly resist any attempt to misuse the position to reward and promote people for other reasons than excellence in teaching.

The format for a senior teacher position description should start with the description for a teacher position and be incrementally added to in ways which reflect the senior status of the position. For brevity, only the additional responsibilities over and above those expected of teachers are included below:

---

1   Title of the position: Senior Teacher of.....

2   Responsible to:

Academic Dean

3   General functions and responsibilities:

Teachers at the senior level are expected to demonstrate excellence in knowledge and skills of their subject. They should model excellence in the implementation of school policy. They assume responsibility for promoting the growth of other faculty members and for evolving the school programme. They also assume team leadership and leadership of professional development activities.

4   Specific responsibilities:

i   Teaching
• Presentations reflect a level of expert knowledge of the subject content
• Models practices of informed teaching and actively participates in the professional growth of other faculty members
• Provides leadership in the selection, modification and implementation of informed practices in the team. This includes direct teaching, cooperative learning, problem-based learning, and mastery learning
• Promotes informed teaching practices by the team
• Problem solves for self and other team members
• Coordinates team effort

---

ii   Programme implementation
- Develops school policy
- Provides assistance to team members
- Undertakes administrative work

iii   Team work
- Ensures the implementation of the concept of the team and team primacy
- Ensures the implementation of the collaborative problem-solving model

iv   Technology
- Undertakes maintenance of hardware and software
- Assists teachers and students in the use of technology
- Leads the team in applications of software to the subject area
- Contributes to the school's technology policy

v   Curriculum (academic and extra-curricular or community education)
- Develops courses/units for the school curriculum
- Serves on the school Teaching and Learning Team

Career Progression: Academic Leadership

Leadership in a school undertaking wholesale re-design is crucial in providing guidance, keeping morale high and gaining and maintaining commitment to the change process. These can only be achieved when leadership at all levels combines excellent human resource management with knowledge and expertise related to the core technology of informed teaching and learning practices.

In many schools, it is surprising how little time administrators devote to instructional and curriculum issues. Re-designing schools around central concepts of informed practices and individualized curricula demands that leaders attend to the most important functions of their schools. Active and direct involvement is important, especially through the stages of the change process, when direction, clarity and commitment are constantly required. Reaffirmation of main goals and purposes is one of the leaders' main responsibilities. Teachers most need support for their classroom work. Leaders can only provide such support when they have the technical expertise in addition to good human relations skills.

As with the senior teacher, the position description for the academic leader is backward mapped from the teacher position description. At the same time, consideration is needed of school policy and the precepts of informed practice. An emphasis is placed on supervision of the academic programme and the practices involved in its implementation. Below is a suggested outline description for the position of academic dean (Bain, 1996).

---

1   Title of the position: Academic Dean

2   Responsible to:

Principal/Deputy Principal

3   General functions and responsibilities:

The Dean plays an instructional leadership role and is responsible for implementation of school policy and particularly the academic and extra-curricular programmes. Responsibility covers both student and staff performance as it relates to teaching and learning. The Dean chairs the school Teaching and Learning Team, monitors the implementation of all programmes, implements the staff appraisal procedure and professional development programme. The Dean is responsible for all Team Leaders.

4   Specific responsibilities:

i   Student and teacher performance
  • Ensures that students make curriculum progress
  • Evaluates student, teacher, team and school performance using appropriate tests and instruments
  • Exercises instructional leadership with respect to the following

ii   Curriculum
  • Develops and implements curriculum development process
  • Assists in design and implementation of courses and units
  • Reviews and selects curriculum resources
  • Problem solves curricular matters pertaining to faculty and students
  • Ensures individualization, student progress and quality of materials and courses

---

iii   Teaching methodology
- Ensures the teaching teams apply informed practice in respect of teaching and learning
- Ensures effective classroom organization and scheduling

iv   Student behaviour management
- Undertakes to manage student behaviour in regard to attendance and conduct
- Oversees consistency between team disciplinary policy and its implementation

v   Student evaluation
- Implements student evaluation and reporting system
- Manages portfolio evaluation and develops evaluation procedures where necessary

vi   Personnel, supervision and evaluation
- Implements school policy on faculty evaluation
- Exercises instructional leadership skills to evaluate staff and to provide feedback
- Serves as member of the personnel team to select new staff
- Implements classroom observation and supervision for professional growth

vii   Instructional support
- Collaborates with Director of Support Services on the implementation of special programmes

viii   Programme integration
- Manages the integration of programmes where appropriate

ix   Team process
- Manages the team model
- Ensures the implementation of the team concept and collaborative problem solving

x   Professional development
- Collaborates with the executive team to implement the professional development programme to include team building; school culture and climate; classroom management; teaching

and learning; technology; community living; the school curriculum
- Integrates all components of the professional development programme

xi Technology
- Responsible for implementing all aspects of the school technology policy
- Provides leadership in the areas of technology for: managing the curriculum; design and implementation of instruction; evaluation of software; all applications; management of the school; and marketing the school

xii Management
- Manages and implements the academic programme including the schedule, major academic activities and events, examinations and parent communication regarding student performance

The same process of backward mapping from the essential core business of the school to decide position descriptions continues back up through the school to include the principal.

A Career Path

The teaching profession has long been criticized for not having established a recognized career progression which rewards those who perform well and who deserve to progress. Teachers in early and mid-career often find their progress blocked as length of service often becomes the main criterion for progression. And this is a poor indicator of performance. What is required is a sequence of career stages, each lasting a determinate period of time, which moves faculty through by rewarding performance.

Bain (1996) suggests the following career steps:

- intern: a one-year programme for students currently enrolled in teaching degrees.
- graduate: the entry level for a career path, including a one-year probationary period.

- instructor: reached after 3–5 years at which time, assuming successful evaluation, moves to the next level.
- teacher: attainable after six years or more of teaching experience; experienced entrants from other schools would be appointed at this level; mid-career.
- senior teacher: performs all the duties of the teacher and in addition, provides instructional leadership and assumes a leading role in professional development.

Whatever the career steps adopted or applied, the present staffing structure of a school would need to reflect the different levels, as appropriate. Very able younger faculty should be able to accelerate through the steps, and this may be one way in which the school can keep such staff. The time spent at each stage in the above example is considerably less than is normally the case in practice.

Budgetary considerations inevitably introduce an air of reality. It is not always the case that rewarding teachers more by paying higher salaries guarantees better teachers and teaching. However, rewarding with average remuneration may firstly enable the school to set and achieve higher than normal expectations of performance, and may secondly enable it to keep in its employ good teachers who might otherwise be tempted to move on.

Selecting Teachers

A clear goal must be to select and promote teachers with the capability and enthusiasm to implement school policy in respect of the curriculum, teaching and learning. It is difficult for professional development to compensate for a lack of ability or commitment to a school policy espousing informed practice in the core technology. However, it may be unrealistic to expect job applicants to already possess the knowledge and skill set necessary to function in the school. Thus, short-listed applicants should be assessed in terms of their potential capabilities, their awareness of the precepts and issues relating to informed practice, and the likelihood of their benefiting from a professional development programme based on informed practice. In other words, selection of suitable staff is based on previous performance and potential performance. All decisions should be referenced to the skills, abilities and predispositions expressed in the relevant position description.

Once the school gathers a reputation for its approach, it will tend to attract teachers who are philosophically committed to, and in agreement with, the precepts that it stands for. Active marketing and presentation of the school's public image in terms of its mission, intentions and programmes is therefore important in attracting applications from competent and empathetic teachers. It is just as important for the applicant to know the philosophy, precepts and practices driving the school to which they are considering applying as it is for the school to ascertain the suitability of the applicant. Essentially, it is a matching process.

It is not the purpose here to describe in detail the various selection tools and processes available to schools. A general rule is that over-reliance on any one technique is fraught with danger. References may be unreliable, especially if the referee is prepared to give a glowing reference in order to rid of a difficult or under-performing colleague. Interviews, too, are notoriously unreliable in their predictive value (Harris and Monk, 1992; Morgan et al., 1984). The interviewee may be able to present an impressive front which bears little relationship to the 'real' person. Nonetheless, the weakness of the interview is also its strength, namely, that it provides an opportunity to interact with the applicant and to gain a sense of the 'whole person'.

Among the battery of selection tools and techniques are application forms, resumés or curriculum vitae, letters of recommendation, rating scales, transcripts, telephone investigations, interviews, tests, analogous tests and demonstration lessons, either live or videotaped. Most procedures rely on the application form, curriculum vitae, references and interview, any or all of which may fail to yield an accurate profile of the applicant. Morgan et al. (1984) therefore strongly endorse the use of analogous tests, where applicants are given problems and in-tray exercises which reflect realistic scenarios likely to be faced in the job. In addition, many selection procedures now include model or demonstration lessons given live if the applicant is *in situ*, or on tape if they are unable to attend in person.

In the United States, use is often made of assessment centres. Shulman (1987a), for example, when working on the Teacher Assessment Project associated with the development of a national certification programme by the National Board for Professional Teaching Standards, recommended the concept of a teaching assessment centre. Among the activities in which such centres engage is to ask candidates to examine several alternative textbooks and to critically compare their merits and demerits, including consideration of the teaching methods assumed, their appropriateness for different groups of learners and the goals to which they are directed. This would test knowledge of their fields. They might then be asked to present an oral and written report of their findings.

Two useful practices can help improve the accuracy and comprehensiveness of performance data used in the selection or promotion process. Both are rarely given due recognition. The first concerns the individual. All teachers and administrators should keep an updated curriculum vitae on computer. The second relates to the organization and its policy with regard to appraisal and professional development. If the school operates a rigorous appraisal system with a detailed and accurate system of records for each staff member, then references can be based on record and hard data rather than on impression and subjective opinion. If the school also links professional development to appraisal, then the applicant may have already begun to address his/her needs. The moral here is that to have been a member of staff in a well managed school can be advantageous in seeking subsequent appointments.

The appointment of new staff or the promotion of existing staff provides an opportunity for administrators and others involved to reaffirm and refresh their own understanding and commitment to the school's precepts and policies. They will want to pool questions to ask of candidates. Bain (1996) gives some examples of the type of questions appropriate to test the previous and potential performance of candidates:

- Having read the school handbook and its philosophy and practices, how does it differ from your present or previous schools?
- Can you tell us how you have adapted instructional materials in the past?
- What steps have you taken in the past to seek professional development to improve your ability to meet student needs?
- What do you see as the role of technology in education? Describe your own technology skills.
- In terms of the position description, evaluate your strengths and needs.

Specific questions are needed to ascertain applicants' characteristics with regard to their philosophical commitment, their current knowledge and skills, their attitudes towards and capacity for change and development, and their knowledge and awareness of the school mission, policy, programme and practices.

Pro formas and summary forms need to be designed to capture the knowledge, skills and attitudes of the candidates and to allow for valid comparisons of their strengths and needs. All of the evidence from the multiple sources of data collection needs to be brought together for this purpose. Underpinning the decisional process is the applicants' abilities to fulfil the mission and policy of the school with respect to its stated curriculum, teaching and learning practices.

Staff Appraisal

Staff appraisal, or personnel evaluation, is an integral part of a personnel policy, which in turn should be grounded in the school's mission and goals. The policy should address the following stages: position description, staff selection, induction, performance appraisal, professional development and, finally, promotion. A fuller exposition of teacher appraisal is included in chapter 11 on evaluating teachers' performance.

There is strong theoretical support for the virtues of appraisal or personnel evaluation. A wealth of research shows that feedback and reinforcement are two effective ways of improving and sustaining performance, for both students and faculty. Appraisal provides an avenue for providing such feedback. There is also general agreement that students, teachers and administrators rarely receive enough feedback on their performance. The traditional culture of schools has been antithetical to feedback.

In practice, there seem to be relatively few examples of successful school appraisal schemes fulfilling meaningful purposes. Among the manifold reasons for this are: the time and effort invested; the tendency to include too much; the human skills required; the technical knowledge which appraisers need; and the confusion of purposes between summative evaluation for promotion and determination of salary and formative evaluation for performance improvement and professional development.

Staff appraisal is a potentially 'powerful' set of activities which can either help bind and confirm the school's commitment to its mission and policy, or derail it. It is an intensely interpersonal process and by definition, heavily judgmental. It needs to be handled with great sensitivity, and to focus on empirical evidence and performance data rather than on opinion or subjective impression. It must be open and transparent, the purposes and procedures clearly understood by all participants, and achieve an appropriate blend of collegial involvement and support with confidentiality.

In the context of the re-designed school, what to appraise and the methods to be used are determined by school policy and the key precepts underpinning that policy. That is, appraisal becomes a tool for reinforcing fidelity to the school precepts of adaptive and individualized curriculum, informed practices of teaching and learning, the embedding and integration of technology, and so on. Teachers and administrators are appraised according to their commitment and contribution to school policy and precepts and the degree of success achieved in their implementation.

An appraisal system referenced in school policy and its undergirding key precepts has significant implications beyond the individual teacher. While most appraisal schemes focus on evaluation of the individual teacher or administrator, the system espoused in this chapter and more fully in the chapter on evaluating teachers' performance generates important benefits for the school as an organisation. For example, by appraising each teacher's and administrator's performance against the common backcloth of school policy and key precepts, the process not only enhances performance at the individual level, but also at the collective or whole-school level. Thus school improvement is a beneficiary from what is ostensibly an individually targeted exercise; a phenomenon which is rarely appreciated with appraisal schemes.

Finally, both formative and summative elements are considered important features of the system. An emphasis on formative evaluation signifies the use of appraisal in promoting the ongoing improvement of teachers as they develop the greater knowledge and skill mastery implicated in individualizing curricula and informed teaching and learning practices. However, summative elements of the appraisal system are also important, particularly as they relate to promotional and salary decisions and to references for staff applying for positions outside the school.

Professional Development

Successful professional development programmes need to be integrated with, and supportive of, the whole-school design process. As Schlechty (1990: 139) says, 'Human resource development becomes the linchpin upon which all improvement efforts are based'. This section outlines the principles of informed approaches to professional development which integrate with school design are outlined.

More recently, policy makers and educators have come to place great importance on professional development as crucial to the successful implementation of restructuring policies. However, few such restructuring policies identify the principles let alone the specifics of supportive professional development programmes. In general, professional development is a weak spot in the school improvement process. There is a need for more robust models of professional development, ones which derive from the images of the reformed, re-designed school.

In most schools and school districts throughout the Anglo-American world (and beyond), too little is invested in ongoing professional development and too much on 'one-off' workshops or talks. Teachers in many systems have minimal non-contact time for collaborative planning. Teachers in the USA typically have three to five hours a week for planning compared with mainland China, where they may have up to twenty hours. In addition, professional development is grossly underfunded, often comprising less than 1 per cent of the education budget, which is meagre when compared with IBM's investment of 10 per cent of its budget in professional development. Too often, there is little incentive in terms of career advancement for teachers to engage in professional development. Moreover, as Darling-Hammond (1996) claims, the way in which teachers' work is organized – in isolation from one another – and the failure to use technologies in teaching, mean that many teachers are ill-prepared for the job they undertake. Darling-Hammond observes that high-performance businesses are abandoning their traditional hierarchical, organizational forms in favour of flatter hierarchies, creating teams and training employees to take on wider responsibilities using technologies to perform their work more efficiently. Schools that have done this are able to provide more time for teachers to work together and more time for teachers to work closely with students.

Guidelines for a new wave of professional development programmes are beginning to emerge, especially in the USA. They are urgently needed, since most restructuring policies emanating from governments, whether Western or Asian, specifically state that the provision of appropriate and high quality professional development is a *sine qua non* for successful policy implementation. Notably absent from these documents, however, is specification of the type, form, standard and quality of professional development required. It is therefore instructive to identify some of the 'new wave' thinking on professional development, bearing in mind that it largely reflects American insights and therefore needs some caution before its application to other cultures.

After reviewing forty-four elementary, middle and high schools in the USA with the purpose of eliciting the conditions for high performance through school-based management, Wohlstetter (1995: 23) concluded, with respect to professional development, that these successful schools had a 'focus on continuous improvement with school-wide training in functional and process skills and in areas related to curriculum and instruction'. Not only was professional development a high priority, but staff participation was regular and on-going. Furthermore:

> Professional development at these schools was used strategically and was deliberately tied to the school's reform objectives ... activities were oriented toward building a school-wide capacity for change, creating a professional community, and developing a shared knowledge base .... These successful schools also expanded the range of content areas for training beyond the typical areas of curriculum and instruction to include participation in decision making, leadership responsibilities (for example, running meetings, budgeting, interviewing), and the process of school improvement.
>
> (Wohlstetter, 1995: 24)

These findings are worth emphasizing and warrant the following substantial recognition. First, professional development becomes meaningful when it is locked in to the school's re-design agenda and becomes a meaningful part of the life of the school (Lieberman, 1995); and second, faculty require more than substantive knowledge and skills in curriculum, teaching and learning. They also need the human management skills associated with the processes of collaboration.

Professional development in the learning-centred school is geared to the improvement of teaching and learning. In designing a professional development programme, it is first necessary to clarify what teachers need to know (Darling-Hammond, 1998). The following list provides a summary of teacher craft knowledge based on earlier chapters on teaching and learning in this book and on the ideas of Darling-Hammond (1998):

- pedagogical content knowledge (Shulman, 1987b), the ability to understand subject matter deeply and flexibly, so that students can be helped to form cognitive maps and to see connections between ideas;
- knowledge of child and adolescent development and ability to support growth in cognitive, social, physical and emotional domains in order to shape productive learning experiences; sensitivity to what students know and believe and to help them engage new ideas;
- knowledge of student differences in terms of culture, intelligence and learning styles;
- pedagogical learner knowledge, linking teaching with how students best learn and motivating them to engage and care about learning; knowledge and ability to vary teaching strategy according to learning goals and learner strengths and weaknesses; ability to evaluate appropriately, to work with special education needs students and to understand how students acquire language;
- knowledge of curriculum resources and technology, including knowing how to connect students with sources of information and knowledge to allow them to explore ideas, acquire and synthesize information, and to frame and solve problems;
- knowledge of the social context of learning, of how to structure interactions among students, to promote shared learning, and collaboration among and between students, teachers and parents;
- knowledge and ability for self-reflection and analysis.

Acquiring this sophisticated knowledge and developing practice that is different from that which teachers themselves experienced as students requires learning opportunities that are more powerful than simply reading and talking about new pedagogical ideas (Darling-Hammond, 1998). Teachers learn best by:

- studying and researching, applying ideas in practice, and reflecting;
- collaborating, sharing and articulating their experiences with other teachers;
- connecting what they do with student work and levels of attainment.

Teacher professional development in the re-designed school therefore needs to be:

- grounded in sound research and inquiry;
- contextualized in real classroom situations or contexts which simulate the reality as closely as possible to provide opportunities for trying and testing;
- based on articulation and evaluation of the experiences and results with colleagues.

Everyday practice and professional development should be seamlessly integrated, just as theory and practice are inextricably linked. As questions and problems arise in the practice of everyday teaching, teachers are professionally developing when they resort to theory, research and disciplined inquiry in order to find solutions. This definition means that professional development is not an activity confined to specially organized events; rather, it is ongoing and integrated in the professional practice of inquiring teachers.

Professional development may therefore take place in a range of settings. It can occur as specially organized school events, off-school site activities or college-based programmes, but it should also be an integral part of the teacher's everyday classroom life. In this latter regard, the teacher becomes a true reflective, inquiring practitioner, and professional development is more an attitude of mind, pedagogical approach, and an evaluation and problem-solving process than it is a formally organized event. Defined in this way, professional development is more resistant to budgetary fluctuations. Whenever stringent budgetary policy threatens educational expenditure, professional development programmes are invariably seen as one of the early casualties. An integrated professional development classroom practice approach, however, is less dependent on budgetary policy.

Darling-Hammond and McLaughlin (1995) identify the following successful professional development strategies for improving teaching:

- experiential, engaging teachers in concrete tasks of teaching, assessment, and observation that illuminate the processes of learning and development;
- grounded in participants' questions, inquiry, and experimentation as well as profession-wide research;
- collaborative, involving a sharing of knowledge among educators;
- connected to and derived from teachers' work with their students as well as to examinations of subject matter and teaching methods;
- sustained and intensive, supported by modelling, coaching, and problem solving around specific problems of practice; and
- connected to other aspects of school change.

In general terms, Darling-Hammond (1998), citing Ball and Cohen (1998), claims that successful professional development programmes which support re-designed core technologies of teaching and learning:

- centre on critical activities of teaching and learning, such as planning lessons, evaluating student work, developing curriculum, rather than abstractions and generalities;
- grow from investigations of practice through cases, questions, analysis and criticism;

- build on substantial professional discourse that fosters analysis and communication about practices and values in ways that build collaboration and standards of practice.

These new programmes typically engage teachers in studying research and conducting their own inquiries through cases, action research, and structured reflections about practice. As Darling-Hammond notes, 'They envision the professional teacher as one who learns from teaching rather than as one who has finished learning how to teach' (1998: 9). The task of professional development is to develop the capacity of teachers to inquire systematically and sensitively into the nature of learning and the effects of teaching.

Many of the tenets of professional development identified above are features of Brewster Academy's re-design programme in New Hampshire, USA. Professional development is regarded as an essential early stage in the re-design process. All teachers contract to undertake a seven-week full-time, hands-on professional development programme focused on school policy based on informed practices of teaching and learning (Bain, 1996). The programme runs each year. Both new appointees and long-serving teachers are involved. Master teachers have gradually taken over responsibility for running the programme in which store is placed on practical demonstrations, modelling and critical peer reflection. Participant teachers are paid an allowance for attendance and satisfactory completion of the programme.

The programme aims to provide sufficient support and infrastructure to ensure that professional development experiences result in improved classroom practice. Among the list of elements which support the school design policy and which are included in the Brewster professional development programme are:

- teaching and learning;
- classroom management and organization;
- technology;
- team building and school climate;
- collaborative consultation;
- community living;
- the school curriculum.

An important feature of the approach is the replication of instructional methods, first as used in the professional development programme, and then as practised with students in classrooms. This fidelity to the school design principles of informed practice enables reinforcement of experience. Teachers first experience the new instructional methods as learners on the professional development programme and then apply them as teachers in their classrooms. Professional development of staff is school-focused, addressing specific school policies and involving functioning teams.

Focus in the above account has been placed on teacher professional development. Equally important, however, is the professional development of administrators who have responsibility for creating the school culture in which the principles and practices of teacher professional development can build. Images and visions of the re-designed school – its form and shape – should contextualize the professional development of principals and administrators (Murphy, 1992). Administrators require sound cognitive maps of the re-designed school, its elements and components, and their connectivity. This means that their professional development needs are based on the following, all of which contribute to culture building:

*   knowledge of core technology, and informed practices of teaching and learning;
*   knowledge of overall curriculum design and evaluation;
*   knowledge of organizational structures;
*   a gestalt capacity to understand the connectivities between the elements making the whole school;
*   ability to understand and develop the school's human resources at both an individual and collective level; and more specifically with respect to change;
*   transformational leadership, that is, the ability to manage the change process in self and others;
*   knowledge of the policy and environmental contexts within which the school will function;
*   capacity to embrace and network the various stakeholders and members of the school community;
*   ability to generate and allocate all resources – human, financial and physical – in ways which promote the school's capacity to re-design.

This list can be summarized in the following three categories of knowledge and skills:

*   technical, substantive knowledge, such as that related to core technology and school design;
*   human resource skills, such as those required to work collaboratively with and to win the involvement and commitment of others;
*   process/structure knowledge, such as that which enables action and implementation.

A similar set of principles applies to administrator professional development as applies to teacher professional development. That is, an important part of development should be integrated with the everyday practice of administration. The concept of inquiry and research-based reflection is as apposite for the administrator as it is for the teacher. Administrator professional development needs to be practice-based and grounded in real world problems faced in leading and managing re-designed schools. Professional development then becomes a problem-based and problem-solving activity engaged in on-the-job as well as in more formal programmes. Research, reading and literature as well as successful experience become the basis on which informed, disciplined inquiry and reflection is possible. Articulating, sharing and collaborating in the professional development endeavour is achieved in at least three forums: the administrator with school colleagues, with administrators of other schools (for example, mentoring) and with academics and researchers.

Cross-Cultural Implications

While the personnel model elaborated in this chapter may be seen as generic or universal in terms of its inherent appeal, the ways in which people in different cultures may filter, adapt, operationalize and even compromise the model, deserve consideration. First, the model is founded on a rational assumption, namely that the person with the most appropriate skills and knowledge for the position should be appointed. Second, it portrays a logical stepped process – at least from an Anglo-American perspective – in detailing position descriptions in terms of the school mission and policy, appointing and inducting the chosen person, appraising for performance to determine feedback and reward, and professionally developing for self and organizational improvement.

Different cultural values may even lead the basic assumption underpinning the model to be challenged. It is a general aim in most Anglo-American schools that appointments are made on the basis of the 'best' person for the job. 'Best' is defined in the West as the person chosen from among the applicants who is thought to have the most appropriate knowledge and skills. Contrast that with the following statement by Cheng and Wong (1996: 44) in respect of mainland China:

> Although schools everywhere are never serious bureaucracies in Max Weber's definition of the term, schools in East Asia are even less so, because factors such as charisma, school traditions and peer norms often have more significant bearings on schools than formal structures and regulations. The extreme case is in China, where personal connections (guanxi) are often seen as a legitimate element in personnel matters such as recruitment and promotion.

Dimmock and Walker (1997) also noted the tendency in Hong Kong for teachers to be appointed to schools either on the basis of their having been a past student of the school, or on the basis of their connections with the principal or a teacher already employed in the school. Of course, the ability and past record of the student might also be considered. While such use of connections might seem 'corrupt' to the Western view, it is seen very differently among Chinese. Their aim is to recruit staff who will be dedicated and loyal to the school; someone who will work hard and do their best for the students. A former student, or a teacher who is known by an existing staff member and is well regarded, are assumed – through their connections – to be more likely to display this loyalty and commitment.

The importance of connections can be understood in the context of the tendency for Chinese teachers to see the school as an extension of the family. As Cheng and Wong observe (1996: 44), 'There is some subtle bonding among teachers in a school, that members of the same school unite and work towards the common goal of the school'. They go on to explain this feature not in terms of rational consensus, but as a 'traditional value where individuals are expected to submit to organizational goals. The general "trust" which is insightfully discussed by Fukuyama (1995) remains the backbone for most schools in East Asia.'

Selection in East Asian schools is thus inclined towards choosing people who will fit into the organization and become loyal, hard-working 'family members'. Contrast this with selection procedures in Anglo-American schools, where such considerations are often overlooked or downplayed in favour of the merits of applicants' past achievements, especially academic performance. Social and interpersonal values and skills together with a capacity to 'fit in' to the school community and to contribute as a dedicated member of the organization may not be given due consideration. As schools in Western cultures press to become more community-oriented organizations, with greater reliance on collaborative methods of working, they should expect to pay greater heed to such aspects.

Cross-cultural differences may also be noteworthy in appraisal and professional development. Such differences as they affect appraisal are discussed in Chapter 11 on evaluating teachers' performance. Suffice to say that Anglo-American ways of handling evaluation and feedback through direct face to face situations seem inappropriate in the Chinese culture, where the primacy of preserving relationships and 'saving face' is given pre-eminence. Resort to more delicate, sensitive and subtle means may have to be made.

Interesting and important cross-cultural differences in relation to professional development are noted by Stevenson and Stigler (1994). These authors observed that teachers in China and Taiwan generally have fewer years of formal education than American teachers. The real training of Asian teachers occurs on the job after graduation. Beginning teachers are still considered novices who need the help and guidance of more experienced colleagues. In Japan, the system of teacher training is like an apprenticeship. The accumulated wisdom of older, more experienced teachers is passed on to the new generation and the idea is to perfect practice in an ongoing way. By law, beginning Japanese teachers must receive a minimum of twenty days of in-service training during the first year. Master teachers, selected for their teaching ability, supervise this training. Many are released from teaching for one year, to concentrate on working with beginning teachers.

In addition, beginning and experienced teachers in Japan and China are expected to perfect their teaching skills through interaction with other teachers. Meetings are arranged by principals and deputy principals for experienced teachers to advise and guide younger colleagues. Discussions are very specific to crafting classroom techniques and lesson plans. Study groups are formed to undertake tasks such as jointly planning a lesson. Subsequently, one of the group might teach the lesson while the others observe and evaluate with a view to improvement. Stevenson and Stigler (1994) note that the use of physical space and teachers' time are both conducive to professional development. In both Japan and China, teachers share large staffrooms where they can communicate with each other more easily. In Western schools, teachers are very often scattered in small workrooms about the school. As mentioned earlier, teachers in China have up to twenty lessons a week of non-contact time, thus promoting more collaboration and joint planning of instruction and lesson planning. By contrast, many Western teachers may only have between three and five non-contact periods a week.

Cross-cultural differences such as those above lead Hallinger and Leithwood (1996) to argue that the concept of culture goes beyond the notion of exogenous variables such as community and institutional context, and the endogenous variable, organizational culture. Rather, it permeates all aspects of schools and the lives of those who work in them. It influences individual teacher and administrator behaviours, practices and experiences, as well as life at organizational and community levels. It therefore follows that, 'the knowledge base that underlies administrative practice will also be influenced by the cultural context in which the administrator works' (Hallinger and Leithwood, 1996: 109). The same conclusion is apposite for teaching and teachers.

Hallinger and Leithwood (1996) go on to note that administrator preparation and professional development programmes in the USA have been criticized for lack of relevance (to the job), for being too theoretical and for over-reliance on traditional delivery modes such as lecture, group discussion and experiential methods. However, they continue:

Perceived inadequacies in the professional training offered to educational leaders are not ... confined to the USA and other 'Western' countries. Both the content and methods used in the administrative training programmes of developing countries have generally been borrowed more or less directly from Western societies. Although exceptions do exist ... this has been the case even when there is neither conceptual nor empirical validation of the knowledge base in the receiving culture. Thus the state of affairs in developing and non-Western countries with respect to administrative preparation may be even more problematic in certain respects.

(Hallinger and Leithwood, 1996: 110)

Recognition needs to be given to the need to contextualize the knowledge base underlying professional development programmes for both administrators and teachers. The questions are: what are the implications of cultural difference for the design and conduct of training programmes? Which elements, if any, may be regarded as universal knowledge and therefore commonly used across cultures? Will the effectiveness and suitability of training methods vary between cultures?

Hallinger and Leithwood conclude by questioning the salience of Western theories of leadership and schooling to administrators operating in other cultures. This is especially the case when much of the knowledge base and professional development is questionable even for American principals. The discontinuities seem more bizarre for non-Western administrators trained in the West, who return to their own societies and feel obliged to implement what they have learned. Hallinger and Leithwood are therefore led to advocate more research in indigenous cultures to explore the empirical base for the application of theoretical knowledge, craft knowledge and school/system policies. Knowledge and learning are, after all, culturally mediated.

Significant cultural differences apply in elevating certain attitudes and moral codes above performance-related skills in Chinese schools. High priority in the leadership of Chinese schools tends to be given to traits such as 'saving face', preserving harmonious relationships, loyalty and dedication, discipline, strong will and persistence. Age, seniority and experience are respected. Gender may also play a role; in some Hong Kong schools known to the author, older male teachers are particularly held in esteem. This contrasts with the Anglo-American concentration on performance-related skills. Such differences mean that training programmes in China include the study of attitudes, morals and the affective domain, an area often omitted from programmes in Western countries. Walker et al. (1996) found that culturally learned interpersonal relationships among Hong Kong Chinese transferred to in-service training settings. Team members deferred to their older more senior colleagues in group problem-solving discussions. Prescriptive behaviours borrowed from Western societies are unlikely to be applied in training programmes in East Asia, let alone be transposed to the workplace (Hallinger and Leithwood, 1996).

In terms of methods used in professional development, there seems to be even more reliance on traditional teaching approaches in East Asian programmes than is the case in Western school systems. As noted by Hallinger and Leithwood (1996), even when case study and simulation exercises are used in Asian settings, they are often based on Western contexts. Like many of their Western counterparts, the programmes often fail to progress past the theoretical knowledge base to deal with applications in practice, let alone within particular cultural settings. Assumptions and customs vary enormously across cultures – even within Asia and the West – let alone between them. For example, training programmes advocating collaboration and participation take on a different hue in the hierarchically organized Asian school when compared to schools in Anglo-American cultures.

Likewise, teachers' professional development needs to be culturally contextualized. In East Asia, this means taking account of large class sizes of forty-five or more, classrooms lacking audio-visual and multi-media technology, confined spaces and overcrowded conditions, hierarchical relationships, teachers who are given relatively high respect and who are expected to know all the answers, and overdependency on textbooks and a mechanistic approach to learning. Thus, when Hong Kong introduced in 1994 a Target-Oriented Curriculum – a student-centred approach to teaching, learning and assessment – it is within a very different setting and tradition from similar student outcomes-based schemes in Australia, the UK and other Western countries. Professional development programmes need to reflect the specific contextual conditions in which policies are to be implemented.

Financial Resources

Resource allocation is crucial in supporting the aims of the re-designed school, especially in promulgating a more individualized curriculum and informed practices of teaching and learning. Patterns of allocation reveal whether the school is truly fostering the learning of all students and whether it has thought carefully about the resource levels necessary for the learning of different cohorts of students (Knight, 1993). It is not the intention here to discuss in detail how the financing of schools, especially public schools, should be reformed. This issue has been raised and covered elsewhere (see Caldwell and Haywood, 1998). Suffice to say that the traditional source of public funding for education, the tax base, is proving increasingly strained and inadequate as time passes. New sources of funding are needed as the capacity of schools to consume resources outstrips governments' capability and willingness to supply them. It seems ever more clear, however, that re-designed schools need re-designed funding mechanisms.

At present, the typical means of determining the funding of a public school involves the application of a formula which includes elements relating to the location, number of students at the school, the age profile and an allowance for students with special educational needs. It is basically an input model, which contains many contentious assumptions. For example, most schemes are weighted in favour of older students. Thus a secondary student might be funded up to five or six times more than a primary school student. Critics argue that this weighting is disproportionately in favour of the older student and that a fairer balance would recognize that children of primary school age, according to cognitive psychologists, are in their most formative years. Once the school receives the money as a lump sum, a line-item budgeting system is normally used, whereby money is tied to objects of expenditure such as supplies, contractual services and equipment. In other words, emphasis is placed on the items which are purchased rather than on the purpose of the expenditure.

Programme budgeting has more appeal than the line-item approach because it ties resources to objectives and curriculum programmes. The budget is based on major courses or functions, such as instruction and support services, which may in turn be subdivided into programmes for the physically handicapped, maintenance of plant and so on. Programme functions normally correspond to the organizational structure, so that academic and financial responsibilities can be integrated. Programme budgeting is preferable to the line-item method by virtue of its inclusion of the objectives of expenditure aligned to function, purposes and programmes rather than objects.

Neither of the aforementioned methods, however, addresses the need for a system of funding which is integrated with the intentions and purposes of the re-designed school. It is a constant theme of this book that the re-designed school elevates student learning and the attainment of student outcomes. All students, irrespective of ability, age, gender and ethnicity, have the right to achieve a level of student learning outcomes as close to the limit of their aptitude as possible. So far, in earlier chapters, we have focused on ways in which the curriculum, teaching, learning, technology and personnel can contribute to the achievement of this goal. But what of the resource implications? How might a system of financial resources best support this objective?

In a school which elevates student learning outcomes to primacy, a system of budgeting is needed which allocates resources in ways that enable all students to achieve that level of student outcomes of which they are capable. Instead of decisions taken on the basis of the costs of mounting each course or program, resources need to be allocated according to the expected costs of enabling students to achieve their respective levels of learning outcomes. That is, estimates would be made on the basis of student need, with 'need' defined in terms of resources required to enable students to achieve levels of student outcomes reflecting their learning capabilities. It would involve teachers, parents and students in ascertaining and estimating student abilities and thereafter setting realistic but challenging learning goals and outcome levels. It would reinforce the press for individualization by identifying the differentials among students in terms of their learning needs and capabilities. Students and schools perform successfully when leaders, teachers and students recognize the need for agreement on goals, when resources are allocated to support goal achievement, and when all parts of the school work consistently and collaboratively towards the same ends. In addition, resources in the re-designed school should be allocated to professional development in ways which support the precepts of informed practice with respect to curriculum, teaching and learning.

The approach to funding described above is student outcomes-related. In an ideal scenario, it is would be the logical system for the re-designed school. At this time, however, it may present too many challenges to be realistic. As Levacic and Ross (in press: 17) assert:

> Ideally, if the formula is to encourage schools to maximize educational effectiveness, a funding agency would wish to allocate finance according to schools' outputs rather than inputs. However, it is difficult to develop appropriate school output measures when expected educational outcomes are diverse, difficult to define, and not readily quantifiable. Those school outputs which are more easily quantifiable, such as test and examination results, are heavily dependent on the characteristics of students, in particular, their social background and ability – and therefore sophisticated statistical proceedings are required to generate 'adjusted' output measures. There are also the important issues of ensuring that output measures are not capable of being manipulated by schools, and that undesirable incentives are avoided so as to prevent the risk of adverse selection of students by schools.

This leads Levacic and Ross to argue for the next best method, which is needs-based school funding. Here, the student is the main unit of funding and it is students as inputs – as measured on the school roll – who are funded. There are four main components of this funding formula:

Component 1: basic student allocation. This would be made up of a basic per student allocation and a supplement for differences between students according to grade level, age, or year group.

Component 2: curriculum enhancement. In addition to differentiation by grade level, some formulae provide for an enhanced curriculum for certain students, often according to ability or aptitude. These programmes usually focus on specific subjects, for instance, music, sport, languages, science or mathematics. This element applies to the costs of enriching the curriculum for selected students or schools.

229

Component 3: student-specific supplementary educational needs. This relates to differences in students' characteristics which result in some students requiring additional resources in order to provide them with the same level of access to the curriculum that is enjoyed by most students at their grade level. Additional expenditure might be needed for those students with special educational needs.

Component 4: school-specific site needs. The unit here is the school site, not the student. Some schools, by virtue of structural factors might incur additional costs because of their state of repair, position or below par materials used in their construction. For example, some schools are more expensive to heat or keep cool than others. Multi-site campuses and remote schools generally involve more cost because of the travel required.

Funding and the allocation of resources, especially finance, but also time, space and equipment, are important issues in enabling all students to achieve their potential. Some would conclude that a needs-based formula is not the perfect solution, but it is a step in the right direction towards an outcomes-driven model.

Conclusion

This chapter has covered a large landscape, from position descriptions, staff selection, professional development and selected cross-cultural implications of a personnel policy, to financial resources and their deployment; all within the context of a re-designed, learning-centred school. In keeping with the precepts of the re-designed school, the chapter has emphasized the need for consistency, coherence and connectivity between the different elements which go to make a personnel policy, and between the personnel policy itself and the rest of the school design plan. Administration and teaching, learning and curriculum need to be seen as interconnected and professional development programmes designed accordingly.

A further purpose of the chapter has been to reinforce the principle of informed practice, especially in regard to professional development. Research-based inquiry and knowledge of relevant research literature on teaching, learning and curriculum, as well as on management and leadership, inject meaning to the concept of reflective practitioner. Unless the teacher or administrator has a research inquiry-driven approach, reflection may be little more than contemplation of subjective experience. At worst, it could mean immersion in ignorance.

Finally, some dangers of generalizing across cultures have been noted. In some Asian societies, for example, personal connections play a major role in selection and promotion. There may be good justification for this, especially when the connections are predicated on issues of loyalty and commitment to the institution. But the very notions of what 'good' leadership and management mean in Asian societies may differ from Anglo-American perspectives. Equally, the customs and traditions governing interpersonal relationships and communication are culturally mediated. Concepts of time and space and teachers' work organization are also culture-bound, and highlight the need for cultural sensitivity and contextualization when designing and implementing personnel and human resource policies.

References

Bain, A. (1996) 'Future school institute at Brewster Academy', unpublished manuscript, Brewster Academy, Wolfeboro, NH, USA.

Ball, D. and Cohen, D. (1998) 'Developing practice, developing practitioners: toward a practice-based theory of professional education', in L. Darling-Hammond and L. Sykes (eds) *Teaching as the Learning Profession: Handbook of Policy and Practice*, San Francisco: Jossey Bass.

Caldwell, B. and Haywood, D.K. (1998) *The Future of Schools: Lessons From the Reform of Public Education*, London: Falmer Press.

Cheng, K. and Wong, K. (1996) 'School effectiveness in East Asia: concepts, origins and implications', *Journal of Educational Administration* 34 (5): 32–49.

Darling-Hammond, L. (1996) 'What matters most: a competent teacher for every child', *Phi Delta Kappan* 73 (3): 193–200.

—— (1998) 'Teacher learning that supports student learning', *Educational Leadership* 55 (5): 6–11.

Darling-Hammond, L. and McLaughlin, M.W. (1995) 'Policies that support professional development in an era of reform', *Phi Delta Kappan* 76 (8): 597–604.

Dimmock, C. and Walker, A. (1997) 'Hong Kong's change of sovereignty: school leader perceptions of the effects on educational policy and school administration', *Comparative Education* 33 (2): 277–302.

Fukuyama, F. (1995) *Trust: The Social Virtues and the Creation of Prosperity*, New York: The Free Press.

Hallinger, P. and Leithwood, K. (1996) 'Culture and educational administration: a case of finding out what you don't know you don't know', *Journal of Educational Administration* 34 (5): 98–116.

Harris, B. and Monk, B.J. (1992) *Personnel Administration in Education: Leadership for Instructional Improvement*, 3rd edn, Needham Heights, MA: Allyn and Bacon.

Knight, B. (1993) 'Delegated financial management and school effectiveness', in C. Dimmock (ed.), *School-Based Management and School Effectiveness*, London: Routledge, 114–41.

Levacic, R. and Ross, K.N. (1998) 'Principles for designing needs-based school funding formulae', in K.N. Ross and R. Levacic (eds), *Needs-Based Resource Allocation in Education via Formula Funding of Schools*, Paris: International Institute for Educational Planning, UNESCO.

Lieberman, A. (1995) 'Practices that support teacher development: transforming conceptions of professional learning', *Phi Delta Kappan* 76 (8): 591–6.

Morgan, C., Hall, V. and Mackay, H. (1984) *A Handbook on Selecting Senior Staff for Schools*, Buckingham: Open University Press.

Murphy, J. (1992) *The Landscape of Leadership Preparation: Reframing the Education of School Administrators*, Newbury Park, CA: Corwin.

Schlechty, P.C. (1990) *Schools for the Twenty-First Century: Leadership Imperatives for Educational Reform*, San Francisco: Jossey Bass.

Shulman, L.S. (1987a) 'Assessment for teaching: an initiative for the profession', *Phi Delta Kappan* 69 (1): 38–44.

—— (1987b) 'Knowledge and teaching: foundations of the new reform', *Harvard Educational Review* 57 (1): 1–22.

Stevenson, H.W. and Stigler, J.W. (1994) *The Learning Gap: Why Our Schools are Failing and What We Can Learn from Japanese and Chinese Education*, New York: Touchstone.

Walker, A., Bridges, E. and Chan, B. (1996) 'Wisdom gained, wisdom given: instituting PBL in a Chinese culture', *Journal of Educational Administration* 34 (5): 12–31.

Wohlstetter, P. (1995) 'Getting school-based management right: what works and what doesn't', *Phi Delta Kappan* 77 (1): 22–6.

11 Evaluating Teachers' Performance

This chapter looks at evaluation, and specifically teacher appraisal, within the context of the re-designed school. It does not purport to cover all aspects of school evaluation indicated by Figure 5 in Chapter 2. Rather, it focuses on teacher appraisal, its purposes and methodologies within a learning-centred school, and draws some implications regarding appraisal in different cultures. Limiting the present discussion to appraisal is justified by the fact that it is, at least potentially, one of the most influential ways of improving the quality of teaching and learning in school. Staff appraisal was also briefly discussed in Chapter 10.

Evaluation is an integral part of the design process, connecting past and present performance with future improvement. It also serves to connect the different elements of the re-designed school, such as the curriculum, teaching and learning, technology, organization, personnel and management. Evaluation is thus geared to two sets of phenomena: that concerning the personnel dimension and another relating to the elements of school design *per se*. Undergirding all of the elements in school design is the human resource, so that evaluation fundamentally targets the skills and competencies of personnel in their fulfilment of curriculum design, teaching, learning, application of technology and so on. In the learner-centred school, however, evaluation is primarily focused on teaching and learning. This means that all of the elements of design are evaluated, but within the context of their respective contributions to enhancing teaching and learning. Thus, teachers are appraised according to their practice and promotion of informed teaching and learning. Senior and middle managers are appraised for their leadership, management, resourcing and culture building and the extent to which these activities are directed at promoting informed teaching and learning outcomes. In addition, key elements of school design such as the curriculum, the teaching and learning model, the personnel policy, professional development, organizational structures and the technology plan and policy are evaluated in relation to their respective contributions to enhancing the quality of teaching and learning. Hence, the design, implementation and outcomes of the various elements are all included for evaluation.

All aspects of the learner-centred school are evaluated systematically in an ongoing way. Figure 2.4 in Chapter 2 represents the cyclical process involved. Over a period of time, the school review process systematically covers leadership, management, resourcing and culture; structures, including the curriculum, and use of time and space; and teaching and learning. For a given period of time, however, with limited time and resources, a school might focus its evaluation endeavours on only one or two of these areas. Recommendations arising from the review and evaluation process then become the basis of the school improvement programme which, as Figure 2.4 indicates, feeds into the school development plan.

It is helpful at this point to clarify the following key terms: evaluation, appraisal, effectiveness and efficiency. 'Evaluation' is defined as the making of judgements about the worth or value of a phenomenon in terms of agreed criteria, such as goals. Among the units which might be evaluated are whole schools, departments, programmes or lessons. Evaluation can thus focus on three levels: the individual, the group and the whole school. 'Appraisal' in the current context is taken to apply to the evaluation of the individual teacher or principal. Other relevant terms include 'effectiveness', that is, the degree to which teachers, students and others approximate to achieving agreed goals, and 'efficiency', which concerns the amount of resources – financial, physical and human – consumed in achieving the goals.

At the heart of evaluation lie the twin activities of data gathering and decision making. Issues of methodological concern, particularly validity and reliability, are crucial in generating trustworthy data on which more informed decisions and judgements can be made. Two central issues concern what and how to evaluate. The answers to both will depend on the purpose(s) of the evaluation. Among the recognized purposes of evaluation are:

- programme justification and improvement;
- personnel performance appraisal;
- school and sub-school performance;
- marketing and school public relations.

In the context of the re-designed school, each of these purposes achieves elevated importance. Justifying and improving school programmes is essential in a change environment; teachers are expected to adopt informed teaching and learning practices; and the school is concerned to inform its stakeholders about the purposes, performances and achievements within the re-design context.

Answers to the key questions – what and how to evaluate – are also provided by the design process itself, which brings definition to each of the elements. For example, informed teaching and learning practices have been identified, as have the roles and responsibilities of teachers, and these direct the focus of evaluation in quite specific ways. Evaluation therefore targets the teacher's ability and effectiveness in practising the methods of informed teaching, including mastery learning, direct teaching, cooperative learning, peer tutoring, problem-based learning and so forth.

A number of schemata setting out the purposes of evaluation may be recognized. One scheme is based on the following

- internal school improvement, the process whereby the school, or part thereof, acquires feedback on its performance in order to improve;
- internal personnel decision making, involving the hiring, firing and promoting of staff;
- external accountability, the process by which the school renders an account for its performance to some external body or stakeholder (for example, Education Department or parents).

Evaluation is a necessary prior stage to accountability, since performance needs to be gauged first before an account can be rendered. In this chapter, the focus is placed on evaluation for internal feedback, and more specifically teacher appraisal, as a means of teacher and school improvement.

Teacher Appraisal

Evaluation, and specifically appraisal, is a potentially powerful mechanism within the gamut of strategies available to school management. As noted in Chapter 10, when designed and implemented successfully, it has strong capacity for improving performance. However, when the reverse is the case, it may have an equally destructive effect on staff morale and performance. If appraisal is to function effectively, it should be seen as part of a personnel system rather than as a discrete entity in itself. In this way, six elements can be distinguished as comprising the personnel system. If staff are to perform effectively they need to be clear about the answers to all six elements below:

1 To whom are they responsible and accountable?
2 What are their roles and responsibilities?
3 What skills, competencies and standards are expected of them?
4 How well are they performing in relation to those standards?
5 What targets are identified for their future development?
6 How will they achieve those targets?

The first of the above questions concerns the establishment of a meaningful accountability system; the second and third depend on clear position descriptions; the fourth and fifth centre on appraisal; and the sixth overlaps appraisal with professional development. In reality, many teachers feel threatened by appraisal on the grounds that they distrust the intentions underlying it. For example, they believe it could be used to sanction or even dismiss them. However, a contrasting perspective is that teachers have a right, as employees, to have clear answers to the six questions listed above. This not only assists them in performing their duties, but also builds in more safeguards against unfair, biased and subjective treatment at work. In this latter sense, appraisal is seen as a right and a safeguard, not as a threat.

In the context of the re-designed, learning-centred school, the potential benefits that can flow from an appraisal system are the following:

- it enables excellence in informed practice to be rewarded;
- it clarifies the skill areas in which staff require further training and development;
- it improves teaching quality and thus the quality of schooling;
- it results in more effective deployment of staff resources;
- it facilitates systematic career planning;
- it clarifies individual and organizational goals and objectives;
- it enables decisions on promotion to be taken;
- it recognizes potential for self-fulfilment and for future promotion and leadership;
- it provides feedback on performance and raises morale;
- it measures progress and improvement and provides a documented personnel file on each staff member;
- it provides more accurate, objective staff references;
- it throws light on the efficacy of school organization and its practices;
- it enables the school to plan future recruitment;
- it provides an opportunity for counselling;
- it minimizes misunderstandings between appraiser and appraisee;
- it clarifies whether staff are well matched with the aims and policies of the school and thereby enables decisions to be made about future employment.

These are all potential benefits. If practitioners lack the skills to implement the system in a positive way, then the benefits may just as easily be transformed into negative consequences. Appraisal should essentially be a systematic (not a one-off) review of performance and potential aiming sympathetically at personal and professional fulfilment within a framework of staff development. According to this definition, appraisal leads to staff development: the two are complementary.

Evaluators, however, have recognized two different but related paradigms concerning appraisal. The first is formative, and is geared to improving performance through staff development; the second is summative, and is aimed at deciding issues such as hiring and promotion. The former is supportive and developmental, while the latter involves the making of final decisions or judgements about the career and financial status of staff. Evaluation for external accountability is also summative, and again may lead to decisions about future resourcing. There is disagreement as to whether it is possible and desirable to keep the formative and summative separate, or whether they are inextricably linked. Arguments for separating them hinge on the reality that where the same appraisers are responsible for both, teachers are less likely to be open and self critical in their formative appraisal, especially if they believe the same information can be used against them when it comes to decisions on promotion or continuation of employ-ment. From the decision makers' viewpoint there are advantages to combining both, simply because they obtain more information about staff.

Guidelines for Designing an Appraisal System

The following principles provide useful guidelines in designing a staff appraisal system for a learning-centred school:

- every staff member, including the principal, is appraised;
- appraisal should integrate with, and be based on, school policy and position descriptions;
- individual and organizational improvement goals should dovetail;
- openness and trust should exist between appraiser and appraisee, hence a positive culture and climate is essential;
- judgements and decisions are based on evidence and reliable informa-tion rather than opinion, although the latter may be important;
- select the appropriate method for the purpose;
- include as wide a range of relevant data sources as possible;
- use meaningful criteria relevant to desired student outcomes;
- evidence, interviews and agreements are documented;
- both appraisers and appraisees receive training in necessary skills;
- teachers are involved in evaluation;
- a handbook is prepared as a source of information on the appraisal scheme;
- a right of appeal to a third party in case of disagreements;
- confidentiality and confinement of personal information to those who need to know;
- agreement on future action is essential as a result of the appraisal process;
- efficiency in time and cost is needed in administering the system.

It is worth commenting on some of these guidelines. Different methods are needed in promoting teacher development as distinct from making personnel decisions, such as promotion or tenure. Teachers should be involved in all phases of developing and operating formative systems, or otherwise the system is unlikely to reflect their aspirations, concerns and interests. Both evaluators and those appraised should be trained in the use of evaluation instruments, especially in the collection of useful, valid data, interpretation of results, the setting of goals and the implementation of action plans. Evaluators should be trained to provide feedback to teachers which is clear, precise and sufficiently diagnostic to promote improvement in teaching (Stiggins, 1988). Evaluation results should be used by teachers, staff developers and school managers to set staff development and training priorities and to evaluate success in achieving personal and organisational goals. Unlike many appraisal schemes, the scheme advocated here integrates individual appraisal and school improvement. Comment on methodological guidelines is offered below.

While few of the guidelines above are contentious, some raise difficult decisions in their execution. For example the last one, on the administrative efficiency of the system, concerns the amount of time which appraisal consumes, both for teachers and for administrators as appraisers and appraisees. In many schools where appraisal is operating, the system is seriously compromised because neither teachers nor administrators are prepared to bear the opportunity costs of investing appropriate time and effort. In the re-designed school, however, informed teaching and learning are central to the mission and purpose. Appraisal is a key vehicle in assisting teachers to adopt informed teaching methodologies which focus on enhancing student learning outcomes. As such, it is too important to the central mission of the school to be seriously compromised. As reflective practitioners, teachers are involved in an ongoing way in collecting data, peer-evaluation and self-evaluation. Administrators are heavily involved in working with teachers, advising and giving insightful feedback, and using informed teaching and learning principles and practices as reference points and benchmarks. In short, a significant proportion of organizational time is invested in appraisal, but this is fully justified in terms of its key contribution to the central mission of the school.

Methodologies for Data Collection

Meaningful analysis of performance is based on valid data from multiple sources, rather than just relying on opinion. Whatever the purpose of the appraisal, a multi-method approach is required to capture valid evidence. Multi-method may mean that both quantitative and qualitative methods of data collection are used. Quantitative approaches involve rating scales, tests and observation schedules, while qualitative methods include interviews, case studies and naturalistic observations. These methods may generate subjective data, such as opinions, and objective data, such as factual evidence from school records and documents. Using a multi-method approach enhances the validity of the data through triangulation, which is the process of comparing and cross-referencing results and evidence obtained from different sources.

When designing an appraisal system, and in particular the multi-method approach to be adopted, cognisance should be taken of the purpose and targets of the exercise. Data collection methods chosen by individual teachers for self-appraisal and by schools for formal appraisal will vary in their emphasis. Self-appraisal and personal reflection may involve the use of diaries, journals and portfolios whereas formal appraisal models involving colleagues may also include observation, document/record analysis and interviews with the appraiser, peers and occasionally parents or students.

In the conception of appraisal being advocated, teachers collect data throughout the year. It is thus necessary for them to adopt a mindset whereby they continuously look for evidence in their teaching preparation, delivery and post-lesson phases as to the contribution they are making to the students' progress and success in achieving desired learning outcomes. The process is thus continuous rather than a once-a-year spot check.

This encourages teachers to keep a portfolio, which might include the following: teaching materials, lesson plans, student work samples, evaluations of student progress, assessment records, video tapes of lessons, diagrams of the learning environment, teaching aids and reports. Supporting documentation might include: educational philosophy, teaching and career goals, teaching experiences, specific information about the students and the course, class resources, reflective commentaries about teaching and a list of pertinent professional development experiences (Lacey, 1996).

Since the focus of appraisal in the learning-centred school is teaching and learning, particular emphasis is given to meaningful performance criteria which attend to desired student outcomes. In other words, evaluation criteria or targets are aimed at curriculum coverage, teaching methods and assessment techniques and the extent to which these enhance student capacity to achieve learning outcomes.

An Appraisal System for the Learning-Centred School

A convincing rationale for an appraisal system suitable for the learning-centred school is provided by Leithwood (1988). He is one of few who pointed out early on the wisdom of appraisal achieving, simultaneously, both individual and organizational development, and accomplishing this while focusing on informed teaching and learning. Leithwood's argument, set out below, matches many of the design principles underlying the ideas presented in this book. By adopting such an approach, it is possible to achieve a whole-school synergistic effect, where all staff work towards the same direction. A further attraction of the model is its restriction to the main priorities of teachers' performance and its modesty in not attempting to be all-encompassing, a pitfall made by many conventional appraisal schemes, which tend to founder as a result.

Leithwood (1988) begins by arguing that school improvement is about reducing the gap between current and desired levels of student outcomes. In order to improve student outcomes, it is necessary to identify the factors which influence them, such as teaching. Thus a more comprehensive conception of school improvement defines it in terms of teachers, administrators and other personnel directly or indirectly influencing student learning. Consequently, a key question to ask is: what roles and practices will teachers need in order to improve student learning? What stages of growth are necessary for them to acquire such practices? What are the obstacles to their growth? Significantly, Leithwood (1988: 86) concludes, 'Performance appraisal contributes to the improvement of schools and schooling to the extent that it provides valid answers to these questions.' Evidence from studies of conventional appraisal schemes indicates that teachers typically see little relationship between the dimensions of practice appraised and those which are instrumental to school effectiveness and improvement.

If appraisal is to be effective, it should not try to cover every facet of a teacher's role. In selecting dimensions and practices, it is prudent to choose those which influence or have the potential for influencing student learning. Thus research on effective teaching practice reveals, for example, that corrective feedback and positive reinforcement both have high effect sizes on student learning (Brophy and Good, 1986; Fraser et al., 1987). A closer inspection of the teaching effectiveness literature reveals that some practices are more efficacious than others in improving student outcomes (see, for example, Fraser et al., 1987); the inference is that these should be high on the adoption list for an appraisal scheme. Once these specific teaching methods and behaviours have been identified, it is necessary to clarify the best ways for teachers to implement and practice them. This involves teachers and appraisers becoming familiar with informed practice (see Chapter 7 on Informed Teaching). As an example, Brophy (1981) distinguishes twelve specific practices by which teachers give effective praise, including rewarding attainment of specific performance criteria, focusing student attention on their own task-relevant behaviour and orienting them towards further challenging problem-solving achievement.

Finally, consideration needs to be given to the contribution appraisal can make to growth in teacher development. When teachers change, they tend to do so incrementally. Leithwood (1988) therefore suggests the construction of a profile of growth in teacher effectiveness, along the lines of the profiles developed to chart student learning and to measure student attainment of key stages and levels of learning. Such a profile of teacher development is relevant for appraisal in both enabling teachers to be located in terms of their development, and to chart their rate of progress. As a possible profile for teacher development Leithwood (1988) constructs a matrix, with one axis consisting of four dimensions of teaching practice – consistency, integration, balance and individualization – and the other axis gauging the extent to which the teacher achieves these four dimensions.

In the following example, I have adapted Leithwood's individualization dimension and suggested four stages of teacher development, progressing from 1 to 4, as follows:

1 The teacher demonstrates an awareness of the differing levels of ability amongst groups of students.
2 The teacher formulates objectives that attempt to match individual interests, abilities and learning styles of individual students.
3 The teacher formulates objectives by making allowance for individualized learning, and manages classroom learning by enabling some students to benefit from individualization.
4 The teacher not only formulates objectives systematically, but manages classroom learning in ways which include all students in individualized learning.

At issue is the contribution that such profiles can make to appraisal schemes and ultimately to teacher growth and professional development. The construction of profiles for various dimensions of teaching practice would, in itself, constitute an invaluable form of reflective inquiry for school faculty.

In summary, the argument presented is that appraisal should focus on the individual in relation to school improvement and change. It should be selective rather than all-encompassing if it is to be geared towards improving student learning and if it is to be workable. Appeal to research evidence on effective teaching helps clarify the key dimensions and practices which are likely to improve student outcomes, and these become the basis for the selection. Further investigation of the teaching effectiveness literature is helpful in elucidating informed practice for each of the selected dimensions. This process of selecting and informing requires teachers and administrators to engage in professional development, inquiry and reflective practice. The construction of profiles of teacher development along key dimensions provides a longitudinal perspective, enabling the progress of teacher growth to be charted. Research literature and experience provides an informative knowledge base for the reflective process underlying all of this to take place.

Exactly the same process is advocated for principal appraisal. In this case, appeal to research evidence and literature on principal effectiveness and school effectiveness plays the same role as teaching effectiveness in the example alluded to above.

Differentiated Supervision

The aim of this section is to describe a model of appraisal which matches and is consistent with the precepts and principles of the learning-centred school. Leithwood (1988) provides a convincing rationale for such a system. However, how would such a system function? In this respect, Glatthorn's (1997) model, known as 'differentiated supervision', not only seems compatible with but reinforces Leithwood's ideas and thus has much to recommend it. The system outlined below is a modified version of Glatthorn's (1997) model of appraisal. Its attractions are as follows. First, it adopts a view of teaching as a true profession rather than as a low-level technical enterprise. Traditional supervisory models view the teacher as having a problem to which the supervisor has a solution. As skilled professionals, teachers benefit from support and feedback, from colleagues and students as well as from administrators. In addition, since the model centres on appraisal in the learning-centred school, it recognizes a part for students as learners in the evaluation of teachers, given appropriate circumstances. Second, school effectiveness research indicates that collegial climates are more conducive to colleagues sharing professional norms and giving feedback and support to each other, and committing to high standards of performance. A differentiated approach emphasizes cooperation and mutual assistance where teachers help each other grow.

Third, supervisors find it impossible under traditional appraisal systems to do justice to all facets of the teacher's role, and for all faculty, because of insufficient time. Differentiated supervision assumes that a standardized approach to appraisal, where it becomes a perfunctory, ritualistic annual activity, is counterproductive; instead, good supervision should involve colleagues and self as well as administrators, and it should be continuous throughout the year rather than an annual event. Fourth, teachers differ in their requirements of appraisal since they are at various stages of development and expertise. Teachers with higher levels of expertise may require less intensive development than inexperienced or problem teachers. In addition, if the school culture is appropriate, teachers are willing to learn from their peers as well as administrators. Fifth, the model may lead to school organizational development at the same time as it achieves individual development. Finally, the model targets improvement in teaching and learning.

Components of Differentiated Supervision

Differentiated supervision involves three developmental and two evaluative elements (Glatthorn, 1997). The three developmental elements are – cooperative, intensive and self-directed; the two evaluative elements are – intensive and standard. However, some teachers may not undertake all of these. All five elements are described in more detail below.

The three developmental elements aimed at professional development

Cooperative development is the mainstay of the model. All teachers work together in their functioning teams (core teaching or course teams) to assist each other to practice informed teaching. Their appraisal and professional growth is directly related to the school improvement plan, school policy and the full variety of informed teaching and learning practices. In a given year or time period, the school priority plan might be for all teachers to success-fully adopt, for example, mastery learning. Appraisal for that period would thus be focused on mastery learning, the success with which colleagues were implementing it and the difficulties they were encountering. Administrators and supervisors would be involved in an advisory capacity, but much of the responsibility for appraisal and development would reside in the hands of colleagues. For example, it would become the responsibility of the team to support the efforts of a colleague to practice mastery learning. The same would apply if appraisal was focused on direct teaching or cooperative learning. Team members would visit each other's classrooms, observe and confer with each other, conduct action research and develop curriculum and learning materials together. In addition, student evaluations of teachers' construction of learning opportunities is included wherever possible. By linking individual appraisal to school improvement priorities based on informed practices of teaching and learning, the school improves at the same time as individual teacher performance improves, and because this element of appraisal is school-wide, colleagues are able to assist each other. For example, some might be expert in mastery learning, and they might adopt a mentoring/coaching role.

Intensive development, on the other hand, requires that only staff with instructional problems would participate in this element. The supervisor (an administrator-cum-mentor) observes, analyses and coaches throughout the year, focusing solely on informed practices of teaching and learning. The effects of supervised teaching on students' learning is a prime consideration to be taken into account.

Self-directed development enables all teachers to set personal goals and to work independently towards them, without supervision, but again with possible feedback from students.

The two evaluative elements

Intensive evaluation is provided to those teachers working in intensive devel-opment. Intensive evaluation is used to make personnel decisions, such as whether to grant or deny tenure and promotion, and whether or not to renew contracts. An intensive evaluation is based on specific research-supported criteria, involves several observations and conferences and evaluates performance of instructional functions. It is carried out by school administrators.

Standard evaluation concerns the rest of the teachers, those who are competent and experienced and for whom a minimum number of observations and conferences are arranged, just to comply with district or state mandates.

Appraisal for promoting the learning-centred classroom

Central to the theme of this book is the design of an appraisal system which targets teaching and learning and student outcomes. In learning-centred schools and classrooms, the focus is on learning outcomes rather than on teaching methods. However, unlike many advocates of outcome-centred approaches, the present account argues that it is important to consider the links between teaching and learning, while still focusing on outcomes. Many advocates of learning outcomes' approaches tend to diminish the importance of the connection between teaching and learning outcomes.

In learning outcome-centred approaches, the teacher is resolute in ensuring that:

1   The lesson outcome is directly related to the unit goal or outcome.
2   The lesson outcome is significant to the subject, for future learning, to the student and for the unit.
3   The lesson outcome is developmentally appropriate, challenging, but achievable (Glatthorn, 1997).

Before the lesson, the teacher visualizes the sequence of meaningful learning tasks, how students will be assessed and how to ensure mastery for all students. Most importantly, learning outcomes are uppermost throughout the lesson. Thus, the outcomes are made explicit at the outset, or, in discovery-oriented lessons, are presented in a way which enables students to be clear about what is expected of them and how it is to be achieved. After the lesson, the teacher reflects in private, with peers or with a supervisor, on whether the outcomes were achieved and whether all students achieved them. As Glatthorn (1997: 26) says, 'the bottom line question is, what did the students learn in that period that they did not know when they walked in to the lesson?'

What are the implications of a learning-centred approach for appraisal? Standard versions of clinical supervision focus just on teaching methods, while Glatthorn (1997), in advocating an outcomes' approach, suggests that teacher appraisal should concentrate on what students learned. The approach adopted here, however, emphasizes the connections between teaching and learning outcomes. That is, teachers are appraised according to what students learned as a result of what and how they were taught.

Thus, it is necessary to adapt and reorient Glatthorn's (1997) reasoning to take account of this different orientation, namely, the teaching–learning outcome connection. The following constitutes a possible scenario for an

appraisal context involving a pre-observation conference, a classroom observation, the observational analysis and a post-observation conference.

The pre-observation conference. The supervisor, whether administrator or
peer, checks whether the teacher is clear about the answers to the following
questions as the basis for the subsequent observation:

1   What are the intended lesson outcomes? Do they relate to the unit
     outcomes? Are the outcomes significant? Are they developmentally
     appropriate?
2   What are the characteristics of the students as learners? For example,
     what are their interests, abilities and learning styles? What work will
     they do to achieve the outcomes?
3   What are the intended teaching methods? Why were these teaching
     methods selected in view of the outcomes? Are they justified by research
     evidence on effective teaching? How will the teacher assess student
     performance; is it authentic assessment?

The classroom observation. The supervisor focuses on observation to
answer these questions:

1   How is the learning outcome and its significance explained? Was it
     connected to the unit outcome? Was it significant to the skills and ideas
     of the subject, the learner and future learning?
2   Did all students seem to master the outcome? If not, who did and did not?
     What is the evidence that learning was occurring or was not occurring?
3   Are all students engaged in learning? What is the quality of their
     learning experiences?
4   What teaching methods is the teacher adopting? Is there evidence of
     flexibility to accommodate individualization and different learning
     styles and experiences, both direct teaching and more constructivist
     approaches? In reality, many more specific questions about the teacher's
     approach would be asked, all related to effective teaching research.
5   How is learning assessed? How often?

Observational analysis. The supervisor analyses and reflects on the data
collected. Were the learning outcomes achieved? By whom? If not, for what
reason? Were the teaching methods appropriate, given the students' learning
characteristics and the learning outcomes?

The post-observation conference. In helping teachers become reflective
about teaching and its contribution to student learning, the supervisor
encourages the teacher to engage in a problem-solving process to work out
answers to the following questions:

1   From your perspective, did the students understand the learning outcome objective? Was it clear?
2   Which of the students mastered the outcomes and who did not? How do you know?
3   What work did the student do to achieve the outcome, and was it a quality experience? How do you know?
4   How do you explain the students' success or lack thereof? What role did teaching play in this?
5   What are the implications for future improvement in teaching and learning?

Many of these are complex issues, especially responses which invite teachers, supervisors and peers to consider connections between teaching methodology and student achievement or non-achievement of learning outcomes. That is why a problem-solving orientation is appropriate. In many, perhaps most, cases it will be impossible to establish precise causal connections. But that is not the point. Rather, what is important is that teachers are encouraged to think about what and how they teach in the context of student achievement of specific learning outcomes. In other words, the learning experiences they provide for students not only decide the intended learning outcomes, but also affect whether, and which, students achieve those outcomes.

A Cross-Cultural Perspective on Appraisal

School restructuring policies have been adopted in many Western and Asian countries. In many non-Western countries where appraisal is found, the basic policy design, including the introduction of formal schemes of staff appraisal, tends to be imported from countries such as the USA, UK and Australia. This raises yet again the vexed question as to the suitability of policies, in this case staff appraisal, forged in Western cultures and imported into societies with different cultures.

Hofstede (1995) has addressed this issue in the context of the business world, noting that performance appraisal systems, strongly advocated in Western management literature, suggest that employees' performance will improve when they receive direct feedback, usually from a superordinate. This may be true, he says, for individualist cultures. Western models of appraisal not only assume direct feedback, open communication and more equal relationships between the superordinate and subordinate, but also that organizational members see themselves as individuals rather than as team or group members. In collectivist societies, however, these assumptions may not hold, and the giving of direct feedback can destroy the harmony which is considered so important in governing interpersonal relationships.

The implication of Hofstede's remarks for introducing appraisal into the collectivist societies of East Asia, is that feedback might be more appropriately given indirectly, 'through the withdrawing of a favour, or via an intermediary person trusted by both supervisor and employee' (Hofstede, 1995: 157). In other words, it may be necessary to adapt appraisal from Western approaches relying on direct face to face feedback between appraiser and appraisee to suit the cultural contexts of East Asian schools.

One of the main channels through which culture manifests itself is at the level of interpersonal relationships and interpersonal communication, both of which are at the heart of the appraisal process. Cultural adaptations to accommodate these concerns might include greater reliance in Asian schools on peer appraisal and on self-appraisal, both of which avoid direct face to face confrontations between personnel at different hierarchical levels.

It is instructive to relate the case of Hong Kong as an example of an Asian school system challenged to introduce staff appraisal. What are the implications of Hong Kong's culture for the introduction of staff appraisal in its schools? Both of the major school restructuring policies of the 1990s – the School Management Initiative (SMI) (Education and Manpower Branch and Education Department (1991) and the Education Commission Report No. 7 (ECR7) (Education Commission Report No. 7, 1997) – are unequivocal about the necessity to introduce a staff appraisal system. The importance of appraisal, as set out in the SMI, is its assessment of staff strengths and weaknesses, its clarification of staff development needs, and its contribution to ensuring a meritocratic basis for promotion. The same arguments are repeated again in the ECR7, only this time appraisal is seen as part of a quality assurance process. By 1998 few schools, even those which had been part of the SMI scheme since its inception, could claim a workable and effective appraisal system. In the absence of strong teachers' unions in Hong Kong, difficulties associated with the introduction of appraisal seem more attributable to practical problems of implementation at the school site.

In many respects the challenge of installing appraisal systems in Hong Kong's schools represents a more general problem concerning the implementation of top-down restructuring policies. In order to facilitate the implementation of appraisal in Hong Kong schools, two Advisory Committee documents (Education Department, 1992, 1993) on appraisal were produced. Neither, however, details clear procedures for operationalising an appraisal system. This situation typifies a key dilemma of reform: the centre, in the form of the Education Department, is either unwilling or unable to provide schools with detailed guidance and direction on implementation. Each school is therefore left to work out its own response. However, for their part schools rarely seem to possess the technical knowledge, expertise, initiative, determination and resources to make such reforms happen. Inertia is often the result.

Recent research on Hong Kong principals found that the maintenance of harmonious (and the avoidance of conflictual) relationships with staff invariably proved the overriding priority in their management of difficult school situations (Walker and Dimmock, 1999). Fears that employees may lose 'face' and with it, personal loyalty to the organization, are uppermost in the minds of many Chinese principals. By the same token, Dimmock and Lim (1999) found from their case study of middle managers in a Hong Kong school, that the most challenging role change faced as a consequence of restructuring, concerned the appraisal of teachers under their supervision and the handling of potentially difficult technical and personnel decisions. They admitted to being underprepared and lacking in appropriate training for the task.

Conclusion

Unlike conventional appraisal schemes, the model of teacher appraisal outlined in this chapter does not focus on the individual teacher *per se*, but on the contribution made by individual teachers to the school mission defined in terms of the best quality teaching and learning for all students. For teachers, this means a focus on the preparation and delivery of curricula to students and the authentic assessment of student attainment. Teachers' work is primarily defined as an iterative process between adopting informed teaching practices and connecting with and enabling successful student learning outcomes. This relationship provides a focus for teacher appraisal and also for administrator appraisal. In the latter case, the issues attend to the extent to which administrators promote, resource and evaluate the delivery of quality teaching and learning outcomes by teachers.

A number of assumptions underpin the model. These include the school having a clear and explicit mission and set of policies concerning quality teaching and learning outcomes for all students, and a driving concern for knowledge-based informed practice regarding teaching and learning, which provides high standard benchmarks against which teachers can be appraised for professional development. The principle of differentiated supervision secures the twin benefits of school-wide and individual flexibility. School-wide agreement to focus on a restricted number of informed teaching and learning practices each year or semester brings many benefits. It achieves school-wide improvement in a synergistic way, as well as individual growth; it promotes peer support and collaboration; and it reduces the personal threat posed by appraisal since the whole school community is focused on the same goals. Equally, because teachers are at different levels of experience and expertise, their development needs vary. Through their own inquiry and research, teachers should play a key role in constructing all stages and facets of the model and its operation.

Finally, although little research has been undertaken on teacher appraisal from a cross-cultural perspective, it is likely that its successful operation in schools across the world depends, at least in part, on the extent to which cognisance is taken of local cultural influences and sensitivities. As school restructuring extends around the globe and teacher appraisal continues to evolve, the tension between internationalization and local cultures will warrant increasing attention, no more so than in the arena of teacher and administrator appraisal.

References

Brophy, J. (1981) 'Teacher praise: a functional analysis', *Review of Educational Research* 51 (1): 5–32.

Brophy, J. and Good, T. (1986) 'Teacher behavior and student achievement', in M. Wittrock (ed.), *Handbook of Reseach on Teaching*, 3rd edn, New York: Macmillan.

Dimmock, C. and Lim, P.H.W. (1999) 'School restructuring in Hong Kong: a case study of the effects on middle managers', *Asia Pacific Journal of Education* 19 (1); 59–77.

Education and Manpower Branch and Education Department (1991) 'The school management initiative: setting the framework for quality in Hong Kong schools', Hong Kong: The Government Printer.

Education Commission Report No. 7 (ECR7) (1997) 'Quality school education', Hong Kong: The Government Printer.

Education Department (Advisory Committee on the School Management Initiative) (1992) 'Staff appraisal in schools', Hong Kong: The Government Printer.

—— (1993) 'The appraisal of the school head', Hong Kong: The Government Printer.

Fraser, B.J., Walberg, H.J., Welch, W.W. and Hattie, J.A. (1987) 'Syntheses of educational productivity research', *International Journal of Educational Research* 11 (2): 147–247.

Glatthorn, A. (1997) *Differentiated Supervision*, 2nd edn, Alexandria, VA: Association for Supervision and Curriculum Development.

Hofstede, G. (1995) 'Managerial values: the business of international business is culture', in T. Jackson (ed.), *Cross-Cultural Management*, Oxford: Butterworth Heinemann, 150–65.

Lacey, K. (1996) *Performance Appraisal and Career Planning*, Melbourne: Macmillan Education Australia.

Leithwood, K.A. (1988) 'Performance appraisal as an instrument for planned change: contributions of effectiveness research', in E.S. Hickcox, S.B. Lawton, K.A. Leithwood and D.F. Musella (eds), *Making a Difference Through Performance Appraisal*, Toronto: Ontario Institute of Education Press, 84–110.

Stiggins, R.S. (1988) 'The case for changing teacher evaluation to promote school improvement', in E.S. Hickcox, S.B. Lawton, K.A. Leithwood and D.F. Musella (eds), *Making a Difference Through Performance Appraisal*, Toronto: Ontario Institute of Education Press, 141–57.

Walker, A. and Dimmock, C. (1999) 'Exploring principals' dilemmas in Hong Kong: increasing cross-cultural understanding of school leadership', *International Journal of Educational Reform* 8 (1): 15–24.

12 Learning-Centred Leadership

In the re-designed, learning-centred school, leadership and management play vital roles in creating, maintaining and developing quality curricula, teaching and learning for all students. This chapter first emphasizes the part played by the backward-mapping and iterative process in identifying the key characteristics of leadership in the re-designed, learning-centred school. Second, it discusses each of the characteristics in turn. Finally, it outlines a cross-cultural perspective of leadership and raises issues relating to cultural differences in the way leadership is exercised.

Earlier chapters have presented conceptions of curricula, learning, teaching, technology, and organizational structures in the re-designed school. Leadership is crucial in securing each of them in a form conducive to the learning-centred school. Only when these aspects of school design are clarified is it appropriate or possible to introduce the conception of leadership advocated. This is justified by the principle of backward-mapping and iteration which runs consistently through the book. According to this principle, clear conceptions of leadership are not independent of the elements which constitute the learning-centred school. Rather, they are derived from the nature and form of the various elements of the re-designed school, and especially its core technology, including learning, informed teaching, technology and organizational structures. Hence, in forming clearer conceptions of the elements, one is at the same time determining and clarifying the nature and form of leadership required. One implication of this approach is that leaders do not exercise discretion as to what constitutes leadership, although there would appear to be latitude as to how they lead and their preferred style of leadership. Using the backward-mapping principle to determine the notion of leadership is not to diminish its importance; on the contrary, it ensures harmony and connectivity between leadership and all of the other elements which comprise the learning-centred school.

Leadership may be defined as the ability, by virtue of taking initiative, to influence the thoughts and actions of others towards achieving agreed goals. In capturing the generality of situations, this definition presents a low key version of leadership. In a stronger version, the leader is seen as inspiring, enthusing and motivating others to contribute higher levels of commitment and effort to secure goals than they otherwise would. Successful leaders generally possess a sense of vision, direction, and goals along with the capacity to persuade, convince and commit others to high levels of effort to secure them.

Leadership in the learning-centred school is assumed to be organization-wide; that is, it is dispersed among faculty and students at different levels. According to this view, teacher leadership is an important phenomenon, as is student leadership, with each being applicable to certain school functions and arenas. Leadership is not therefore seen as a zero-sum concept with all of it vested in the person of the principal. Rather, part of the principal's exercise of leadership is the empowerment of leadership in others. Thus leadership in the learning-centred school is seen as a nested concept, the lowest level of which applies to students, the next layer to teachers, another layer to senior teachers, then deputy principals and finally, the overarching layer, to the principal.

The Eleven Components and Seven Dimensions of Leadership in the Learning-Centred School

Following the process of backward mapping from ideas presented in earlier chapters and from previous research on the design of learning-centred schools (Dimmock, 1995a; Dimmock, 1995b), a conception of leadership is derived which emphasizes eleven components. While the components are presented as discrete entities for the present purpose of analysis, in reality they dovetail closely and overlap. The components are as follows:

1   Goal orientation, especially towards student learning outcomes;
2   Technical knowledge, and management, of curriculum design, development and evaluation;
3   Technical knowledge, and management, of effective teaching and learning;
4   Understanding and advocacy of research findings on effective teaching and learning, school effectiveness and school improvement as basis of practice;
5   Knowledge and management of technology;
6   Knowledge and management of organizational structures for service delivery of teaching and learning;
7   Capacity and willingness to model desired and desirable behaviours, including ethical, social and learning-oriented;
8   Building organizational culture to value learning for all and a positive, collaborative climate of human relations;
9   Leadership of human resources and management of other resources in support of enhancing learning for all;

10 Monitoring and reviewing performance at school and sub-school levels for quality assurance in order to provide feedback, positive reinforcement and accountability;

11 Strategies for organizational change and innovation towards the learning-centred school.

These eleven components can be grouped into eight dimensions, as follows:

1 Educational leadership: components 1 through to 4;
2 Technological leadership: component 5;
3 Structural leadership: component 6;
4 Moral leadership; component 7;
5 Cultural and symbolic leadership: component 8;
6 Human resource leadership and non-human resource management: components 9 and 10;
7 Political leadership: particularly affecting components 9, 10 and 11;
8 Strategic and transformational leadership: component 11.

Each of these dimensions is now discussed.

Educational Leadership

A major shift in the mind-set of school leaders is prompted by the centrality of students and learning in learning-centred schools. Principals and teachers are goal-oriented in respect of improving student learning outcomes, interpreting their work roles and judging their performance in terms of the contribution they make to enhancing learning (Levine and Lezotte, 1990). They conceptualize school problems in these terms, using students and their learning as goals and benchmarks against which to assess the effectiveness of their own performance. They adopt collegial and professional, rather than hierarchical, stances in problem solving (Moore Johnson, 1990). They encourage teachers to conceptualize issues bottom-up, from the students' viewpoint, rather than top-down, from their own perspective. Above all, they hold students' welfare uppermost in their values, believing that they are in school primarily to serve the interests of all students. These school leaders are goal-oriented with respect to learning at two levels: they possess a school-wide perspective, viewing the school and parents as a learning community; and they are acutely concerned, through a heightened sense of justice and equity, for the interests of each student and their learning needs (Leithwood and Montgomery, 1982; Reilly, 1984).

Leadership in the school for quality learning and teaching focuses on learning, pedagogy and curriculum (Hord et al., 1984; Leithwood and Steinbach, 1993). Principals and other administrators exercise instructional leadership based on a strong technical knowledge of curriculum design, development and evaluation, and effective teaching and learning. Such technical knowledge is a *sine qua non* for leading and managing both teachers as professionals and subject experts and students as inexperienced learners; both groups are engaged in a set of activities, namely teaching and learning, which are both esoteric and complex. In addition, technical knowledge of curriculum design, development and evaluation becomes increasingly important the more these curriculum processes become school-based. Without such knowledge, school leaders are likely to find professional dialogue and interpersonal communication on key school issues, as well as relationships between themselves and other school members, to be seriously deficient. Principals and senior staff who are well versed in the theory and practice of curriculum design, implementation and evaluation and with knowledge of effective teaching–learning principles are empowered leaders of their learning communities (Duke, 1987). They possess the technical knowledge to relate to teachers and students on classroom-level issues as well as provide whole-school perspectives on curricular and pedagogical issues.

As learners, principals and senior staff demonstrate that they value the importance of research findings as guides to informed practice and future innovation (Rossow, 1990). They encourage teachers to be cognisant of research on effective teaching and learning by obtaining and disseminating relevant literature and by resourcing and arranging staff development to keep staff informed (Duke, 1987). These school leaders familiarize themselves with research on principal effectiveness, school effectiveness and school improvement and seek appropriate opportunities to apply important findings (Leithwood, 1988). In regard to research, they demonstrate in their own behaviour the value they place on reading, understanding, reflecting, conceptualizing and transforming ideas into practice.

Technological Leadership

So important is technology in the re-designed school that it becomes an integral part of leadership. Leaders need to be conversant with the capabilities and potentialities of technology. As Chapter 8 illustrates, the integration of technology into the learning-centred school should conform to a carefully engineered plan built on the fundamental principles of access for all and embeddedness across the whole curriculum. If these precepts are unattainable in the short term, they should certainly figure as long-term goals towards which the school is headed.

Computer technology is central to the delivery of the curriculum programme and the attainment of student outcomes in the learning-centred school. Its centrality means that it can be a vital catalyst for change in school re-design. Its intrusiveness into the heart of the classroom means that traditional notions of teaching and learning are re-configured. The respective roles of teacher and learner are transformed. With the adoption and implementation of whole-school policies involving the application of computer technology into classroom teaching and learning, school re-design penetrates into the classroom. While many other aspects of school re-design fail to penetrate inside the classroom, this is not the case with computer technology. An essential responsibility of leadership is to ensure the visions, goals and policies concerning technology are adopted and implemented across all faculty.

Leaders must themselves believe in the centrality of computer technology to student learning in the information and knowledge-based society. They require at least basic technical knowledge in order to appreciate its potentialities and possibilities within the re-designed school. Equally, they need to empower and encourage others, particularly those with specialist expertise, to promote and implement a coherent school-wide technology policy.

The creation of a school technology plan and policy requires broad input from a number of people, including teachers, administrators and outside business representatives. Such a plan should first identify the student learning outcomes desired (Whitaker and Moses, 1994). Using the backward mapping strategy, the school should then envision and plan its teaching–learning models of informed practice. These are the approaches to teaching and learning which it believes will deliver the student outcomes. At this point, the technology plan should integrate with the overall teaching–learning strategy. A school technology plan which enjoys integrity can only be conceived when the school has a clear idea of its student outcomes and its teaching–learning policy. For example, decisions need to be taken on how technology can be used to enhance the quality of interpersonal communication between teacher and students and between students, both inside and outside the school. How will technology complement other more traditional teaching–learning methods? Leadership is instrumental in ensuring a rigorous and thoughtful planning process, employing backward mapping and encouraging iteration to check backwards and forwards for coherence and consistency.

Finally, leadership is instrumental in providing support and resourcing for relevant and high quality staff training. Training should integrate the features of hardware and software with the school curriculum, teaching and learning. Ideally, teachers need to understand the possibilities that the hardware and software offer within the contexts of the curriculum they are delivering, and the teaching–learning models they are adopting. Whitaker and Moses (1994) argue that when deciding the technology budget, approximately one-third should be devoted to the hardware, one-third to the software and one-third to staff training. Considerable funding will be required to maintain and update the system.

Structural Leadership

Successful implementation of new conceptions of teaching and learning depends on major reconfiguration of school organizational structures. As Chapter 9 indicates, these structures include new forms of student and teacher groupings as well as reformed timetable arrangements and curricula. At stake is the capability to plan, design and implement new structures on the basis of backward mapping from student outcomes, and from the model of teaching and learning to be realized. The design and configuration of structures should support, not hinder, the delivery of a quality curriculum to all students. Backward mapping ensures that structural design is dependent on, and derived from, informed practices constituting the core technology. Typically, the reverse is the case. Structures have come to assume such dominance that key elements of core technology have been determined by structural parameters. Thus standard lesson times, inflexible, standardized curricula, regimented timetables and traditional times of school operation have come to govern decisions about core technology.

Effective school leaders realize the importance of managing structures in the promotion and achievement of desirable practices, professional relationships and school-wide goals. An understanding of schools as organizations and the range of viable alternative structures is required (Ubben and Hughes, 1992). A knowledge of organizational theory and analysis, including current thinking on flexible organizational designs, is a key part of the leader's role in school re-design. An ability to select appropriate structures conducive to the effective delivery of the new curriculum, teaching and learning model is axiomatic. Above all, the structures have to be feasible and workable. The ability to reflect critically on the extent to which existing and new structures facilitate and obstruct the delivery of quality teaching and learning depends on the leader's ability to backward map and to make connections and to predict consequences and outcomes. This is a neglected concern in the study of leadership. In the initial stages of re-designing schools, traditional structures may need demolishing, especially if they are incompatible with the flexible delivery of curricula to all students. Effective leadership thus recognizes the importance of organizational structures in enabling the core technology to function productively (Dimmock, 1993; Murphy et al., 1985).

Moral Leadership

The discussion of leadership so far has assumed it to be behaviourally based; that is, leaders try to change the behaviours of others. However, as Sergiovanni (1992) reminds us, an even more fundamental responsibility of leaders is to foster among staff and students a quest for an understanding of the meaning underpinning their behaviours. Here, the emphasis is on faculty and students understanding and articulating what they are doing, and why.

Addressing these issues, and understanding the meaning of their behaviours would appear to be an important prior stage to persuading or convincing them to change, especially if they are professionals and if they are to receive the respect they are due.

Moral leadership, however, is more than putting faculty and students in touch with the meanings undergirding their behaviours. As Sergiovanni (1992) explains, it is a dimension of leadership centred on purpose, values and beliefs, all of which are powerful attributes capable of transforming schools from base organizations to tight communities possessing commitment, devotion and service. Legitimizing emotion and the expression of guiding principles by which to live fosters authentic relationships with others while keying into their innermost values. Appeal to and connection with this deep level of values and beliefs is a more promising way of achieving true collegiality, based on shared work and common goals. It creates a natural rather than contrived interdependence among teachers.

Moral leadership also includes promulgating a view of teachers as true professionals and students as authentic learners. It involves motivating teachers and students by appealing to emotion and social bonds within a context of informed professional ideals and practices. Public declarations of values and purpose are part of the expected responsibility of leaders. The same set of values should permeate individual relationships and the formal and hidden curriculum.

Moral authority is a qualitatively different basis for the exercise of leadership from the more common bases of research evidence, bureaucratic authority or charismatic qualities. It generates obligations and duties derived from widely shared values, ideas and ideals (Sergiovanni, 1992). It also helps provide a practical definition of leadership, viewing it as enabling teachers as professionals and students as active learners to assume more responsibility and authority for their performances. Sergiovanni (1992) refers to this as a servant view of leadership, a perspective which is compatible with the backward mapping principle of leadership espoused in this book. In other words, appropriate leadership backward-maps to and derives from the characteristics of the core technology of curriculum, teaching and learning. It cuts away obstacles and hindrances preventing teachers and students from adopting informed practice.

In the learning-centred school, leaders deliberately and consciously demonstrate in their own professional work the core values and behaviours they wish to promulgate in others. They model the behaviours and values they advocate for teachers and students (Dimmock, 1995a, 1995b). With the leader as role model, desirable values and practices are deliberately replicated at different levels. In advocating a school focus on student learning, effective principals and teachers approach their own professional work with a learning orientation (Barth, 1990). The problematic nature of many issues and the value of inquiry in determining their resolution is publicly demonstrated in leader behaviour from the principal through teachers to students. For example, collaborative learning among students is reinforced when paralleled by teacher collaboration in and out of the classroom and when collaboration through all levels of school operation is publicly valued. Encouraging students to problem solve in their learning is reinforced when students observe teachers modelling the same processes in their teaching and in the wider school setting of administration and policy making. These processes are more evident where students are involved with staff in school decision making.

The same modelling and reinforcement applies at different levels in the school to leadership, goal-directed behaviour and preparedness for risk-taking. The concept of leadership density entails its exercise throughout the school, with leadership exercised by students in the classroom, by teachers and by senior staff. Encouraging students to set goals for their learning is paralleled by teacher and school goal-setting. Powerful reinforcement occurs where these sets of goals align. Likewise, developing in students a confidence to take risks and learn from mistakes is supported where students observe these values and behaviours operating across other levels of the school, including school leadership and management.

Ability and willingness to involve all participants in the school community, especially teachers, students and parents, reflects the school leaders' awareness of the importance of democracy and equality in building a healthy school climate for enhancing teaching and learning. These leaders realize the importance of democratic values, such as tolerance and respect for the rights and values of others, participation, concern for equity, and ability and opportunity to make judgements and choices in one's own and others' interests. These and other democratic values become embedded in the curriculum, school structures and core processes of learning, teaching and decision making (Dimmock, 1995c). Uppermost in the value system is the equal valuation of all students, irrespective of their abilities, ethnic backgrounds or gender. A healthy democratic school climate where students are encouraged to participate in, and are consulted about, the running of their school is as much a valuable part of their learning as the acquisition of subject knowledge. Effective school leaders realize the one form of learning is likely to promote the other.

Cultural and Symbolic Leadership

According to Bolman and Deal (1991), many of the significant events and processes in organizations are ambiguous or uncertain; it is often difficult to know what happened, why it happened or what will happen next. Rational approaches to analysis, problem solving or decision making are not always possible. Faced with uncertainty and ambiguity, human beings create symbols to resolve confusion and to bring direction and predictability to their work lives. Many school events and processes are important more for what they express than for what they produce: they are myths, rituals, ceremonies, public displays and values which help members retain a sense of mission and direction for what the school stands. At the same time they serve to bolster a sense of belonging, attachment and commitment to the school mission and above all, success in the mission. The cultivation and promotion of the cultural and symbolic is a key function of leadership in the learning-centred school.

Tight coupling and synergy is achieved when all parts of a school share common values, goals and practices. Forging cultural and to a lesser extent bureaucratic linkages between the parts of a school helps dismantle the barriers and internal divisions which have sustained loose coupling in the past and creates a unifying energy to achieve school goals in the future. These are achievable when the school is tightly coupled, not through heavy-handed bureaucratic and hierarchical administration, but through common cultural linkages and shared professional practices supported by a necessary modicum of bureaucracy (Wilson and Firestone, 1987).

New configurations of teaching and learning are dependent on school leaders taking responsibility for building a culture which supports learning for all and a positive climate which values productive human relations (Ubben and Hughes, 1992). Effective school leaders recognize the multiple and mutually reinforcing strategies available to them in building supportive learning cultures. These range from more explicit forms of verbal communication with all groups in the school community to include modelling and demonstrating through their own behaviours, as well as more subtle uses of symbols, ceremonies and rituals (Parkay and Hall, 1992). High but realistic learning expectations are conveyed, rewards, recognition and resources for learning are provided, and learning time is protected (Smith and Piele, 1989).

Leadership in the Human and Non-human Resource Dimensions

High levels of learning productivity in schools are underpinned by human resource leadership. Aspects of human relations critical to effective teaching and learning are motivation, collaboration and care. High performance is attained when teachers and students are motivated to achieve. Successful leaders are distinguished by their capacity to enthuse. They also exert a capacity to bring people together to work collaboratively. In schools where each student is valued as an individual learner, where a strong sense of equity and social justice permeates policy and practice, where teachers assume joint responsibility with students for learning outcomes, care, concern and commitment permeate relationships. Students care for each other, teachers care for students as well as for each other and principals care for teachers and students.

Part of this care and concern shown by leaders includes a recognition that teachers be encouraged to develop as professionals. Teachers require the opportunity to professionally develop collaboratively and individually. They need to be accorded the respect and integrity to develop as inquiring, reflective practitioners. For teachers to become inquiring, reflective practitioners, however, most of them will need a more robust knowledge and skill base of informed teaching and learning practices than they presently possess. It is the responsibility of the concerned leader to ensure that these conditions are created for teacher development.

Collaborative and collegial decision making is more likely when the principal and senior staff are not buffered from the core technology. Principals and administrators as instructional leaders are able to set priorities for nurturing the quality of teaching and learning in the school. They accept the broadening of managerial responsibilities that comes with school-based management, but contain these additional tasks by framing their importance within the context of teaching and learning. Financial management, for example, is conceived more in terms of how it can influence resource allocation to enhance the core technology rather than regarded as intrinsically important in itself (Duke, 1987). The focus on instructional or educational leadership by principals and senior staff sets the school culture and prevailing values. The school is valued as a learning community, with the principal as chief learner alongside staff and students (Barth, 1990). Traditional role divisions between administrators, teachers and learners become blurred and frequently inverted. Students adopt teaching as well as learning roles, while teachers adopt learning as well as teaching roles. School leaders encourage these more fluid roles and relationships, recognizing their importance in enhancing the school as a community of empowered learners.

Learning-centred leaders realize that new conceptions of teaching and learning are predicated on collaborative relationships throughout the school (Rosenholtz, 1989). Teachers, for example, are able to create successful collaborative classroom experiences for students as well as collaborate effectively among themselves in planning, teaching, evaluating and school decision making (Moore Johnson, 1990). Effective school leaders realize the need to nurture collaboration by establishing a framework of trust, respect, congeniality and collegiality. The ways in which they as leaders relate to teachers, students and parents help establish the norms of behaviour desired for others. Instances of genuine teacher collaboration seem hard to achieve in traditional schools, where teachers have relied on individualized methods of working; the 'one teacher to a class' syndrome is the norm. In the learning-centred school, however, better quality and more informed decisions and actions are seen as emanating from combining the professional knowledge and expertise of teachers. Teachers are grouped in year or course teams, with overall responsibility for the academic and personal welfare of students entrusted to their care (see Chapter 9). They plan, prepare and share curriculum materials and units of work to ensure vertical and horizontal integration of the curriculum. They develop and share lesson plans and assessment schemes. They take collective team decisions on all cases reviewing student academic progress, behaviour and discipline. In the learning-centred school, student academic and disciplinary records are fully computerized, so that each staff member can attend meetings in possession of all the necessary information available on their laptop computers. The level of information thus brought to bear on decision making can be sophisticated: first, through profiling student academic and disciplinary progress, and second, through combining the views of team members and seeking a consensus decision.

In the initial stages of establishing collaborative team decision making, teachers may need appropriate training. Formalized procedures may need to be followed to ensure that the principles of collaborative decision making are implemented in a disciplined way. This ensures informed practice is established and routinized in team decision making and problem solving, in much the same way as informed practice pervades teaching and learning. At Brewster Academy in New Hampshire, for example, teachers were initially drilled in a number of sequenced procedures on the conduct of successful team meetings. Each team, consisting of no more than seven members, has a team leader, who is mainly responsible for the operation, evaluation and accountability of the team performance. Team members divide and rotate roles over a period of time, including chairing, recording and time-keeping. Meetings are not to last more than one hour. Each member of the team is formally offered the opportunity to contribute to each stage of the decision-making process, beginning with a statement of the issue or problem, reviewing all of the relevant facts and evidence and giving their interpretation, moving to possible alternative strategies to address the issue, and finally selecting the preferred course of action, which must be taken on a team consensus basis. Leadership in the learning-centred school is thus exercised importantly through the medium of teamwork.

Resource allocation is crucial in supporting the quality school for learning and teaching. Patterns of allocation reveal whether the school is fostering the learning of all students and whether it has thought carefully about the resource levels necessary for the learning of different cohorts of students (Knight, 1993). As remarked in Chapter 11, program budgeting ties resources to objectives and curriculum programs and is a marked advance on simple line-item budgeting which still pervades schools. A further stage beyond program budgeting involves tying resources to student outcomes. Instead of decisions taken on the basis of the costs of mounting each course or program, resources are allocated on the expected costs of individuals or groups of students achieving certain levels of learning outcomes. Students and schools perform well when leaders recognize the need for agreement on goals, when resources are allocated to support goal achievement and when all parts of the school work consistently and collaboratively towards the same ends. Resources are allocated to professional development which, in turn, supports improvements in teaching and learning. Professional development of staff is school-focused, addressing school policies and involving functioning teams aiming at attaining student learning outcomes.

Effective schools monitor and review their performance at whole school and sub-school levels (Cuttance, 1993). Their school communities express interest in the quality of teaching and learning, the appropriateness of structures, culture and climate, as well as the quality of leadership and management, by adopting and institutionalizing evaluation procedures. School leaders contribute directly through their personal involvement in monitoring and reviewing, and indirectly by establishing a culture and climate supportive of the engagement of others in review. Effective leaders in the learning-centred school realize the importance of monitoring and reviewing as pre-requisites for providing feedback and positive reinforcement, both of which are consistently found among the factors contributing most to learning (Fraser et al., 1987). In their capacity as leaders, they give abundant feedback and positive reinforcement to teachers and students and at the same time build the culture for these behaviours to permeate all levels and members of the school community. Furthermore, they appreciate that review and evaluation are pre-requisites for accountability to their constituents. They realize that accountability is part of the social, political and professional contexts within which the school functions and they maximize the opportunities it creates for bringing recognition and possibly resources, to the school.

Political Leadership

Although political aspects of leading the learning-centred school have not received due emphasis in this book, they are nonetheless vital in its successful functioning. All organizations are political. They are composed of individuals and groups pursuing aims to further their interests. In the process, they exercise power and consume resources. Politics is about the exercise of power in the pursuit of interests, and the consequential decisions to allocate finite resources to achieve goals which serve those interests. The exercise of effective political leadership in the learning-centred school harnesses the energy produced by individual and group pursuit of interests and channels it towards the school mission of enabling all students to achieve appropriate learning outcomes.

Skilful leadership recognizes that some problems can best be dealt with through political means. Bolman and Deal (1991) argue that leaders need the flexibility to reframe or reconceptualize problem situations in terms of four perspectives and associated abilities, namely, structural, human resource, cultural and symbolic, and political. They attest to most principals using the structural and human relations frames, but rarely the cultural-symbolic and political frames. This leaves them ill-equipped to deal with the full gamut of difficult situations confronting them. Inappropriate or injudicious choice of strategies tends to worsen problems rather than mitigate them.

Adroit political leadership harnesses different sectional interests and energies in the school by means of bargaining and negotiation, striking deals and exchanging agreements. It focuses effort and resources on overall goals, appealing to the primacy of learning for all students. In this way, power and influence are exercised to unite the school by taking cognisance of sectional interests and then uniting them to focus on, and secure, the big picture goal of ensuring all students achieve success in terms of learning outcomes. In summary, the political dimension to leadership is crucial in creating a whole-school perspective and preventing fragmented sectional interests from achieving dominance, and in allocating resources in ways consistent with the school mission.

Strategic and Transformational Leadership

The learning-centred school is constantly looking for school improvement. Two aspects of leadership are central to school improvement: strategic and transformational. In relation to strategic leadership, Caldwell (1998a, 1998b) has utilized Boisot's (1995) typology of four different strategic leadership responses. Each response is appropriate to certain levels of turbulence in the environmental conditions and the capacity of the organization to extract and process useful information from that environment (level of understanding).

Low turbulence and low understanding mean that strategic planning is not possible. Only an *emergent strategy* is appropriate and possible, that is, an 'incremental adjustment to environmental states that cannot be discerned or anticipated through a prior analysis of data' (Boisot, 1995: 34). Such conditions may have applied in education several decades ago.

Low turbulence and high understanding environments mean that *strategic planning* is possible and appropriate; that is, the formation of medium to long-term plans on the basis of an environmental scan. Strategic planning is a rational response to more predictable environments; it is unsuited to school environments which are restructuring and re-designing.

High turbulence and low understanding environments favour *intrapreneurship*. This is the equivalent of entrepreneurship, but is carried out within the organization. Since the formulation of organization-wide strategies is disfavoured in such situations, individual initiatives may be possible and those which are successful may later be adopted by the organization.

High turbulence and high understanding environments favour *strategic intent* as a response. Conventional strategic planning is made difficult by the degree of turbulence. On the other hand, reliance on individual initiative and opportunism is inadequate for whole-school design. Strategic intent is a process of coping with turbulence and at the same time providing direction and guidance to a school through a direct, intuitive understanding of what is occurring, a kind of 'intuitively formed pattern or gestalt – some would call it a vision – to give it unity and coherence' (Boisot, 1995: 36).

As Caldwell (1998b: 41) notes, citing Boisot (1995), strategic intent is 'the distinguishing mark of the learning organization, and by implication, an essential part of its strategic repertoire'. Caldwell (1998a) also argues that schools are now facing these highly turbulent environmental conditions and that they need to develop a capacity to process information and acquire understanding which will enable them to make timely and effective responses to fast changing conditions. If Caldwell's conclusion is accurate, then his argument provides a strong justification for this book, the purpose and contents of which are intended to provide a gestalt whereby schools acquire the capacity to re-design themselves. Visions, however, are insufficient. They need to be filled out. Starting with the precepts of school design in Chapter 2 and charting, in subsequent chapters, the different elements which make up the whole school, this book has sought to provide the information necessary for strategic intent. Moreover, through the principle of backward- and iterative-mapping, it has pointed up the connections between the different elements of the school as an organization.

Strategic leadership needs to be combined with transformational leadership to ensure that plans and initiatives are actioned. Both aspects of leadership characterize the learning-centred school, an organization which is adaptive, responsive and flexible in its teaching and learning model. With new students entering the school each year, change is endemic. These schools are constantly searching for better ways of service provision to a clientele which is fluid and changing. Principals and senior administrators are transformational leaders (Leithwood and Jantzi, 1990); they promote, support and evaluate change according to its positive influence on teaching and learning. They are discriminatory in investing only in change which fits the school agenda and are comfortable in handling the change experience. They are also enthusiasts for promoting change across their communities. A focus on instructional leadership combined with transformational leadership holds out promise for improving the quality of teaching and learning. Their technical knowledge of teaching, learning and curriculum enables them to be selective in adopting change (Fullan, 1991). Their expertise as leaders and managers of the change process with respect to the implementation of new forms of teaching and learning enables them to handle opposition or conflict which may come from students, teachers and parents. Leading and managing a community of learners entails responsibility for ensuring that all participants are well informed about, aware of and involved in the arguments for change. Effective school leaders recognize the importance of timing in managing change and that ultimately it is students and teachers who hold the key to improving student outcomes.

A Cross-Cultural Framework for the Comparative Study of Leadership

Although studies of educational leadership have proliferated over the last decade, they have mostly focused on Western school settings. Leadership in non-Western school settings has largely been ignored, with the result that little is known about the influence of culture on the beliefs and actions of school leaders across national boundaries. As a consequence, comparative educational leadership as a sub-set of comparative educational administration has, on the whole, failed to materialize (Dimmock and Walker, 1998a, 1998b). In short, few studies have been completed of comparative leadership from a cross-cultural perspective. This leads to the conclusion that until comparative studies of school leadership are undertaken across different societal cultures, it is unwise to assume that theories and practices of leadership espoused in, for example, Anglo-American cultures are universally applicable to other cultures, including those of Asia.

In order to address this vacuum, Walker and Dimmock (1999a) are presently conducting research aimed at developing a cross-cultural understanding of educational leadership in particular, and of school management, organization and schooling in general (see also Dimmock and Walker, 1998b). This section presents a brief look at this work, bearing in mind that it is developmental (see Chapter 3 for a full discussion of the need for a cross-cultural comparative approach to school leadership and management).

A necessary starting point is a clarification of culture, defined here as the enduring sets of beliefs, values and ideologies underpinning a society's structures, processes and practices. As culture constitutes the context in which school leadership is exercised, it exerts a substantial influence on how and why leaders think and act as they do. Leadership, like other social acts, has to be viewed within its cultural context for an accurate understanding of its characteristics. In addition, culture can be conceptualized at a number of interrelated levels, from the micro (school) level to the macro (national) level, all of which may influence leadership thought and action. While considerable research into various aspects of school organization culture has already been undertaken, little is known about the influence of national cultures in explaining school leadership practices or in comparing leaders across different national or societal cultures.

Basing our ideas on those of a number of scholars in the field of international and comparative business management (Hofstede, 1980, 1991; Trompenaars and Hampden-Turner, 1997), our framework for comparative investigation of educational leadership is conceptualized around six dimensions of societal culture (Walker and Dimmock, 1999a). A fuller explanation of the six dimensions is given in Chapter 3. The six dimensions are:

1   Power-distributed/power-concentrated: relates to the distribution of power in a society.
2   Group oriented/self-oriented: relates to whether a society is collectivist or individualist.
3   Consideration/aggression: relates to the degree to which a society is caring as opposed to competitive.
4   Proactivism/fatalism: is concerned with whether the society believes it is in control of its destiny or whether it is fatalistic.
5   Generative/replicative: this relates to the degree to which a society is innovative compared with imitative.
6   Limited relationship/holistic relationship: this applies to how relationships are conducted, according to firm rules, or by connections and personal influence.

It is worth noting that, in reality, leadership practices result from a complex interplay, *inter alia*, between the personality and motives of individuals, organizational culture and societal culture (Hofstede and Bond, 1984). The complex interrelationships between these phenomena remain to be investigated, especially as it seems that leader behaviour is resultant from the interplay of all three. However, for the present purpose, focus is placed on societal culture and its impact on school leadership. The following analysis presents a brief account of how societal culture may influence school leadership through some of the six dimensions identified.

Applying the Cross-Cultural Framework to Principal Leadership

A main reason for developing a cross-cultural comparative framework is to increase understanding of how national or societal culture may influence educational leadership. As recognized above, there is a marked absence of research which specifically targets the influence of culture, as distinct from country studies, on the conception and practice of school leadership. Indeed, it is difficult to locate any studies which systematically compare school (principal) leadership using the construct of societal culture as the main mode of analysis. A justification for the framework is its attempt to address this void. The following discussion is tentative and is provided as exemplification of the types of cultural influences which may be identified by applying the framework.

McAdams (1993) suggests that one of the main distinctions between the US and Japanese societies is the Japanese group orientation and American individualism. Cheng (1998) agrees, holding that Chinese societies, such as Hong Kong and mainland China, are more collectivist than individualist.

Both these observations are supported by Hofstede's (1991) empirical findings. In terms of the framework presented, this suggests that Japanese and Chinese principals are more group-oriented than self-oriented. One repercussion of this in schools, and on principals' beliefs and actions, is that principals in many English-speaking and non English-speaking Western societies are more inclined to consider the individual needs of both teachers and students in the operation of schools. As Cheng (1998: 16) states: 'In European nations such as Germany, France and the Netherlands, schools cater to students with different aptitudes and interests.' In East Asian societies, such as China, Thailand and Japan, on the other hand, education is seen as a means by which students adapt to the expectations of the community. In such group-oriented societies, the role of the school and the principal may focus on developing and ensuring harmony among staff and enforcing common, standard approaches to governance, organization, curriculum and instruction.

Both Hofstede (1991) and Trompenaars and Hampden-Turner (1997) suggest that cultures attribute status, respect and power according to different cultural norms. For example, in Chinese societies respect may be attributed to position, age or family background, whereas in New Zealand it is attributed more to personal or on-the-job competence (Trompenaars and Hampden-Turner, 1997). In societies where power is linked to extrinsic factors, leadership tends to be from the 'top' and exercised in an authoritarian or autocratic manner. An example of this is India, where Sapra claims 'beneath (the) superficial slogan-mongering level, lies real India – unchanging, feudalistic or paternalistic and class ridden. The authoritarian set-up of (our) society with its hypersensitivity towards caste-distinctions makes a mess of policy decisions' (1997: 122). He continues by claiming that, given the Indian social ethos, it is unsurprising that school principals are authoritarian. In terms of the framework, Indian principals would conform to the power-concentrated rather than the power-distributed pole. Principals in other societies would be placed more toward the power-distributed pole. For example, McAdams found that German principals, because of their relationships with staff and their route to the principalship were collaborative and collegial, even more so than 'is typically the case in the United States' (1993: 118).

Different cultures deal with conflict and participation in different ways. According to Bond (1991), for example, the disturbance of interpersonal relations and group harmony by conflict can cause lasting animosity in Chinese cultures. As a result, the Chinese tend to avoid open confrontation and assertiveness. In the school or group context, this may be manifested through teachers and principals avoiding open disagreement by a tacit acceptance that it is always the leader's view which prevails (Walker et al., 1996). Principals in such cultures therefore may exhibit a tendency to avoid situations which risk conflict and to rely instead on authoritarian decision-making modes. As a consequence of conflict avoidance and of the requirement for harmonic relationships, decisions and policies are seldom challenged or approached creatively by the group. In such cultures, which may be classified as replicative systems, principals and schools may accept policies and edicts easily and tend toward preserving the status quo.

As noted, some cultures tend to be more group-oriented than self oriented. Hofstede (1991) suggests that most Southeast and East Asian societies, such as Singapore and Hong Kong, and South American countries, such as Venezuela and Columbia, are collectivist (also see Cheng, 1998). Countries which tend more toward a self-orientation include the USA, Australia, France and Germany (Hofstede, 1991; McAdams, 1993). In these Western societies, organizations generally focus on task achievement rather than the maintenance of relationships. Principals in such societies may have a tendency to put the task before relationships and judge staff on the basis of performance and the 'bottom line'. Such principals may be classified according to the framework as engaging in limited relationships.

Hofstede (1991) and others (Trompenaars and Hampden-Turner, 1997) suggest that cultures differ in their approach to change. In countries such as Australia there tends to be a reasonably high tolerance of change, and school personnel take a proactive stance to influence the effects of change on their work lives. Policy and operational changes are challenged, questioned and negotiated at the school level. In other societies, change and uncertainty is accepted almost as a coup de grace, as the way things are meant to be. Principals in countries such as mainland China which tend toward this fatalistic view may rely on established philosophies, responsibilities and power relationships to provide staff with security while accepting and implementing change, whether or not they agree with the change.

Such insights as those above begin to throw light on the cultural influences on principalship practices. Making value judgements as part of any comparison must be resisted, since cultures place different emphases on what they consider as effective practices. While the application of the framework for cross-cultural comparison is capable of exposing interesting and worthwhile insights, it is only a starting point. Many issues remain outstanding in the construction of a cross-cultural comparative approach to leadership.

The Influence of Culture on Principals' Handling of Dilemmas

Further light on how culture seems to play a significant part in influencing school leadership has been shed by recent studies conducted in Australia and in Hong Kong on principals' leadership dilemmas (Dimmock, 1996; Walker and Dimmock, 1999b). The rationale behind these studies is that culture moves particularly to the fore when principals are faced with crises or extreme situations or what might be termed dilemmas. Empirical data were collected on how principals perceived the source and nature of the dilemmas they faced, how they managed and coped with them, and with what results. As the following summary reveals, interesting insights were gained, especially as to how some Chinese principals in Hong Kong perceived and reacted to dilemmas. The data confirms that how principals make sense of and react to their workplace problems is culture-dependent.

Exemplification of how Chinese principals perceive and manage their dilemmas and how culture intrudes into the process is illustrated in the following cases. In one dilemma, an expatriate teacher who was highly valued by the principal for his excellent English language teaching (such teachers are all too scarce in Hong Kong and schools are reluctant to lose them) refused to conform to school policy on teaching. The Vice Principal (VP), with responsibility for teaching in the school, made frequent efforts to get him to conform. Eventually, life for the teacher became so uncomfortable that he threatened to resign. The principal tried unsuccessfully to arrive at a compromise, but to no avail; the teacher resigned and the school lost a valued asset who was difficult to replace. As a result, harmony was maintained with the VP and other staff, but the principal was left disappointed and grappling with contradictory feelings. In the principal's words:

> I was sorry to see the teacher go because of his excellent classroom ability, but in a way I was relieved because it released some of the fighting which had been disrupting the panel (department). Most staff agreed that he had to go in order that we have a more harmonious situation between the teachers. In Chinese we say 'two tigers cannot get on together'.

In the case of a second principal, a dilemma was created by a request from the school supervisor (who is senior to the principal in the hierarchical chain and to whom the principal reports) to promote a relative who was a teacher in the school. The performance of the teacher, however, was considered by the principal and colleagues not to warrant promotion; indeed, there were many more deserving teachers than the supervisor's relative. The principal saw the dilemma in terms of respecting hierarchy, maintaining harmony and preserving relationships with both teachers and the supervisor. He saw himself in a no-win situation; to promote the teacher would alienate staff and to refuse would, at the least, disturb the harmonious relationships with his superior. He linked the need for harmony to Chinese cultural values: 'I think harmony is culture. Harmony is central to Chinese culture, I honestly believe that in our Chinese society, harmony comes first.' What appeared to give him the most dissonance was the possibility of harmony being disturbed by conflict. Whichever way he turned, harmony was bound to suffer. If he promoted the teacher, he would lose the respect of other teachers, but would satisfy the supervisor and school managers who had appointed him and could dismiss him. If he did not promote the teacher he might incur the wrath of the supervisor and school managers, but enjoy the confidence of his staff. He expressed his feelings thus:

> The need for harmony makes me feel lonely as a principal. I was annoyed that I was pushed to promote one teacher by one of my managers ... this made me very upset. I tried to put forward my point that we want equity, we want performance. I put all of these to my supervisor – to gain harmony.

The principal chose a coping strategy which acquiesced with the request from his supervisor. Somewhat misleadingly, he thought this to be a 'compromise'. His choice of coping strategy illustrates the apparent importance of hierarchy and respect for position so deeply embedded in Chinese society. The primary consideration ultimately was maintenance of harmony with the supervisor, his superior, rather than retention of faith and trust from his staff.

In a third case, the dilemma arose from a tension between cultural values and the principals' beliefs about teaching and learning. The dilemma situation was grounded in the bi-sessional school structure, where two primary schools – a morning and an afternoon school, each with its own principal – share the same building. The dilemma would not have emerged had it not been for this structure. The principal of the afternoon session (PM), a recent graduate from a local university, believed that the school could better meet the needs of the students by revamping the student reporting system to be more flexible in reflecting individual differences. She secured the agreement of most of her staff. However, the morning principal (AM), her senior in terms of age, experience and the informal hierarchy, disagreed with what he saw as progressivism. When the afternoon principal went ahead and introduced the change, she was, as she put it, 'informally, but obviously punished'. Her dilemma was now accentuated, since if she continued doing things in her own way she risked further 'punishment', while if she discontinued the practice, she risked a lowering of staff morale. As the principal stated, 'if I do everything he (the AM principal) says, my teachers would not be happy'. The principal's chosen coping strategy was to back down and accept the seniority and power of the AM principal, claiming 'I just have to live with it, nothing will change'.

Although each of the above cases is complex and has a number of factors combine to produce the dilemma, it is the distinctive contribution of culture which is of interest. In each case, the values of harmony and respect for hierarchy were pervasive, a phenomenon well recognized in Chinese culture. Cheng and Wong (1996), for example, suggest that in Chinese societies group harmony is seen as more important than individualism (see also Hofstede, 1980). It is assumed that maintenance of group harmony is in the best interests of the individual. Cheng and Wong continue, 'This is quite different from the Western notion of the individual–group relationship where the group cannot thrive unless and only after individuals in it thrive' (1996: 38). According to Bond (1991), the disturbance of interpersonal harmony through conflict can cause lasting animosity in Chinese cultures.

If most of the dilemma situations were rooted in the need for harmony, they were equally involving of respect for hierarchy and seniority. According to Cheng (1995), groups and organizations in Chinese societies are more likely to be ordered around hierarchical sets of relationships and the rule of behaviour which govern them, than are their Western counterparts. Fei (cited in Cheng and Wong, 1996: 38) holds that Chinese societies are governed by a hierarchy 'where people are born into a certain position in the social hierarchy, and behave accordingly. This is in contrast with societies in the West where, in an *association configuration*, social structures and norms are formed acceding to *ad hoc* needs among individuals' (emphasis in original). The values of harmony and hierarchy are about maintaining relationships and power structures. In Chinese societies, and as reflected in the dilemmas studied, relationships are paramount and play a predominant role in peoples' lives. Redding (1977) in fact suggested that organizational behaviour in East Asian organizations was relationship-centred, while in the West it tends to be 'ego-centred'.

Some dilemmas are heightened by elements of a 'culture clash'. That is, they are caused or accentuated by the attempt to import Western beliefs and values about education into a traditional Chinese cultural setting (Dimmock, 1998). When these 'different' values clash, new dilemmas result or existing ones worsen. Evidence of such is seen in the third dilemma described above.

Emergent patterns were discernible in how principals coped with their dilemmas and the ways in which coping strategies related to the sources of a dilemma. Cultural values appeared to be implicitly arranged in a hierarchy, with harmony, hierarchy, seniority and age, rather than teaching and learning beliefs or personal reasons, predominant. For example, in the case of the first dilemma, the basic cultural value was the need for harmony with the more senior teacher; in the second and third dilemmas, it was the need to respect and maintain harmony with the supervisor and management board. Coping strategies in these cases suggest the existence of a hierarchy of values in the Hong Kong Chinese culture, with hierarchy, seniority and harmony predominant.

These conclusions raise a number of questions for the learning-centred school. First, if the pursuit of harmonious relationships is the predominant driver of coping strategies, even when dilemma sources are multifaceted, how does this influence the prime function of the school, namely, teaching and learning? Second, if principals tend to cope with dilemmas through allegiance to the system of seniority, can they secure the commitment of teachers towards school improvement? In other words, what implications follow for teacher empowerment, involvement and dedication to the school? Third, is it possible for principals to develop alternative coping strategies when the powerful cognitive and practical influence of cultural values, such as harmony and seniority, are held in such high esteem? Fourth, how does allegiance to such cultural factors affect principals' feelings about their jobs and work lives? Finally, are principals' dilemmas and coping strategies likely to change with the introduction of Western-style restructuring policies designed to re-configure the roles, rules and relationships in Hong Kong's or any other Asian school system?

Conclusion

This chapter has explored the notion of leadership in the learning-centred school. It has also presented a cross-cultural perspective on school leadership and empirical data to support the claim that principals' perceptions and actions are, to an extent, culture sensitive. Arguments presented are grounded in two fundamental axioms which, it is claimed, have received minimal acknowledgement in the field of educational administration. The first concerns the importance of the way in which images of leadership are forged. Rather than deductively listing the desired characteristics of leaders in redesigned schools, this chapter has attempted to arrive inductively at a conception of leadership, starting from a detailed blueprint of what the learning-centred school looks like. This process necessitates what is called a backward-mapping and iterative-mapping process, involving images of student outcomes, which then suggest appropriate learning and teaching approaches; these in turn generate supportive organizational structures and so on back through the organization to leadership, culture building and resourcing. Such a process is likely to offer a more authentic and legitimate image of leadership in the learning-centred school than are more conventional approaches.

The second, equally important axiom is that studies emanating from the West, particularly the English-speaking Western countries, continue to assume that research findings and prescriptions on leadership apply universally. Those in non-Western countries also appear to accept unquestioningly these apparent 'universalities'. This illustrates the convincing case for more culture-specific studies on school leadership and administration. In the meantime, researchers could more carefully and specifically contextualize their studies within defined cultural boundaries. When useful and valid comparisons of similarities and differences between leadership and school administration in different cultures begin to emanate, the field will be well on the way to refining its theoretical and practical knowledge base.

References

Barth, R.S. (1990) *Improving Schools From Within: Teachers, Parents and Principals Can Make the Difference*, San Francisco: Jossey-Bass.

Boisot, M. (1995) 'Preparing for turbulence: the changing relationship between strategy and management development in the learning organisation', in B. Garratt (ed.), *Developing Strategic Thought: Rediscovering the Art of Direction-Giving*, London: McGraw-Hill.

Bolman, L.G. and Deal, T.E. (1991) *Reframing Organizations: Artistry, Choice and Leadership*, San Francisco: Jossey Bass.

Bond, M. (1991) 'Cultural influences on modes of impression management: implications for the culturally diverse organisation', in R. Giacalone and P. Rosenfield (eds), *Applied Impression Management: How Image-Making Affects Managerial Decisions*, Newbury Park, CA: Sage.

Caldwell, B.J. (1998a) *Beyond the Self-Managing School*, London: Falmer Press.

—— (1998b) 'Leadership in the creation of world class schools: beyond the self-managing school,' paper presented at the Leadership for Quality Schooling Conference, Hong Kong: University of Hong Kong.

Cheng, K.M. (1995) 'The neglected dimension: cultural comparison in educational administration', in K.C. Wong and K.M. Cheng (eds), *Educational Leadership and Change: An International Perspective*, Hong Kong: Hong Kong University Press.

—— (1998) 'Can educational values be borrowed? Looking into cultural differences', *Peabody Journal of Education* 73 (2): 11–30.

Cheng, K.M. and Wong, K.C. (1996) 'School effectiveness in East Asia: concepts, origins and implications', *Journal of Educational Administration* 34 (5): 32–49.

Cuttance, P. (1993) 'School development and review in an Australian state education system', in C. Dimmock (ed.), *School-Based Management and School Effectiveness*, London: Routledge, 142–64.

Dimmock. C. (1993) 'School-based management and linkage with the curriculum', in C. Dimmock (ed.), *School-Based Management and School Effectiveness*, London: Routledge, 1–21.

—— (1995a) 'School leadership: securing quality teaching and learning', in C. Evers and J. Chapman (eds), *Educational Administration: An Australian Perspective.* Sydney: Allen & Unwin, 274–95.

—— (1995b) 'Restructuring for school effectiveness: leading, organising and teaching for effective learning', *Educational Management and Administration* 23 (1): 1–13.

—— (1995c) 'Building democracy in the school setting: the principal's role', in J. Chapman, I. Froumin and D. Aspin (eds), *Creating and Managing the Democratic School*, London: Falmer Press, 157–75.

—— (1996) 'Dilemmas for school leaders and administrators in restructuring', in K. Leithwood, J. Chapman, D. Corson, P. Hallinger and A. Weaver Hart (eds), *International Handbook of Educational Leadership and Administration*, vol. 1, Dordrecht: Kluwer Academic Publishers, 135–70.

—— (1998) 'School restructuring and the principalship: the applicability of Western theories, policies and practices to East and South-East Asian cultures', *Educational Management and Administration* 26 (4): 363–77.

Dimmock, C. and Walker, A. (1998a) 'Towards comparative educational administration: building the case for a cross-cultural, school-based approach', *Journal of Educational Administration* 36 (4): 379–401.

—— (1998b) 'A cross-cultural comparative approach to educational administration: development of a conceptual framework', *Educational Administration Quarterly* 34 (4): 558–95.

Duke, D.L. (1987) *School Leadership and Instructional Improvement*, New York: Random House.

Fei, H-T. (1985) *Xiangtu zhongguo* (Earthbound China), Hong Kong: Joint Publishers.

Fraser, B.J., Walberg, H.J., Welch, W.W. and Hattie, J.A. (1987) 'Syntheses of educational productivity research', *International Journal of Educational Research* 11 (2): 147–247.

Fullan, M.G. (1991) *The New Meaning of Educational Change*, London: Cassell.

Hofstede, G.H. (1980) *Culture's Consequences: International Differences in Work-Related Values*, Beverly Hills, CA: Sage.

—— (1991) *Cultures and Organizations: Software of the Mind*, London: McGraw-Hill.

Hofstede, G.H. and Bond, M. (1984) 'Hofstede's cultural dimensions: an independent validation using Rokeach's value survey', *Journal Of Cross-Cultural Psychology* 15 (4): 417–33.

Hord, S.M., Stiegelbauer, S.M. and Hall, G.E. (1984) 'How principals work with other change facilitators', *Education and Urban Society* 17 (November): 89–109.

Knight, B. (1993) 'Delegated financial management and school effectiveness', in C. Dimmock (ed.), *School-Based Management and School Effectiveness*, London: Routledge, 114–41.

Leithwood, K.A. (1988) 'Performance appraisal as an instrument for planned change: contributions of effectiveness research', in E.S. Hickcox, S.B. Lawton, K.A. Leithwood and D.F. Musella (eds), *Making a Difference Through Performance Appraisal*, Toronto: Ontario Institute of Education Press, 84–110.

Leithwood, K. and Jantzi, D. (1990) 'Transformational leadership: how principals can help reform school cultures', *School Effectiveness and School Improvement* 1 (4): 249–80.

Leithwood, K. and Montgomery, D.J. (1982) 'The role of the elementary school principal in program improvement', *Review of Educational Research* 52 (Fall): 309–39.

Leithwood, K. and Steinbach, R. (1993) 'The consequences for school improvement of differences in principals' problem-solving processes', in C. Dimmock (ed.), *School-Based Management and School Effectiveness*, London: Routledge, 41–64.

Levine, D.U. and Lezotte, L.W. (1990) 'Unusually effective schools: a review and analysis of research and practice', Madison, WI: National Centre for Effective Schools Research and Development.

McAdams, R. (1993) *Lessons From Abroad: How Other Countries Educate Their Children*, Lancaster, PA: Technomic.

Moore Johnson, S. (1990) *Teachers At Work: Achieving Success in Our Schools*, New York: Basic Books.

Murphy, J., Weil, M., Hallinger, P. and Mitman, A. (1985) 'School effectiveness: a conceptual framework', *The Educational Forum* 49 (3): 361–74.

Parkay, F.W. and Hall, G.E. (1992) *Becoming A Principal: The Challenges of Beginning Leadership*, Boston: Allyn & Bacon.

Redding, G. (1977) 'Some perceptions of psychological needs among managers in Southeast Asia', in Y. Poortinga (ed.), *Basic Problems in Cross-Cultural Psychology*, Amsterdam: Swets & Zeitlinger.

Reilly, D.H. (1984) 'The principalship: the need for a new approach', *Education* 104 (Spring): 242–7.

Rosenholtz, S. (1989) *Teachers' Workplace: The Social Organisation of Schools*, New York: Longman.

Rossow, L.F. (1990) *The Principalship: Dimensions in Instructional Leadership*, Englewood Cliffs, NJ: Prentice Hall.

Sapra, C. (1991) 'The school principal in India', in W. Walker, R. Farquhar and M. Hughes (eds) *Advancing Education: School Leadership in Action*, London: Falmer, 119–30.

Sergiovanni, T.J. (1992) *Moral Leadership: Getting to the Heart of School Improvement*, San Francisco: Jossey Bass.

Smith, S.C. and Piele, P.K. (eds) (1989) *School Leadership: Handbook for Excellence*, 2nd edn, Eugene: ERIC Clearinghouse on Educational Management.

Trompenaars, F. and Hampden-Turner, C. (1997) *Riding the Waves of Culture*, 2nd edn, London: Nicholas Brealey.

Ubben, G.C. and Hughes, L.W. (1992) *The Principal: Creative Leadership for Effective Schools*, 2nd edn, Boston: Allyn & Bacon.

Walker, A., Bridges, E. and Chan, B. (1996) 'Wisdom gained, wisdom given: instituting PBL in a Chinese culture', *Journal of Educational Administration* 34 (5): 12–31.

Walker, A. and Dimmock, C. (1999a) 'A cross-cultural approach to the study of educational leadership: an emerging framework', *Journal of School Leadership* 9(4): 321–48.

—— (1999b) 'Exploring principals' dilemmas in Hong Kong: increasing cross-cultural understanding of school leadership', *International Journal of Educational Reform* 8 (1): 15–23.

—— (in press) 'School principals' dilemmas in Hong Kong: sources, perceptions and outcomes', *Australian Journal of Education*.

Whitaker, K.S. and Moses, M.C. (1994) *The Restructuring Handbook: A Guide to School Revitalization*, Needham Heights, MA: Allyn and Bacon.

Wilson, B.L. and Firestone, W.A. (1987) 'The principal and instruction: combining bureaucratic and cultural linkages', *Educational Leadership* 45 (1): 18–23.

13 Community, Connectivity and Consistency in the Learning-Centred School

This book provides blueprint models, frameworks and ideas for schools in re-designing themselves as learning-centred institutions. It also highlights societal culture as an important factor in schooling. It is argued that important cultural differences exist in the way students learn, teachers teach, and schools are organised, led and managed. The purpose of this concluding chapter is to provide a synthesis of the main arguments espoused in preceding chapters and hence to present a summary. By so doing, it attempts to connect the many elements and components involved in the design of the learning-centred school.

Five precepts or tenets were recognised in Chapter 1 to underlie the arguments and ideas presented. They are:

- the onus to re-design is on each school;
- re-design should focus on teaching, learning and the curriculum;
- school design needs to be holistic, emphasizing the interconnections between all parts of a school;
- no single blueprint of school design is appropriate for all schools, but there are generic precepts and approaches which provide sensible guidelines and directions;
- it is important to contextualize models and blueprints of school design within the societal culture in which they have developed; what is appropriate for one culture will probably require adaptation when implemented in another.

These precepts provide a guiding frame for this concluding chapter.

A main aim of the book is to bring definition to the core technology of schooling and to the organizational structures and leadership and management functions which support it. In the re-design process to achieve the learning-centred school, teaching and learning and student outcomes assume pride of place at the forefront. The concept of the learning-centred school is underpinned by two assumptions: first, that students of all abilities deserve a more individualized education, one that specifically addresses their achievement history, intellectual characteristics and learning style prefer-ences; and second, that a school needs to be more tightly coupled as a professional organization if it is to be successful in addressing individual student needs and if teachers are to feel supported in the process. These provide base reference points for decisions that need to be taken on many issues. In the experience of schools which have undertaken re-design, the process continues to evolve even after five to ten years.

Essentially, creating the learning-centred school involves the following:

- A curriculum differentiated by level and teaching materials within each class, and designed on the basis of student outcomes.
- A curriculum which integrates informed teaching practices with the content of subject areas taught, thereby assisting teachers to decide when and how to use different teaching approaches, schedule different groups, differentiate learner needs and abilities by level of achievement and manage a multi-level classroom to reflect student-centred learning and a more individualized education for students.
- Teachers work as teams in an on-going cycle of feedback, support and evaluation.
- Technology is infused into all school activity, especially teaching and learning, and an intranet is employed to manage both the logistical (attendance, behaviour and discipline) and programmatic dimensions of school operations (for example, curriculum design tools, teacher promo-tion portfolios); technology is embedded in the curriculum and is accessible to all students.
- The configuration of physical space and time is conducive to a wide range of teaching approaches and allows teaching teams to work collab-oratively with groups of students.
- Faculty position descriptions referenced directly and definitively to quality teaching, classroom and student performance; the personnel policy is built on recognizing and rewarding mastery of informed prac-tices.
- Administrators actively support the delivery of student-centred learning by being instructional leaders, spending time in the classroom managing the program, giving expert advice and evaluating.
- Systematic and ongoing professional development for teachers which addresses the skills in curriculum, teaching, technology and classroom management necessary to implement the program.
- Administrators lead and manage the following in ways which support teaching and learning outcomes:
  i   build organizational structures
  ii   promote professional development
  iii allocate human and other resources
  iv   build culture

   v   encourage collaboration and teamwork

   vi   involve all elements of the school community and build a sense of community.

All of these indicate the need for whole-school restructuring, where each of the parts is mutually reinforcing. Everything the school does should be questioned as follows: how does this serve student-centred learning? and, how does this serve the process of teaching and learning?

Re-designing schools is beset with many dilemmas. Schools as organizations are conventionally complex and ambiguous in nature. The individualist culture which has pervaded them accounts for the absence of an agreed professional skill set in the culture of teaching. Yet the challenge of creating the learning-centred school targets more informed classroom practices and improved student learning outcomes; in short, the most impenetrable part of schools.

Moreover, the effort to change this complex organization, with its loosely-coupled parts, warrants a change process and methodology which is itself complex and comprehensive and demands a high degree of connectivity. For example, consider the relationship between curriculum, technology, professional development and best practice. If it is assumed that a more sophisticated individualized curriculum is necessary, then there is an implication that teachers will need to use different texts and multiple teaching approaches; all at the same time. To build a curriculum design model to do that in the absence of an infusion of improved skilling of faculty is to invite failure. This means that professional development, the teaching-learning model and the curriculum must all be designed and implemented simultaneously. Furthermore, it is impossible to change all of the foregoing without considering the use of physical space, computer technology, better leadership and management structures and so on (Bain, 1996). Change has to be comprehensive and intentional, since it constitutes a very significant intrusion into the existing culture of the loosely-coupled school.

To summarise, schools are complex structures characterised by loose, internal coupling; the teaching profession does not have a clearly agreed and approved skill set. Moreover, the change process demands high connectivity among its parts to be successful. How to re-design, given these conditions?

In response, this book has argued the need to bring definition and intentionality to the design process. This is achieved by firstly, developing a vision of the learning-centred school and its constituent elements, how they connect and models of informed practice. Secondly, it is achieved by the principle of backward-mapping and iteration as a means of ensuring connectivity between all of the elements and aligning the whole system consistently with student learning outcomes. Backward-mapping, as Chapter 2 shows, involves the elevation of student outcomes to pre-eminence and backs up through the school, taking account of the students and their learning processes and theories and appropriate teaching approaches drawn from informed practice. The process of backward mapping continues through the organization with the use of computer technology, use of space and time, other organizational structures, leadership, management, professional development and resource allocation and evaluation. Each derives from the configuration of elements earlier in the process to ensure consistency and alignment with student learning outcomes. At each stage, a backward-forward or iterative checking process should take place to ensure fidelity to student outcomes.

Developing a vision of the learning-centred school with models of informed practice and utilizing a backward-mapping process is not to impose rigid, straitjacket solutions aimed at de-professionalizing schools and those who work in them. For one thing, schools presently tend to be decoupled organizations with minimally agreed professional skill sets and standards. Rather, the models and practices advocated in support of the learning-centred school attempt to introduce higher levels of professionalism and greater flexibility and choice in regard to informed practice. Improving the knowledge base and skills set of teachers and administrators is to extend their repertoire of possible practices and thus to professionalize them. A higher level of professionalism comes with teachers selectively choosing teaching strategies and approaches to suit the particular curriculum outcomes to be achieved and the characteristics of the students as learners. Bringing definition and intentionality to the process of schooling, where little currently exists, is more likely to raise than lower professionalism and performance. In other words, professionalism depends on a more robust core technology.

The Role of Leadership and Management in Implementation

Developing a vision, identifying the key constituent elements of the learning-centred school, exercising backward-mapping and including detailed models of informed practice form the 'technical' part of school re-design. The other is the human enterprise part. Both parts need to be managed in concert.

Framing the re-design process, given its complexity, in terms of a comprehensive, coherent model, helps overcome many of the dilemmas normally associated with whole-school reform, such as lack of clarity and purpose. It has, however, created other dilemmas. For example, like all models it is underpinned by assumptions and values about the nature of schooling and the roles of teachers and students. It is comprehensive in affecting all aspects of schooling. It demands engagement by all faculty, or else its effects will be diluted. For these and other reasons, the managerial challenge in winning the wholehearted conviction and acceptance of faculty and administrators and securing their willingness to implement may be formidable.

A key question concerns how much of the whole-school design should school leaders have in place at the outset of the process? At one extreme, it would be unwise – even if it were possible – for leaders to articulate in detail the design of the learning-centred school 'up front'. This would make it difficult for staff to feel they could make an input and thus to gain their ownership and commitment. Conversely, it would be equally imprudent to begin the process without clear definitions and intentions, given the ambiguous nature of schooling and school management, the lack of definition given to informed teaching and learning practices in particular, and to school design and restructuring in general. An appropriate tack therefore is for school leaders to begin the process with a clear and intended direction and an outline of the design they wish their school to follow. Core tenets or precepts should be identified early in the process and should not be compromised. Skilful leaders will need to decide, on the basis of knowing their school communities, how much they should present 'up front' and how much they 'steer from behind', encouraging others to 'arrive at similar conclusions'. The main issue for school leaders is that the school community is embarking on wholesale change which is too important to be undertaken without direction. It is equally important, however, that for the process to be successful, all groups in the school community feel included and consulted. As the design evolves over time and detail is brought to the process, the community makes a key contribution. Involving others is time consuming; leaders require patience and must resist the temptation to rush, but they also need to keep the momentum for change going if it is not to stall.

An important issue concerns the role of the principal in relation to other administrators and to the whole re-design process. At the same time as the school is being re-designed, it should continue to function with minimal disruption. As discussed below, a stepped introduction of the new design year by year means that part of the school changes while the rest retains the status quo. The school still has to be managed and administered at the same time as it is being dramatically changed. This raises the issue as to whether the role of change agent, whose prime responsibility is to architect the re-design process, can be successfully combined with the everyday management and administration of the school. Whether responsibility for the change process is handed over to a change agent who is not the principal will depend on the availability of suitable personnel and their relative workloads and strengths.

A comprehensive and coherent model of school design is thus necessary to frame the process, even though it will evolve and gain detail with time. Equally, managing the human side of the change process and handling the implementation is critical if the model is to be brought to fruition. There are four developmental phases through which faculty need to be managed:

preparation, design, implementation and evaluation. These are not necessarily linear; the design may take place at the same time as preparation, and evaluation may occur at any time.

Leading and managing the implementation process is a delicate act because of the comprehensiveness of the change process and the interrelatedness of the components. It would be a mistake to tackle only one of the elements or to try to tackle them algorithmically, for example, changing first teaching, then curriculum, then technology and so on. At the same time, tackling all of them simultaneously could mean that faculty are overawed by the sheer magnitude of the intrusion on their school work. For this reason, a pilot process and staged introduction year by year or grade level by grade level, starting with the youngest in the school and working up through the school, is desirable. Piloting offers the dual advantage of facilitating comprehensive change while containing the magnitude of the intrusion on the school.

A further strategy concerns the provision of high quality professional development early in the process to equip staff with an improved professional skill set attuned to deliver more individualized learning and a broad range of teaching approaches aligned to the vision of the learning-centred school. This programme of professional development needs to be systematic and ongoing, framed to meet the requirements of the learning-centred school yet leaving room for ownership by the faculty. It needs to cater to all staff, yet be sufficiently flexible to accommodate different interests, levels of experience and expertise. The focus of the programme should be informed practices of teaching and learning aimed at enhancing the learning achievements of all students. Faculty have a right to professional development of an appropriate kind and quality if the expectation of the organization is that they implement a whole-school model. Professional development is thus provided to meet individual staff needs only in so far as it enables each to fulfil the demands and expectations placed on them by the collective school community.

A reference point for leading and managing faculty is whether the interests of teaching and learning are served. If the organization is seen as an inverted triangle built on successive tiers, then students are at the top, teachers below and administrators are below teachers. Every tier, even that at the base of the triangle where administrative duties assume paramount importance in the office of the principal and where control over resources is greatest, needs to justify its existence in relation to the reference point of classroom practice. Towards this end, the school needs to be reconstructed around teams to allow for significant faculty participation in decision making. In addition, administrators spend a high proportion of their time in the classroom, supporting, giving feedback and running workshops. Importantly, the principal and administrators, as instructional leaders, symbolise the clear connect between the activity, skill and expertise of the leadership and the provision of high quality, more individualized, student-centred learning.

If faculty are to perform to high levels of professionalism they need the resources to do the job. Classrooms need to be adequately equipped. The centrality of computer technology in future learning-centred schools demands a campus computer network (intranet), with laptop computers for all faculty and all students, a congenial physical environment in which teams can meet and teach, and classroom space designed to enable a student-centred approach supported by technology. All of this requires an infrastructure of programs and management systems that call upon informed practice regarding evaluation and monitoring of student progress.

A system built on the attainment of student outcomes requires a rigorous evaluation system to assess and record the progress and achievement of individual students across the cognitive, affective/social and physical/behavioural domains. All aspects of student assessment are computerised and available, on a restricted basis, to all staff on the campus network.

Effective human resource management demands a personnel policy based on the precepts of school design. Promotion and career paths of faculty should reflect the principle of informed practices of curriculum, teaching and learning. Position descriptions, for example, reflect the fundamental precepts of the model, such as informed practices. Criteria for teacher appraisal and professional development likewise reflect the fundamental tenets of informed practice.

Building Community, Involving Parents and Making Connections

Creating the learning-centred school as advocated in this book is not to impose bureaucratic top-down procedures. Nor is it to standardize or routinize the complex educative process. On the contrary, the models and informed practices described in this book provide an extended knowledge and information base, one which increases the range of choice for school communities to take charge of the re-design process. As Sergiovanni (1998) claims, good schools reflect the values of their particular communities – students, parents, teachers – and each will be different. Through their uniqueness they not only gain the connections between the elements constituting the school design, but among the stakeholders: families, teachers and students. A truly 'connected' learning-centred school will have the bonding that comes from the collective community with shared interests. Sergiovanni (1998) argues that this bonding can only come from shared values, purposes, ideas and ideals.

A possible source for shared values derives from religious beliefs. Catholic schools, for example, may find it rather easier than secular schools to secure a strong common bonding of values. But another source of shared values for a community may come from the precepts and tenets of the learning-centred school, such as those espoused in this book. Once the learning-centred school distinguishes a set of shared values, the nature of leadership changes, as Sergiovanni (1998) points out. The basis of leader decision making ceases to be bureaucratic rules or personal persuasion and becomes moral authority; that is, the leader is morally bound to exercise leadership in ways which are consistent with the community's shared values. However, as he also admits, such morally authoritative leadership can be dangerous if the shared values are allowed to become fixed, immutable and unquestioned dogma. School communities are often fast-changing environments: many are already multicultural. Identifying shared values and common purposes in a postmodern world presents further challenges for many school leaders. The main aim is to create true communities with shared core values from groups exhibiting divergence. Diversity of view can make for a healthy community, as long as relationships and communication between the divergent parts remain intact and as long as there is shared agreement about main goals and problem-solving procedures.

Although parental involvement has been mentioned in Chapter 4 as a key element in initiating re-design, subsequent chapters have not highlighted the key role that parents can make to the learning-centred school. Epstein (1995) has developed a useful taxonomy of ways in which parental involvement can be engineered, based on the notions of home–school partnerships and the school community. She identifies six forms of parental involvement as the basis of home-school partnerships:

1   Parenting: aimed at helping families establish home environments to support children as students. These include parent education, family support programmes, and home visits.
2   Communicating: focused on designing effective forms of school-to-home and home-to-school programmes and student progress. These include yearly parent conferences, portfolios of student work sent home, student-led conferences, new informative ways of reporting student achievement and clear information on student course choice and activities.
3   Volunteering: aimed at recruiting and organizing parent help and support. These include surveys to identify parent interests and talents and parent duties such as safety patrols.
4   Learning at home: geared to providing information and ideas to families about how they can help students at home with homework and other school decisions. These can include booklets on the skills required to complete subject exercises and information on homework policy and expectations.
5   Decision making: covers parental involvement in school decisions and developing parent leaders and representatives. These include active

parent/teacher associations, training for parents to play a decision-making role, and networks for families to connect with parent representatives.

6   Collaborating with the community: aimed at identifying and integrating resources and services from the community to strengthen school programmes, family practices and student learning and development. These include information for families on community health, cultural, recreational and social support services, and ways in which students can serve communities.

Many scholars agree that three themes underpin most of the recent programmes aimed at achieving greater parental involvement (Davies, 1991). All three are consistent with the precepts of the learning-centred school:

*   Providing success for all children. Convincing parents and students that schools can be organized in ways that enable all students to experience learning success.
*   Serving the whole child. Social, emotional, physical and academic growth are interlinked and must be addressed by schools, families and other institutions.
*   Sharing responsibility. In order to promote the social and academic development of children, the key institutions must change their practices and relationships with one another.

Steinberg et al. (1996) were able to separate cause and effect in looking at parental involvement and school performance. They found that school success motivated parents to become more involved in their children's education. However, the reverse is also true: being an involved parent can actually lead to student success. The clear conclusion is that parental involvement and home–school partnerships have an important part in the re-design of schools.

The importance of conceptualizing the re-designed school within the context of its local community is highlighted by the undeniable fact that the problems facing schools, particularly those serving societies with chronic economic and social problems, run well beyond the capacity of the school itself to address. A solution is thus seen to rest with policies which embrace the wider social environment. A raft of economic and social welfare programmes are advocated, all integrated into a coherent package. This may be a useful way forward, although the difficulties in changing society may be much greater than those experienced in changing schools. The argument for broader community reform should not, however, detract from the need for the school itself to re-design. Advocates of the community reform thrust argue that decades of school reform have failed to address the problems of drop-out students and unsuccessful learners. However, it is also the case that past school reforms have been limited in their conception. They have not targeted whole-school restructuring and have not been based on the principles and precepts of school re-design, such as those enunciated here.

The Cross-Cultural Dimension and the Learning-Centred School

The cross-cultural accounts in this book have been mostly confined to comparisons between the Anglo-American Western culture and the Confucian-heritage (largely Chinese) Asian culture. Both of these cultures are far from homogeneous and are becoming more diffuse and multi-cultural, making generalizations increasingly difficult. The 1990s has witnessed a growing interest on the part of Anglo-American societies in East and Southeast Asian education. In particular, the empirical work of Stevenson and colleagues (for example, see Stevenson and Stigler, 1992) at the beginning of the 1990s compared the performances of students and schools in Japan, China and the US and the reasons underlying them. They recommended that the USA could learn from East Asian countries, rather than vice versa. Subsequently, Reynolds and Farrell (1996) among others suggested that UK schools had much to learn from the superior academic performance of students in Taiwanese, Japanese, Singaporean and Korean schools. These trends indicate the development of a new phenomenon, a reciprocal East–West interest in school and student performance, as argued below.

A growing interest in Asian education as a source of inspiration for American and British education has continued throughout the 1990s and is particularly noteworthy. For most of the post-1945 period, it has been Asian countries which have been interested in importing Western educational policies and ideas. While this is still the case, the 1990s has seen the development of a reciprocal interest, whereby Anglo-American countries have become intrigued by the performances of some Asian school systems. The proposal that the politically and economically most advanced countries have something to learn about education and schooling from less strong and less advanced countries (even allowing for Asia's fast economic growth rates for most of the 1990s) is indeed a rarity (Hatano and Inagaki, 1998). Even though few societies today are insulated from external cultural influence, it is conventionally the more powerful political societies which seek to impose their cultural ideas and practices on other less powerful societies. As Serpell and Hatano (1997) argue, this imposition was formerly by hegemonic means, but is now replaced by the modernization theory. This holds that less advanced countries can develop, both economically and socially, by importing technologies and systems such as education from more advanced countries. A consequence is the phenomenon of policy cloning noted in Chapter 3. Hatano and Inagaki (1998: 83–4) state:

It has become almost a universalistic principle to justify the transplanta-tion of many Western cultural inventions in to other societies. Even when it takes the milder form of recommending that less powerful groups import advanced tools deliberately and with some adaptation, the direction of the influence is almost always from the western to the non-western countries.

Serpell (1993) agrees, arguing that by adopting Western systems of schooling and incorporating Western ideas, many non-Western countries believe they can enhance their economic and social development. The break-up of the Communist bloc and the growing influence of international financial institutions such as the IMF and the World Bank has served to increase this trend. Hence the phenomenon of reciprocity of interest, which has seen the fascination of American and British educators with the perfor-mances achieved by some East and Southeast Asian school systems represents a new departure.

Growing reciprocal East–West interest in each other's school systems holds out the promise of greater understanding and mutual benefit. However, it is also fraught with danger. If policies and practices are simply transported and crudely adopted without an understanding of the societal cultural influences underpinning them, then problems are likely to ensue. That is why education researchers and policy makers need more robust frameworks, research instruments and empirical studies of a cross-cultural kind. Country comparisons will not do. We need to identify cross-cultural dimensions for true comparisons of similarities and differences to be gauged (Dimmock and Walker, 1998a, 1998b).

A key question concerns the extent to which the precepts and principles underlying the learning-centred school apply cross-culturally. In addressing this important question, it is tempting to conclude that most if not all of the precepts are applicable in different cultures. The basis of this conclusion is that, first, schools in different societies face similar problems and challenges. For example, creating schools which cater to all students' needs is a major challenge for every society. In a similar vein, there is scope for every school to improve its curriculum in terms of relevance, balance, integration and so on, as well as improve the quality of teaching and learning. Secondly, the precepts of school re-design espoused in this book as guidelines for addressing the problems and challenges do not appear to be culture-sensi-tive. To restate the seven precepts, they are:

1   student outcomes provide goal direction for learning;
2   schools exist primarily for teaching and learning; learning and the indi-vidual learner are made the centrepiece of all that happens in the school;

3   teaching focuses on learning and teaching for understanding; a balance and variety of teaching strategies is achieved, a combination of methods from didactic and expository to constructivist;

4   the curriculum is tailored to suit the diverse needs of students;

5   learning and teaching shape and dictate school structures and organization, including technology and the use of space, which are designed to support and facilitate the principles and practices of learning and teaching;

6   learning and teaching determine professional development, leadership and management, resource allocation and culture/climate, all of which are dedicated to supporting a service delivery designed for quality teaching and learning;

7   at all stages and in all activities, especially teaching, learning and leadership, the school adheres to 'informed practice'.

Moreover, the design principle of backward mapping from student outcomes and informed practices of learning and teaching to the other aspects of the learning-centred school appear as valid for schools in Asian as Western societies. If these precepts are not culture-sensitive, then what is the significance of culture in school design? Where and how is it necessary to consider culture? It is argued below that culture plays a key influential role in influencing the interpersonal relations and communication which lie at the heart of school implementation. In other words, culture is especially poignant at the point where the precepts are operationalised.

The foregoing questions about the significance of culture assume added salience with the likely continuation of school system restructuring within a globalized and internationalized educational policy environment. The phenomenon of policy cloning, seen as part of the globalization of education, enables the process of policy formulation to be hastily completed – often a prime motive of policy makers – with the consequence that minimal attention is paid to the receptivity of the host culture to the imported policy.

It is not, however, at the policy formulation or policy adoption stages that the impact of culture is most felt. Rather, it is at the policy implementation stage, which centres on the school. Autochtony and adaptation tend to fall on the shoulders of principals and teachers working at school level, where cultural dimensions find expression in the processes of teaching and learning and in leadership and management, and where students carry cultural values from the home and family into the classroom. As Hallinger and Leithwood (1996) note, citing Hofstede (1976), how people approach space, time, information and communication are shaped by the cultural context and appear broadly to differentiate Eastern (high context) and Western (low context) cultures. They go on to claim, 'we view culture as having an impact on schools at the institutional level, on the community context, on the beliefs and experiences of administrators, on administrative practice, and on a school's particular culture' (1996: 108).

Reconciling Generic School Design Principles with Cultural Difference

If the above line of argument is valid, then the precepts of school design hold true across different cultures. The essential issue then becomes one of reconciliation between the precepts of school design which appear to be generic, and much of societal culture which is deeply ingrained and which we cannot hope, and should not expect, to change. The resolution to this situation is that each society work out its own adaptation and cultural inter-pretation of the school design precepts. The following provides illustrations of how this might work.

It has been noted in Chapter 3 that a cultural characteristic of Chinese and many other Asian societies is high power distance or power concentra-tion, a situation where power is unevenly invested in the few at the top of the society and its organizations. Operating against this, however, is the school design principle which places emphasis on collaboration, teamwork and participative decision making and the creation of flatter, more collegial structures. A reconciliation in this instance is for collaboration, teamwork and participative decision making to take place in the lower and middle levels of organizations, leaving the higher echelons intact.

A second illustration of how schools within and across different societies interpret and shape their response to the school design precepts in a cultur-ally-dependent way relates to informed practices of teaching, learning and leadership. While the broad shape of teacher appraisal might conform to generic principles, how a particular scheme actually functions in a given school and society may well depend on culturally specific features of that society. Thus, in Chinese schools, where 'loss of face' and the maintenance of harmonious relationships is often all-important, appraisal might not involve the same degree of emphasis on face-to-face feedback between a supervisor and supervisee. Alternative emphases such as peer and self-super-vision might be more culturally appropriate.

A third example concerns individualization. How Asian schools interpret individualization and institutionalise it might well differ from Anglo-American versions. There should be no attempt – even if it were possible – to convert Asian cultures from more collectivist to individualist in orientation. The collectivist nature of Asian cultures, however, does not necessarily preclude the institutionalization of more individualization in curriculum, teaching and learning. It simply involves adaptation of individualization to fit Asian cultural values. For example, greater emphasis than in Western schools might be placed on designing differentiated curriculum, teaching and learning programmes around the group as opposed to individual needs. In addition, the collectivist nature of many Asian cultures should allow their schools to capitalise on those powerful features of school design, such as informed practices of cooperative learning, and collaboration and teamwork, which are favoured by collectivism. Similarly, as Stevenson and Stigler (1992) reveal, Asian teachers and students often seem to apply the principles of direct teaching – itself an effective informed practice – to good effect. Students tend to be more willing to listen and concentrate and teachers appear to be more adaptable in combining direct teaching, individualized questioning and constructivism than are many of their Western counterparts.

A further factor to be considered regarding adaptation in line with cultural harmony is the difference in resource and logistical parameters. In many Chinese schools there may be sixty students in a class. In Hong Kong, forty-five is commonplace. Classrooms are often crowded and ill-equipped. Teachers may have few audio-visual aids to work with. Under these conditions, Asian teachers are wise to select carefully from the range of informed practices those which lend themselves to the physical and material conditions. Direct teaching, as opposed to lecturing, may be one such approach.

In other words, culture is reflected, *inter alia*, in the way people engage and relate to each other and in the way they act in and react to power and influence relations. This is as true for life in school as it is for the family. As Stevenson and Stigler (1992) show, cultural differences between Japan, China and America in terms of family customs and socialization combine with cultural differences in pedagogy and the organization of teaching and learning to account for different student and teacher performances in those societies.

If the above analysis is correct and the impact of culture is felt chiefly at the school implementation level, then this places a heavy burden on principals and teachers in particular. With more cross-cultural research, it should be possible for system-level policy makers to become better informed and more attuned to the significance of culture as it impacts on the implementation of policies which they have formulated and adopted. In this way, they may eventually be able to backward map and allow for culture in the formulation of policy. In addition, with more refined cross-cultural frameworks and instruments, it should eventually be possible for policy makers and others to predict what will and will not travel across cultures.

Cultures are changing. In countries such as the UK, USA and Australia, societies are becoming more multicultural as they reflect migration patterns. In East and Southeast Asia, rapid economic growth has opened economies and societies to world markets and competition and to international tourism and the media, all of which is grafting aspects of Western culture on to indigenous cultures. This is clearly the case in Hong Kong, and is becoming so in China. Younger generations hold different cultural values from their more traditional parents and grandparents. As Cheng and Wong (1996) note, with the spread of education in East Asian societies involving entire populations rather than just a select few, the present emphasis on conformity and effort may change. Will the present faith in work effort as a means of achievement be undermined by Western philosophies geared to catering for individual needs and adaptive teaching? Will a tension develop in Asian school systems between progressive teachers who advocate change on the one side and traditional teachers and conservative-minded parents on the other? How much attention will be paid to special needs and heterogeneous abilities? Will schools be expected to adapt to the diversity of their clientele rather than expect the clientele to adapt to schools, as at present? Will the traditional hierarchical structures give way under capitalist-style market reforms? How will societies like Hong Kong reconcile Eastern and Western values and trends in their education systems? Paradoxically, with the convergence of educational policies and school systems around the world, the need for greater understanding of cultural divergence and autochtony increases.

Conclusion

School restructuring and its globalization has exposed two important weaknesses in the fields of educational administration and education policy. The first is the relatively few models of whole-school design which have been developed and fully articulated. The second is the predominance of Western-centric, largely Anglo-American, theories and practices and the accompanying assumption that these are universally applicable. The purpose of this book has been to address both of these issues.

In respect to the first, the book has attempted to map the key elements or components that comprise a learning-centred school, identify informed practices within the elements, and to make the all-important connections between them. It has highlighted the importance of bringing intentionality, connectivity and reinforcement and consistency to the school design process. It has also assumed that schools themselves should accept the main responsibility for their re-design.

In respect to the second, it has questioned the universality of Western theory and practice by highlighting the importance of culture in contributing to differences in teaching, learning and leadership between Western (Anglo-American) and Asian (Chinese) societies. It has been argued that while it is possible to identify generic precepts or tenets of school design which apply across cultures, cultural differences should not be ignored at the level of implementation, where decisions of operational detail are taken. In the future, policy makers should take cognisance of culture when formulating policy.

There is a clear need for robust cross-cultural comparative research in schooling, school leadership, management and organization. Developments along these lines are dependent on the emergence of valid cross-cultural frameworks, models and dimensions, research instruments and empirical studies which identify similarities and differences, convergences and divergences, and the cultural explanations underlying them between schools in different societies. When the field of educational administration and policy begins to move along these lines, it will be well on the way to developing a sophistication of theory and practice befitting the twenty-first century.

References

Bain, A. (1996) 'The future school institute handbook', unpublished manuscript, Brewster Academy, New Hampshire, USA.

Cheng, K.M. and Wong, K.C. (1996) 'School effectiveness in East Asia: concepts, origins and implications', *Journal of Educational Administration* 34 (5): 32–49.

Davies, D. (1991) 'Schools reaching out: family, school and community partnerships for student success', *Phi Delta Kappan* 72 (5): 376–80.

Dimmock, C. and Walker, A. (1998a) 'Towards comparative educational administration: building the case for a cross-cultural, school-based approach', *Journal of Educational Administration* 36 (4): 379–401.

—— (1998b) 'A cross-cultural comparative approach to educational administration: development of a conceptual framework', *Educational Administration Quarterly* 34 (4): 558–95.

Epstein, J. (1995) 'School/family/community partnerships: caring for the children we share', *Phi Delta Kappan* 76 (9), 701–12.

Hallinger, P. and Leithwood, K. (1996) 'Culture and educational administration: a case of finding out what you don't know you don't know', *Journal of Educational Administration* 34 (5): 98–116.

Hatano, G. and Inagaki, K. (1998) 'Cultural contexts of schooling revisited: a review of "the learning gap" from a cultural psychology perspective', in S.G. Paris and H.M. Wellman (eds) *Global Prospects for Education: Development, Culture, and Schooling*, Washington, DC: American Psychological Association, 79–104.

Hofstede, G.H. (1976) 'Nationality and espoused values of managers', *Journal of Applied Psychology* 6 (2): 148–55.

Reynolds, D. and Farrell, S. (1996) 'World's apart? a review of international surveys of educational achievement involving England', London: Her Majesty's Stationery Office.

Sergiovanni, T.J. (1998) 'Moral authority, community and diversity: leadership challenges for the 21st century', paper presented at the inaugural meeting of the Centre for Educational Leadership, Hong Kong: University of Hong Kong.

Serpell, R. (1993) 'The significance of schooling: life-journeys in an African society', Cambridge: Cambridge University Press.

Serpell, R. and Hatano, G. (1997) 'Education, schooling and literacy in a cross-cultural perspective', in J.W. Berry, P.R.Dasen and T.S. Saraswathi (eds), *Handbook of Cross-Cultural Psychology*, vol. 2, Boston: Allyn & Bacon.

Steinberg, L., Brown, B. and Dornbusch, S.M. (1996) *Beyond the Classroom: Why School Reform Has Failed and What Parents Need To Do*, New York: Simon and Schuster.

Stevenson, H.W. and Stigler, J.W. (1992) *The Learning Gap: Why Our Schools are Failing and What We Can Learn From Japanese and Chinese Education*, New York: Touchstone.

Index

academic orientation: Confucian-heritage societies 97, 104, 125; curriculum 84, 97, 104
accountability 2, 10, 25, 26, 235, 261
adaptive education 112, 139–40, 152
administration 2, 25, 27, 39, 41, 44, 276–7, 280–1; computer technology and 169; cross-cultural comparative framework 50–3; and evaluation 248; and leadership 252, 259, 263; and resources policy 203, 209–12, 222–3, 225–7; *see also* management
Africa 40, 51
Anderson, L. 140
Anglo-American education *see* United Kingdom; United States; Western/Asian education
Anglo-American influence *see* Western influence
appraisal *see* evaluation and appraisal
architecture 193
Asian education *see* Western/Asian education *and individual countries*
Australasia *see* Australia; New Zealand
Australia 21, 40, 41, 47, 48, 49; curriculum 78, 84, 89–91; leadership 267; organizational structures 188, 189, 190, 194–5; physical environment 110; restructuring 12, 41; Schools Council 31, 188, 189; teaching 156, 157; technology 176–7
Azuma, M. 162

backward mapping 28, 29, 33, 35, 36, 277–8, 286, 288; curriculum design 94, 96; and leadership 250, 251, 254, 255, 256, 263, 271; and learning 113, 116; and organizational structures 187; and resources policy 204, 205, 207, 210, 212; and teaching 132
Bain, A. 64, 74, 169, 170, 171, 175, 200, 205, 210, 212, 215, 221, 277
Ball, D. 220
Barnett, B.G. 80
Bechtol, W.M. 89, 116, 117, 118, 122, 123, 141, 144, 147, 148
behavioural theories 11, 112, 137–8, 144, 152
Berger, S. 178
best practices 21–3
Biggs, J.B. 41, 101, 102, 127, 128, 157, 159–63
Blake, R.R. 54
Block, J.H. 94, 112, 140, 144
Bloom, Benjamin 96, 112, 140–1
Blunt, P. 51
Boisot, M. 4, 5, 262–3
Bolman, L.G. 44, 257, 261
Bond, M. 265, 266, 270
Bray, M. 44
Breivik, P. 173
Brewster Academy, New Hampshire, USA 64, 171, 175–6, 181, 193, 200, 221–2, 260
Brickley, D. 186
Bridges, E.M. 149
Britain *see* United Kingdom
Brophy, J. 144, 150, 240
Brown, D.J. 31
Bruner, J.S. 112
bureaucracy 185, 186

Caldwell, B.J. 31, 32, 227, 262, 263
Canada 40, 173
Carnegie school structure 191
Carroll, J.B. 112, 140
Carroll, J.M. 184, 191

change agent 69–70, 71, 172, 279
Cheng, K.M. 44, 101, 223, 224, 265, 266, 267, 269–70, 288
Child, J. 58
China 15, 40, 41, 42, 49, 284; application of backward mapping 36; leadership 265–6, 267; learning 107, 110, 126; organizational structures 184, 191; parental involvement 76; personnel policy 217, 223–5, 226; reconciling generic principles with cultural difference 287, 288; resources 288; teaching 157, 158, 159, 160, 161, 162–3; technology 182
Chinese Culture Connection 46, 49
Chinese societies 35, 41, 42, 58, 97; effort 101, 126, 163, 289; harmony and preservation of relationships 100, 224, 226, 248, 266–7, 268–71, 287; leadership 265–71; and learning 124–9; and teaching 154–65; and technology 178; *see also individual countries*
Chubb, J.E. 11
cognitive processes and skills: curriculum and 84–5, 87, 89, 100, 102; and learning 109, 127–8, 147; *see also* problem-based learning; problem solving
cognitive psychology 11, 110
Cohen, D. 220
collaboration 5, 33, 287, 288; Hong Kong 102, 128–9; leadership 257, 258, 259–60, 261, 266; learning and teaching 128–9, 163, 188–90, 257, 259–60, 276; personnel policy 224, 227
collaborative consultation model 200, 259–60
collectivism *see* individualism/collectivism
community building 281–4; *see also* organizational culture
comparative education studies 43, 44–5
comparative psychology 46
competition 48, 52, 101, 156
computers *see* technology
Confucian dynamism *see* short term/long term orientation
Confucian-heritage societies *see* Chinese societies
connectivity 2, 3, 8, 9, 14, 16, 277, 281–4, 289; curriculum 80, 103–4; and

models, frameworks, precepts for school design 21, 29–31, 33; and organizational structures 186–7; resource policy 230
consistency 9, 16, 30, 36, 68, 277–8, 289; resource policy 230; *see also* backward mapping; iterative mapping process
constructivism: East Asian teaching 161, 288; psychology 11; teaching 138; and technology 177, 181, 182
cooperative development, differentiated supervision model 243
cooperative learning 22, 68, 69, 101, 102–3, 110, 121, 123, 134, 135, 137, 139, 140, 146–9, 150, 152, 174, 177, 189, 193, 201, 243, 288
Copernican Plan of school organization 191–2
core technology 2, 3, 80, 132, 278; and models, frameworks for school design 28–9; organizational structures 187–8, 255; rigidity 11–12; *see also* curriculum; learning; teaching and teachers
cross-age tutoring 103, 189, 191
cross-cultural comparative approach 39–59, 289–90; case for culture and cross-cultural comparative framework 43–6; comparative framework for educational administration and policy 50–3; comparative framework for leadership 264–71; comparative framework for organizational culture 54–7; comparative frameworks in international business management 46–50; need to consider culture 40–3
cross-cultural perspective 13, 15, 37, 289–90; curriculum design 97–104; evaluation 246–9; implementation of design process 284–90; initiating design process 75–6; learning 107, 124–9, 155–7; organizational structures 201; resources policy 217, 223–7, 230–1; teaching 154–65; technology 178–83; *see also* cross-cultural comparative approach
cross-cultural transferability 12–13, 20, 36–7, 40–1, 66, 107, 129, 154, 164, 182, 246, 264, 270, 284–6
Cuban, L. 173
cultural borrowing *see* policy cloning

cultural leadership 257–8, 261, 262
culture *see* organizational culture;
    societal culture
culture clash 270
curriculum 1, 2, 3, 14; element in school
    design 18, 21, 25, 28, 29, 30;
    evaluation of 234
curriculum design 15, 21, 28, 78–104,
    275, 276, 277, 287; cross-cultural
    implications 97–103; financial
    resources 227, 228, 229; key design
    issues 82–8; and leadership 252, 253;
    and learning 79–80, 81, 85–6, 89–104
    passim, 109; model for implementing
    student outcomes' curriculum
    approach 91–6; operationalizing
    outcomes-oriented curriculum 88–91;
    and organizational structures 184,
    192–3, 201; and personnel policy 204,
    205; precepts for and dimensions of
    80–2; and teaching 79–104 *passim*,
    140, 141, 147, 277; and technology
    81, 82, 170, 171, 172, 173, 175, 179,
    180, 181, 182

Darling-Hammond, L. 203, 217, 218–21
Davies, D. 283
Davis, O.L. 21
Deal, T.E. 44, 257, 261
decentralization 25, 26, 40–1
democracy 257
design: definition of concept 9; reasons
    for introducing 9–12
design of learning-centred school 1–16;
    community, connectivity and
    consistency 275–90; elements and
    strategy 3–5; generic precepts,
    frameworks and models 14–15,
    18–37, 275, 285–6; globalization,
    internationalization and
    ethnocentrism 12–13; holistic and
    intentional process 1, 9, 14, 16, 68,
    186–7, 275–8, 289; need for school
    design 9–12; reasons for focusing on
    learning-centred school 1–3; reasons
    for introducing 9–12; reconciling
    generic principles with cultural
    difference 287–9; school effectiveness
    and school improvement context 5–8;
    terminology 8–9
design process, implementation 278–90;
    building community, involving
    parents and making connections

281–4; cross-cultural dimension
    284–7; reconciling generic principles
    with cultural difference 287–9; role of
    leadership and management 278–81;
    see also individual aspects e.g.
    curriculum design
design process, initiating 15, 63–76;
    assessment of needs 63, 64, 68–73,
    75; cross-cultural issues 75–6;
    formulating policy 74; identifying
    forces for change 64–6, 70, 74, 76;
    using research evidence on informed
    practice 66–8, 70, 74
Dewey, John 85
Dimmock, C. 12, 28, 43, 53, 75, 81, 187,
    223, 248, 264–5, 267
Direct Teach Model (M.Hunter) 144–6
direct teaching 22, 68, 69, 102–3, 135,
    138, 139, 140, 144–6, 150, 165, 193,
    243, 288
discovery/experiential approaches to
    teaching 135
Doyle, D.P. 185
Dunn, K. 117, 118
Dunn, R. 116, 117, 118

East Asian societies *see* Chinese societies
    and individual countries
Eastern Europe 40
economic systems 58–9; changes in
    10–11, 64–6; and culture 288; and
    curriculum 97, 100; and teaching 154;
    and technology 178–9
Economist, The 59
educational leadership 252–3
effective learning 19, 36, 39, 41, 66,
    107–8, 135–6, 253
Effective Schools Productivity Systems,
    Research Assistant database 67
effective teaching 39, 41, 135–6, 182,
    189; literature on 19, 22, 36, 66,
    134–5, 240, 241, 253
Eisner, E.W. 84
Elmore, R.F. 10, 11, 28, 133
Epstein, J. 282
equality 257
equity 2, 11, 12
ethnocentrism 12–13, 41, 107
evaluation and appraisal 3, 15, 233–49,
    278, 281; appraisal system for
    learning-centred school 239–41;
    cross-cultural perspective 246–9, 287;
    definitions 234; differentiated

supervision model 242–6, 248;
leadership and 261; methodologies
234, 238–9; and personnel policy
214–17, 224; purposes 234–5

Farrell, S. 41, 42, 124, 284
Fei, H-T. 270
Fisher, A. 196
flexibility 4, 278; adaptive education
approach 139–40; case studies of
innovative schools 194–200;
leadership 261–2; and organizational
structures 184, 186, 187–93
Fok, L. 41
4MAT system of learning 119–21
France 40, 267
Fraser, B.J. 150, 151, 152–3, 240
Fukuyama, F. 224
Fullan, M.G. 31, 33

Gagnè, R.M. 107, 113–16
gender, personnel policy 226
Germany: leadership 266, 267;
organizational structures 195–9, 201
Gipson, S. 181
Glaser, R. 112
Glatthorn, A. 242, 244
Glennan, T. 173
globalization 12–13, 37, 40, 45, 59, 164,
249, 286, 289
goal-directed learning 28, 111–12
goal-setting, leadership and 229, 257,
260, 262
Good, T. 144, 240
Goodlad, J.I. 86
Gouldner, A. 55
government policy *see* policy
Gow, L. 128
groups, work 101, 102–3, 147;
organizational structures 188–9, 193,
197–8
guided inquiry 174
Guskey, T.R. 94, 96, 140

Hall, G.E. 172
Hallinger, P. 44, 149, 225–7, 286
Hampden-Turner, C. 49–50, 51, 52, 53,
264, 266, 267
Hancock, V. 168, 173–5
Hargreaves, A. 33
Harris, A. 136, 137
Hartle, T.W. 185
Hatano, G. 284–5

Hau, K.T. 163
Haywood, D.K. 227
Hess, R.D. 162
Heuston, D.H. 182
Ho, D.Y.F. 41
Hofstede, Geert 46–50, 51, 52, 54, 55,
100, 101, 127, 155–7, 246–7, 264, 265,
266, 267, 269, 286
Holweide School, Cologne 195–9, 201
Hong Kong 35, 41, 42, 47, 48, 49, 58,
288, 289; curriculum 78, 97, 98–103,
104, 179, 227; initiating re-design
process 75, 76; leadership 265,
267–71; learning and teaching 42,
110, 127, 128, 154–63 *passim*;
organizational structures 184, 193,
201; personnel policy 223–4, 226,
227; resources 110, 288; restructuring
12, 41; staff appraisal 247–8;
technology 178–80, 181
Hughes, P. 83
human resources *see* personnel policy
humanistic psychology 85
Hunter, Madeleine 144, 146
Hutchins, C.L. 11

Inagaki, K. 284–5
inclusion, policies of 11, 12
independent and private schools 79, 88;
and technology 173, 175–7, 207
independent learning 177
India 40, 266
individualism/collaboration in education
5, 102; *see also* collaboration
individualism/collectivism 46, 47–8,
287–8; applied to comparative
framework for education
administration and policy 51–2; and
curriculum 100–1, 102, 103; and
evaluation 246–7; and leadership
265–7, 269–70; and learning 127, 128;
and teaching 155, 157, 162
individualization 139, 275, 287–8; of
curriculum 80, 99–100, 101, 104, 277;
of learning 118, 133, 173, 177, 187–8,
192, 193, 198, 241; teaching 140, 152
information society 10–11
informed practice 5, 21, 36, 66–8, 69, 70,
278, 287–8; and computer technology
173; distinguished from 'best
practice' 15, 21–3; evaluation 240,
248; organizational structures 187–8,

201; and resources policy 204, 205, 213, 227, 230
informed teaching practices 15, 68, 132–65, 182, 276
Ingvarson, L. 176–7
intentionality 74; curriculum 81, 91; design process 1, 9, 68, 289
International Achievement Tests in Maths and Science 40, 41, 42, 102, 124, 154, 159, 160
International Association for the Evaluation of Educational Achievement (IEA) 42
international business management 46–50, 246–7, 264–5
internationalization 12–13, 37, 40, 59, 249, 286
iterative mapping process 35, 36, 277, 278; curriculum and 91; evaluation 248; and leadership 250, 263, 271; and learning 113, 116; and resources policy 204, 205; and teaching 132

Japan 41, 42, 47, 58, 284, 288; leadership 265–6; parental involvement 76; physical environment and learning 110; professional development 224–5; and teaching 154, 157, 158, 161, 162, 163, 164
Jigsaw 148
Johnson, D. 148
Johnson, R. 148
Jones, M. 51
Joyce, B. 33, 137, 138

Kember, D. 128
Knight, B. 190
Kolb, David 120
Korea 41, 47, 58, 284; teaching 154

Latham, G.P. 31, 111
leadership 2, 3, 15, 16, 45, 51; components and dimensions 251–64; cross-cultural framework for comparative study of 264–71; curriculum and 80; evaluation 234; initiating re-design process 65, 68–73; learning-centred 250–71, 278; literature on 8, 13; models, frameworks and precepts for school design 18, 20, 21, 25, 27, 29, 30, 33, 34; and organizational culture 54, 56; personnel policy 209–12, 226, 231;

role in implementation of design process 278–81, 282; and technology 181
learning 1–3, 11–12, 14, 15, 107–30, 275, 277, 280; context and conditions for 109–11; cross-cultural perspective 107, 124–9 (implications of learning differences 129); and curriculum 79–80, 81, 85–6, 89–104 *passim*, 109; evaluation 234; goal-directed 111–12; informed practice 68, 201, 204, 287–8; lack of success 11; and leadership 252–3, 254, 255, 257, 258, 259, 263; literature on 8, 13, 19, 36, 41, 66; models, frameworks and precepts for school design 18–37 *passim*, 108; and organizational structures 109, 147, 184, 187–9, 194–5, 196–8, 199, 201; place in school design 109; and resources policy 109, 110, 204, 228–30; styles 109, 116–24; and teaching *see* teaching and teachers; and technology 168, 169, 170, 173, 175–7, 180, 182; *see also* outcomes
learning-centred school: community, connectivity and consistency 275–90; definition of 1; reasons for focusing on 1–3; *see also* design of learning-centred school; design process
learning theory 8, 13, 66, 112–16, 144, 187
Learning Together 148
Lee, Shin-ying 125, 126
Leithwood, K.A. 44, 225–7, 239–41, 242, 286
Lester, R.K. 178
Levacic, R. 229
Levin, H.M. 12
library(ies) 171, 178, 191, 192
lifelong learning 155, 157
Lim, P.H-W. 75, 248
Little, J.W. 33
Locke, E.A. 31, 111
long term/short term orientation *see* short term/long term orientation
Loper, S. 117
Loucks, S.F. 172
Louis, K.S. 33

McAdams, R. 265, 266, 267
McCarthy, B. 119–21
McDonald, H. 176–7

McLaughlin, M.W. 220
Malaysia 47
management 2, 15, 278; culture and 231; curriculum and 80; evaluation 233, 234; initiating re-design process 63, 68–73; learning-centred 250; models, frameworks for school design 18, 20, 21, 25, 27, 29, 30, 33, 34; organizational structures in innovative school 197; resources 8; role in implementation 278–81; *see also* administration
management theory 13
Marton, F. 127, 133
masculinity/femininity 46, 48, 50; applied to comparative framework for education administration and policy 52; and teaching 156
Massachusetts Institute of Technology, study of Hong Kong economy 178–9
mastery learning 68, 94, 96, 104, 112, 134, 138, 140–4, 152, 243
Melmed, A. 173
memorization *see* rote learning
Methodist Ladies College (MLC), Australia 176–7
Miles, M.B. 33
minority groups 11, 12
models 15, 18–37, 289; Gestalt model 33–5; to guide school re-design 25, 27–33; school–system relationship 23–5, 26
modernization theory 284
moral leadership 255–7, 282
Morgan, C. 214
Morris, P. 41–2, 98, 103
Mortimore, P. 107, 112
Moses, M.C. 254
Mouton, J.S. 54
multicultural element 12, 49, 282, 288; and curriculum 84, 104; and teaching 157
Murphy, D. 85–6
Murphy, J. 10–11, 31, 187–8

New Zealand 40; leadership 266; organizational structures 190–1

Oatlands School, Tasmania 194–5
O'Donoghue, T.A. 82–7
OECD 40
O'Neil, J. 116
organizational culture 3, 14, 15, 44,
48–9; comparative framework 54–7; and curriculum 80; and evaluation 234; implementation of design process 281–4; initiating re-design process 63–76; and leadership 257–8, 259, 261, 264, 265; and learning 109; literature 8; models, frameworks and precepts of school design 21, 25, 27, 29, 30, 31, 32–3, 34; and organizational structures 186
organizational structures 2, 3, 15, 184–201, 278; case studies of innovative schools 194–200; cross-cultural issues 200–1; evaluation 234; flexibility 184, 186, 187–93; and leadership 255; and learning 109, 147, 184, 187–9, 194–5, 196–8, 199, 201; models, frameworks and precepts for school design 21, 25, 27, 28–9, 30, 31, 34; principles for re-designing 187–8
organizational theory 8, 13, 66, 255
Ornstein, A.C. 110, 151
outcome-based education (OBE) 86–7, 94–5, 96, 104, 112, 140, 187
outcomes 1, 2, 3, 10, 278; curriculum and 78–104, 276; and evaluation 239, 240, 244–6, 248; and leadership 254, 255, 264, 271; learning and teaching 109, 111, 132, 140, 141–2, 144; model for implementing student outcomes' curriculum approach 91–6; models, frameworks and precepts for school design 20, 23–35 *passim*; operationalizing outcomes-oriented curriculum 88–91; organizational structures 187; and resources 228–30
Owens, R.G. 185
Oxley, D. 196

parents 281–4; and curriculum in Hong Kong 99, 101, 104; initiating re-design process 64, 68, 75–6; and learning 125, 126; and organizational structures 198, 199
'pause, prompt and praise' model of teaching 138
peer appraisal 247, 287
peer learning/tutoring 69, 102, 103, 110, 128, 135, 148, 177, 189, 193, 197–8
personalized instruction 152
personnel policy 3, 15, 203–31, 276, 281; appraisal 215–17, 224; cross-cultural implications 223–7, 230–1; position

descriptions for teachers, senior
teachers and administrators 205–12;
professional development 217–23,
224, 225–7, 229; selection 33, 213–15,
223–4; and teacher appraisal 236–7
physical space and environment 193,
195, 201, 276, 278, 288; and
computer technology 171, 174–5,
176, 179; evaluation and 234; Hong
Kong curriculum 102–3, 104; and
learning 109–10; and models,
frameworks, precepts for school
design 21, 25, 28, 30
Piaget, J. 112
policy 2, 9–10, 18–19, 21, 27–8, 36;
cross-cultural comparative approach
and framework 39, 44, 50–3, 288,
289–90; curriculum 98, 102, 104;
force for change 64–5;
internationalization/globalization 12,
37, 40–3, 45, 286; *see also*
restructuring
policy cloning 12, 40–1, 45–6, 284–5,
286; *see also* cross-cultural
transferability
political leadership 261–2
Porter, A.C. 150
postmodernism 282
power distance (power distributed/power
concentrated) concept 46–7, 50, 287;
applied to comparative framework
for educational administration and
policy 51; and curriculum 100;
initiating re-design process 75; and
leadership 266; and learning 127; and
teaching 155, 156–7
principal effectiveness literature 253
principals 45, 56, 68, 70; and appraisal
241, 247–8; and implementation of
re-design process 279, 280, 288;
leadership 251, 252–3, 256, 259, 261,
263, 265–71; personnel policy 212
Print, M. 85
private schools *see* independent and
private schools
problem-based learning (PBL) 68, 139,
149–50
problem solving 89, 102, 191, 192, 257
professional development 13, 276, 277,
278; and computers 170, 172, 180–1,
182; curriculum and 80, 103;
implementation of re-design process
280; informed teaching 164; and

leadership 259, 261; models,
frameworks and precepts for school
design 21, 25, 29, 30, 31, 32, 33, 34;
and organizational structures 199;
resources policy 214–15, 217–23, 224,
225–7, 229, and teacher appraisal
236, 242–3
professionalism 22, 134, 278; and
organizational structures 186;
resources policy 212–23
progressivist theory 85–6
psychology: and culture 46; and
curriculum 85; learning theory 110,
112; and social and economic change
11
Purkey, S.C. 34

quality school: definition 18; design of
23, 36 (seven precepts 20–1, 67–8); for
learning 124

Raburn, R. 86
Ramsden, P. 133
Ratski, A. 196
Rebore, R.W. 33
Redding, G. 270
reform, educational 2, 10; approaches to
5–8, 19; definition 8–9; *see also*
restructuring
religion 281
Renshaw, P. 127
repetitive learning 161
resource management literature 8
resources 3, 15, 203–31, 278, 281, 288;
cross-cultural implications 217,
223–7, 230–1; curriculum and 80
(Hong Kong 103, 104); evaluation
234; financial 227–30; leadership
258–61, 262; and learning 109, 110,
204, 228–30; and models, frameworks
and precepts for school design 21,
25–34 *passim*; organizational
structures and access to 191;
technology and 178
restructuring 10, 12, 15, 18–19, 286, 289;
and curriculum 89, 103; definition 9;
evaluation and 246, 247, 249; and
leadership 271; and learning 129;
literature on 8, 31, 66, 89; models,
frameworks and precepts for school
design 23–5, 26, 31, 33, 37; and
parental participation 75–6; societal
culture and 39, 40, 41

Reynolds, D. 41, 42, 124, 284
Rosenholtz, S. 32
Ross, K.N. 229
rote learning 102, 127–8, 161
Rubin, I. 136

Salili, F. 163
Sapra, C.L. 266
Schlechty, P.C. 10, 217
school: holistic nature 2; organic system
    14
school design *see* design
school effectiveness 4, 5–8, 13, 19, 22,
    31, 36, 37, 39, 41, 44, 66, 67, 68, 253
school improvement 5–8, 13, 19, 22, 36,
    37, 39, 41, 66, 68; evaluation and 238,
    240; and leadership 253, 262–4
school mission: curriculum design 92;
    and evaluation 248; initiating re-
    design process 64, 66, 68, 70, 74;
    leadership and 258, 262; resources
    policy 205, 262
school systems 21; models and
    frameworks of school–system
    relationship 23–5, 26
Shulman, L.S. 151, 214
scientific management 185–6
Scott, L. 194
self-actualization, curriculum and 85, 86
self-appraisal and supervision 247, 287
self-efficacy theory of learning 112
Senn, J. 173
Sergiovanni, T.J. 255, 256, 281, 282
Serpell, R. 284, 285
short term/long term orientation 46, 49;
    Hong Kong curriculum 101; and
    teaching 156
Showers, B. 33
Silver, H. 116
Singapore 35, 41, 42, 47, 48, 58, 284;
    curriculum 97; leadership 267; and
    teaching 154; technology 178, 180–1
Slavin, R. E. 12, 113, 147, 148
Slee, R. 7
Smith, M.S. 34
social change, schooling and 6, 10–11,
    64–5
social justice issues 2, 11, 12;
    incorporation into curriculum 85
social learning theory 112
social problems 11
social reconstruction, curriculum and
    85, 86

socialization 6, 101, 162
societal culture 3, 12–13, 14, 15, 34, 35,
    36, 37, 39–59, 275; case for culture
    and for a cross-cultural comparative
    framework 43–6; comparative
    framework for organizational culture
    54–7; complexity 57–9; cross-cultural
    comparative framework for education
    administration and policy 50–3;
    cross-cultural comparative
    frameworks in international business
    management 46–50; and curriculum
    design 97–103; and evaluation 246–9;
    implementation of design process
    284–90; initiating design process 66,
    75–6; and leadership 264–71; and
    learning 107, 124–9, 155–7; need to
    consider 40–3; and organizational
    structures 201; personnel policy
    223–7, 230–1; and teaching 154–65;
    and technology 178–83
sociology 55
Sorenson, J.S. 89, 116, 117, 118, 122,
    123, 141, 144, 147, 148
South America, leadership 267
South Korea *see* Korea
Spady, W.G. 94–5, 112, 140, 187
specialist teachers 190
Spinks, J. 31, 32
Steinberg, L. 283
Stevenson, H.W. 76, 125, 126, 157, 160,
    161, 162, 224, 225, 284, 288
Stigler, J.W. 76, 157, 160, 161, 162, 224,
    225, 284, 288
'stimulus and response' model of
    teaching 138
strategic intent (Boisot) 4, 5
strategic leadership 262–4
structural-functionalist models 43, 44,
    45
structural leadership 255, 261, 262
Student Teams-Achievement Divisions
    (STAD) 148–9
students: assessment 80, 81, 192–3;
    evaluation of teachers 243; leadership
    251; *see also* learning; outcomes
symbolic leadership 257–8, 261, 262

Taiwan 35, 41, 42, 49, 58, 284; learning
    125–6; physical space 110;
    professional development 224; and
    teaching 154, 157, 158, 161;
    technology 178

Tang, C. 102, 128
task group to complete needs assessment
71
Taylor, Frederick 185
teacher training 164, 182; Japan 224–5
teaching and teachers 1, 2, 3, 11–12, 14,
15, 275, 276, 277, 280; appraisal *see*
evaluation and appraisal; approaches
138–50; as artistry and professional
practice 134–6; cross-cultural
perspective 154–65; and curriculum
79–104 *passim*, 140, 141, 147, 277;
implementation of design process
287, 288; informed practice 15, 68,
132–65, 182, 201, 276, 287–8; and
initiating re-design process 65, 68, 75,
76; knowledge, behaviours and skills
68, 150–4; and learning 109, 113–16,
117–18, 121–4, 128, 129–30, 132–65
passim; literature on 8, 13, 19, 36, 41,
66, 134–5, 150–4; models,
frameworks and precepts for school
design 18–36 *passim*; models of
136–8; and organizational culture 55;
and organizational structures 184,
186, 189–90, 194–5, 196–7, 199, 201;
resources policy 203–4, 205–9,
212–27, 231; status 42; and
technology 168, 169, 170, 172, 174,
175–7, 180, 182; *see also* leadership
team teaching 190, 192
teamwork 189–90, 198, 199, 200,
259–60, 276, 280, 288; *see also*
collaboration
technological leadership 253–4
technology 3, 13, 15, 168–83, 276, 277,
278, 281; creating school technology
plan 171–2; cross-cultural perspective
178–83; and curriculum 81, 82, 170,
171, 172, 173, 175, 179, 180, 181, 182;
descriptions of integrated technology
schools 173–7; key principles for use
169–70; models, frameworks and
precepts for school design 21, 25, 28,
30; and organizational structures 184,
185, 191, 192, 193; resources 178, 204
Thailand 47; leadership 266; technology
181
thematic teaching 174
thinking skills *see* cognitive processes
and skills
Thomas, R.M. 44

time and timetabling 28, 190–2, 195,
199, 234, 276, 278
transformational leadership 262–4
Trompenaars, F. 49–50, 51, 52, 53, 264,
266, 267
tutoring 152

uncertainty avoidance 46, 48–9; applied
to comparative framework for
education policy and administration
52–3; Hong Kong curriculum 101;
and teaching 156
United Kingdom 47, 48, 49, 58;
curriculum 78, 84, 98; parent
participation 75–6; restructuring 12,
41; teaching 154, 156, 157
United States of America 47, 48, 49, 58,
284, 288; curriculum 78, 84, 88; lack
of learning success 11; leadership
260, 265, 266, 267; learning 125–6;
organizational structures 185, 186,
191, 193; parent participation 75–6;
personnel policy 203–4, 214, 217–18,
221–2; restructuring 12, 41; social
and economic change and
educational reform 10–11; teaching
154, 156, 157, 158, 159; technology
168, 171, 173–6; *see also* Brewster
Academy
university–school partnerships 164

Vallance, E. 84
value-added concept 2
Van Horn, R. 182
Vasquez, B. 147
Vecchio, R. 47
Volet, S. 127
Vygotsky, L. 112

Walberg, H.J. 189
Walker, A. 43, 53, 194, 223, 226, 248,
264–5, 266, 267
Wang, M.H.G. 112, 139–40
Watkins, D.A. 101, 102, 127, 128, 160
Weick, K.E. 33
Weil, M. 137
Westerberg, T. 186
Westerman, D. 153–4
Western/Asian education 12–13, 15,
36–7; and curriculum 97–104; and
evaluation 246–8; importance of
societal culture 39–59; initiating re-
design process 75–6; and leadership

264–71; learning-centred school 284–90; and organizational structures 201; personnel policy 217, 223–7, 230–1; student learning 107, 124–9, 155–7; and teaching 154–65; and technology 178–83

Western influence: dominance 39, 40, 41, 43, 45, 289; restructuring 12; *see also* cross-cultural transferability

Whitaker, K.S. 80, 254

Wiggins, G. 80

Wilkinson, B. 58

Winter, S. 102, 128

Wohlstetter, P. 218

Wong, K.C. 101, 223, 224, 269–70, 288

Wynne, E.A. 189